# AMERICAN HISTORY GOES TO THE MOVIES

Whether they prefer blockbusters, historical dramas, or documentaries, people learn much of what they know about history from the movies. In *American History Goes to the Movies*, W. Bryan Rommel-Ruiz shows how popular representations of historic events shape the way audiences understand the history of the United States, including American representations of race and gender and stories of immigration, especially the familiar narrative of the American Dream.

Using films from many different genres, *American History Goes to the Movies* draws together movies that depict the Civil War, the Wild West, the assassination of JFK, and the events of 9/11, from *The Birth of a Nation* and *Gone with the Wind* to *The Exorcist* and *United 93*, to show how viewers use movies to make sense of the past, addressing not only how we render history for popular enjoyment, but also how Hollywood's renderings of America influence the way Americans see themselves and how they make sense of the world.

**W. Bryan Rommel-Ruiz** is Associate Professor of History at the Colorado College in Colorado Springs.

# AMERICAN HISTORY GOES TO THE MOVIES

## Hollywood and the American Experience

*W. Bryan Rommel-Ruiz*

 Routledge
Taylor & Francis Group

NEW YORK AND LONDON

First published 2011
by Routledge
711Third Avenue, New York, NY 10017

Simultaneously published in the UK
by Routledge
2 Park Square, Milton Park, Abingdon, Oxon OX14 4RN

*Routledge is an imprint of the Taylor & Francis Group, an informa business*

© 2011 Taylor & Francis

The right of W. Bryan Rommel-Ruiz to be identified as author of this work
has been asserted by him in accordance with sections 77 and 78 of the
Copyright, Designs and Patents Act 1988.

Typeset in Bembo by
Keystroke, Station Road, Codsall, Wolverhampton

*Library of Congress Cataloging in Publication Data*
Rommel-Ruiz, W. Bryan.
American history goes to the movies : Hollywood and the
American experience / W. Bryan Rommel-Ruiz.
p. cm.
1. United States–In motion pictures. 2. National characteristics,
American–In motion pictures. 3. Motion pictures–United States–
History. 4. Hollywood (Los Angeles, Calif.)–History. I. Title.
PN1995.9.U64R66 2011
791.43'65873–dc22
2010028995

ISBN 13: 978–0–415–80219–2 (hbk)
ISBN 13: 978–0–415–80220–8 (pbk)
ISBN 13: 978–0–203–83373–5 (ebk)

# CONTENTS

# ACKNOWLEDGEMENTS

I was born in Hollywood, California, and raised in the shadow of the film industry. As a child, I attended movie openings and screenings, watching countless hours of film. My father worked as a cameraman at KWHY-TV, where I would spend many weekends observing the technical side of television. Later, I fell in love with the discipline of history as an undergraduate at the University of California, Berkeley, so in many ways it was only a matter of time that I would write a book about film and history. Still, there are many organizations and people whom I wish to thank for helping me write this book. First, I wish to thank the Robert J. Cosgrove Endowment, the Social Science Executive Committee, and Dean Susan Ashley and Associate Dean Victor Nelson Cisneros of Colorado College for providing funds that enabled me to purchase computer equipment, software, and films for my research. My colleagues at Colorado College's History Department have been immensely supportive. In particular, I want to thank Dennis Showalter for our conversations about Westerns, especially John Ford's *The Searchers*. I am grateful to Anne Hyde for last-minute bibliographic references on Native American history and to David Torres-Rouff for our conversations about Western films and Jeffersonian ideology. I want to extend special thanks to my colleague John Williams. John and I taught a seminar entitled "Religion, Witchcraft, and the Occult," where he indulged my last-minute impulse to show *The Exorcist*, a decision that not only provided an engaging class discussion but also encouraged me to write the chapter on evil and the history of American religion. I am indebted to the students in that class for provoking many ideas that I have incorporated in Chapter 1, and to John for reading a draft of this chapter.

Portions of Chapter 2 and Chapter 3 were presented at Film and History League conferences and the Southwest American Popular Culture conference. I appreciate the comments and criticisms of commentators and fellow panelists, which helped me refine ideas in these chapters. While I have been able to write *American History Goes to the Movies* during the last couple of years, I began my research many years ago when I first taught my "American History, American Cinema" course at Colorado College. In many respects, this book could not have been written without the engaging intellectual exchanges from my students in these classes. Although there are too many students to acknowledge, I hope that any student who took those courses knows how much I appreciate our invaluable class discussions. It is to the students of Colorado College that I ultimately dedicate this book. I especially want to thank David Shively, whose senior research paper about the Kennedy assassination and Oliver Stone's *JFK* I supervised. Many of our conversations found their way into the JFK chapter in this book.

I am indebted to my wife Terri Lynn for her emotional support throughout the writing process. Finally, I want to thank my children, Emma and Javier. One of the fun things about writing this book has been sharing my ideas with my children, who have shown a real interest in this work. My 13-year-old daughter Emma and I spent hours watching Civil War films, and it has been rewarding to see her become interested in American history and watch films critically. Likewise, my 10-year-old son Javier learned to see that a movie like *Batman Begins* is more than a superhero film. He may still question the way I see connections between the movie and September 11th, but that he can challenge his academic father and critique the film himself rather than simply accept my conclusions makes all the time I put into this project well worth it. While these have been fascinating teaching moments with my children, it has been more gratifying as a parent to watch their intellectual interests grow.

# INTRODUCTION

At the end of Martin Scorsese's *Gangs of New York*, Amsterdam Vallon (Leonardo DiCaprio) stands in a cemetery across Manhattan Island with Jenny Everdeane (Cameron Diaz), reflecting upon the violent devastation New York City just endured following the notorious draft riots of 1863. Amsterdam has come to bury his father Priest Vallon's razor, a memento symbolizing the tribal wars between American nativists and ethnic immigrants in nineteenth-century New York history. Scorsese's film began with Priest (Liam Neeson) using this razor to mark his face as he prepared to battle his rival Bill "The Butcher" Cutting (Daniel Day-Lewis), a street war intended to determine whether the nativists or immigrants would control the Five Points district of Lower Manhattan. Later in the movie, Amsterdam would similarly use his father's razor to again fight Bill, who now wielded enormous power in the city upon defeating Priest Vallon, having earned a reputation for unleashing violence upon the ethnic communities in Five Points and notoriety among the city's political leaders. During those epic days in 1863, Amsterdam avenged his father's death by killing Bill during another street battle, and his headstone now lies next to Priest Vallon's. As he buries his father's razor, Amsterdam also buries a volatile period in the city's history, one defined by men like Priest Vallon and Bill Cutting, who together represented a generation of Americans torn by nativist and ethnic prejudices in the years before the American Civil War. Recalling his father's words as he observes a smoldering Manhattan, Amsterdam ponders upon the ways New York City was transformed that day in 1863, a city now "born of blood and tribulation just as we are born into this world."[1] Yet Amsterdam regretfully notes in the film's final scenes how future generations will forget about men such as Bill and his father, as well as this contested period in mid-nineteenth-century American history when the young republic stood at a cultural crossroads. Even though such pivotal moments periodically have occurred throughout United States history, it was during this era when Americans intensely fought over the sociological definition of their country, according to *Gangs of New York*. With the Civil War as the historical backdrop, Martin Scorsese's film points to this critical moment in US national history when Americans determined whether all citizens, regardless of ethnic or racial background, should be extended the rights and privileges to participate in their rapidly growing democracy.

Despite Amsterdam's optimism that a new multicultural and democratic New York City emerged from the ruins left in the wake of violent rioting, he recognized that progress and moving forward in history would nonetheless exact a tragic price from future generations of Americans. As the film closes, Amsterdam states, "Everything we knew was mightily swept away [that day in 1863]. No matter what they did to build this city again . . . for the rest of time it would be like nobody knew we was [sic] ever here."[2] To punctuate Amsterdam's epigraph, the following scenes portray New York City rapidly transforming over the next century and a half, presenting images of an early-twentieth-century Brooklyn Bridge, followed by those of Manhattan's spectacular skyline at mid-century, and finally images of the Twin Towers of the World Trade Center—notably camera shots filmed before the terrorist attacks of September 11, 2001.[3]

As this closing sequence accelerates New York City's history, we observe the advent of modernity over the course of the twentieth century, and its powerful symbols of progress. However, the cemetery on the other side of the Brooklyn Bridge where Bill Cutting and Priest Vallon were buried gradually vanishes, neglected and then ignored over time, disappearing in the omniscient shadow of Manhattan's powerful skyscrapers. As *Gangs of New York* fades to the credits, viewers are left with a lasting image of a touch of sunlight radiating upon the Twin Towers, while dark clouds shroud the rest of Manhattan, signaling foreboding rain. With this juxtaposition of the sunlit Twin Towers and darkened city, the film provokes us to remember a time in American history when "everything we knew was mightily swept away" on an equally devastating day in September 2001, when the nation was again transformed by tragic events. Whatever one believes about Martin Scorsese's decision to include these controversial images of the World Trade Center in his movie so soon after the events of 9/11 (the film was released in December 2002), these closing scenes demand that we consider the meaning of American history in the face of progress, and the ways Americans engage with their national past.

Americans have a problematic relationship with their history. Despite claims that they do not have a history, Americans actually do have an extensive past defined by significant events that have influenced the trajectory of world history, particularly since the dawn of the twentieth century. Perhaps they cannot claim a deep past that stretches over 5,000 years like the Chinese, or live among the remnants of ancient civilizations as do the people of Europe, India, and the Middle East. And while the United States is a young republic founded barely 250 years ago, it possesses rich traditions that extend back to European antiquity when one considers its religious, aesthetic, and intellectual worldview, as well as its political and economic institutions. Even within the past couple of centuries, Americans have contributed to Western politics, political economy, and the natural and medical sciences, not to mention that it continues to maintain a significant international presence as a leading political, military, and economic power in the twenty-first century. Beginning with the American Revolution in the late eighteenth century, the United States demonstrated that forging a republic based upon the liberal principles of the Enlightenment was possible at a time when monarchical absolutism reigned in continental Europe. Since the early twentieth century, the United States has shaped global politics, economics, and perhaps more controversially, popular culture, defining a period in world history aptly known as the "American Century." Thus, it is baseless to claim Americans do not have a national past; the more pressing question, however, is whether they actually connect with their "history."

We should be clear to distinguish the "past" from "history." Throughout this book, I will be drawing upon the definitions of history articulated by the eminent American historian Charles Beard in his presidential address to the American Historical Association in 1934, a time when Beard believed the historical profession faced an epistemological crisis about the future directions of the profession. In this published address, Beard defined two forms of history: history as past actuality and history as thought. He stated,

> History as past actuality includes . . . all that has been done, said, felt, and thought by human beings on this planet since humanity began its long career. History as record embraces the monuments, documents, and symbols which provide such knowledge as we have or can find respecting past actuality. But it is history as thought, not as actuality, record, or specific knowledge, that is really meant when the term history is used in its widest and most general significance. It is thought about past actuality, instructed and delimited by history as record and knowledge—record and knowledge authenticated by criticism and ordered with the help of the scientific method.[4]

In this regard, history as thought provides the intellectual framework to interpret the past, providing us with an explanation or understanding of significant past events and people, and the rich world they created. However, it is precisely the issue of history as thought and the matter of historical interpretation, or more precisely, finding historical meaning in the past, that presents a significant challenge for Americans when they engage with their history. For it is when Americans attempt to derive historical understanding from the past that they may discover how their history can conflict with a vision of their nation that fundamentally celebrates the United States as a country more oriented towards its progressive future rather than its past. Americans believe their nation is a land of unlimited opportunity that provides people chances for renewal and redemption, forgiving of their past in order to start anew, allowing them to move forward towards a future that offers potential happiness. Yet, this belief in a progressive future essentially requires Americans to detach from their past, otherwise it can hold them back from achieving their ambitions, aspirations, and dreams. In other words, remaining connected to their history can prevent Americans from concentrating upon the potential bounty that the future promises.

In this regard, Americans believe in a worldview best articulated by Scarlett O'Hara (Vivien Leigh) in Victor Fleming's *Gone with the Wind*, another historical film that points to the American Civil War as the pivotal moment in American history that defined the future of the American character. Throughout Fleming's film, Scarlett, despite her romantic and economic challenges, maintains an indomitable faith that nothing will hold her back from starting over and achieving her goals in the future. For Scarlett, to look towards the past and dwell upon what she has lost would place her in the suffering position of her longtime love, Ashley Wilkes (who resists Scarlett's amorous advances, although not always convincingly). Even as the South rebuilds and moves forward in time during Reconstruction (1865–1877), Ashley (Leslie Howard) continues to live in a romanticized past, so enslaved to a vanishing vision of a gallant antebellum South that he remains disconsolate and disoriented in the present, and hopeless about the future.[5] For most of the movie, Scarlett shares Ashley's sorrow of a civilization "gone with the wind," even as she demonstrates a powerful spirit that enables her to survive apocalyptic devastation to her family and their home, Tara, in the wake of the Confederacy's defeat. As she learns, Tara and the rural worldview it embodies give her the strength to gradually rebuild a life, and eventually prosper in post-Civil War Atlanta.

Ultimately, she realizes that reliving the lost world tied to Ashley only chains her to an illusion, and actually prevents her from achieving a potential future that is more promising and enriching, an ideal symbolized by her relationship with her estranged husband Rhett Butler (Clark Gable), who has firmly embraced the future and the promises it holds for him and a New South. As if speaking for most Americans, Scarlett announces her future without history as she disconnects from Ashley to pursue Rhett, who has left her in the closing moments of the film in order to rebuild his life in his native Charleston. In the film's final scene, she decides to return to Tara and leave her tarnished past in Atlanta, believing the future holds the opportunity to reconcile with Rhett. Precisely because she has faith in the future detached from the past, she states at the close of the film: "Tomorrow, I will think of some way to get him back. After all, tomorrow is another day."[6]

America has been a land of "new beginnings" since the time of Jamestown (1607) and Plymouth Rock (1620), and Americans remain the intellectual descendants of Thomas Jefferson, who imagined an independent nation free from the historical corruption that plagued Europe, and as president secured the Louisiana Purchase (1803) in order to ensure that the bountiful land in the

American West would continually offer native and immigrant Americans redemption and renewal should their opportunities become limited in the East. Because of Jefferson, the United States can be a land of perpetual Huckleberry Finns who will "light out for the Territory" to start their lives anew if they ever became frustrated and disenchanted with modern, "sivilize" [sic] life, and "can't stand it."[7] But just as Jefferson could envision an America of unbounded equal opportunity and individual freedom while ignoring his personal history with slavery, Americans arguably will not enslave themselves to their past if it interferes with their pursuits of wealth and happiness. Thus, the United States is not a country free *from* history, but offers Americans as well as immigrants the freedom to escape their past should they choose, and celebrates this as an essential value of the American character.

It is this tenuous connection with history that apparently alarmed Martin Scorsese, and his montage of recent New York City history in the final scenes of *Gangs of New York* reflects a perspective about the tragic relationship Americans have with their past. In this sequence, we are meant to marvel at the technical achievements of modernity such as the incredible bridges and skyscrapers humanity has ingeniously produced in New York City; but we are also provoked to ponder how Americans are just as quick to demolish anything that stands in the way of these technological symbols of progress. Indeed, this is the ironic purpose of saving older buildings with state and national registries: these buildings that we are meant to value for their local and national historical significance must be protected from us because we would otherwise destroy them in the name of urban progress. Perhaps this is the poignant point Martin Scorsese wants us to consider when he concludes his film with a New York City urban landscape that still includes the Twin Towers of the World Trade Center.

*American History Goes to the Movies*, however, maintains that Americans do want to know about their history, and films provide an essential media for them to engage with their national past. In fact, historical films arguably rival academic histories as the primary way Americans connect with their history. Although history textbooks may provide factual knowledge about the American past, movies enable us to see substantive historical significance in the past in ways history textbooks cannot. People crave stories because they are meaningful; and herein lies the attraction of films as historical narratives and why Americans prefer cinematic historical representations to that of academic monographs, the primary form professional historians present their scholarship. Fundamentally, the issues that separate these two forms of historical presentation are as much epistemological and ontological as they are representational, and center upon the ways academics practice history. Precisely because academic history evolved as a social science, historians objectify the past and detach themselves from the subjects they study. Films do the exact opposite. Professional historians value time, place, and historical context, stressing change and difference between the past and present. Filmmakers narrate a past that is a history of the present.

Cinematic historians practice a form of history similar to that of nineteenth-century historians like George Bancroft. These amateur scholars grounded their historical narratives in archival research, and some even held advanced degrees from eminent European universities where many later professional academic historians would receive their doctorates. Nevertheless, these academics dismissed the works of "gentlemen historians" like Bancroft because they wrote histories that approximated mythic narratives which told stories about the ways Americans emerged as an exceptional people and celebrated the United States as a democratic nation.[8] The rise of the modern university and the categorization of history as a discipline in the social sciences moved the legitimate, professional practice of history away from men like Bancroft towards academics with doctorates in the discipline.

This change produced an epistemological shift in the ways professional historians were expected to study the past. As Peter Novick describes in his history of the American historical profession, scholars in the late nineteenth century embraced the more social scientific approach of reputable European historians like Leopold Von Ranke. Following the principles of Von Ranke, American academics pursued objective history in order to relate the past "as it actually happened," researching data and letting the facts "speak for themselves." For these more "scientific" historians, the emotional literary flourishes that made earlier historical narratives attractive to the American public wrongfully positioned the historian at the authorial center of their historical narratives as they constructed plots, protagonists, and used other literary conventions to tell stimulating stories about the past. In their minds, historical narratives violated the basic methodological and epistemological tenets of scientific history. For them, objective history intentionally detached the historian from the story he was relating, whose role is to assemble and write up historical facts they discovered while conducting rigorous research.[9] To ensure objective history was produced, an entire professional academic apparatus based upon peer review was constructed to legitimize historical scholarship. The omniscient footnote became the terrain to demonstrate historical objectivity and the way for historians to police each other to ensure that professional rules were followed.[10] From historian J.H. Hexter's perspective, peer review discourse defines the professional parameters of the historical community and protects it from interlopers who practice shoddy history.[11] Nevertheless, the establishment of a academic historical society has led to a restrictive professional community that essentially practices history for itself.

Since academic historians have set the terms of debate about what constitutes history, historical films have been judged by these professional standards. In the following pages, this book will demonstrate that we are applying the wrong standard to cinematic histories. Instead of expecting films to relate "the past as it actually happened," or in Charles Beard's terms "history as past actuality," we should approach them as historiography, or "history as thought." As numerous scholars of film and history have pointed out, the demands of cinema and the centrality of narrative fundamentally make it impossible for a historical film to tell the "past as it actually happened."[12] Filmmakers must tell a good story, and if plot and character development require historical exaggeration or even fabrication, historical facts are likely to be sacrificed to advance the narrative.[13] Yet, this does not mean historical films do not raise significant historical questions. In fact, they often engage the same historical issues that animate academic historiography. Rather than ruminating over the question about historical accuracy in films, the following chapters will illustrate that there is incredible historical value in American cinema when we examine films as historiography. The first four chapters work in this vein as they take a selection of films and connect them with particular historiographic issues in the fields of American religious history, the Civil War and Reconstruction, and the American West. As these chapters examine historical ideas concerning the ways people have understood the sociological problem of evil throughout time, the problem of race and freedom during the Civil War period, and the vitality of Jeffersonian ideology during westward expansion, they offer a different interpretive approach to the study of film and history.

In the ensuing chapters, *American History Goes to the Movies* explores the relationship between film and history in a more professional and philosophical context as well. Chapters 5 and 6 illustrate the ways films about the American immigration experience and the pursuit of the American Dream connect closely with immigration historiography, whether that is the European American or Mexican American experience. However, this chapter begins an intensive discussion about the problem of historical narrative and the ways it reflects a substantive gap between cinematic and academic history. Curiously, historical films best reflect the purpose and aspirations of American social history, an academic field that gained prominence in light of the civil rights and women's movements of the 1960s. The academic goal of social history has been to demonstrate that the historical experience of American everyday life and marginal peoples is just as significant as the history of political institutions and leaders. Average Americans outside the sphere of the national government were as political as their leaders, affecting local communities, and occasionally, municipal, state, and federal policy. In fact, cinematic history illustrates how social history can be engaging as it allows viewers to connect with the lives of average Americans, and experience their triumphs and tragedies in American history. Martin Scorsese's *Gangs of New York* and Francis Ford Coppola's *Godfather* saga are just two successful examples of powerful melodramas that draw audiences into the everyday life of the American immigrant. Curiously, academic social history has not found the kind of widespread audience, and arguably legitimacy, among the American public as cinematic social history. Chapter 6 interrogates this issue and connects it with the problem of historical narrative and the project of social history more generally.

Chapters 7 and 8 explore the ways cinematic and academic history approach the dilemma of historical trauma in our recent past. Looking at films and academic histories of the assassination of President Kennedy and the 9/11 terrorist attacks, these chapters describe the ways historical narratives are critical for Americans to understand these national tragedies, enabling them to find historical meaning and significance in these traumatic events. Precisely because historical narratives provide closure to the problem animating a film's plot, they can offer resolution to historical questions that focus upon how and why these events happened, questions that continue to haunt Americans. Indeed, historical narratives may provide the necessary catharsis for people to work through their trauma and find historical meaning in tragic events like the JFK assassination and 9/11 terrorist attacks. And herein lies the attraction of historical narratives and how they address historical trauma. Where historical narrative demands historical engagement and provides historical understanding, academic history promotes objectivity and disinterest as it examines the past in a historical context distant from the present. As we will see, an academic approach to the JFK assassination and 9/11 has proved elusive. Conspiracy theories abound, and sifting through available evidence has been challenging because so much remains classified for reasons of national security (thereby further feeding the conspiracy theories), hamstringing any scholar who attempts to objectively research partially selected documents provided by the government.

Given Von Ranke's principles of practicing history "as it actually happened" it is practically impossible to write an academic history of these events. Consequently, professional historians have largely removed themselves from the historical debates surrounding these national tragedies. This is not to say that there are no academic histories of these events; just not notable ones written by professional historians. As we will see, scholars from other academic fields, such as English, political science, and physics, have attempted to write academic histories of the JFK assassination and 9/11. They vie for the historical legitimacy often accorded to the official government histories such as the Warren Commission's report and the 9/11 Commission's report. However, since these government commissions admitted that their reconstructed histories are limited because agencies such as the Central Intelligence Agency (CIA) purposely withheld evidence, critics have been able to find Americans willing to lend credence to their counter-narratives. Whether one wants to call them conspiracy theories or counter-narratives, these academic studies have gained legitimacy because they operate as historical narratives, providing historical resolution and historical meaning to these traumatic national events for Americans in ways the Warren and 9/11 Commission reports have failed.

Furthermore, direct cinematic representations of the 9/11 terrorist attacks such as Paul Greengrass's *United 93* and Oliver Stone's *World Trade Center* purposely avoid critical historical and political questions that would help viewers understand why these events occurred, even more so than the 9/11 Commission's report. Interestingly, superhero movies like *Batman Begins* and *Iron Man* address the historical issues better than the transparent 9/11 films *United 93* and *World Trade Center*, as we will see. Still, it is notable that the 9/11 Commission self-consciously wrote a "narrative of this report" and presented it as a history.[14] In fact, the 9/11

Commission manipulated time and historical events in order to construct a compelling narrative that is as much emotionally engaging as it is informative. Clearly, the 9/11 Commission recognized the psychological and political power of narrative as a way to convey the historical significance of those momentous days in September 2001. Will conspiracy theories and counter-narratives about 9/11 dominate the American historical consciousness as they now do for the JFK assassination? Part of the purpose of *American History Goes to the Movies* is to explore this question, and understand why cinematic history and counter-narratives have emerged as convincing historical narratives to rival the "official" history.

# 1

# EXORCISING THE DEMONS WITHIN

## Gender, Race, and the Problem of Evil in American History and Cinema

At various moments in the first half of William Friedkin's *The Exorcist* (1973, 2000), a ghoulish, demonic cloaked figure randomly flashes between scenes, almost unnoticed, provoking the viewer to question its presence in the film. Moreover, the viewer is left pondering the filmmaker's larger purpose of inserting these flashlit shots in a movie that centers upon the demonic possession and exorcism of a young girl in 1970s America. The answer, of course, is that William Friedkin's jump-cuts of the cloaked demon have nothing and everything to do with his film about the problem of evil. The apparent incoherence and opaqueness of these scenes illustrate why these flashlit shots remain controversial among some viewers who argue that the film sends demonic subliminal messages.[1] Nevertheless, the flashing demonic figure is a critical narrative device that illuminates the movie's central religious themes. Although not conventionally connected to the film's plot, the flashing ghoul nonetheless embodies the symbolic horror of the movie: the randomness of evil. Viewers often comment upon the ways *The Exorcist*'s shocking pornographic imagery and vulgarity horrifies them, not to mention the ways the movie blasphemes sacred Christian symbols and rituals. But considering this film blasphemous would be nothing further from the truth. In a profound way, *The Exorcist* is a provocative, and some would say conservative, religious film that philosophizes upon the nature of evil in the modern world.[2] Indeed, the film's major premise pivots upon Chris MacNeil's (Ellen Burstyn) initial turn to medical and psychiatric science to resolve her daughter's afflictions, only to reject rational science and empiricism because they fail to "cure" her daughter Regan (Linda Blair). With modern science unable to "treat" Regan, Chris appeals to Father Damien Karras (ironically a trained psychiatrist who doubts his own faith) and the Catholic Church to perform an exorcism in order to cast out the demon possessing her daughter. Arguably, Chris's appeal is a validation of the power of Christianity and

Catholicism to confront and defeat evil. This was evidently one way a Catholic newspaper interpreted the film.[3] However, the apparent victory of the demon over Father Merrin (Max von Sydow), and Father Karras's (Jason Miller) invocation to the demon to possess him actually reveal a much more ambivalent and terrifying conclusion that doubts the power of Christian faith and Catholic rituals to triumph over evil.[4] To suggest that evil remains impervious to modern science and traditional religious rituals is perhaps even more blasphemous than the film's graphic imagery and gore could ever be.

Throughout the film viewers are reminded of evil's power. Although *The Exorcist* suggests reasons why the demon possessed Regan, the film ultimately remains inconclusive about why and how the demon specifically inhabited Regan. The movie begins with an archeological dig led by Father Merrin in Iraq that may have unearthed the artifact that unleashed the demon into the world, although the connection between the artifact and Regan's possession remains suggestive. When the unearthed artifact finds its way to Chris and Regan's home in Washington, DC, the viewer is left unsure of how it arrived there.[5] Like the subliminal demonic figure flashing throughout the first half of the movie, *The Exorcist* maintains that evil is random, and efforts to derive its reason, causality, and meaning will always remain elusive.

In this respect, *The Exorcist* challenges our common understanding of evil and the function of religion as a cultural system. In one of the more enduring explanations of religion, Clifford Geertz notes that the concept of evil exists to help humans understand why bad things happen to good people.[6] Evil thus provides a significant epistemological need: it offers a supernatural reason for causality in the natural world. Thomas Luckman maintains that causality is one of the essential components that shape our worldviews,[7] and in this respect evil provides a critical cognitive framework for humans to understand the world around them by looking for explanations and meaning beyond the known natural world. Given the significance of evil and the epistemological function it supposedly serves, then, *The Exorcist* assaults and horrifies us precisely because it demands us to reject the idea that evil can be rationally understood: that is, the film posits that evil is beyond human comprehension. Nevertheless, the film also asks us to consider the historical context of 1970s America and the changing gender and family roles produced by the social transformations of the 1960s and 1970s. Chris is a single mother who works as an actress, making a film in Washington, DC about radical student politics and the Vietnam War, entitled *Crash Course*. While viewers observe Chris's intimate and loving relationship with her daughter, they also see her throwing a lavish party that includes a Catholic priest, Father Dyer (William O'Malley), playing the piano and singing with guests. This is also the scene that introduces Regan's aberrant behavior when she tells an astronaut he "will die up there" and proceeds to urinate in view of the guests. In another scene, we observe Chris bemoan the absence of Regan's father in his daughter's life (he will not even talk to his daughter on her birthday), and it is clear that the deteriorating traditional family structure has produced instability in Chris's household. Although concerned, Chris does not seem to rebuke Regan for playing the Ouija board and provoking conversations with the supernatural. As much as she is a caring mother, she is initially blind to the malevolent forces enveloping Regan as her acting career and romantic relationship with the film's director absorb her. Could her questionable career, licentious secular lifestyle, and broken family be as much to blame for Regan's demonic possession as the mysterious demonic artifact?

From this perspective, *The Exorcist* engages in a classic historiographic debate among scholars of religious history: to what degree do we interpret religious life, ideas, and behavior from a functionalist perspective and to what degree from a substantive one? That is, how do we understand religion in terms of what it *does* (functionalist) and how do we understand it in terms of what it *is* (substantive).[8] More often, scholars are simultaneously interested in functionalist and substantive approaches to religious phenomena, but usually one methodological approach emerges as the major heuristic approach that frames their research and analysis. Films such as *The Exorcist* offer interpretations of religious phenomena from a functionalist and substantive approach as well, and provoke us to ponder critical issues such as the purpose and nature of evil in the modern world. When we place *The Exorcist* in a broader context about religion in American history, it becomes part of a historical conversation about religious interpretations of power, gender relations, and social change in American society. In this way, Friedkin's film connects to a historical trajectory that reaches back to colonial American history and the Salem witchcraft trials of 1692, particularly in the ways in which people drew upon religion to help them understand changing social and cultural phenomena.

This chapter, then, examines films with religious themes and the ways they address the problem of evil. In particular, it explores how Christianity and its construction of evil operate as an interpretive lens through which some Americans comprehend social turbulence and the empowerment of women and minorities in American history. In many respects, these films reflect scholarly interpretations about the history of Christianity, Satan, and witchcraft. This chapter takes a decidedly functionalist approach to religious phenomena to help us understand how religious films and scholarship explain palpable anxieties about social and political transformations enveloping American society at particular moments in American history. Moreover, by comparing American religious history with similar non-Western religious historical phenomena, we will see the broader ways religion and its interpretation of evil offer explanations for people to understand the turbulence of social and political change across time and space. However, we will also see how the Christian construction of Satan as a model of, and model for, evil uniquely defines Western religious history. The ways in which people in the West, particularly Americans, identify Satan with supernatural power and malevolent forces has framed the way in which some people interpret how powerless and oppressed peoples have empowered themselves as historical agents to challenge more dominant power structures. Whether it is women during the Salem witchcraft trials of the 1690s or women and minorities during the women's liberation and civil rights movements in post-World War II America, people looked to Christian eschatology and Satan to help them understand these social movements. In profound ways films with religious themes, particularly in the horror genre, reflect these anxieties and fears about tectonic shifts in American society.

However, as much as Christianity has offered an explanation for these social and political transformations, it also has demonstrated its limitations to explain these changes. As we will see, when Mel Gibson released his film *The Passion* in 2004, he faced public outcry for the film's anti-Semitic themes.[9] Significantly, the film is actually quite faithful to the Gospels as this chapter will demonstrate, particularly the Gospel of John. Nonetheless, changing views about Jews in American society in recent American history informed the reaction to the film's anti-Semitism. Both the film and the firestorm it engendered reflect a broader historical transformation about racial ideology in America. Over the course of the twentieth century, particularly following World War II and the Holocaust, racial ideologies in America changed to such a degree that Jews went from being categorized as a distinct non-white race, to a distinct cultural, arguably "ethnic," group included within a more elastic definition of whiteness in the post-war period.[10] However faithful Gibson's film was to the biblical Gospels, a segment of modern America would not tolerate his interpretation because his *Passion* recalled medieval Passion plays, and the violent assaults upon European Jews that sometimes followed Easter Passion reenactments. Still, that the film grossed over $300 million,[11] and spawned a relic cult clearly reveals that certain enduring racial ideologies and religious constructions of evil remain potent in modern America. As one church sign in Denver posted following the release of *The Passion*: "Jews Killed the Lord Jesus, 1 Thess. 2:14, 15. The Holy Scriptures."[12]

## Religion, Gender, and Witchcraft in Early American History

Few events have captured the American historical imagination as the Salem witchcraft trials of the 1690s. Since the nineteenth century, historians have debated whether the Salem witchcraft scare was reflective of similar scares in early American and European history or something that was altogether unique.[13] Furthermore, since Arthur Miller's 1953 play (and 1996 film adaptation) *The Crucible*, Americans have asked themselves whether the Salem witchcraft scare was a religious episode specific to Puritan New England, or a psychological pheno-menon characterized by mass hysteria and paranoia, which under certain historical conditions could erupt again. Of course this was the parable of Miller's 1953 play, as the Salem scare was an allegory for the post-World War II anticommunist "witch-hunt." Miller's *The Crucible*, and his adapted screenplay for Nicholas

Hytner's 1996 film, provides gripping drama even though the plot involving John Proctor, Elizabeth Proctor, and Abigail Williams is fictional. Nevertheless, the play and film are arresting in the ways they champion individuals such as John Proctor over the course of Miller's narrative. Proctor and others accused of witchcraft become examples of courageous individuals who resist mass hysteria and its corrosive consequences, while vilifying those who capitalize upon it, such as Abigail Williams, who empower themselves at the devastating expense of others in their community.

Although Arthur Miller offers a disclaimer that *The Crucible* is historical fiction, he nevertheless did historical research and drew upon Marion Starkey's then classic, *The Devil in Massachusetts*.[14] While researching for the play, Miller immediately recognized that the Salem witchcraft trials were connected to a broader American narrative to which he only provided dramatic emplotment and interpretation to this seemingly provincial story. As Miller noted, "Salem is one of the few events in history with a beginning, middle, and end."[15] Admittedly, Miller fictionalized historical data (the historical John Proctor was about 60 at the time of his trial and Abigail Williams was about 11) in order to emplot his narrative, but taking these dramatic licenses empowers his larger historical interpretation that seeks to find meaning and significance in this tragic historical episode. And though some may see Miller's play as an historical artifact grounded in 1950s America and McCarthyism, the 1996 film adaptation still demonstrates its historical and literary potency by reminding us of the tragic human drama associated with the Salem witchcraft outbreak. Viewers do not need historical reminders of the anti-communist crusade that may have made the play prescient when it was originally presented in 1953. The struggle for John Proctor to find human dignity in the travesty of mass hysteria and injustice (and also the powerful performance given by Daniel Day-Lewis as Proctor) continues to give us historical insight into events like Salem throughout American history.

In this regard the film *The Crucible* reflects this book's recurring theme that narrative fiction can articulate grander historical truths while rendering historical details and context marginal. Rather than dismissing cinematic histories as historically deficient, we need to remember their historical value to tell stories about the human condition in the American past. Nevertheless, recent scholarship in Early American history reveals how historical context remains critical in order to understand the Salem witchcraft craze of the 1690s. Where Miller's play and Hytner's film represent these adolescent girls as opportunists who unleash mass hysteria, recent scholarship has raised questions about gender, Anglo–Indian military conflict, and Salem's struggle with the Anglo-American political economy. Collectively, this scholarship complicates Miller's characterizations of the accusers and those accused of witchcraft in his literary adaptation, requiring us to consider numerous factors that enabled the Salem witchcraft scare to possess New England in the 1690s. And though much of this scholarship was published after the initial dramatization of Miller's *The Crucible* in 1953, Hytner's cinematic adaptation incorporates some of the scholarly themes explored in these academic histories while retaining the integrity of Miller's play. Where scholars and Hytner may disagree about historical detail and representation, they fundamentally appear to agree that Salem was not "actually" about witchcraft per se. That is, they agree that religion may have been the vocabulary and cultural script deployed by the Salem community to interpret what afflicted their Puritan world, but ultimately it was other political, social, economic factors that created the "perfect storm" that erupted into the Salem witchcraft scare of the 1690s.

Determining "what actually happened" in Salem during the 1692 witchcraft hysteria remains widely debated among colonial American historians. Historians of gender in early America have brought to our attention the marginal social positions of women in seventeenth-century New England, particularly the afflicted adolescent girls, and how this factored considerably in the history of the Salem witchcraft episode. Indeed, Carol Karlsen argues that the social marginality of the accusers influenced the ways they directed their accusations at certain prominent women in the Salem community.[16] In a different interpretation, Mary Beth Norton has described the ways Anglo-Indian colonial warfare was critical to the Salem witchcraft scare, especially in terms of the ways the consequences of these military conflicts affected New England's social demographics and who emerged as the accusers and the accused in Salem.[17] Norton contends that some of the accused girls had limited social prospects as orphans of frontier wars, remaining socially marginal members of the Salem community. As accusers, these girls assumed powerful positions and intensified the hysteria. They in turn inversed the community's social structure, enabling them to maintain positions of authority in a patriarchal and theocratic society that otherwise would never have allowed them such power. Finally, historians such as Paul Boyer and Stephen Nissenbaum argue that the eruption of the witchcraft craze in Salem was the consequence of Salem's internal social and economic struggles as it became integrated into the transform- ing Anglo-American Atlantic world.[18] Collectively, these historians demonstrate how the Salem witchcraft outbreak was unique to its historical context, thereby challenging Miller's parable that the Salem witchcraft episode was a historical phenomenon connected to other moments of mass hysteria in American history.

Historians have long recognized Arthur Miller's literary brilliance in his historical rendering of the Salem witchcraft trials. As Paul Boyer and Stephen Nissenbaum state, "When Arthur Miller published *The Crucible* in the early 1950s, he simply outdid historians at their own game."[19] In part, Miller's success rests on the powerful story he tells, but the play is also successful because Miller presents a historical interpretation about a gripping human story in early American history that continues to remain elusive to us. Moreover, Miller recognizes that the Salem witchcraft craze requires a level of historical imagination and interpretation since key legal documents regarding depositions and testimonies are lost. The Salem witchcraft trials, thus, necessitate emplotment and interpretation precisely because so many critical documents are missing, and Miller's *The Crucible* masterfully provides this historical narrative. But the absence of important documents has not detracted historians. Indeed, historians have produced their own historical narratives as well, including constructing emplotments and interpretations that offer explanations as to "what actually happened" to Salem in 1692. In one of the more compelling accounts, Paul Boyer and Stephen Nissenbaum locate the Salem witchcraft scare in the broader history of homogeneous seventeenth-century New England communities and their transformation into more socially and culturally heterogeneous societies by the early eighteenth century. Written in the early 1970s, their book, *Salem Possessed*, works in the tradition of American social history and much of the community studies that characterized colonial American scholarship in the 1970s and 1980s. The interpretive thread of these micro-social histories is quite similar, although a few diverge from the main argument.[20] In brief, these community studies contend that as the Anglo-American Atlantic world became more integrated economically and politically in the late seventeenth and early eighteenth centuries, these structural changes produced social and cultural anxieties about the future of these predominantly Puritan communities, particularly among those New England communities that had envisioned their colonial religious experiments to be immune from the enveloping forces of English commerce and imperial control. A variety of New England communities responded to this cataclysmic changes differently, and often through a religious lens. Indeed, Boyer and Nissenbaum point out that in 1734 adolescent girls of Northampton, Massachusetts were afflicted with physical paroxysms and claimed to be taken by religious spirits like the girls of Salem in 1692.[21] However, in the mid-eighteenth century this religious episode produced a religious revival that led to what some historians call the Great Awakening. As Boyer and Nissenbaum argue, however, a similar religious tremor was seen not as the hand of God, but as the work of Satan in Salem. How do we account for this difference? For Boyer and Nissenbaum, the answer lies within the internal social and economic struggles of Salem as well as the broader political struggles in colonial Massachusetts, and the ways town leaders chose to interpret the event as the consequence of evil.[22] As colonial Massachusetts' initial charter was revoked and the colonial government was beset by political and imperial instability in the late seventeenth century, legitimate colonial authorities could not intervene in the Salem outbreak until late in the witchcraft scare. By then, the local hysteria had metastasized into a much wider outbreak that spread beyond Salem and enveloped Essex County, of which it was a part. Within this political vacuum, historic tensions within Salem surfaced and witchcraft became a weapon by which enemies could attack one another. As Boyer and Nissenbaum note, witchcraft accusations and trials were part of New England culture and society; however, the unique nature of the Salem witchcraft hysteria was symptomatic of subterranean social and economic tensions that surfaced at this moment in time in this particular New England community.[23]

In her book, *In the Devil's Snare*, Mary Beth Norton reminds us of two significant facts: the Salem witch-hunts occurred within a broader context of

Anglo-Indian conflict in colonial New England; and that the larger imperial issues, political and military, informed the progress and extent of the Salem witchcraft hysteria, itself part of an interconnected movement of political and social anxiety that swept Essex County.[24] Significantly, Norton stresses that we need to understand Salem within a specific theological and cultural worldview where people accepted witches and the Devil as part of their cosmology and believed spiritual forces could manipulate human behavior. Historians such as Jon Butler see the Salem episode as an intensification of more pervasive and traditional views about witchcraft generally held by Anglo-American colonists. Butler demonstrates that witchcraft cases in the seventeenth and eighteenth centuries, from New England down through the Chesapeake, reveal extensive popular witchcraft beliefs with a long tradition connected to a deep European medieval past.[25] Working in this intellectual vein, Richard Godbeer has demonstrated the extensiveness of magical practices in New England, their popularity among lay people, and how they were not necessarily equated with witchcraft, despite contrasting declarations by the Puritan ministers.[26] Yet, the scholarship of Butler and Godbeer, while expanding our knowledge of the history of magic and popular religion in New England, minimizes the Salem witchcraft outbreak to such a degree that one could forget that this Puritan community was possessed by social convulsions and mass hysteria in 1692. Perhaps historians (and by extension Americans) have overly focused on the events in Salem. Godbeer apparently believes so, as he documents an overlooked witch-hunt that enveloped Stamford, Connecticut in 1692 as well.[27] But these efforts to historicize the Salem witchcraft episode are more than attempts to recover the conditions that made the outbreak possible. Within the history of Salem lie grander narratives about the human condition and human tragedy, enigmatic stories that act like a gravitational vortex that commands our attention. Salem remains historically significant because Americans believe, if general interest, artistic representations, and voluminous studies on the subject are any indication, that this historical event demands explanation and interpretation.

Mary Beth Norton evidently sees this. In contrast to Butler and Godbeer, Norton recognizes that Salem's magnitude and hysteria ultimately were unique to its historical context, where colonial New England remained locked in an ongoing frontier struggle with Native Americans, and how the unstable, not to say impotent, colonial government failed to address these Indian–settler conflicts, let alone deal with the initial accusations and trials erupting in Salem.[28] For Norton, then, the trial records, however incomplete, remain critical to her narrative because they reveal the complex and multiple levels of social, military, and political conflicts that enabled the local Salem witchcraft outbreak to metastasize into a regional epidemic.[29] Simultaneously provocative, although perhaps disconcerting for traditional historians, Norton's book periodically ventures into the realm of historical inference in order to provide historical interpretation of this arresting episode in American history, particularly where documentation remains sparse or missing. Perhaps recognizing that some academics will be uneasy with these interpretations, she sets these historical discussions in gray boxes following certain chapters. Arguably working in the intellectual vein of Hayden White, Norton sees the historical, perhaps literary, value in the narrative that Salem reveals.[30] Yes, this narrative depends on sparse documentation of legal proceedings, but enough information is available to emplot the narrative. Limited documentary information may limit historical explanation of the Salem tragedy if one follows a traditional social science approach to historical research and analysis. Nevertheless, there remains historical merit in presenting historical research and then interpreting one's scholarship as Norton does in order to find historical meaning and significance in this tragic moment that continues to haunt American history. Granted, Norton's repeated interpretive asides in these gray boxes detract from the book's argumentative thrust by marginalizing critical points she advances. Nonetheless, she recognizes that these interpretive moments, while inferences based on scarce source material, enable readers to see deeper historical issues surrounding the Salem witchcraft scare. Although some of these interpretive asides concern fundamental historical questions that animate people's interest in witchcraft trials such as the veracity of the accusations or motivations of the afflicted girls, other times Norton uses these moments of narrative disjuncture to directly engage the multiple historiographic arguments surrounding the history of witchcraft in colonial America that have yet to provide a satisfactory interpretation.[31]

If the function of a historical narrative is to provide a story that satisfactorily resolves historical questions (that is interpret understanding and meaning in historical moments, connecting the past with the present), then the historiography of the Salem witchcraft scare has yet to offer Americans this desired historical catharsis.[32] In some ways, Norton's intellectual and interpretive transparency reflected in these aside gray boxes allow the reader to see a richer, complex, and fundamentally more human story. Too many scholars claiming to explain the "true" reasons underlying the Salem witchcraft outbreak dismiss the "world of wonders" that informed Puritan worldviews. These scholars prefer to amplify more secular issues such as the veiled accusations against innocent members in the Salem community as a way to attack one's enemies for personal, secular material or political gain, or to search for environmental or medical factors (such as the pharmacological connections between local plants and their ability to create hallucinations) that produced mass hysteria in Salem.[33] In contrast, Norton respects the worldview and cosmology of seventeenth-century New Englanders, weaving a narrative that more accurately represents the beliefs and fears of a people in their place in time. Norton's sympathetic rendering of Salem's history enables readers to emotionally engage with their past. Her book may not entirely provide the kind of cathartic conclusion we want from a historical narrative of the Salem witchcraft scare (and perhaps we will never achieve this), but it offers a level of historical understanding in ways that recalls Arthur Miller's literary efforts and also seeks to recover historical significance in this tragic episode in American history.

Norton's interpretive and intellectual achievements aside, her narrative's attempt to stress the broader political, imperial, and military conflicts influencing the 1692 witchcraft outbreak overshadows the gender and sexual politics in the history of witchcraft in New England, no matter how much she tries to remind us that these issues were evident in the Salem outbreak. Carol Karlsen, however, describes the ways in which the Salem hysteria was a more intense manifestation of the history of gender in New England Puritan society. True, Salem was particularly unique in the ways in which those who comprised the accusers and accused were predominantly women, but the nature of the accusations and the fact that women predominantly numbered among the accused and the executed reflected a longer ambivalent history of gender, sexuality, and power in colonial Puritan society. Karlsen notes that Puritans had constructed a more flexible theology regarding gender relations compared with medieval Catholicism. Where the medieval Roman Catholic Church had uniformly categorized women as the embodiment of sin with few redemptive possibilities (based upon Eve's temptation with the serpent in the Garden of Eden and subsequent tempting of Adam with the apple from the Tree of Knowledge), Puritans constructed a theology that placed women as more (but not exactly) spiritual equals with men. In Puritan theology, women had the possibility to be among God's predestined elect, a theological position that encouraged educational and religious opportunities. For example, Puritanism (and Calvinism more generally) encouraged literacy among its followers regardless of their gender, as reading the Bible was valued in order to engage with God and lead a spiritual life in the secular world.[34]

But these theological views had their limitations, as Karlsen notes. Anne Hutchinson most famously demonstrated the reluctance among Puritans to fully accept women as spiritual equals as most Puritan religious leaders rebuked her claims to be a minister of God's word. Accusations of witchcraft and Satan's influence surrounded Hutchinson's religious movement, and she eventually left Massachusetts with her followers to the more religiously tolerant colony of Rhode Island to avoid persecution. According to Karlsen, Hutchinson tested the gender limits of Puritan theology.[35] Moreover, this Puritan worldview, which firmly believed in witchcraft, struggled to reinforce a gender hierarchy in colonial New England society in the seventeenth century. These efforts were complicated as women acquired property as widows, holding sufficient power to either maintain that property or distribute it among their children according to her deceased husband's or her own wishes. When some widows refused to remarry, in part to maintain control of their property, they became marginal members of Puritan communities. Karlsen contends that these social and economic conditions made these women vulnerable to accusations of witchcraft.[36]

Furthermore, witchcraft was the category through which Puritans interpreted female sexuality. If Puritanism contained sexual impulses (some would say repress) in order for followers to maintain a proper Christian life, it was believed that witchcraft, sorcery, and other forms of pagan religious practices unleashed sexual activity, particularly among women. Puritans did not fully disagree with their Catholic contemporaries that women were more susceptible to sexual temptations given their collective beliefs in the Eve narrative. They believed women who were under the spell of witchcraft or influenced by the Devil transgressed strict gender hierarchies, especially when they challenged authorities, who in some cases included Puritan ministers.[37] Jane Kamensky notes how afflicted girls, whether entranced or pretending, would employ and deploy the discourse of witchcraft to subvert accepted gendered norms, even lash out at leading Puritan ministers such as Cotton Mather.[38]

Here, historians of women and colonial New England connect with some of Arthur Miller's interpretive arguments about the history of Puritanism and witchcraft in Salem. While Miller's 1953 play contains and codes female sexuality, his adapted screenplay for Nicholas Hytner's 1996 film is more explicit regarding Puritan attitudes about gender and sexuality. In both the play and film Abigail Williams confesses to her uncle the Reverend Samuel Parris that she and other adolescent girls were dancing in the forest when they were discovered by Parris. Her uncle interprets the frolic as "some obscene practice" even as Abigail defends the girls' behavior as "sport." In disbelief, Parris states,

> I saw [his black slave] Tituba waving her arms over the fire when I came on you. Why was she doing that? And I heard a screeching and gibberish coming from her mouth. She was swaying like a dumb beast over that fire!

And though Abigail feigns innocence to her uncle, Parris confronts her with the fact that he saw a discarded dress in the forest, declaring to Abigail, "And I thought I saw—someone naked running through the trees."[39] In this exchange, Abigail continues to deny what her uncle claims to have witnessed. In the play the girl's illicit sexual behavior is described in this dialogic exchange, leaving the audience to determine the degree to which the girl's behavior in the woods actually occurred, or whether Reverend Parris's Puritan attitudes about pagan religious practices and sexuality overly scripts the way he interprets the scene in the woods. Hytner's 1996 cinematic adaptation, however, accepts the girl's unbridled sexuality and the ways dancing in the woods and participating in Tituba's pagan, perhaps voodoo, religious practices were a wanton release from Puritan repressive sexual and gender constraints. Indeed, in Hytner's film viewers see the ways the girls and Tituba were "screeching" with "gibberish coming from [their] mouth," to rephrase Miller's play. And together, they were all "swaying like a dumb beast over that fire!"

In fact, Hytner begins his film with the girls escaping to the woods, bringing charms to conjure magical spells which they hope will influence their romantic relationships and fantasies.[40] Yet, in a stunning scene nowhere evident in the play, Abigail Williams (Winona Ryder) seizes and dismembers a chicken, smearing its blood over her face and body in a lurid and sexual manner, hoping that conjuring spirits will supernaturally consummate her romantic fantasy to marry John Proctor. Although initially horrified by Abigail, the rest of the girls then shriek and undress, dancing and participating in a libidinal religious frolic to invoke the power of the pagan spirits. In the film, Parris does in fact discover the girls in their hyper-sexualized state while participating in the pagan rituals. When the girls see Parris, they flee back to Salem hoping to hide their transgressive behavior. Indeed, it is the fear that accusations of their "diabolical" activities could lead to criminal charges of witchcraft that provoke the girls to confirm rumors that Salem has been bewitched by diabolical forces, afflicting them and controlling their aberrant behavior. Thus, to defend their sexual transgressions and subversive gender roles, the afflicted girls drew upon Puritan cosmology and theological scripts to confirm the fears that Salem was within the grips of the Devil and his minions, who now lived among them, working to undermine God's work in this Puritan society. In Hytner's *Crucible*, the conditions that produced the Salem witchcraft hysteria in 1692 were thus ones rooted in Puritan values about gender roles and sexuality. Moreover, the ability of the afflicted girls to empower themselves by accusing socially respectable figures in the Salem community reinforced a worldview that believed witchcraft unleashed sexual and gender disorder. Like the works of Karlsen and Kamensky, Hytner's *Crucible* grounds the Salem witchcraft trials and the ensuing social disorder in the historical context of a Puritan worldview that defined and stressed hierarchical gender relations. Collectively, these cinematic and academic historical interpretations stress the ways in which the discourse of evil was deployed in colonial New England to marginalize and criminalize women who transgressed these strict social and theological gender categories.

## Satan and Evil in a Comparative Cultural and Historical Context

As much as historians, artists, and Americans have focused upon the Salem witchcraft trials in American history, witchcraft hysteria was unique neither to this Puritan community, nor to the American colonies in general. Indeed, historians of European witchcraft have also documented similar witchcraft outbreaks, noting how the seventeenth century was notable for spasmodic episodes of witchcraft accusations, trials, and executions.[41] Some of these historians have also stressed the critical dimensions of gender in the history of European witchcraft.[42] While a number of historians have demonstrated the ways social, political, and economic conditions contributed to European witchcraft hysteria, some have also noted how the Protestant Reformation, Catholic Counter-Reformation, and the ensuing religious wars factored considerably into the extensiveness and violence of witchcraft hysteria in seventeenth-century Europe.[43] In this respect, the Salem witchcraft outbreak is part of a broader history of witchcraft and the social construction of evil in the West. Indeed, as we compare witchcraft outbreaks in the West to other moments of religious hysteria in non-Western cultures, we see historical connections to the ways these episodes of mass hysteria are manifestations of wrenching social, economic, and political transformations. However, the centrality of Satan in Christian cosmology, and the ways he represents the embodiment of evil manipulating the natural and supernatural world reflects a fundamental difference between these histories of mass hysteria. By interpreting broader structural changes in their communities as the work of Satan, people in the West elevated local conflicts into a cosmological moral battle between those who worked for the forces of God and those who worked for the forces of the Devil. Connecting witchcraft accusations and trials to this transcendent spiritual struggle between good and evil could only lead to a worldview that legitimized violence, eliminating those people believed to be transgressing and subverting the will of God.

In 1768, a sorcery scare enveloped late imperial China similar to those that erupted in seventeenth-century Europe and the American colonies. In East and West, the fusion of popular religious culture and state power magnified local fears into mass hysteria that involved leading political authorities, resulting in state violence. However, where the witchcraft outbreaks were diverse and diffuse in the West, the sorcery scare was concentrated in China's Lower Yangtze region. More important, the 1768 sorcery cases involved the imperial bureaucracy and arrested the attention of the Chinese Emperor Hongli, intensifying and centralizing the role of the state in this sorcery scare. Based upon accusations of "soulstealing" and queue-clipping, popular peasant religious fears became a vexing political problem for the Emperor, creating political conditions that challenged his authority and the legitimacy of his ruling dynasty. Much as Mary Beth Norton connects the Salem witchcraft crisis to colonial military and political conflicts in New England, Philip Kuhn attributes the 1768 sorcery scare to the political, military, and social problems facing the Emperor Hongli. Hongli's army faced humiliating defeats against the Chin-ch'uan peoples of western Szechwan and King Aungzeya of Burma further south. As Kuhn speculates, "might Hongli's fury and frustration have spilled over into domestic politics" as his armies "floundered" in these military campaigns?[44] Although Kuhn grounds the sorcery scare in popular Chinese religious beliefs, he offers a more functionalist approach to this Chinese history of religious mass hysteria like many scholars of Salem. For Kuhn, the Chinese sorcery scare of 1768 reflects the social and political tensions troubling the Manchu dynasty, and its ability to exercise power over an imperial bureaucracy largely controlled by a Han elite.[45]

Kuhn's interpretation of the 1768 sorcery scare does not challenge beliefs in soulstealing and the fears it engendered in late-eighteenth-century China. But like scholars of witchcraft in the West, Kuhn begs the question of why the soulstealing scare erupted into mass hysteria and involved the Chinese imperial government. Soulstealing has a long history in traditional Chinese popular religion and other soulstealing episodes erupted in 1810 and 1876, but they were never as extensive socially nor politically. For Kuhn, the Lower Yangtze region was ripe for such an outbreak of religious hysteria. First, China's wrenching transformation into a more commercial society by the late eighteenth century also produced a socially mobile population that in turn created social and cultural anxiety. Laborers and beggars drifted into previously more homogeneous and traditional societies, coming under increased suspicion for problems that vexed local communities as a consequence of social and economic changes. Added to these broader structural transformations, the uncertain legitimacy of the minority Manchu dynasty ruling over the majority Han population produced further tensions. As a result of a Manchu imperial edict, all Chinese males were required to dress their hair in a queue, a Manchu custom and the political and cultural signifier of popular allegiance to Manchu imperial hegemony. Furthermore in popular Chinese religion, hair held religious significance as it was believed to be an extension of the soul. Was queue-clipping a sign of sedition against Manchu political authority or soulstealing? For Kuhn, in 1768 China, it was both, and his study reveals why fears of soulstealing reached the level of mass hysteria, as well as providing reasons why the Emperor Hongli became invested in the prosecution of soulstealing cases. Local courts and the imperial bureaucracy were slow to prosecute local soulstealing accusations, frustrating the emperor who proceeded to call into question the allegiance of the Han officials overseeing the soulstealing cases.

While there were episodes of mass hysteria leading to the torture, and in some instances, execution of a few accused soulstealers in local Chinese communities, the grinding and halting machinery of the imperial bureaucracy limited the breadth and scope of the 1768 sorcery scare, much to the consternation of Emperor Hongli and Chinese commoners who believed sorcerers were traveling throughout China stealing souls. For Kuhn, however, the elaborate and complex imperial bureaucracy that operated by its own rules, laws, and traditions prevented this episode of limited religious mass hysteria, albeit one that intensely held the interest of the emperor, from escalating into widespread state terror. This is not to conclude that China's eighteenth-century imperial bureaucracy was "modern" if rationality and constitutional legal mechanisms define modern bureaucratic culture.[46] The imperial bureaucracy, nevertheless, adhered to a rule of law and tradition that could serve as a barrier against the political whims of the emperor, and the hysteria of the Chinese populace in its efforts to ensure that traditional definitions of justice and due process were followed. As Kuhn states,

> Nobody mourns the old Chinese bureaucracy. The social harm it did, even by the standards of the day, went well beyond the crushed ankles of helpless vagrants. Yet its nature impeded zealotry of any sort, whether for good or ill. Without that great sheet-anchor, China yaws wildly in the storm. Without a workable alternative, leaders can manipulate mass fears and turn them with terrible force against the deviants and scapegoats of their own day—anyone vulnerable to labeling, either for his social origins or his exotic beliefs—with none to stand between.[47]

In his historical representation of the political struggle between Emperor Hongli and the Han-controlled imperial bureaucracy, Kuhn finds interpretive meaning in his narrative of the sorcery scare of 1768. The steadfast truculence of the Han imperial bureaucracy ultimately minimized the soulstealing hysteria. For Kuhn, therein lies the historical significance in this episode of religious mass hysteria, statecraft, and imperial power.

Yet, there may be more to this story of the 1768 soulstealing crisis. Can we also draw another conclusion from this sorcery scare that considers the cultural construction of evil in Chinese popular religion? Seen from this light, the sorcery scare might illuminate how cultural categories of evil in Western culture were fundamentally different, and why the witchcraft hysteria in Salem was much more lethal despite being more limited to a few New England communities. Here, the figure of Satan in Christian cosmology and his spiritual struggle with God provides critical insight to understanding the ways Puritans defined evil and Satan's ability to manipulate the natural and supernatural worlds, including human behavior. As much as religious systems stress hope and offer optimistic beliefs and rituals to confront our everyday lives, they also provide moral philosophies and cosmologies that help people understand the just, the unjust, and the reasons why people suffer. As Clifford Geertz points out, evil is a powerful epistemological construct that explains "why rain falls on the just, but not on the unjust."[48] Through categories and symbols of evil, people are able to rationalize life's horrors and injustices. Evil, then, is an ethical and supernatural explanation that imparts meaning and order upon the otherwise capricious world we live in.

In this vein, various religious systems have developed symbols of evil, often represented in a culturally constructed demonology. In Chinese popular religion, demons, known as *kuei*, are malevolent spirits "who are responsible for any untoward happening, any sort of trouble that cannot be readily explained by a more obvious cause." But, according to Laurence Thompson,

> it is especially significant that in the last analysis the depredations of malignant spirits were not a principle of evil working for its ends but the functioning of *karma*. The *kuei* were after all maleficent because they had been wronged . . . [t]heir vengeful natures might cause them to harm those who were apparently innocent, but if one could know all the facts, one would find the karmic process working in the long run with perfect justice.[49]

Satan, in contrast, does act malevolently for his own ends, and towards God's defeat in the cosmological struggle between good and evil. Where propitiating the gods and leading a pious life can ward off demons and lead to good karma in Chinese popular religion, humans have little to no power over Satan's behavior in Christian cosmology. As Thompson further notes, a variety of religious cultures practice forms of exorcism to cast out demons.[50] However, Chinese popular religion and Western Christianity fundamentally approach exorcism and demon possession differently. Chinese popular religion recognizes the capricious nature of spirit possession, but humans have the ability to expel demons from the possessed once they have satisfied the wronged malevolent spirits.[51] In Christianity, however, any kind of spiritual negotiating or bargaining with Satan is incomprehensible. To acquiesce to God's spiritual antagonist would only validate his supernatural power. Therefore, while some Christians, notably Catholics, recognize the power of exorcism, the victory over the Devil is ultimately only temporary, as the fundamental battle between Satan and Christians is locked in a perpetual spiritual conflict until Jesus Christ's Second Coming and Armageddon, the cosmological war that ostensibly will lead to Satan's defeat.

The 1768 sorcery scare in China was unique for enveloping important imperial officials in this episode of religious hysteria, most notably the Emperor Hongli. However, more conventional moral panics based upon Chinese popular religion, rumor, and fear of malevolent spiritual forces have erupted throughout Chinese history. As in Western societies, marginal and vulnerable people were often accused as perpetrators bringing evil and calamity to local communities, according to Barend J. Ter Haar. Ter Haar notes that none of these more localized moral panics in Chinese history ever reached the scale of the sorcery scare of 1768, but they could involve local magistrates and spread rapidly from one community to another, facilitated by a wildfire of repeated rumor. Indeed, the power of the rumor, grounded in perceived social, political, and/or economic realities and anxieties empowered popular Chinese ghost stories. Collectively, these stories and rumors enabled these narratives of malevolence to take on social and political power, stirring up moral panic, and often leading to local violence against those suspected of bringing evil to these local communities.[52] According to Ter Haar, witchcraft and scapegoating in China paralleled those in Western communities in this regard, particularly in the ways rumors and ghost-witchcraft stories could explain local fears and anxieties, which periodically led to episodes of mass violence. Rumors, it must be remembered, are powerful modes of discourse because they are sources of information based upon possibilities, and in these cases, possibilities of malevolence, and whether the information communicated is factual remains fundamentally immaterial. That people who spread these rumors believed them to be true, becoming enveloped in these episodes of moral panic and mass violence, reveals the degree to which we need to take seriously the power of rumor and narratives of evil as communicative discourse. Furthermore, Ter Haar reminds us that ghost-witchcraft stories in Chinese history are significant in order for us to understand popular religious culture and the ways they illuminate moral and epistemological systems that inform people's worldviews across pre-modern (and some would argue even in modern) cultures and societies. We should remember that Satan is the ultimate boogey-man story. He is the antagonist in religious narratives told among Christians that describe the ways Satan unleashes his malevolent powers to harm and ensnare them, opposing the work of God in their communities. As with Chinese ghost stories, Satanic narratives fundamentally provide meaning and coherence in Christian cosmology that explain the presence of evil in the natural and supernatural world.

As mentioned earlier, Satan remains a distinct religious construction in Western Christian cosmology in contrast to other figures of malevolence in various cultural demonologies. Evil, for Satan, is not a means to an end, but an end unto itself. That end, of course, is the destruction of God and his plan for human redemption. However, there are other critical points of religious difference in these cultural constructions of malevolence. In Chinese popular religion, evil is regarded as an outside force, often embodied in marginal or outside figures in local communities. In Western Christianity, in contrast, Satan is the "intimate enemy," the one within a closely connected community who betrays trust and friendship in order to achieve evil ends. Satan, or Lucifer, after all, was God's most revered angel, but who believed himself to be higher than God and his beloved human creations. For Lucifer's sin of pride, he was cast out of heaven to reign in Hell, to be forever at war with God. As Elaine Pagels demonstrates in *The Origin of Satan*, the figure of the satan actually has its origins in Judaism, where the satan (the capitalization would come over the course of the history of Judaism and when Christians personified him as the Evil One) could be a force of either good or evil, serving fundamentally as an obstacle for humans in their spiritual paths.[53] Even as Satan takes on a more malevolent character over time in the evolution of Judaism, it is never clear whether he is working for or against God in this religious tradition. In the Book of Job, for example, Satan attempts to undermine Job's faith and relationship with God by negotiating with the Lord to strip Job of his material wealth, destroy his family, and inflict physical ailments upon him. In the narrative of Job, Satan has argued to God that if disasters were to befall Job, then his faithful servant would turn away from him. The Lord, in turn, allows Satan to take everything from Job, knowing he will continue to have faith in God despite his calamities. While the moral of this story is Job's persistent faith despite his inflicted misery, we should remember that Satan remains an ambiguous figure of malevolence in this narrative and throughout most of the Judaic religion, sometimes working with and sometimes working against God's plan for human redemption.[54]

In her social history of Satan, Elaine Pagels contends that early Christians transformed Satan into the "intimate enemy" as a way to explain critical historical and theological questions about the history of Jesus Christ and the centrality of the crucifixion and resurrection in Christian theology.[55] One of Judaism's remarkable contributions to the world's religions has been its moralization of the universe.[56] In this cosmological battle between good and evil, malevolent forces challenge God's chosen people, and hinder their ability to fulfill their religious covenant with him. Pagels further notes that Christians transformed this supernatural moral struggle,[57] recasting Satan as the evil force undermining the mission of God's son, Jesus Christ, to redeem the sins of humanity. Christ's crucifixion and resurrection are central to Christian theology because Christ's death, according to orthodox Christianity, is the ultimate human sacrifice that renewed the religious covenant between God and humanity. If one believes that Christ died for his sins, then his sins are redeemed, leading to reunification with God in paradise. According to Pagels, numerous questions surrounded the historical Jesus, most notably why one of his disciples would betray him and turn him over to authorities; why the Jews largely rejected him, even though he initially came to them, claiming to be the savior whom the Jewish prophets of old had foretold would emerge among them, and restore Israel to greatness; and why he was tried as a seditious criminal, first by Jewish religious leaders, and then by the Roman governor Pontius Pilate, who had Christ tortured and crucified.

Pagels argues that Christians established Satan as the evil force responsible for these multiple acts of human malevolence that led to Christ's crucifixion.[58] Beginning with the Gospel of Mark, which many scholars maintain is the foundational narrative for the four canonical Gospels, Christ's human narrative accelerated when Satan tempted him in the desert following his baptism and dedication to God. After Christ had been fasting for forty days, Satan visits and tempts the physically weakened Christ three times, but is ultimately rebuked by Christ. As he retreats, Satan remarks that he will return at a later date to triumph over Christ. This enigmatic statement foreshadows how later human actions will be part of a greater struggle choreographed by Satan working through Jewish religious leaders and even through one of Jesus' disciples to explain how ordinary human beings could overpower and determine the death of a divine savior. Yet, for Pagels, this narrative of spiritual warfare and betrayal needs to be examined within the broader historical and political context of Roman-occupied Judea. As she points out, there are numerous approaches to reading the canonical four Gospels, and looking at the New Testament Gospels as wartime literature is another historically significant way to interpret the social history of the Early Christian Church and the development of Satan in Christian cosmology.[59]

The Jewish War in 66 CE was the signature historical event that influenced the theological trajectory of Satan in Christian cosmology, according to Pagels.[60] At this historic moment, when numerous Jews rebelled against Roman rule, Jewish leaders and their followers fought among themselves. Some leaders (including important religious leaders) believed that Jews should capitulate to Roman rule to protect their religious traditions; others wanted to end the Jewish uprising, seeking closer cultural ties with Roman culture and the Hellenistic tradition; and yet other leaders persisted in their military resistance against Roman rule. The civil wars among the Jews produced lasting enmity, and when the Romans defeated the remaining Jewish rebels, they destroyed the Jewish Temple, and thus the power of the Jewish religious hierarchy. The destruction of the Temple transformed Judaism from a centralized religion centered on the Temple and its religious leaders to one that was a more decentralized, fragmented religious community; where the Torah and local rabbis replaced the destroyed Temple and its leading religious clerics as the centers of religious authority in dispersed Jewish communities throughout the Mediterranean world, and beyond.[61] In this environment, the nascent Christian church moved from being a cult within Judaism to its own religious movement, developing a demonology of Satan to explain why Jews widely rejected Christ as their prophetic savior, and how he had worked among Jewish clerics to undermine Christ's earthly mission. In league with the Devil, according to the canonical Gospels, Jewish religious leaders plotted Jesus' death, waiting for the moment when they could eliminate him and his influence.[62] This moment arrived when Jesus' disciple Judas Iscariot, who the Gospels also claim was under the influence of Satan, turned him over to Jewish religious leaders. In this rendering of history, these Jewish leaders, under Satan's aegis, are Christ's enemies. The Roman authorities (although historically the real powerful figures who authorized and conducted crucifixions) succumbed to the pressures of the Jewish leading clerics. The four canonical Gospels fundamentally narrate this story of Jewish betrayal, beginning initially with the high Jewish religious leaders in the Gospel of Matthew to the entire Jewish people in the last of the Gospels, that which tradition calls the Gospel of John.[63]

This religious and historical interpretation of Jewish culpability and Christ's crucifixion informs Mel Gibson's film *The Passion*. Although the film does not explicitly present Jewish religious leaders, and Jews in general, as working on behalf of Satan to destroy Jesus Christ (and by extension, the Christian Church), their sinister behavior in Gibson's movie is part of a longer history of accusing Jews as "intimate enemies" and minions of the Devil undermining Christianity described earlier. More than the numerous films portraying the life of Jesus Christ, Gibson's film connects with recent historiography about early and medieval Christianity such as Pagel's *The Origin of Satan* and to some degree, Caroline Walker Bynum's *Holy Feast* and *Holy Fast*, particularly in the ways the film identifies violent suffering with spiritual transcendence.[64] While the choice of presenting the film in the ancient languages of Latin and Aramaic transparently evokes the film's attempt to represent historical accuracy, it is actually the demonization of Jewish leaders and the graphic violence of Christ's Passion that achieves a measure of historical accuracy. Provocatively, the film's historicity closely follows the canonical Gospels, particularly the Gospel of John. As Pagels states,

> Writing c. 100 C.E., John dismisses the device of the devil as an independent supernatural character . . . Instead, as John tells the story, Satan, like God himself, appears incarnate, first in Judas Iscariot, then in the Jewish authorities as they mount opposition to Jesus, and finally in those John calls, "the Jews"—a group he sometimes characterizes as Satan's allies, now as separate from Jesus and his followers as darkness is from light, or the forces of hell from the armies of heaven.[65]

While the demonization of one's enemies transcends cultures over time and space, the centrality of this demonization, particularly towards Jews, defined early Christianity and shaped the history of anti-Semitism in the West.

Gibson's film fundamentally reflects the Passion plays reenacted in medieval Europe that were similarly anti-Semitic. The medieval ethos of the film is most evident in the brutal violence Christ endures during his trial, torture and crucifixion in the movie. The film bluntly shows Christ's body eviscerated, bleeding and violently torn apart to amplify his suffering. The movie wants viewers to emotionally and spiritually engage with this violent reenactment that only films can accurately portray. Despite the long tradition of Passion reenactments in Western history, only cinematic techniques can realistically portray Christ's violent and visceral suffering. In this way, the film signifies medieval Christianity's ideal of *Imatatio Christi*, the powerful belief that one could approximate Christ's divinity and spirituality by reenacting his physical suffering endured during his Passion by violently torturing their bodies in order to achieve the spiritual sublime.[66] As Caroline Walker Bynum has noted, numerous Christian saints such as St. Francis of Assisi practiced *Imatatio Christi* in their religious asceticism, but particular female saints were attracted to this religious practice because of their ambivalent relationship with their bodies. While female ascetics attached spiritual significance to food and their bodies (women's bodies, like Christ's flesh transubstantiated in the Eucharist, were valued as sources of nourishment) they also believed that the flesh symbolized worldly desires and led to mortal sin. In *Holy Feast and Holy Fast*, Bynum demonstrates how particular medieval female saints endured *Imatatio Christi* because they maintained that only through bodily suffering could one transcend the body's physical limitations, strengthen spirituality, and reach divinity.[67]

This ideal of *Imatatio Christi* signifies the horrific gore in Gibson's film and its brutal representation of Christ's Passion and crucifixion. His film fundamentally wants viewers to see the ways in which Christ's suffering was greater than any other that humans have endured, and how Jesus' triumph over extreme torture and crucifixion reveals his divine love for humanity. Brutal violence, then, is the film's necessary aesthetic to amplify its rhetoric of human suffering, redemption, and spiritual transcendence. In this regard, Gibson's reenactment of the Passion demands that the audience participate in a virtual form of *Imatatio Christi*. It draws us into its gory and visceral universe in order for us to understand the historical and religious meaning of Christ's crucifixion, reliving his Passion in order to achieve sublime divinity. Notably, Gibson's *Passion* spawned a relic cult that encouraged people to remember and reenact their cinematic religious experience. People can purchase relics through Gibson's production company, such as nails that resembled those used in the film for Christ's crucifixion. This relic cult further reveals how *Imatatio Christi* is not simply an archaic medieval form of Christian asceticism predicated on bodily torture. Even in this more symbolic and commercial form, Gibson's relic cult illuminates the ways in which variations of *Imatatio Christi* remain a religious ideal for some Christians in our contemporary world as a way to seek spiritual fulfillment.

Gibson's *Passion* was a financial success, exceeding $370 million in the United States alone. Yet, his film represents Jewish leaders nefariously, and this portrayal produced widespread outcries claiming that the movie is anti-Semitic. Whether intended or not, Gibson's movie recalled those medieval Passion plays that vilified Jews as "Christ-Killers," and fanned anti-Semitic flames following its cinematic release in 2004. As earlier noted, a church sign in Denver, Colorado cited biblical scripture that stated "Jews killed the Lord Jesus."[68] Still, given the power of Christian Fundamentalism in the United States, it is quite remarkable that these anti-Semitic accusations dominated media attention and stunned Mel Gibson, requiring him to defend his cinematic interpretation of Christ's Passion and ultimately forcing him to re-edit the film.[69] Yet the film cannot entirely escape anti-Semitism, even in its toned-down version, because the historical sources that inform the film, namely the canonical New Testament Gospels, ultimately vilify Jewish leaders, and all Jews in the case of the Gospel of John, as working on behalf of Satan. Nonetheless, it can be argued that the success of the film's critics to persuade Gibson to change the movie's overt anti-Semitism hinged upon a reevaluation of Jews in contemporary American society. As Matthew Frye Jacobson notes, Jews have been socially and politically marginalized throughout most of American history, an example of how a people's religious faith defined them as a distinct race.[70] As Pagels' book demonstrates, Christians have been vilifying Jews throughout Christianity's history, affirming the centrality of gentiles in Christian theology because they accepted Christ as humanity's savior, while demonizing Jews for rejecting Christ as the prophetic redeemer.[71] The history of Jews in America continued this historical trajectory. However, with the advent of empirical science and eugenics at the end of the nineteenth century, Jews were eventually viewed as a biologically distinct race. Jewish claims to naturalization and citizenship, along with other recently European immigrants, were viewed with suspicion by the dominant white Anglo-Saxon Protestant American community.[72] Since the 1790 naturalization law that established the process by which "free white persons" could become American citizens, "whiteness" has been a contested cultural and political, not to mention racial, category, and Jews have been viewed as not white until recent history. Anglo-Saxon Protestants equated whiteness with virtuous citizenship, the necessary ingredient for a stable, self-governing republic. By restricting the definition of whiteness to themselves for most of our national history, Anglo-Saxon Americans denigrated people excluded from this category as unfit to exercise responsible citizenship, even if these excluded Americans who followed the naturalization process or were born in the United States.[73]

Yet, over the course of the twentieth century, particularly as a result of the racial violence of World War II and the Holocaust, white American views of Jews changed, along with racial attitudes more generally. As Matthew Frye Jacobson contends, the history of race in America transformed in the post-war period as whiteness became a more elastic category, now including those once excluded immigrant European nationalities and Jews. As the African American civil rights movement accelerated in the 1950s, the American conversation about race focused on the binary categories of white and black.[74] As Jews "became" white in the post-World War II era, and the Holocaust represented the ultimate signifier of racial violence, anti-Semitism is now less tolerated in American society. Criticisms of Mel Gibson's anti-Semitic portrayal of Jewish leaders (and Jews more generally) reflects these seismic changes in American racial attitudes, forcing Gibson to alter his film. Nevertheless, that the film was wildly popular among American Christians reflects how views regarding Jewish culpability for Jesus Christ's death remain persuasive in powerful parts of the Christian community.

Gibson's *Passion* thus needs to be viewed in the context of the long history of Satan and demonizing antagonists within one's religious community as the "intimate enemy." As Elaine Pagels notes, Christians would fundamentally signify evil by vilifying those who challenged its orthodoxy based on the canonical Gospels and the Roman Church's authority, and once Christianity disconnected from its Judaic foundations.[75] The emerging Roman church was centralizing its authority in Late Antiquity as it established a hierarchical organizational structure and a theological orthodoxy. It thus branded those Christians who denied their ecclesiastical legitimacy, such as the Gnostics, as heretics in league with Satan, working to destroy Christianity. More threatening than pagans and other non-believers, these declared heretics were intimately and dangerously familiar with the Christian faith, but the Roman Church pronounced that these heretics perverted the "true faith" and led their followers astray. It is this legacy of fear, suspicion, and anxiety surrounding the diabolical "intimate enemy" within the Christian community that has led to vehement and violent attacks against insiders who have challenged various orthodoxies, whether they are religious, social, or political.

This history of demonization in Western Christianity has also defined the history of Western Civilization, beginning with the early Roman Church's attack against, and then elimination of heterodox Christian beliefs in Late Antiquity through the Middle Ages (perhaps including the religious Crusades and wars against Muslims). This history continued with the Protestant Reformation and the European religious wars in the sixteenth and seventeenth centuries, leading perhaps inexorably towards Salem. However one chooses to interpret this history of Satan as the intimate enemy, his powerful narrative of malevolence continues to terrify and horrify even those who do not consider themselves practicing Christians. Whenever Americans are collectively gripped with fear and anxiety, whether that was in our colonial past or in our more secularized present, Satan has resurfaced as the signifier to explain our collective decline from a traditional moral, social, and political order into an abyss of hedonism, licentiousness, and social disorder. Like Puritan ministers sermonizing their Jeremiads of hellfire and damnation, voluble social, political, and religious critics in recent history have maintained that the United States has fallen from God's grace into a morass of moral and social decline largely due to the women's, gay, and (to some degree) minority, civil rights movements, as well as the sexual revolution of the 1960s and 1970s. Indeed, some scholars have argued that the palpable fears and anxieties provoked by the systematic transformation of American social and cultural institutions as a result of these social movements, including fundamental changes in Constitutional interpretations regarding protected privacy rights, the make-up of the nuclear family, and the secularization of American public schools, significantly contributed to the moral panic of the 1980s, widely known as the "satanic cult scare."[76] That some of the principal people accused of being satanic cult leaders during this moral panic were once-trusted teachers and day-care providers speaks volumes about the ways in which social anxieties were connected to the increasing numbers of women in the workforce, the growing number of children in child care, and the marginalization of religion in American public schools.[77] Moreover, the 1980s satanic cult scare reveals the persistence of Satan's signifying power, and the fear of the "intimate enemy" in recent American history.

## *The Exorcist,* Gender, and Sexuality in Recent American History

Critically, the number of horror films released in the late 1960s and the following decades, including *Rosemary's Baby, Dawn of the Dead*, and the countless "slasher" films of the 1980s, touch upon some of these themes of social and cultural anxiety in the political wake of the 1960s social movements and sexual revolution.[78] Indeed, Gregory Waller notes that the premieres of Roman Polanski's *Rosemary's Baby* and George Romero's *Dawn of the Dead* in 1968 were more than coincidental, as this was the year of Robert Kennedy's and Martin Luther King's assassinations, and Richard Nixon's presidential election. As a genre, horror films represent our anxieties and nightmares, and their entertainment value lies in reliving and confronting those nightmares, an experience that ultimately leads to a catharsis that overcomes the terror inherent in our anxieties, at least in the context of the movie. *Rosemary's Baby* and *Dawn of the Dead* are two films in the horror genre that explore the decline of the nuclear family and the impotency of our political institutions, aptly reflecting collective American fears surrounding the chaos of the late 1960s.[79] Nevertheless, nothing had prepared Americans for the horror, sacrilege, and sheer emotional violence of *The Exorcist* in 1973, despite the widespread popularity of the book upon which it is based. In this singular film, generational and gender anxieties collide with graphic religious symbolism and terror, interconnecting a story of an innocent young girl possessed by a horrific demonic force with a broader story about an innocent, adolescent nation also possessed by unseen malevolent forces seemingly destroying American society. Recent history only confirmed collective fears that the country was becoming unhinged. Americans believed their political institutions had betrayed them, first with the Vietnam War and then Watergate, both of which were taking over the national consciousness. The assassinations of charismatic and hopeful leaders in the 1960s, the explosive Chicago Democratic Convention which exposed generational conflict, and the decline of the nation's industrial manufacturing base at the outset of the 1970s only increased this palpable unease and fear. Americans seemed to be sleepwalking through a collective nightmare in the early 1970s.

It is within this context we need to understand the film's terrifying narrative about the power of evil and the pathological ways we want to signify and explain the horrors that envelope us. Yet, people searching for a singular moral story that offers catharsis and narrative closure in this movie will be unsatisfied. While the film is segmented in three parts (the Iraq archeological dig, Regan's diagnosis, and the exorcism) traditional emplotment and narrative patterns elude us. In fact, the disjointed plot reinforces the film's general theme about the conflict between rationality and irrationality. In this regard, the film maintains that evil is rationally incomprehensible, and that modernity cannot offer an explanatory theological or epistemological system to understand order and disorder in the natural and supernatural world. Some scholars contend that *The Exorcist* reinforces Christian mythology and simplifies the conflict between good and evil.[80] As we will see, however, the film's horror actually lies in a story of random evil in a morally disruptive universe, and how the innocent are not immune from the malevolence that haunts our world, no matter how much we hope to shield them from its terror and violence.

There are numerous ways to interpret *The Exorcist*, a film so rich with symbolism. Although critics contend that the film is about satanic possession, or associate the demon inhabiting Regan as the devil of Christian mythology, the film never specifically identifies Satan as the perpetrator of evil. The pagan demon Pazuzu is the closest the film comes to identifying evil, and even his culpability in Regan's supernatural possession remains suggestive. Father Merrin calls the malevolent force possessing Regan "the devil" and draws upon Christian theology and Catholic rituals to exorcise the demon, but the film proceeds to illuminate the spectral image of Pazuzu during the exorcism, not iconic images of Satan. In *The Exorcist*, evil is multivalent and discursive, and the movie's ambiguous moral universe resists an anthropomorphic embodiment of evil. Those who consider the movie satanic not only are mistaken, but also reinforce the significant degree to which Satan consistently remains the dominant symbol of evil in American culture, even in scholarly interpretations of the movie.[81]

While this chapter will examine the nature of evil in *The Exorcist*, it will mostly focus on the ways this movie challenges viewers to think about religion, gender, and modernity in relation to the socio-political turbulence of 1970s America. From the opening scene in Iraq, the film juxtaposes traditional and modern values, highlighting the historic tension between religion and modern science, and the ways this persistent struggle reflects humanity's yearning for cures to their debilitating afflictions. The film also challenges modernity's reification of possessive individualism and its philosophy of history. In this regard, *The Exorcist* undermines the legitimacy of what Jürgen Habermas has called the Enlightenment Project,[82] calling into question the social progress promised by the various social movements of the 1960s, themselves political struggles connected to visions of human emancipation embodied in Enlightenment ideas of political rights and historical agency. The film actually recalls Walter Benjamin's critique of modernity and its philosophy of history. In "Paris, Capital of the Nineteenth Century," Benjamin contends that history is not the story of human progress: rather it is the inter-relationship between past and present, where the present neither repeats nor progresses from the past; instead the present intensifies and amplifies the past by rendering significant only that which connects to the present.[83] History is phantas-magoric, an optical illusion that intensifies or diminishes the past in relation to what the present signifies as important. From this perspective we can understand the importance of the film's Iraq sequence. The film signifies the unearthing of ancient artifacts of good and evil and repeatedly displays them throughout the film because they intensify and amplify a historic cosmic moral battle between good and evil in the modern context of Regan's exorcism. The film may deny progress and rebuke modernity by collapsing the time between past and present, a theme represented in the camera shot of the stopped clock in the Iraq sequence, but it does not necessarily valorize the persistent power of religious traditions. The film's views about religion are strikingly ambivalent, as we will see, even as it critiques the Enlightenment's celebration of empirical science, historical subjectivity and human progress. Still, the movie presents religion as a symbolic cultural system that helps us understand the chaotic historical forces transforming American society. In this vein, the film engages in a historical conversation about religion's power to render meaning to social changes produced by the modern world, thereby provoking epistemological questions connecting the movie to the histori-ography of American religious history and the 1692 Salem witchcraft hysteria.

*The Exorcist* presents religion and modern science literally struggling for Regan's soul, deploying religious rites, scientific methods, and medical procedures to control her body and alleviate the afflictions haunting her. While Carol Clover contends that this conflicting relationship between religion and science is paradigmatic of possession films (sometimes referred to as the struggle between White and Black Magic), *The Exorcist* elevates this historic conflict to a broader critique of modernity and ideas of human progress. The film's narrative structure establishes this conflict immediately as it opens up with Father Merrin supervising an archeological site in Iraq. Here, modern academic and scientific methodologies collide with ancient religious symbols as diggers recover a medal of St. Joseph and a figurine of the malevolent deity Pazuzu. Immediately our mental equilibrium is shaken as we try to rationalize the discovery of these objects and their logical relationship to the main narrative of Regan's spirit possession that we know will follow. As we wonder why and how this medal of a Christian saint arrived in Mesopotamia, so far from Western Christian civilization and so near a symbol of pagan evil, this film sequence establishes an important tone: logic and reason are fleeting and we live in an uncertain universe, where worlds collide, and life is a series of random events. These early scenes in Iraq are critical because they introduce the viewer to Father Merrin, a tortured priest who confronts evil forces whenever he appears in the film. Despite his limited screen time, Merrin's character nonetheless offers the possibility of a logical narrative structure as the initial brief scenes of the archeological dig suggest that unearthing the Pazuzu figurine may have unleashed the evil that possesses Regan. The appearance of the spectral Pazuzu during the exorcism only reminds viewers of Merrin's confrontation with a life-like statue of the malevolent deity at the beginning of the film. In these scenes with Father Merrin, we wonder if there is a narrative pattern to the film's emplotment, or if the film is a series of dramatic moments connected simply by coincidences.

In fact, *The Exorcist*'s narrative instability propels our emotional disequilibrium (the primary cinematic device essential to the horror film) and contributes to the aura of terror that cloaks the film. Moreover, as the film's Iraq sequences suggest randomness and coincidence, we are presented with an important irony: that an archeologist (and interestingly a Catholic priest), someone whose academic field employs scientific methods to uncover the mysteries of the ancient past, may actually be responsible for unleashing the supernatural evil terrifying the principal characters of the film, namely Chris, Regan, and Father Damien Karras. Camera shots of time pieces in an Iraq sequence, particularly a stopped clock, further signifies how the "progress" of time has been disrupted, and past and present, the modern and the ancient, have become enveloped. Father Merrin often has been viewed as a symbol of religious and folk tradition in the film because of his faith in exorcism, and is the foil to contrast Father Karras, whose skepticism and intellectual grounding in empirical science represents the modernist dimension of Catholicism.[84] However, Merrin's role as an archeologist and his pursuit to know the meaning of the artifacts he unearthed as he visits other "experts" in Iraq is more complicated. Placed in the context of the frequent scenes of hospitals and asylums later in the film, ostensibly symbols of human progress, the archeology sequence challenges empirical science and the human hubris to know the mysteries of our universe. Indeed, the film points out that our human desire to know our natural world is not only limited, but efforts to objectify it and subject it to scientific analysis can also lead to our own destruction. That these scenes of ancient Iraq quickly (and randomly) transition to modern Washington, DC suggests that the ancient and modern worlds, in other words, the past and present, remain interconnected,[85] and spiritually bounded. The movie only reinforces this theme by juxtaposing the chaos in the streets of Iraq with scenes of urban chaos and traffic in contemporary Washington, DC. In effect, these scenes illuminate how modern America is no more progressive than the ancient and traditional cultures that define "lesser" developed regions of the world, no matter what the automobiles in the nation's capital and other modern symbols of technology signify to the contrary.

The stark and violent scenes of Regan's medical diagnosis are among the most graphic in *The Exorcist*. Although the pornographic cross-masturbation sequence receives the most attention, the ritual violation of young Regan's body by doctors conducting medical procedures is equally graphic and gory. Mark Kermode contends that the syringe injection scene (where the needle penetrates Regan's body and an orgasmic flow of blood showers her body) is as rich with psycho-sexual meaning as the cross-masturbation scene that follows later in the film.[86] The violent ways these medical and religious symbols are collectively deployed in the movie signify Regan's sexual violation and a perverse rite of passage to womanhood. *The Exorcist*'s religious and scientific themes interconnect in the film sequence focusing on the doctors' visit to the MacNeil home, which is the sequence that also concludes the second part of the film. This scene mocks the powers of medical science while affirming the demonic possession narrative that will now dominate the movie. This film sequence heightens our disequilibrium as we are searching for answers to Regan's violent hysteria. At this moment, our perspective aligns with Chris MacNeil's narrative point-of-view,[87] now focused on the belief that something evil is controlling Regan. Terrified after seeing Regan having an apparent violent epileptic seizure, Chris calls the doctors and implores them to come help her daughter. While viewers have witnessed Regan's epileptic attack along with Chris, they have also seen her bed violently shake during this episode, revealing to us that something supernatural has taken over Regan and her room. Following Chris into Regan's room, the physicians now enter the bowels of terror. A hysterical Regan violently resists the doctors, shouting "Fuck Me" as they inject a sedative serum with a syringe, again attempting to take control of her body.[88] This critical sequence accelerates the movie's narrative as the plot descends into the violent and horrific supernatural universe that defines the rest of the film. In the doctors' visit sequence, the film exposes the irrelevance of the physicians' medical expertise, as Chris, and even the doctors, lose faith in medical science's ability to cure Regan. While the narrative structure of the film has been leading us towards this revelation, we now realize the futility of empirical science, and now believe that Regan is "truly" possessed by a malevolent force. We ultimately accept this conclusion once the doctors admit they cannot help Regan, telling Chris to look for a priest to help her afflicted daughter. Importantly, the narrative logic of the film's plot has become increasingly believable as a result of the series of camera shots focusing upon the exterior of Regan's room, emphasizing the point-of-view of the film's characters as they enter.[89] This camera position is designed to have viewers sympathize with the characters affected by Regan's possession, emotionally engaging the audience and enabling them to become a part of the characters' intimate community. Collectively, the characters and audience witness the supernatural horror inhabiting Regan's room as well, effectively drawing all participants into the film's universe of terror.

Shortly after this scene, viewers watch the more graphic sexual cross-masturbation and cunnilingus scene that will amplify the themes of ritual violence and psycho-sexual disorder. Arguably the previous syringe scenes are less horrifying, but such an innocuous response to the gore connected to medical procedures while feeling shocked at the sexual violation of a sacred religious symbol reveals both the power of religion as a cultural system and the widespread legitimacy (not to mention the banality) of modern science. Yet, the juxtaposition of these scenes calls our assumptions about religion and science into question. In fact, the conflict between religion and science represented in the film reflects our broader cultural ambivalence towards either one as a paradigmatic epistemology. Although we might think we have transcended this historic struggle, *The Exorcist* challenges the primacy of science to provide answers to our human ailments. Ever since the Scientific Revolution, leading figures of the Western scientific community such as Francis Bacon and René Descartes have promised that empirical science will conquer the mysteries of our universe, leading to human and social progress.[90] *The Exorcist*, however, dismisses modern scientific empiricism and its authoritative claims to "know" the natural world. Chris's initial, and what viewers would see as a "natural," decision to seek help from the medical community and her faith that they will diagnose and cure Regan's "disorder" are ultimately rendered ridiculous as the multiple examinations, procedures, and pharmacological treatments fail. That these doctors eventually suggest to Chris, an apparent non-believer, to seek help from a priest and consider exorcism to "cure" Regan, reflects how the film rejects empirical science's truth-claims and modernity's affirmations that science will lead to human progress.

Upon taking the point-of-view of Chris and others, the audience becomes convinced that evil has taken over her house of horror: Chris's fear now becomes our fear. For example, in the scene just before the doctors' visit, the camera follows Chris climbing the stairs that lead to Regan's room. With the camera positioned from Chris's vantage, she opens the door, and we see her face express horror: the viewer and Chris simultaneously see Regan's violent gyrations and her bed shaking. This cinematic device fundamentally affirms the veracity of the film's plot. Like Chris, we have witnessed the plethora of evidence that this scene explicitly proves: that something mysterious, even malevolent controls her daughter. Consequently, we will reject the medical diagnosis that Regan is simply afflicted with a hysterical disorder. Now that we inhabit this narrative universe of the supernatural with Chris, we sympathize with her terror and also believe Regan's demonic possession. Furthermore, we can accept the possibility that Fathers Karras and Merrin can exorcise the demon(s) possessing Regan now that we have fully entered this supernatural world. While the subject of whether the exorcism is ultimately successful will be discussed shortly, it is important to note at this point why viewers could believe in the "possibility" that Catholic religious rites and rituals possess exorcising power. In his study of the sorcerer and his magic, Claude Lévi-Strauss emphasizes that more than the sorcerer and the afflicted believing in the sorcerer's curative magical powers, the wider community with whom they share religious values must also accept the patient's supernatural affliction as well as the sorcerer's power. Consequently, when the sorcerer successfully exorcises the spirits haunting the afflicted, the patient is cured and, more importantly, the values of the community are affirmed. This collective abreaction thus heals the patient and provides catharsis for the community; for the integration of the patient back into the community confirms the legitimacy of the community's supernatural beliefs, its cultural construction of evil, and the power of religion as a cultural system to resolve collective anxieties. Lévi-Strauss contends that religion, in this context, is pathological and displaces (perhaps represses) more progressive, scientific ways to address cultural and social problems.[91]

Nevertheless, religion cannot be easily dismissed as a misplaced fabrication of reality, as Lévi-Strauss suggests. In performing his magical ritual, the sorcerer also validates the community's ontological system of meaning,[92] and it is within this context we need to understand the ritual of exorcism in *The Exorcist*. Once we accept Regan's demonic possession, we also believe in exorcism's possibility as a magical practice, and the power of the film's sorcerers-cum-priests to expel the demon. In the film's climactic scene, Father Karras exorcises the demon possessing Regan by imploring it to inhabit him. When Father Karras then propels himself through the bedroom window in order to destroy the malevolent spirit, we participate in a collective abreaction along with Regan and Father Karras. At this point, the exorcism provides a collective catharsis, releasing our terror, and confirming the film's ontology. In other words, this moment of abreaction validates the fears we have experienced throughout this film and how we have accepted its systems and symbols of meaning. Perhaps our modern, secular intellect might have previously doubted the possibility of supernatural possession, but the emotional experience of watching this movie is our empirical evidence that we ultimately believe that demons stalk the earth and randomly possess people, even if only for the couple of hours while viewing the film. Nonetheless, if Regan's exorcism produces an abreaction and catharsis, what narrative closure does it provide that signifies greater historical significance and meaning for an American audience? This, of course is another issue we need to examine as we consider the other critique of modernity embedded in *The Exorcist*—whether historical subjectivity actually exists, and whether human emancipation is possible.

Modernity is a slippery, complex word that has a variety of meanings.[93] This chapter, however, focuses upon two of its features particularly connected to the larger Enlightenment vision of human progress: rational empirical science and historical subjectivity. In his examination of modernity's philosophical tradition, Jürgen Habermas recognizes the limits of modernity and its promises for human emancipation and progress, especially in light of how such philosophical claims have led to the horror and terror of the twentieth century, a theme reflected in *The Exorcist*. Nevertheless, Habermas believes that the essence of this Enlightenment Project is salvageable and worth pursuing in order to make our world a better place.[94] *The Exorcist*, however, is very ambivalent about the future of the Enlightenment Project and the belief that empirical science and individual agency will lead to human progress. The former issue has already been examined in terms of the conflicts between religion and science and their claims to "know" and "explain" Regan's body. The latter issue emerges in the film as particular characters struggle to assert individual agency to control their fates in a narrative universe taken over by supernatural forces. *The Exorcist*'s overarching narrative arc focusing upon the randomness of evil partly connects to the theme of human agency, as it rebukes one's ability to interpret a pattern or see causality in Regan's demonic possession. The inability of medical science to diagnose, let alone cure, Regan's affliction also reveals the limitations of human intellectual faculties to know the natural world, let alone control it. The film further addresses this theme in the narrative surrounding Father Karras's psychological struggles, his religious faith, and Regan's exorcism.

*The Exorcist* introduces Father Karras during the filming of Chris MacNeil's movie *Crash Course* at Georgetown University, where he is a practicing psychiatrist for his fellow priests. Although we initially see him laugh along with other observers of the film, he proceeds to leave the crowd, walking alone across campus. This sequence not only presents the human side of Father Karras, but also suggests the lonely, solitary life he leads. In the first half of the film, we shortly learn of the demons possessing Karras: the guilt he feels for abandoning his aging mother, and his declining faith in Catholicism. While Karras will become instrumental in the demonic possession narrative, his story connects to the broader theme of the American Dream in contemporary America, a story of individual agency, success, and freedom. These may be virtues and goals generally championed by American culture and society, but the film quickly reveals stories where one's pursuit to achieve this American Dream exacts a price on the American family. In this regard, Father Karras's story parallels Chris MacNeil's and her hope to have a successful acting career and a loving family. The deterioration of their respective families eventually brings them together, literally at the moment when the possessed Regan speaks in the voice of Father Karras's mother, piercing the emotions of the guilt-ridden priest. As Father Karras and Chris increasingly realize, their hope for personal redemption lies in exorcising their personal demons, as well as those possessing Regan.

The film illuminates Father Karras's tortured soul during critical scenes with him and his mother, his meetings with Father Dyer, and in the extended dream sequence. In the dream sequence, a ghoulish-looking demon sporadically appears along with other seemingly random surrealistic images, including one of a medal of St. Joseph eerily resembling the one Father Merrin unearthed in the Iraq archeological dig. Perhaps the random ghoul suggests the priest's personal demons, but like so many things about *The Exorcist*, looking for narrative patterns in the dream remains elusive. These scenes are just as likely to be a series of coincidences with no narrative logic. The film, however, informs us that Father Karras feels responsible for abandoning his mother, an emotional tension driving his self-alienation and his cynicism with his religious faith. As his uncle will remind him, his decision to become a priest prevents him from being with his mother who is ill and lives alone. In one particular scene, his mother tells Father Karras that she sorely misses him, and fears losing her independence because family members want her to live in a convalescent home. She wants Father Karras's promise that this will not be her fate. Shortly thereafter, we see Father Karras walking through a women's mental ward in a decrepit public hospital, where we see his mother strapped down on a gurney, living among mentally disturbed women. We will return to this scene as it relates to the film's theme of gender, madness, and social disorder, but this scene critically reveals Father Karras's struggle with historical agency and the costs of the American Dream. This scene dramatizes the ways Father Karras believes he failed his mother in his pursuit of his dream of higher education and the priesthood. His guilt is reinforced by his uncle who tells him that as a Harvard educated and trained psychiatrist, Father Karras would be wealthy if he lived a secular life, and would be able to afford to place his mother in a reputable home for elderly people. Apparently the son of immigrants, he has achieved the American Dream as an Ivy League educated priest and Johns Hopkins trained psychiatrist, now working at an elite American university. Despite his commitment to the Church (which actually financed his education), he is spiritually unfulfilled as a priest, and believes his individual choices to achieve his American Dream has betrayed his mother. Father Karras has become so cynical about his life and detached from his religious faith by the end of the first half of the film that he initially dismisses Regan's demon possession when Chris inquires about exorcism. Indeed, Father Karras is so absorbed in the world of modern psychiatry and has drifted so far away from his spiritual life, he instinctively turns to his more pronounced beliefs in scientific rationalism and empiricism to diagnose Regan's condition. However, he does begin to believe that a malevolent supernatural force controls Regan once she speaks in the voice of his mother, exclaiming "Why have you done this to me, Demy?"[95] While Father Karras's faith in exorcism remains problematic until the film's climactic scene when the demonic force possesses him, his religious faith grows stronger the more he confronts the demon possessing Regan, recognizing that her salvation depends upon his redemption as well.

In fact, the film's exorcism sequence is so critical because it fundamentally critiques modernity's promises of historical subjectivity and human emancipation. Father Merrin, who was brought in to lead the exorcism, ultimately dies in his effort to expel the demon, without success. Father Karras initially registers serious doubt in the ritual itself and whether a man who has lost so much religious faith as himself could be an instrument of God's power to exorcise evil. Arguably, Father Karras's invocation to the demon to possess him, and then hurtling himself through the window to his and the demon's death, is an affirmation of human agency to control supernatural evil. This dramatic scene can be interpreted as Father Karras's moment of redemption, having saved Regan and then taking last rites from Father Dyer as he lays dying at the bottom of the stairs outside the window. However, Father Karras's invocation to the malevolent spirit is also validation that the Catholic ritual of exorcism failed. When provoking the demon, he does not follow religious rites, but in a fit of anger seduces the demon to take a faithless priest. This is neither a moment of religious affirmation, nor one celebrating God's triumph.

Instead it is Father Karras's recognition of how much power this supernatural evil holds over the natural world. Fundamentally, the priest is not redeemed; rather he is damned for betraying his faith and his God. If the exorcism was a ritual where God was working through human agents to expel malevolent forces, the failure of this ritual to expel the demon from Regan's body only confirms that evil controls this narrative universe. However, this does not mean there is no individual agency in the movie, for Father Karras chooses to forsake his religious beliefs to save Regan. The film, then, challenges our optimism about historical subjectivity but does not reject it altogether.

The Exorcist presents an ambivalent narrative in this regard; for Father Karras chooses to reject Catholic ritual and concedes triumph to evil, but his individual action to accept the demon saves Regan from damnation. Appropriately, the film does not provide narrative closure or catharsis. Following Father Karras's death, Chris and Regan prepare to leave Washington, DC and Father Dyer arrives to say goodbye. Just previous to this scene, Chris says goodbye to the nanny, who proceeds to give her a medallion of St. Joseph, which the nanny has "found in Regan's room." Is this Father Karras's medallion? Or is it Father Merrin's from his Iraq archeological dig? When Father Dyer arrives, Chris tries to give him the medallion, who in turn returns it to Chris. Although Dyer's desire for Chris to keep the medallion is clearly a sentimental memento to remind her of Regan's demonic ordeal and Father Karras's "sacrifice," perhaps providing ostensible narrative closure to Karras and Chris's American Dream stories, the medallion's true significance (like so many things in the movie) remains elusive. Indeed, the memento further challenges a traditional motif in the ideology of the American Dream: that progress and optimism lie in the future, full of promises with new beginnings; and most importantly, that we can escape from our past. Clearly, Chris and Regan want to leave Washington, DC and their haunted house, in an effort to escape this horrific past for the promise of a better tomorrow. Yet, by telling Chris to keep this religious icon, Father Dyer demonstrates that she can never escape hers and Regan's history. Chris may tell the priest that her daughter does not remember what happened, but the film then closes with a powerful image of the film's title in red letters overlaying a black background, recalling the film's introduction, and initially playing the haunting "Tubular Bells" film score and then screeching cacophonic noise. Chris and Regan may hope for a new start and the promises of better tomorrows, but the closing music and titles actually return us to the film's beginning, suggesting they will be forever haunted by their past.

While Father Karras's narrative is important to the film's narrative discourse about demon possession and spiritual redemption,[96] the film also focuses upon gender, sexuality, and the social anxieties generated by the liberation movements of the 1960s. The generational conflict that marked this decade arrests our attention in Chris MacNeil's film Crash Course where she implores protesting students to work for social and political change within the system—that is, pursue reform rather than revolution, but only for the students to reject her plea. That

Georgetown University, an academically elite Catholic institution, is chosen as the site for Chris's film reinforces the film's conservative theme, one that stresses restoring order to the destructive chaos plaguing contemporary American society. The women's liberation movement was among the most transformative of the period, challenging traditional gender relations and conservative ideas about the nuclear family. Contemporary political and religious critics focused most of their attacks on the gender and sexual revolutions of the 1960s as much as the hedonism of the hippie counterculture. Collectively, these events revealed that "Satan was alive and well on Planet Earth," to invoke the title of one popular apocalyptic religious text published in this period.[97]

*The Exorcist* addresses these issues of hedonism and family upheaval in the second part of the film. Chris MacNeil is a working single mother, but one who works in an industry with questionable morals, has a romantic relationship with her film's director, Brook Jennings, and employs a nanny to care for her daughter. As much as Chris evidently cares for her daughter, she shields her romantic relationship from Regan, who learns of it through gossip magazines. Perhaps Chris wants to protect Regan's innocence by not bringing her daughter into the seedier sides of her profession, but she has also neglected Regan in her pursuit of her career. The mise-en-scène of the kitchen film sequence powerfully reveals the moral ambiguity of Chris's American Dream and its consequence for her family. Regan confronts her mother about her romantic relationship as they both share an intimate moment in the kitchen. In this scene, the film highlights family domesticity, only for outside forces, movie-industry gossip and Captain Howdy, to overshadow this moment of intimacy between mother and daughter. Chris's surprise that Regan has been playing with a Ouija board and communing with spirits only amplifies the ways in which her working life and neglect of Regan has led to her family's destruction; for Regan's "game" with Captain Howdy is suggestive of the malevolent spirit that will possess her later in the film. Upon her discovery of Regan's conversations with Captain Howdy, Chris wants her daughter to stop playing this supernatural game, although her plea is perhaps too late. Regan's confession of her supernatural conversation is an omen that in Chris's absence, the supernatural world has already brought her within its grasp.

Evidently, Chris's American Dream is to pursue her career as an actress while simultaneously having a family. Yet, we soon discover the difficult relationship she has with her ex-husband, who enrages her when he fails to call Regan on her birthday. Chris has imagined an ideal relationship with her daughter, but the film suggests the cost of her having an active career outside the home has destabilized her family. Moreover, the hedonistic culture associated with her profession intrudes on her family life as well. Shortly following the kitchen scene, Chris throws a party at her home, where we see an intoxicated Brook Jennings as well as a spirited, libertine Father Dyer playing a piano and singing along with party guests. Indeed Father Dyer reflects how the Church has been infected with 1970s hedonism as it has attempted to modernize following the Vatican II synod and reforms of the late 1960s. Not only does Dyer fantasize about heaven as a grand nightclub with him as the headliner, but also he exposes the homoerotic tensions in the priesthood, at least that which is represented in the film, by discussing homosexuality with Father Karras. In one particular exchange, Father Dyer states, "[Chris] can help us with my plan for when we both quit the priesthood." Karras asks, "Who's quitting the priesthood?" To which Dyer replies, "Faggots. In droves. Basic black has gone out . . ."[98] With Father Karras's scientific skepticism and Father Dyer's relaxed morals and questionable sexuality, the film suggests that the Church's move away from its conservative traditions as it has adjusted to the modern world, has only led to its corruption. That Regan's afflictions begin to manifest during this lavish party further illuminates how a licentious American lifestyle has "possessed" the American family and the Catholic Church. Her erratic behavior portends to the horror that will follow. During the party, she descends the stairs in her pajamas, interrupts a conversation to tell an astronaut that he "will die up there." She proceeds to urinate on the carpet, shocking Chris and her guests. Of course their surprise is nothing compared to the ensuing graphic violence, but in these early scenes the film slowly presents a narrative of an unraveling family and the dark side of the American Dream.

While *The Exorcist* examines themes related to the women's liberation movement and its consequences on the American Dream and family (and in provocatively negative ways) through Chris's narrative, the film explores the theme of female sexuality and youth culture in contemporary America through Regan's story. As noted earlier, the film initially presents an innocent Regan, clearly on the cusp of adolescence, whose virginal innocence is initially violated by the syringe injection film sequences, and then in the similarly graphic, although much more symbolically shocking, cross-masturbation scene. As her psychological disorder morphs into spirit possession, Regan's sexuality increasingly becomes unleashed, and ultimately unhinged. Possessed by supernatural demons, Regan becomes hypersexual, spews sexual epithets, and overpowers authority figures, whether they are doctors, priests, or her mother. In the film's second part, Regan's sexual rites of passage begin with the medical procedures to diagnose her disorder as earlier noted. The mise-en-scène establishes the decidedly masculine power position of medical professionals. Doctors and nurses stand over Regan as her body is strapped to a gurney, piercing her body and spilling her blood while injecting fluids in her, searching in vain for the scientific answers to her afflictions. Yet this sexualized scene also establishes Regan's growing assertiveness as she provokes doctors with sexualized vulgar language and becomes more physically confrontational.

In the 2000 re-released DVD version, a sequence has been added to suggest that Regan is slowly descending into lunacy and madness. This additional scene clearly connects to the one of the women's mental ward that Father Karras visits. The asylum and hospital sequences draw attention to female power, lunacy, and unbridled sexuality, and the ways medical science diagnoses these female attributes as disorder and hysteria. Much like Michel Foucault's critique of prisons and asylums, *The Exorcist* highlights the discursive power of medical science and professionals, and locates their power in an Enlightenment episteme that has solidified their control over our bodies.[99] Like Foucault, the film rebukes modern medicine's truth-knowledge-power praxis by lampooning the doctors' efforts to diagnose Regan's affliction. Regan's uncontrolled sexuality, initially in the context of her sexualized epithets at the doctor's office, but more evident when she clutches the doctor's crotch in a later scene, appear only to validate the doctors' initial diagnosis that she is hysterical and suffers from a medical disorder. As described earlier, these film sequences must be viewed in the context of the cross-masturbation and cunnilingus scene, although now we need to consider these scenes in the context of female sexuality, and how they demand that we associate unbridled female sexuality with demonic possession. Before the doctors inject Regan for a second time, she cries "Fuck Me." And in the cross-masturbation scene, she exclaims, "Let Jesus Fuck You" and buries her mother's face between her legs, shouting "Lick Me." [100] In these scenes, the secular and the religious become enveloped, connected by sexual profanity, sacrilege, and Regan's uncontrolled sexuality. Apparently, Regan's empowerment is as blasphemous as her sacrilegious sexual intercourse with the Christian cross. Her sexuality unleashes uncontrolled power, enabling her to enforce her will over the doctors, priests, and her mother. And though her hypersexuality empowers her as she dominates these authority figures, the film asserts that her power is unnatural and destructive, leading towards disorder and evil.

In this way, *The Exorcist* takes a decidedly religiously conservative position about gender and sexuality, although interestingly, a position oddly similar to that of postmodernists such as Michel Foucault. Carol Clover contends that Regan's body, while uncontrollable and mysterious, is nonetheless a site of knowable truth for doctors and priests: the film reverses the historic one-sex model where the female body is now the source of knowledge and power rather than the male body.[101] In the movie, Regan's body performs, displays, and articulates whatever evil force that is imprisoning her, and seemingly "embodies" those truths about the nature of evil in the universe. If these men can unlock and control those mysteries inhabiting Regan, she and they will be free from this supernatural evil. However, the film has demonstrated that however much the doctors and priests try to command Regan's body, their efforts are to no avail as the mysterious spirits continue to imprison her and mock their furtive attempts to overpower the supernatural.

In one of the most arresting scenes in the movie, Regan's body spells "Help Me," apparently scripted from an entrapped Regan struggling with the demons inside her own body. Her body may have become a site of epistemological discourse about the knowledge and power of evil, as Clover contends, but it is unclear whether reading her body's semiotics will reveal the truths to conquer the irrational being controlling Regan, and free her from its grips. Perhaps Father

Karras emancipates her by becoming a feminine spiritual portal himself, penetrated by the malevolent spirit, and plunging to his death through the other mysterious portal in Regan's room, the bedroom window. By destroying his body and taking last rites from Father Dyer, has Karras become emancipated from the spiritual and psychological demons possessing him? Perhaps, but in his case, knowing and controlling his body did not lead to freedom, neither physical nor spiritual. Becoming possessed led to his death and damnation. Father Dyer may perform last rites, but Karras has already rejected the ritual of exorcism, and by extension his Catholicism, surrendering his body, God's creation, to the malevolent spirit. In this regard, the film, like Foucault, challenges modernity's assumption that knowledge of our bodies and our sexuality reveal natural truths about our identities, or that this knowledge can lead to our freedom.[102] In fact, *The Exorcist* asserts that uncontrolled sexuality results in disorder and destruction. Consequently, the film dismisses the women's movement and the sexual revolution of the 1960s and 1970s. While these social movements claimed they embraced the Enlightenment Project and its promise of individual freedom and social progress, this horrifying film suggests that these liberation movements have only led to the disintegration of American society, not human emancipation.

*The Exorcist*, then, is part of a larger history about gender and power, and the social anxieties this history has provoked in American religion and society throughout time. Moreover, this 1970s horror film connects to those narratives about the Salem witchcraft hysteria such as Arthur Miller's *The Crucible*. Together, these artistic representations address the toxic mix of religion, female adolescent sexuality, and power, which they believe has unleashed social disorder, death, and destruction throughout American history. As scholars of women's and religious history have noted, various cultures have connected female power with unbridled sexuality, which they believe have led to familial and social disharmony, as well as moral decline. This idea informed the Puritan worldview and precipitated the witchcraft crisis that gripped greater Essex County in 1692 (for it reached beyond Salem). A similar worldview informs Christian Fundamentalism and contributed to a similar moral panic in the "satanic cult scare" of the 1980s. In both cases, the changing role of women in American society and redefinitions of gender and family relations provoked a backlash.

In the 1970s and 1980s, the emergence of Jerry Falwell's Moral Majority and Pat Robertson's Christian Coalition galvanized evangelical and Fundamentalist Christians, who became active in American politics to curb what they believed to be the evil excesses of the women's liberation movement and the sexual revolution of the 1960s, and (in their minds) the destructive social transformations these movements engendered. Like Puritans in New England, contemporary Christian evangelicals also sought to exorcise the demons they believed afflicted American society. *The Exorcist* was a prescient film of its time; and for a number of Americans in the 1970s, it was not just the demons possessing innocent Regan MacNeil that needed to be exorcised, but their collective demons as well, which seemingly kept them ensnared in a perpetual psychological malaise. Perhaps it was only fitting, and some would say prophetic, that it was Ronald Reagan who would exorcise the nation's demons, promising a revolution to recapture America's foreordained place in history as the "City upon a Hill," that "Beacon of Light" for the world to marvel as a shining example of virtuous self-government. President Reagan drew upon this history in his 1989 "Farewell Address to the Nation," summarizing his achievements and his revolution of national renewal. In his speech, he recalled a continuous thread in American religious history, one that connected the nation's future with its Puritan foundations, signifying its past and present in a profound religious and historical narrative of redemption and new beginnings.[103]

# 2

# REDEEMING THE SOUTH, REDEEMING THE NATION

## Representations of Abraham Lincoln, the Civil War, and Reconstruction in American Film, Television, and Historical Scholarship

In 1922, President Harding, Chief Justice William Taft, Civil War veterans, and Dr. Robert Moton of Tuskegee College led the ceremony commemorating the Lincoln Memorial on the National Mall in Washington, DC. The presence and speeches of these distinguished men illuminated the controversy over the nation's historical memory of President Lincoln: was he the man who saved the Union? Or was he the man who freed the slaves? While we may think that he did both, the answer was not so simple for a nation which seven years prior to the memorial's dedication was commemorating the fiftieth anniversary of the Civil War's termination. For the majority of white Americans, the dedication of the Lincoln Memorial was another in a series of events to salute national reconciliation. For African Americans, of course, the commemoration ceremony was about the ambivalent (not to say bloody) legacy of emancipation and Reconstruction, and Tuskegee President Moton said as much: "The claim of greatness for Abraham Lincoln lies in this, that amid doubt and distrust . . . he put his trust in God and spoke the word that gave freedom to a race."[1] Lest anyone was confused about the reasons for the gathering and Lincoln's Memorial, President Harding reminded them that "the supreme chapter in American history is [union,] not emancipation."[2]

Images of President Lincoln embody the American nation's ambivalent historical memory about the meaning of the Civil War, and nowhere is this more evident than in Civil War films and historical interpretations of Reconstruction. In both cases, President Lincoln (particularly his assassination) embodies the controversial history which the trauma and bloodshed of Southern Reconstruction provoked. Specifically, filmmakers and historians have raised the issue of what form Reconstruction would have taken had Lincoln survived his presidency. The myth and memory of Lincoln, of course, were invoked by partisans after the Civil

War ended, contending that their respective programs of Reconstruction championed Lincoln's vision.[3] By the early twentieth century, historians and filmmakers alike continued this debate, with strikingly similar perspectives.

Moreover, representations of Lincoln in Civil War historiography and cinema connect to larger themes about contemporary fears among Americans in the early twentieth century about the ways rural and Jeffersonian America receded in the face of modernity. Although Lincoln's presidential administration participated in the centralization of the American nation-state as well as the construction of economic policies that would become the foundation of modern industrialization, Lincoln was recast as a state-rights Jeffersonian challenging the radical forces of political and economic centralization in films such as D.W. Griffith's *The Birth of a Nation* and the scholarship of early-twentieth-century historians such as John Burgess and William Dunning. Scholars like Burgess and Dunning argued that Lincoln's Reconstruction policies would have been more local and state-oriented had he not been assassinated. These cinematic and historiographic representations of President Lincoln as a pre-modern Jeffersonian connected to broader nostalgic historical interpretations of the antebellum South, Civil War, and Reconstruction popularized in Lost Cause literature, films, and historiography.[4]

Lost Cause narratives romanticized Southern agrarian and plantation life, celebrating an age of yeomanry, honor, and racial social order that evaporated with the Confederacy's defeat in the Civil War. Although a literary phenomenon following Reconstruction, Lost Cause visions of the past were also reflected in historiographic interpretations of Southern history leading up to the Civil War (or the War Between the States). In this historical interpretation, the South seceded in order to protect Jeffersonian yeoman democracy, and fought a gallant war to preserve Southern civilization. However, the Confederacy lost the war because of overwhelming Northern military and industrial might. White Southerners remained nostalgic for this Jeffersonian past even as Reconstruction and Redemption (the triumph of Southern white supremacy and politics after the end of Reconstruction) brought industrialization to the South. The eviscerated South following the Civil War was no longer a Jeffersonian agrarian world, and was now integrated into modern industrial America. Yet, through Lost Cause literature and films, Southerners maintained that they were still part of that antebellum Jeffersonian world. With films such as *The Birth of a Nation* and *Gone with the Wind*, white Americans throughout the nation could also long for this distant Jeffersonian past as they collectively faced industrialization and its consequences in the twentieth century. In part, the power and persistence of the Lost Cause narrative lies in its nostalgia for a lost paradise from which Americans had fallen. Industrial capitalism did not bring progress; instead it brought corruption, social conflict, and devastation, leading to the Great Depression in the minds of many Americans. That the film *Gone with the Wind* was released at the height of the Great Depression reveals that part of its popularity lay with imagining a bucolic agrarian America that had been shattered by modernity and the Great Depression.

In 1915, D.W. Griffith released *The Birth of a Nation* to correspond with the fiftieth anniversary of the Civil War's end. Despite the film's controversial narrative, he could expect an audience who surprisingly held a nearly unanimous opinion about Reconstruction's failure. Not everyone would have agreed with Griffith's view that the Ku Klux Klan saved the South from corrupt Northern officials and ignorant black politicians; but historians and white Americans would not have contested his portrayal of vindictive Radical Republican and unqualified black legislators. In fact, historians such as John Burgess and William Dunning rose to prominence in their discipline for demonstrating these points.[5]

Collectively, historical scholarship and American cinema negatively portrayed Reconstruction as a "tragic era" of black misrule and corruption, celebrating its end as the beginning of national reconciliation. While the racist narrative of Griffith's *The Birth of a Nation* became more muted by the release of Victor Fleming's *Gone with the Wind* in 1939, the fundamental (mis)representations of slavery and black freedom remained strikingly similar. A few scholars such as W.E.B. DuBois would challenge these historical interpretations, but the historical profession and Hollywood could expect a national white audience to support their historical interpretations about black inferiority and the triumph of white supremacy.

This chapter begins with a focused exploration of cinematic and scholarly representations of Abraham Lincoln and then examines broader interpretations of Reconstruction. Much like the controversies surrounding the Lincoln Memorial, cinematic and historical representations of President Lincoln raised profound issues about the definition of the American nation. Involved were competing narratives about national reunification, freedom, and democracy. Visions of sectional reconciliation and racial equality were fundamentally at odds given the success of Southern Redeemers who were intent upon solidifying their power by reinstating a brutal racial caste. Despite the important writings of black scholars such as W.E.B. DuBois,[6] a number of these early historians degraded the role of blacks and Radical Republicans as they wrote their national histories of Lincoln and Reconstruction. Like Griffith's *The Birth of a Nation*, their works would shape the perspectives of generations of Americans about Lincoln, Reconstruction, and white supremacy.

## The Civil War, Abraham Lincoln, and the Meaning of Nation in Early Civil War Films

The Civil War had been the subject of numerous plays, nickelodeons, and short films well before the release of Griffith's *The Birth of a Nation*. In fact, Griffith himself had starred in a play and directed eleven one-reelers about the war, preparing him for the spectacle he would later direct and produce.[7] While *The Birth of a Nation* is a landmark film in cinematic history for its technique, and presents Griffith's particular vision of the Civil War,[8] many of the film's themes are grounded in established conventions and tropes about the conflict. As David Shepard states, "Legends of the Old South and the Civil War were permanent fixtures in popular culture," before the release of the picture in 1915.[9] These conventions often described the war as a tragedy that divided families, friends, and lovers, showing battles that emphasized the miseries and sufferings of war. Since the 1880s, Northern and Southern publishers fed a voracious literary market wanting to memorialize the conflict. Invariably, these stories portrayed a lost world of loyal slaves, idyllic social relations, and pastoral bliss destroyed by war. As David Blight notes in *Race and Reunion*, literary works of reconciliation and reunion sentimentalizing antebellum life recaptured this "lost world," particularly popular in an age of rapid industrialization and tense race relations.[10] Thus, when Griffith declares in the opening scenes of *The Birth of a Nation*, "If in this work we have conveyed to the mind the ravages of war to the end that war may be held in abhorrence, this effort will not have been in vain,"[11] and then shows the god of war defeated by the loving presence of Jesus Christ at the end of the film, he is articulating sentiments with which many audiences were well familiar.[12]

The images of union and family were not new to American audiences going to the movies in the early 1900s. Abraham Lincoln, of course, invoked the family as metaphor when he stated that "a house divided against itself could not stand."[13] For filmmakers the family tragedy melodrama was among the more popular themes in their productions of the Civil War. Closely tied to it was the lovers' romantic quarrel and inevitable reconciliation. These narratives of families and lovers divided and then reunited obviously paralleled the national struggle, enabling filmmakers to personalize complex issues that revolved around questions of regional politics, economy, culture, and society. Two early films that embody these formulas are *The Battle of Shiloh* (1913) and *The Crisis* (1916). In *The Battle of Shiloh*, two women, Ellen Winston and Ethel Carey, have tried to discourage their respective brothers Tom Winston and Frank Carey from joining the Union and Confederate armies, only to save them from execution and imprisonment after they have been captured in the war. During the war, Frank and Ellen emerge as lovers while Ellen becomes a spy for the Confederacy. After the brothers leave the prisoner camps, Ethel and Tom likewise become romantically involved. By the end, the film's themes are quite clear: first, family and love define the film's characters, establishing inviolable ties which even the Civil War cannot break, and second, the "marriage" of the two regions is the basis of the American nation.[14]

Instead of employing the divided family theme, *The Crisis* focuses upon lovers (from the different regions) quarreling and reconciling. Unlike *The Battle of Shiloh*, the plot connects the Civil War to historical figures like Abraham Lincoln and the issue of emancipation. In this film, Stephen Brice, a lawyer from Boston, recently arrived in the South, seeks the love of Virginia Carvel. Although attracted to Brice, Virginia rejects him because of his abolitionism, and chooses Clarence Colfax, a Southern gentleman. While fighting for the Union, Brice is wounded and then becomes an aide to President Lincoln. In the mean time, Virginia has lost interest in her relationship with Colfax and calls off their engagement. However, when he is captured by Union forces and is condemned to death, she seeks President

Lincoln and pleads for Colfax's life. Lincoln, wanting to show his mercy on the defeated South, commutes Colfax's death sentence. Seeing Brice as the president's aide, she remembers her feelings for him. The two lovers embrace, and the film ends with them looking towards the future.[15]

*The Crisis* reveals what *The Birth of a Nation* demonstrates more forcefully: how the collision between historical figures and events humanize and dramatize history, while shaping the meaning of historical issues. In this case, abolitionism drives a wedge in an otherwise harmonious relationship between the North and South. Lincoln himself is not seen as an abolitionist (let alone the Great Emancipator) but a leader distraught over the fate of his country. The Civil War is fought over the folly of abolitionism, and it is incumbent upon the president to reconcile the true principles of the nation—unionism. In this context, his pardon of Colfax is emblematic of his true feelings for the South: prodigal son needs to be shown mercy so the family can be reunited. The future marriage between Virginia and Stephen is the foundation of the new family (which Lincoln helped reunite), and whose children will symbolize the consummated relationship between the two regions.

## Representations of Abraham Lincoln in *The Birth of a Nation*

The relationship of blood, race, and nation and the role Lincoln plays in their definition in post-Civil War America is most provocatively shown in Griffith's *The Birth of a Nation*. Based closely upon Thomas Dixon's *The Clansman*, the film traces the origins of the Civil War, Southern defeat and humiliation under Radical and Black Reconstruction, and the "Redemption" of white Southern power through the "heroism" of the Ku Klux Klan. For Griffith, "The bringing of the African to America planted the first seed of disunion," a point demonstrably made from the film's beginning. While this film weaves two major themes of the Civil War genre—the divided family and quarreling lovers—Griffith adds a critical dimension to his interpretation: for him, the central question of the Civil War and Reconstruction was the history and future of African Americans in America. Ironically, scholars at the opposite end of the political spectrum such as W.E.B. DuBois would argue the same point.[16] Where DuBois contended that blacks needed to be extended civil rights and integrated into political society, though, Griffith argues that they must be disenfranchised, and, in an earlier version of his film, expelled from the United States (in fact the deletion of the scene where blacks are herded upon a ship suggests an even crueler fate—that their assault on white women and society deserve nothing less than extermination).[17] Again, Griffith could claim connection to President Lincoln, as the president had advocated African colonization and racial separation during his presidency.[18] While it is unclear what Lincoln believed about slavery's history in America, for Griffith the importation of African slaves set the stage for a family divided, and for fratricidal conflict.

The image and portrayal of Lincoln pivot on his relationship with the two families whose war experiences determine the film's narrative. Austin Stoneman is a Northern Congressman whose staunch support of abolitionism and lust for his mulatto servant has clouded his concern for his family and by extension the nation.[19] His sons Phil and Tod will serve in the war, and his daughter Elsie will be the love interest of the film's hero, the Southerner Ben Cameron, as well as the film's antagonist Silas Lynch, Stoneman's mulatto henchman who intends to destroy Southern white society, and establish black rule. Ben Cameron is the eldest son of the Cameron family, whose idyllic plantation embodies the social and racial order that was antebellum South Carolina.

The narrative begins with Ben inviting his former schoolmate Phil and his brother to the Cameron plantation, where Phil meets and falls in love with Ben's sister Margaret. In this scene, Griffith also introduces the other members of the Cameron family. In the film, the elder Cameron, the honorable patriarch of the family, will represent the political emasculation and social humiliation of the fallen antebellum South during Reconstruction, but whose masculinity and dignity will be restored, or redeemed, by Ben through the founding and triumph of the Ku Klux Klan. Mrs. Cameron is the sacrificing virtuous matron who, after losing a son in the Civil War, will plead with Lincoln to save her surviving son. Finally, there is Flora, the "pet sister," the embodiment of the innocent, virginal white Southern girl who will be preyed upon by the family's former slave, Gus.

During the Stonemans' visit, Tod quickly befriends one of the Cameron brothers. The initial squabbles and friendly jostling suggest that these boys have become friends, perhaps closer to one another than to their respective brothers. By highlighting the humor and closeness between the two boys, Griffith draws the audience into an emotional relationship that will be tragically destroyed by the Civil War. At the end of the Stonemans' visit, the boys promise to see one another again. Griffith fulfills this promise by having them meet on the battlefield fighting. After the Cameron brother falls, Tod rushes to stab him with his bayonet, only to recognize his friend. As he attempts to help Cameron, Tod is shot, and they both die in each other's arms. The powerful brother versus brother theme that continues to arrest Americans, manifests poignantly in this riveting scene. It was this moment that President Lincoln had feared in the film, and it is to his perspective and representation that this chapter will now turn.

## President Lincoln and Reconciliation in *The Birth of a Nation*

The audience is introduced to the president as he signs a proclamation raising 75,000 volunteers. In fact, Griffith begins this scene with the notation, "An historical facsimile of the President's Executive office on that occasion (the raising of troops after Ft. Sumter), after Nicolay and Hay in *Lincoln, a History*."[20] This is the first of numerous efforts Griffith makes to connect his film to real events and figures by replicating historical moments, using them as rhetorical devices to persuade the audience of his historical interpretation. Much as Martin Scorsese's *Gangs of New York* and Oliver Stone's *JFK* cite documentary sources to support their historical arguments, Griffith's *The Birth of a Nation* draws upon primary and secondary sources to reinforce the film's contention that it is narrating history "as it actually happened." And where *Gangs of New York* and *JFK* recall the positivist tradition in recent history, Griffith's film is firmly grounded in this American historiographic tradition along with contemporary historical scholarship of the early twentieth century. Likewise, *The Birth of a Nation* reenacts historical scenes with the cinematic purpose of advancing the film's historical argument just as Scorsese's and Stone's films. In the above sequence, Lincoln is tentative and reluctant to call upon Americans to fight one another. His advisors, not Lincoln, present him with the proclamation. Lincoln paces and ponders before he decides to sign the proclamation. After this scene, Griffith inserts an inter-title stating, "Abraham Lincoln uses the Presidential office for the first time in history to call for volunteers to enforce the rule of the coming nation over the individual states." The following shot shows Lincoln signing the document, and after his advisors leave, he sits alone, takes a handkerchief from his hat, wipes tears from his eyes, and clasps his hands in prayer.[21]

For Griffith, Lincoln is not the rabid abolitionist Southerners feared and reviled on the eve of the Civil War. He is the distraught father of a divided family, and the noble leader keeping the Radical Republicans at bay. The next time the audience sees Lincoln, he is hearing Ben Cameron's mother plead for her son. Mrs. Cameron has come to Washington to tend to her son who was captured, and has been taken to a hospital to recover from his wounds. At the hospital Ben finally encounters his love, Elsie Stoneman, whose picture he has kept with him since Phil had given it to him at their last meeting. Upon hearing that Ben has been condemned to be hanged, Elsie says to Mrs. Cameron, "We will ask mercy from the Great Heart." In the next scene, Mrs. Cameron implores the president to pardon her son. After the president declines her appeal, and turns to leave, Elsie beckons her to ask Lincoln again. At first, President Lincoln declines her second request, but then concedes. With her kneeling next to him in supplication, Lincoln sits at his desk and writes Ben Cameron's pardon. After Mrs. Cameron and Elsie leave for the hospital, Griffith shows Lincoln remaining at his desk and removing his glasses; a gesture in perfect symmetry with the earlier scene when Lincoln wept for calling forth the volunteers. With this juxtaposition, Griffith demonstrates how Lincoln's pardon of Ben Cameron forgives the president for raising an army against the South. To reinforce this point, he has Mrs. Cameron say to her son, "Mr. Lincoln has given your life back to me."[22] By accepting Mrs. Cameron's plea (a mother who has sacrificed a son for the war) and saving Ben's life, Lincoln has honored the dignity of those who fought and supported the Confederacy. In this dramatic sequence, Lincoln has begun to restore the South into the national family, a point Griffith will further stress with the confrontation between President Lincoln and Austin Stoneman.

In the same room where Lincoln signed the proclamation and Ben Cameron's pardon, the president welcomes Stoneman, who has come to "protest against Lincoln's policy of clemency for the South." The comparisons are quite clear. Lincoln will treat all Southerners as he treated Ben Cameron. Just as Ben was condemned to be hanged, Stoneman has come to Lincoln declaring that the South's "leaders must be hanged and their states treated as conquered provinces." As Stoneman wildly protests Lincoln's ideas, the president calmly replies, "I shall deal with them as though they had never been away." Stoneman leaves in anger, while Lincoln stands reflectively. According to Griffith, Lincoln would have the South direct its own reconstruction. The following scene directly pronounces this interpretation, as it begins with the title, "The South under Lincoln's fostering hand goes to work to rebuild itself."[23] Ben Cameron is then shown rolling up his sleeves, and, with other members of his family, sets about putting their lives back together. Here, Griffith affirms contemporary historiographic arguments that contend Lincoln intended to have former Confederate states rebuild themselves as they re-entered the Union, continuing a tradition of limited government and state's rights that was the hallmark of Jeffersonian political ideology.

This optimism is abruptly punctured with the following scene—the assassination of President Lincoln. As Griffith states, "And then, when the terrible days were over and the healing time of peace was at hand . . . came the fated night of April 14, 1865." Among the longer scenes in the film, Griffith dramatically restages the tragic night of the president's assassination to signify how this moment determined the course of Reconstruction. Instead of a benevolent rebuilding of Southern society, the former Confederacy will be treated as Stoneman's conquered provinces. The following two scenes reinforce this point as Griffith shows Stoneman and his mulatto servant Lydia plotting their scheme of Black Reconstruction, and then shows a mournful Cameron family reading a newspaper describing the assassination (a facsimile of the *New South*, dated April 22, 1865). Upon reading the paper, Ben Cameron says, "Our best friend is gone. What is to become of us now!" In the next shot, Ben looks grimly at his father, who, in a gesture similar to Lincoln after he had signed the volunteer proclamation, puts his hands over his eyes and bows his head.[24]

It is significant that the first part of the film ends here. Cameron's mourning of Lincoln suggests a peaceful and reconciliatory rebuilding of the nation. From this perspective, the South was willing to accept defeat and restore its society under "Lincoln's guiding hand." Accordingly, Griffith's Lincoln was not an interventionist nor would have undermined southern institutions (of course how abolitionism would factor into his interpretation is unclear) in the Jeffersonian political tradition. This brilliant juxtaposition does more than provoke the audience to sympathize with the Confederacy, which demonstrates emotional attachment to the president (he forgives them for seceding, and the South forgives him for calling the volunteers), but it legitimizes the actions the South will take under the Ku Klux Klan. From this perspective, terrorizing blacks and undermining Radical Reconstruction not only redeems the South, but also redeems Lincoln's memory. Just as Lincoln had honored their efforts to return peacefully to the national family, they have honored Lincoln by amputating Radical Reconstruction, and restoring the society that Lincoln would have allowed.

Griffith's representation of Lincoln as one sympathetic to Southern defeat may appear exaggerated and perhaps odd to the modern viewer, but this perspective was not too far from the views of contemporary white Americans. Since Lincoln's assassination, white Americans began constructing myths of the president because he died at such a pivotal time in history. As Barry Schwartz notes, his death symbolized the hope and anxiety of the post-war period.[25] With most Americans disappointed in Reconstruction by its end in 1876/77, Civil War pageants and holidays (such as Memorial Day) became sights of reconciliation and mythology.[26] It was at these moments when the mythological Lincoln helped Americans define the meaning, anxieties, and hopes of the conflict and nation. A Lincoln emerged who bore little resemblance to the president who led the nation in the Civil War. While he had promoted unionism, in historical memory he became an advocate of reunion and reconciliation for numerous white Americans, not emancipation. Significantly, this is the portrait of Lincoln post-war historians would write about in their scholarship about the Civil War and Reconstruction.

## President Lincoln, National Reconciliation, and the Historical Profession

Although historians would dispute Griffith's portrayal of Reconstruction as a visceral, bloody race war,[27] their accounts clearly document the racial antagonism that was produced by abolitionism and black suffrage. In fact, Griffith would draw upon historical scholarship to legitimize his interpretation of Reconstruction. The film's second part begins with the titles, "Reconstruction. The agony which the South endured that a nation might be born. The blight of war does not end when hostilities cease." The following title states, "This is an historical presentation of the Civil War and Reconstruction Period, and is not meant to reflect on any race or people today." As evidence to support he excerpts Woodrow Wilson's *History of the American People*. In a brilliant use of historical ventriloquism, Griffith quotes passages such as

> Adventurers swarmed out of the North, as much enemies of the one race as of the other, to cozen, beguile, and use the negroes . . . In the villages the negroes were the office holders, men who knew none of the uses of authority, except its insolences.

He further quotes, "The policy of congressional leaders wrought . . . a veritable overthrow of civilization in the South . . . in their determination to 'put the white South under the heel of the black South' " (Griffith's underlining). Finally,

Griffith quotes Wilson stating, "The men were roused by a mere instinct of self-preservation . . . until at last there had sprung into existence a great Ku Klux Klan, a veritable empire of the South, to protect the Southern country."[28]

More than simply quoting the prominent historian and president, Griffith uses these passages to frame the narrative of the film's second part, divided into the rise of the black South, the disenfranchisement and emasculation of the white South, and the restoration of white supremacy. In effect, Griffith dramatizes a historical perspective held by eminent scholars. From this scholarly template, he can extend an historical interpretation that vilifies African Americans and legitimizes lynching and Jim Crow laws. At this point, Griffith's film moves from spectacle to the level of history: like a historian, he presents an argument, marshals evidence to support it, and offers an assessment of the American past and its possible future. It is precisely because the film works as history not epic spectacle that President Wilson would note that *The Birth of a Nation* was "History written in Lightning."[29]

While Griffith quotes the historian Woodrow Wilson in his epic, much of the film's historical background is consistent with the leading scholarship about the Civil War and Reconstruction. John Burgess, for example, argues that Reconstruction under Lincoln had already been instituted in states like Louisiana, Arkansas, and Tennessee, where he intended to let the states manage their own return to the Union. In these "States," men who swore allegiance to the Union and accepted abolitionism were appointed to manage their return. According to Burgess, the "States" that joined the Confederacy were still part of the Union, and thus did not need to be reconstituted. They needed only to be controlled by men who had supported the Union in the 1860 election or had pledged allegiance to the Constitution.[30] Lincoln recognized that federal intervention was necessary at times during these early years of Reconstruction; but Burgess thought this (and the necessity of one-tenth of Loyal supporters needed to establish a "State" government) were "erroneous" and "destined to result in mischievousness."[31] Even though such federal mandates violated the concept of a "State" according to Burgess, Lincoln's intention to allow states to fundamentally rule themselves was contrary to what certain members of Congress had in mind since they viewed the former Confederates as enemies, redefining him as a Jeffersonian who believed in limited national government and state sovereignty.[32]

Griffith's encounter between Lincoln and Stoneman simulates Burgess's portrayal of Lincoln and the radicals in Congress. Griffith could quote Lincoln stating "I will treat them [the secessionists] as if they never left," because historians such as Burgess were arguing the same points. Burgess's Lincoln and his Reconstruction policy mirror that displayed in *The Birth of a Nation*. Indeed, Burgess concludes his chapter on this topic by describing the peaceful re-entry of states in the Union like Tennessee and then poignantly stating, "Such was the condition of things when the assassin's bullet ended the life of the great and good President and brought the Vice-President, Mr. Johnson, into the office."[33] In *The Tragic Era*, Claude Bowers went even further than Burgess, stating, "Nowhere did the murder [of Lincoln] fall so like a pall as in the South." Quoting a Georgian, Bowers writes, "Then God Help us! If [Lincoln's death] is true, it is the worst blow that has yet been struck the South."[34] This statement could have worked nicely as the final title for the film's first part. In fact, it closely parallels Ben Cameron's final statement at this point of the film, "Our best friend is gone. What is to become of us now!" Bowers' *Tragic Era* corresponds with Griffith's film more closely than any other early-twentieth-century scholarly history of Reconstruction. According to Bowers:

> Never have American public men in responsible positions, directing the destiny of the Nation, been so brutal, hypocritical, and corrupt. The Constitution was treated as a doormat on which politicians and army officers wiped their feet after wading in the muck. Never has the Supreme Court been treated with such ineffable contempt, and never has that tribunal so often cringed before the clamor of the mob.[35]

Like Griffith, Bowers believed Southern Redemption ended this period of political corruption and restored the virtue of Southern civilization. Much as Griffith valorizes the restoration of white Southern rule, "[t]hus, too, the brilliant and colorful leaders and spokesman of the South are given their proper place in the dramatic struggle for the preservation of Southern civilization and the redemption of their people" in Bower's *Tragic Era*.[36]

Similar to Burgess's account, William Dunning describes Lincoln's approach to Reconstruction as a matter of state determination in his *Essays on the Civil War and Reconstruction*, thereby connecting the Republican president to the democratic Jeffersonian tradition. According to Dunning, "Lincoln stated his conviction that the Union could not be broken by any pretended ordinance of secession . . . [and] that the inhabitants of states [which had seceded] were to be in insurrection against the United States."[37] To understand Lincoln's vision of Reconstruction, according to Dunning, Americans need to examine his attitudes about federalism and secession. As Dunning describes, Lincoln "issued a proclamation . . . which recited the subversion of the state governments by persons in rebellion and hence guilty of treason, and the desire of certain of these persons to reinaugurate loyal governments 'within their respective states.' "[38] Discussing the ten percent rule, Dunning notes that Lincoln would pledge to recognize state governments composed of men who swore to a Loyalty Oath.[39] Dunning thus concludes:

> Mr. Lincoln was thus true to the position assumed at the outbreak of the war. The executive department, in short, was fully committed to the doctrine that the corporate existence of the seceding states was not interrupted by the war.[40]

In other words, the president would treat them as if they had not seceded. Again, this is very close to the line Lincoln states in *The Birth of a Nation*. However, where

Dunning and Burgess concede that Lincoln would allow more state control over rebuilding, they are circumspect over the issue of Southern social institutions like slavery.

On this matter, Dunning notes that Lincoln required states to accept federal laws, even those made during the war. Dunning was unsure about the degree to which this included the issue of slavery, noting that the *Emancipation Proclamation* "was merely presented as a rallying point, which might bring people to act sooner than they otherwise would, and was not intended as a final solution of all the delicate questions involved."[41] That is, it was a wartime measure which loyal Southerners would be allowed to coordinate in their respective states. To underscore the problem of slavery during the war, Dunning points to the issue of runaway slaves to Northern armies. Even before the *Emancipation Proclamation,* slaves had run away from Border and Confederate Slave States. While modern historians see flight among slaves as acts of black agency and freedom, scholars such as Dunning argued that, "Commanders were seriously embarrassed by the great crowds of improvident blacks that attached themselves to the armies in their campaigns" and by caring and providing for these runaways, the "status of the negroes thus seems to have been practically that of wards of the national government, with rights totally undetermined."[42] Dunning's perspective on freedmen and slavery during the conflict is important because it frames his view of Radical Reconstruction, describing blacks as unqualified and ignorant freedmen who were dependent upon the federal government for material needs and political support. Dunning's argument (like others concerning black empowerment, white disenfranchisement, and Radicals like Thaddeus Stevens) would be major themes that guide Griffith's vision of Reconstruction in the second part of his film.

The works of John Burgess and William Dunning were among the more influential early works on Reconstruction. Their histories stand among the many written in the early twentieth century whose objective was to reconcile the Southern narrative in the larger national drama of the Civil War and Reconstruction. The historian Peter Novick notes that these historians emerged in a social climate that had seen Reconstruction as a failure and accepted black inferiority. Burgess wrote, "a black skin means membership in a race of men which has never of itself succeeded in subjecting passion to reason."[43] Dunning would write that blacks "had no pride of race and aspiration or ideals save to be like the whites."[44] In his history of the profession Novick states, "The near unanimous racism of northern historians . . . made possible a negotiated settlement of sectional differences in the interpretation of the Civil War and Reconstruction." Consequently, "they became harshly critical of the abolitionists as they were 'irresponsible agitators'." They agreed with Southern historians to denounce the "criminal outrages" of Reconstruction. Although they would agree that slavery was wrong and secession was unconstitutional, Burgess would say that Reconstruction was a "punishment so far in excess of the crime that it extinguished every phase of culpability upon the part of those whom it was sought to convict and convert."[45]

Dunning viewed Reconstruction as such an "unmistakable disaster, leading among other atrocities, to 'the hideous crime against white womanhood which now assumed new meaning in the annals of outrage'."[46] Dunning's observation is of course the fundamental premise of Griffith's history of Reconstruction. In Griffith's version, interracial marriage and miscegenation were the ultimate goals of black politicians, and those motivations lay behind white disenfranchisement. Black pursuit of white women fundamentally legitimized the organization of the Ku Klux Klan and their effort to redeem the South from black rule, according to *The Birth of a Nation*. Despite efforts among historians to distance themselves from Griffith's picture, the history of Lincoln's role in the Civil War and Reconstruction corresponded and legitimized Griffith's more demonstrably racialized portrait of this controversial period. Moreover, the historical profession adapted the Lost Cause narrative from a sentimental literary genre to a historiographic interpretation that would define the field of Reconstruction until the civil rights movement of the 1950s and 1960s with the publication of scholarship by historians such as Kenneth Stampp.[47]

## The Lost Cause Narrative, *Gone with the Wind*, and the Great Depression

With the Lost Cause narrative defining academic and cinematic history in the early twentieth century, white Americans throughout the United States were presented with an historical interpretation of a lost Jeffersonian agrarian past that connected to contemporary concerns about modernity and industrialization. How could a particularly Southern interpretation of the Civil War and Reconstruction define a national history? In part, the tropes of struggle, tragedy, and triumph in films like *Gone with the Wind* resonated with Americans, native as well as immigrant, anxious about modernity and the epistemological crises presented by industrialization. Jeffersonian republicanism promised the availability of land to ensure personal independence. However, the advent of modern industrialization in the late nineteenth century required a wage labor force wherein laborers were dependent upon an employer to provide their income. Historically, wage labor was seen as a temporary condition to accumulate capital, so that one day a wage laborer could purchase land and become an independent yeoman farmer. Political ideologies such as anti-monopolism remained powerful in the late nineteenth and early twentieth centuries because Americans wanted to ensure the availability of land for private ownership and production so that one day tenants and wage laborers could be independent landowners.[48] People held onto these ideologies of political economy for no other reason than to maintain the belief that they could have the possibility to acquire land and live out a life of Jeffersonian independence to pursue their happiness as independent yeoman farmers despite the changing economic and political landscape. In other words, they did not want to concede that a permanent working class would define American labor. Even as Frederick Jackson

Turner presented his "The Significance of the American Frontier in American History" essay in 1894, political and social movements such as anti-monopolism, the Grangers, and Populism reflected that Americans wanted to maintain a world where people could become, and remain independent landowners.[49]

If industrialization produced an epistemological crisis that questioned the transformation of rural America at the turn of the twentieth century, the Great Depression challenged fundamental American ideals of economic independence and the American Dream. Where Americans traditionally believed in historical agency to pull oneself "up-by-their-bootstraps" by working hard and playing by the rules to achieve their American Dream of opportunity and independence, the Great Depression shattered those ideals as millions of Americans tried to make sense of how this economic crisis outside of their control shattered their lives. It is within this context we need to understand the power of Lost Cause narratives into the mid-twentieth century in films such as *Gone with the Wind*.

Through the character of Scarlett O'Hara (Vivien Leigh) audiences relive not only a world of bucolic antebellum plantation life, the tragedy of the Civil War and Reconstruction, but also the ways she struggles and endures hardship in *Gone with the Wind*. Throughout the film, Scarlett can be cruel, mean, and manipulative to achieve her ends; but she also is a survivor who is shrewd, cunning, and clever in order to endure multiple crises. Scarlett O'Hara's narrative may be an allegory for a Southern civilization "gone with the wind," but it is also one that is optimistic, believing that "tomorrow is another day," as Scarlett states at the end of the film. Thus, Scarlett O'Hara transforms from a naive planter's daughter who is precocious and spoiled, scheming to acquire her beau Ashley Wilkes (Leslie Howard), to become an independent, strong-willed survivor of the devastated South. We can only imagine how this story of survival and endurance connected to an American audience that was naive about economic liberalism and industrial capitalism and now witnessed the devastation and demoralization of the Great Depression. At the end of the first part of *Gone with the Wind* Scarlett O'Hara has become the leader of a motley crew comprised of her family (her two sisters and father), her sister-in-law Melanie Wilkes (Olivia de Havilland) and Melanie's son, and a rag-tag group of former Confederate soldiers who collectively live on the ruined, hollowed-out O'Hara plantation.[50]

As this final scene of post-war life ends, Scarlett becomes fed up with taking care of everyone, is hungry, and runs to the garden. She digs into the soil with her hands and savagely devours sickly, wilted turnips. Stopping to reflect upon what she has been reduced to, she proclaims, "As God is my witness, I will never go hungry again." Moreover, Scarlett says that she will do whatever it takes to survive, even if it means she has to "lie, cheat, or kill."[51] We can only speculate what American audiences of Dust Bowl farmers, displaced Americans and immigrants, and unemployed workers recognized in Scarlett O'Hara's words. What we do know is that the film became one of the highest grossing films of the twentieth century and won Oscar awards for Best Actress and Best Film. The film may celebrate the paradise of a lost Jeffersonian America, but it engages history and constructs a historical narrative about socio-economic devastation and human endurance during Reconstruction. Recent scholarship about Reconstruction reveals the factual inaccuracies of the film and how it misrepresents the historical complexity of the post-Civil War South, particularly its depiction of slavery and emancipation. However, it nonetheless represents contemporary historiographic interpretations and more universal historical truths about the ways white Southerners believed they endured the destruction of Southern civilization.

While *Gone with the Wind* reflects these larger universal historical themes that shape the way viewers engage with history, it also neuters the politics of the Civil War and Reconstruction which was so evident in Griffith's *The Birth of a Nation*. With its treatment of slavery, race and black emancipation, *Gone with the Wind* delicately recalls the Lost Cause tradition that permeated Griffith's film, while minimizing *The Birth of a Nation*'s racism and socio-historical interpretations. *Gone with the Wind* simultaneously replays themes of loyal and dutiful slaves while projecting images of ignorant freedmen, although muting Griffith's harsh racism. In one short scene, Scarlett and her faithful, former slave, now servant, Mammy (Hattie McDaniel) fight off leering freedmen who are also listening to an apparent government official who is offering them "40 acres and a mule if you vote for your friends."[52] A freedman echoes these words in minstrel black dialect. Although this scene is a brief moment in the film, the audience understands what is coded about the folly of black emancipation: freedmen are ignorant about politics, unprepared for emancipation, and are the tools of corrupt Reconstruction officials. This interpretation of Reconstruction and black emancipation had become so pervasive in American culture and history by the film's release in 1939 because this historical interpretation had been argued by academics and filmmakers alike throughout the early twentieth century.

Despite this powerful representation of race, emancipation, and Radical Reconstruction, *Gone with the Wind* minimizes other Lost Cause interpretations, particularly the role of the Ku Klux Klan in "Redeeming" the South. For example, after Scarlett has been assaulted (and saved by her former slave Sam), a group of men including Rhett Butler (Clark Gable), Ashley Wilkes, and Scarlett's husband Frank Kennedy (Carroll Nye), search out the person who assaulted Scarlett.[53] Although called a "political club" these men actually represent the Ku Klux Klan attempting to save the virtue of a white woman, a common trope in the Lost Cause cinematic and literary tradition, and again connects to Griffith's *The Birth of a Nation*. However, this is also another moment where the filmmakers of *Gone with the Wind* attempt to neutralize the representation of the Klan by calling it a "political club" while staying true to the Lost Cause tradition.

Yet the Jeffersonian agrarian tradition remains the film's premise. Throughout the film, Scarlett is reminded of the integrity of land and landownership. Scarlett embodies the South's struggle with its relationship to its antebellum traditions, signified in Scarlett's pursuit of Ashley Wilkes, and its ambivalent relationship with the modern South, signified in Scarlett's intense, complex, and aborted relationship with Rhett Butler. When Rhett leaves Scarlett, she proclaims that she will pursue Rhett, but first she must return to Tara, where ties to the land will forge her economic and personal independence in the traditional vision of Jeffersonian political economy. In this vein, the film has recast Southern history as a Jeffersonian narrative that has resisted modernity and whose legacy has remained a reservoir of agrarian independence. Or at least this appears to be the film's intention: industrial capitalism led the United States into the Great Depression, but the Jeffersonian yeoman tradition celebrated in *Gone with the Wind* and maintained by rural America during the turbulence of the Great Depression may yet save the country from the corruption and destruction produced by modernity. While the historiography of Southern slavery and the American South reflects scholarly debates about the degree to which the antebellum South resisted or contributed to the growth of liberal capitalism, the film clearly contends that agrarian Southern life, that which is now "gone with the wind," nonetheless maintained a commitment to Jeffersonian ideology until the Civil War, while the industrial North betrayed Jefferson and the ideals of the American Revolution.[54]

In this respect, *Gone with the Wind* corresponds with leading historical scholarship of the Great Depression era such as Howard Beale's *The Critical Year* (1930). For Beale, the 1866 election embodied the history of Reconstruction. In this "critical year" the Reconstruction policies of President Johnson were defeated in the Congressional elections in favor of Radical Reconstruction championed by key Republicans such as Thaddeus Stevens and Charles Sumner. For Beale, key economic policies more than black male suffrage and the Fourteenth Amendment transformed the nature of southern Reconstruction. As Beale notes, these economic policies were designed to encourage capital investment and industrialization in the reconstructed states. For Beale, the 1866 elections "decided that henceforth New England bred economics and social standards, rather than those of the frontier and plantation, should rule America." With the advent of Radical Republicanism, the Jeffersonian political tradition that nurtured American democracy, liberty, and independence receded during the Early Republic. According to Beale, the industrial transformation of the United States during Radical Reconstruction killed the Jeffersonian soul of America. He states that in 1866,

> an industrialized Northeast, dominated by business principles that were to create the machine made America of today, faced an agrarian South and West contending for those time-honored principles of frontier individualism which had dominated an America that was passing.[55]

Writing in 1930, just as the pall of the Great Depression covered the nation, Beale suggested that the economic policies of Radical Reconstruction that extended Northern industrialization throughout the nation (and in this way he anticipates recent revisionist historical scholarship that demonstrates the ways

Reconstruction was national in its scope and not just regionally focused upon the South) produced the economic devastation of his time. As with *Gone with the Wind*, Beale celebrates Jeffersonian political economy and is nostalgic for a time in American history before modernity wreaked havoc upon American traditions of yeoman democracy and economic independence. Whether or not the Jeffersonian political tradition ever existed in the ways *Gone with the Wind* and academic historians such as Howard Beale revered, the social and economic turmoil produced by the Great Depression made Americans long for this Jeffersonian past.[56] In the process, they framed American history, particularly Reconstruction, in this interpretive vein, constructing a historical epistemology to find solace and meaning in their contemporary world.

## Lincoln and Reconstruction in Recent Historiography and Films

Our modern understanding of Lincoln and Reconstruction has changed significantly since the 1950s. The civil rights movement of the 1950s and 1960s radically transformed American visions of justice and democracy. Accordingly, historical scholarship on the Civil War and Reconstruction has revised previous interpretations about race, emancipation, and political economy. Today, historians discuss the role of African American soldiers in the war and describe the civil rights legislation that the Radicals in Congress promoted.[57] Indeed, the Radicals who were too extreme for the earlier generation of historians are now seen as progressive, and men ahead of their time. The social and cultural revolution engendered by the civil rights movement has extinguished much of the controversy over Lincoln and emancipation. In fact, debating Lincoln's sincerity about emancipation encourages outrage among students who have grown up with the firm belief that Lincoln freed the slaves.[58] Despite the transformation in the scholarship on Reconstruction, however, filmmakers, and the American people more generally, are reluctant to fundamentally alter their vision of the Civil War, and thus its larger meanings. While films like Edward Zwick's *Glory* have substantively altered American understanding of the role of blacks in the Civil War, television docudramas such as Andrew McLaglen's *The Blue and the Gray* or David Wolper's *North and South* series continue to retell the traditional stories of families, friends, and lovers divided by the conflict, demonstrating their intertextual relationship with early-twentieth-century films of the Lost Cause genre rather than substantive engagement with recent academic historiography.[59]

In *The Blue and the Gray*, slavery is an issue minimally explored and mostly serves to drive the dramatic tension in the early part of the docudrama, propelling John Geyser to reject his family at the onset of sectional conflict. However, those who evidently take an ideological stance on slavery and abolitionism, in particular Preacher Welles and John Brown, are portrayed as demented, even maniacal in their beliefs, and never principled. *The Blue and the Gray* tries to address slavery as a national issue by presenting John Brown (Sterling Hayden) and his hanging, as well as the hanging of Jonathan (perhaps an intentional juxtaposition), a free black man who is lynched by Preacher Welles (Warren Oates) and the local sheriff for harboring runaway slaves.[60] But the constituent stories of John Brown and Preacher Welles and their apocalyptic sermonizing only reinforce interpretations of slavery and abolitionism as fanatic ideologies that misguided a distraught nation towards war, which apparently the film's principal characters want to avoid, including President Lincoln, John Geyser, and John's parents. Slavery may animate *The Blue and the Gray*'s early narrative, but it becomes marginalized after Jonathan's lynching, allowing the "divided family" narrative discourse to drive the remainder of this television docudrama. It is the tragedy of the war and the way it divided the nation that fundamentally defines *The Blue and the Gray*. While John's brothers and cousins hope for war, the docudrama presents their exuberance as youthful and innocent male bravado, learning the true horrors of war during the conflict, a trope characteristic of many Civil War military narratives such as *The Red Badge of Courage*. *The Blue and the Gray* does not avoid politics, but mostly illuminates them as a narrative device to emplot the narrative discourse. Ultimately, however, it summarily dismisses recent historiography and interprets contemporary politics and political convictions as the source of an avoidable and tragic conflict.

Interestingly, though, David Wolper's *North and South* miniseries does not shy away from the politics of Reconstruction. Perhaps this is due to the ways in which the docudrama maintains the spirit of John Jakes' novels and his talent as a master storyteller who sees as much narrative power in history as in stories about sex, war, and political intrigue. Perhaps this is also due to David Wolper's experience producing the *Roots* television docudramas in the 1970s, and having retold the history of Reconstruction and the emancipation narrative in these earlier television historical docudramas. For whatever reasons, *Book III: Heaven and Hell*, almost reinvents the Civil War melodrama by simultaneously telling the reunion narrative and emancipation narrative. Furthermore, though *Book I: North and South* and *Book II: Love and War* initially draw upon the Lost Cause narrative to tell the stories of friends and families divided in the years leading up to and during the Civil War, *Book III: Heaven and Hell* vilifies the Lost Cause white supremacy narrative that traditionally defined literary and cinematic narratives of Reconstruction.[61] More than demonstrating an intertextual relationship with early narratives of the Civil War and Lost Cause genre such as *The Battle of Shiloh* (1913) and *The Crisis* (1916), *North and South* draws upon the genre's major motifs to engage and critique Griffith's *The Birth of a Nation*, and to some degree *Gone with the Wind*.

*The Blue and the Gray* and the *North and South* series cannot ignore the black civil rights movement even as they try to retell their reunion narratives. Moreover, as much as they may want to escape David Wolper's landmark and historically powerful *Roots* docudramas televised in the 1970s, these later Civil War docudramas engage in an intertextual dialogue with the *Roots* series as much as the Lost Cause narratives. In fact, that these historical docudramas were televised in 1980s Reagan America reveals that they are as much about reuniting an American national narrative severed by the 1960s civil rights and social movements that empowered women and minorities, and the conservative reaction to these movements in the 1970s and 1980s. And though *North and South* is technically a more inferior film, it nonetheless aggressively engages the politics of Reconstruction where *The Blue and the Gray* adheres steadfastly to its reunion narrative, and minimizes and marginalizes the emancipation narrative, while avoiding Reconstruction altogether.

In *The Blue and the Gray*, the film's protagonist, John Geyser (John Hammond) leaves his family's Virginia farm after the state secedes and his black friend Jonathan (Paul Winfield) has been hanged for sheltering runaway blacks.[62] The docudrama presents John as a marginal member of his family from the beginning. He is an artist while his father and older brothers are farmers. John apparently is against slavery (although it is unclear if he is an abolitionist) and maintains a friendship with Jonathan, a free black man renting land on the Geyser property.[63] Although John's friendship is unique to this docudrama, *The Blue and the Gray* ultimately maintains an intertextual relationship with the Lost Cause narrative genre. Much of *The Blue and the Gray* is derivative of Griffith's *The Birth of a Nation* and other early romantic Civil War films. The major romantic relationship in *The Blue and the Gray* closely resembles Elsie and Ben Cameron's, as John's lover, Kathy Reynolds (Kathleen Beller), is the daughter of an Austin Stoneman-like character, Senator Reynolds (Robert Vaughn), and she works as a nurse during the war. Reversing the theme of the film *The Crisis*, John Geyser rejects his family because it tolerates slavery, although it is unclear whether the Geyser family actually holds slaves (the family has a female servant, who is romantically involved with Jonathan, but we are never specifically told if she is enslaved). In the end, though, John fights for his family farm after serving as a neutral war correspondent when it is attacked by Union soldiers, and it becomes clear to him that his family and its land ultimately define his identity. John has returned full circle. He left his family following Jonathan's "murder," refusing to join his brothers and fight for the Confederacy. When John's brother Mark rebukes him because he will not "defend his home . . . our land," John replies:

> Our land? This sacred soil? A man was murdered on this soil . . . the biggest crime is to side with a black man . . . my friend's hangin' from a tree . . . What's wrong with this land that produces such a bitter crop . . . Don't ask me to fight for this handful of dust.[64]

Yet, at the end of the docudrama, John does defend the family farm, rejecting his neutrality (or in his family's eyes, his treason and apostasy) demonstrating his commitment to his family and its land, grounding the docudrama in the Jeffersonian tradition of agrarian independence. The film concludes with his marriage to Kathy Reynolds, an event that takes place on the Geyser farm, and bringing the remaining Geyser clan (two of John's brothers died in the war), their relatives from

Pennsylvania (some of whom, of course, were Union soldiers), John's close friend and Union officer Jonas Steele (Stacey Keach), and Senator Reynolds.[65] As in Griffith's *The Birth of a Nation*, the divided family is united and the nation's unity is reconciled in a marriage between Southerner and Northerner. And similar to *The Crisis*, the film ends here with promise of reunion, never exploring Reconstruction or its consequences on the nation. In *The Blue and the Gray*, Reconstruction is hinted towards, but never examined.

As in *The Crisis* and *The Birth of a Nation*, President Lincoln (Gregory Peck) plays a significant role in *The Blue and the Gray*. Like the earlier films, he is portrayed as a paternalistic figure who observes the war destroying families. In one scene, he advises John Geyser to become an illustrator for a national magazine so he does not have to "raise a gun against his family" and maintain his anti-slavery ideas.[66] It is John's dilemma that becomes the national problem, and we follow him throughout the film as an impartial observer of the war's horror and tragedy, sympathizing with Northerners and Southerners alike. Preacher Welles emerges as the film's major villain as he is driven by a messianic mission to murder Union and Confederate soldiers, believing he is on God's mission to turn the Civil War into a spiritual Armageddon. Following the death of his son Homer, Preacher Welles, now an officer in the Confederate Army, begins murdering Confederate and Union soldiers alike, clearly demonstrating the madness and dementia of the war. Initially the Preacher/Major Welles constituent story seems like a distraction; however, it actually connects with the television docudrama's narrative discourse about the ways in which fanaticism (again, whether abolitionism or pro-slavery ideology) has produced the Civil War and tragically divided American families, North and South. Moreover, the madness which Preacher/Major Welles signifies also reflects the ways in which ideological and political fanaticism led to the ultimate tragedy: the assassination of the beloved President Lincoln.

As in *The Birth of a Nation*, Lincoln is intimately tied to the main characters in *The Blue and the Gray*. Thus his death feels more personal and distressing. Much as Ben Cameron states in Griffith's film, "Our best friend is gone. What is to become of us now!" the major characters in the 1982 Civil War docudrama lament the national loss of President Lincoln, and his guiding hand to reunite the divided nation. However much the characters (and by extension the viewers) connect with President Lincoln in *The Blue and the Gray*, this personable Lincoln is nevertheless a depoliticized president. He signs the *Emancipation Proclamation*, but his positions about Reconstruction and the future of African Americans, democracy, and freedom are largely ignored. The docudrama tries to signify his signing of the *Emancipation Proclamation* as a historical event by presenting this scene as a moment of great deliberation for Lincoln as he hears competing arguments from his Cabinet members about the judiciousness of signing the measure. Once Lincoln signs the *Emancipation Proclamation* he comments that the nature of the war has changed— it is a war about freedom. But whose freedom? Black slaves, apparently, although Lincoln never explicitly states this, nor does he articulate his plans as president to ensure their freedom. The historical docudrama apparently leaves these vague questions unanswered. Moreover, it completely overlooks how blacks were historical agents in their quest for freedom during the Civil War.

When John Geyser arrives upon a community of slaves (it is never mentioned whether they are runaways or castaways) outside Vicksburg, Mississippi, it is he who delivers them the news of the *Emancipation Proclamation* rather than the slaves learning on their own about Lincoln's executive order. The docudrama accurately points out that only slaves in the seceding states were to be free as a result of Lincoln's *Proclamation*, and correctly states in a dialogic exchange between John and one of the slaves, that actual freedom would happen and be secured only once the Union troops arrived and defeated the Confederacy. Nevertheless, *The Blue and the Gray* eviscerates black freedom struggles by having the slave community effectively genuflect to Abraham Lincoln for emancipating them. It is actually quite clear that these slaves have already lived free as a black community, although in hiding in the Mississippi swamps. While these (former?) black slaves live in fear of renegade Union and Confederate soldiers, they nonetheless have an established community and leadership structure that the docudrama minimizes in order to valorize Lincoln as the "Great Emancipator" and John Geyser for delivering the news of their freedom. Despite how transparently obvious that this is a free black community, though in seclusion (and what free black communities in the war-torn South were not), these black men and women feel free only once John tells them that they are emancipated, and that Lincoln has freed them. African Americans and the issue of slavery are merely historical prop pieces or narrative devices for this historical docudrama that is more concerned with national reunion and reconciliation for white Americans torn apart by the Civil War.

*The Blue and the Gray* clearly overlooks the inroads of recent historical scholarship that examines how black Americans engineered their own freedom and forced the Union Army and President Lincoln to address the issue of emancipation during the war, fundamentally transforming the nature of the Civil War.[67] In fact, even traditional questions about states' rights and the Federal Constitution are largely ignored. By marginalizing the issue of slavery and federalism, the docudrama effectively depoliticizes the meaning of the Civil War. In this context, Lincoln's assassination is a tragedy but has no repercussions on Reconstruction. The nation perseveres after his death. It reunites and reconciles in his absence, embodied in the film by the marriage of the Virginian John Geyser and Kathy Reynolds from Massachusetts (with his aunt, uncle and cousins from Pennsylvania attending). Indeed, the marriage between Northern and Southern lovers promises a reunification that belies the more traditionally sanguineous portrayal of Reconstruction.

While David Wolper's *North and South* trilogy seemingly follows a traditional Civil War genre narrative like *The Blue and the Gray*, the third episode, entitled *Heaven and Hell*, differs significantly from recent television and cinematic representations of the Civil War and Reconstruction. Rather than amputate these two significant historical moments, *North and South* apparently recognizes, along with current academic scholarship, that the Civil War and Reconstruction are interwoven events much like the War for American Independence and the Constitutional Convention in the period of the American Revolution. For this reason, the *North and South* series has a more intertextual relationship with *The Birth of a Nation* and *Gone with the Wind* than the more antiseptic historical docudrama, *The Blue and the Gray*. Arguably, the latter is a better film: it is a tighter narrative, and frankly, the acting performances are better, not to mention its teleplay is more intelligent. Wolper's *North and South* series apparently believes that viewers desire sexual and political intrigue as much as the Civil War as gripping historical narrative. *The Blue and the Gray* cannot completely escape these issues either, reflecting how television studio executives, producers, and directors decided that their historical docudramas needed these salacious elements for television ratings, not altogether surprising given the popularity of nighttime serials like *Dallas* and *Dynasty* throughout the 1980s.

Adhering to these serial sexual and political conventions, however, undermines much of the historical value in *The Blue and the Gray* and the *North and South* series. Still, we can admire *North and South* for addressing major political and historical issues of the Civil War and Reconstruction that *The Blue and the Gray* chooses to marginalize or ignore. Wolper's docudrama attempts to weave the reunion narrative with the emancipation narrative, a Herculean task since these narratives have traditionally been at odds with each other, as historians such as David Blight have argued.[68] The reunion narrative historically privileges concessions to the Southern Lost Cause narrative and its story of honorable defeat and Southern Redemption while undermining black freedom struggles and diminishing the racial violence that defined much of Reconstruction.[69] *North and South Book III: Heaven and Hell* attempts to redefine the reunion narrative by vilifying white supremacy as it valorizes black freedom struggles (albeit with the principal white characters leading these movements). Like so many Civil War and Reconstruction narratives, however, it privileges reunification between North and South over emancipation, and is characteristically signified by a marriage uniting the two regions.

Though the Reconstruction segment of *North and South* presents a revised history of race relations in the post-Civil War period, *Book I: North and South* and *Book II: Love and War* follow classic narrative conventions of this period to the point of banality. These two segments tell the story of Orry Main (Patrick Swayze) and George Hazard (James Read), two friends who meet at West Point just prior to the Mexican–American War (1846–1848), but eventually find themselves supporting their respective regions once the Civil War begins. Orry is the unorthodox son of a South Carolina planter who desires the soldier's life, much to his father's consternation, as he wants his son to become a planter patriarch like himself. Similarly, George chooses to attend West Point instead of participating in his family's ironworks factory located in Pennsylvania.[70] *North and South* immediately connects with the historiography of antebellum America even as the conventional plot unfolds. Perhaps because this docudrama is an adaptation of John Jakes' novel, it can draw upon his experience as a writer of historical fiction. Still, we should not dismiss David Wolper's involvement and his previous experience producing the *Roots* miniseries. With *Roots*, Wolper successfully introduced major themes in African American history to the American television audience in the 1970s, and so we would expect him to include issues of race and slavery in the *North and South* docudrama. Consequently, American history is ever present in *North and South* rather than relegated to superficial scenery like so many historical dramas. In this miniseries, North and South are not simply two diverse geographic regions, but two sections with fundamentally different ways of life—even worldviews.

Through the Hazard family we observe an industrialized and urbanized North with class divisions and prejudices. The Hazards employ Irish immigrants, and we observe the social and economic struggles free blacks face because of systematic racial discrimination. Not all Northerners in *North and South* are rabid abolitionists like George's sister Virgilia (Kirstie Alley), but they universally believe slavery is wrong. In this vein, the Main family is tied to their agricultural and paternalistic Southern way of life, believing slavery as socially and economically beneficial to whites and blacks alike. As much as George and Orry reflect their respective regions, *North and South* presents them as the sensible and moderate voices of worlds propelling towards the extremes. Virgilia is a crazed abolitionist who always vilifies Orry and his family for being inhumane slaveholders. In response, Orry points out that the slaves on his family's plantation are better treated than the impoverished immigrant workers in the Hazard factory. In fact, the miniseries supports both contentions. When an explosion devastates the Hazard ironworks, we watch George plead with his family to help their wounded workers, only to see the callousness with which his brother and father dismiss his concerns.[71]

In turn, Orry recognizes that slavery is an antiquated system preventing the South from becoming modern, and wants to emancipate his family's slaves because he believes his family would better prosper from free wage labor and form closer ties with the industrialized North. Though his family treats their slaves well, we see the brutality of slavery in another context, principally the cruel treatment of slaves by Justin LaMotte (David Carradine), another South Carolinian planter who also happens to be married to Orry's lover, Madeline Fabray LaMotte (Lesley-Anne Down). In *North and South*, abolitionism, slavery, and secession are the viruses contaminating the nation, and George and Orry are the moderate voices trying to prevent the extremes from splitting the nation They are reformers who want to change the worse dimensions of their respective regions, and hope their friendship can be the basis of closer, more productive relationship between North and South.[72]

Nevertheless, the narrative appears so familiar because it directly recalls D.W. Griffith's *The Birth of a Nation*. Just as the Cameron and Main families are from South Carolina, the Stoneman and Hazard families are from Pennsylvania.

Trans-regional friendships attempt to fight against the tide of growing sectionalism only to succumb to provincial loyalties as abolitionism, slavery and civil war divide the families. With the Main and Hazard families, *North and South* draws upon classic narrative devices whereby friends and families become divided by war and tragedy, though ultimately reconciling and reuniting during Reconstruction. As in Griffith's film, abolitionism is a radical, even deranged ideology driving a wedge between North and South. However, Wolper's docudrama presents slavery as fundamentally wrong and holding back Southern society. Like George, Orry disagrees with human bondage, but he finds himself supporting it in the face of Virgilia's passionate and relentless attacks, though more so in the context of defending the Southern way of life. Despite recent historiography, then, *North and South* reflects a historical interpretation of abolitionism more closely connected with academic scholarship at the beginning of the twentieth century that maintained that abolitionism and its corresponding view of racial equality exacerbated regional tensions. Through Virgilia, abolitionism is presented as irrational and maniacal, destabilizing American society as much as driving a wedge between North and South. In fact, the docudrama even reproduces Griffith's most controversial and vile views about abolitionism, race, and sexuality. When Virgilia accompanies her brother to the Main plantation, she encourages one of their slaves, Priam (David Harris), to run away. Although Priam is unsure and apparently well treated by the Main family, Virgilia convinces him that life as a free man in the North is a much better than the one he leads as a slave in South Carolina. Besides her impassioned abolitionism, however, she is equally motivated by her lust for Priam, having sex with him as she helps him flee slave catchers. As in *The Birth of a Nation*, abolitionism and racial equality are actually about interracial sex in *North and South*. As we later discover, life has become worse for Priam in the urban North than it was on the Main plantation. Though he has married Virgilia, they are pariahs in the eyes of the Hazard family for their interracial marriage. Furthermore, Priam cannot find work because of Northern racial discrimination, and reluctantly joins John Brown's militant band because Virgilia wants them to participate in the slave rebellion Brown intends to launch in Virginia. Priam poignantly dies during Brown's raid upon Harper's Ferry, leading viewers to believe that he was mistaken to have run away from the Main plantation. From the perspective of *North and South*, lunatic abolitionists like Virgilia and John Brown lead the North, and cruel slaveholders and secessionists like Justin LaMotte lead the South, marginalizing more sensible Americans like George and Orry, who find themselves inevitably fighting each other as civil war grips the nation.[73]

Though trite, even silly narrative devices structure *North and South Book I: North and South* and *Book II: Love and War*, virtually retelling *The Birth of a Nation* to a more contemporary American audience, *Book III: Heaven and Hell* actually challenges the historical interpretation of Reconstruction and Redemption originally presented in Griffith's film. By *Book III*, Madeline has escaped Justin's cruelty and married Orry. Though Orry survived the devastation of the Civil War, he is tragically murdered by Elkanah Bent (Philip Casnoff), his longtime enemy since their days as cadets at West Point, shortly after the fall of the Confederacy. Following Orry's death, Madeline is reduced to near poverty, and plans to work with her former slaves to rebuild her plantation, establishing a sharecropping system and a school for freedmen, women and children.[74] While sharecropping will eventually become a form of black debt-peonage that closely resembled slavery, early in the history of this labor system black freedmen and women agreed to this arrangement because they believed it enabled them to maintain lives as economically independent yeoman farmers and protect their nascent freedom, in effect live a version of the Jeffersonian dream.[75] This apparently is also Madeline Main's intent, or so it is interpreted in this way by her brother-in-law, Cooper Main (Robert Wagner), who is shocked by Madeline's plans. She describes her plans as "the new way" so that she can survive and pay the mortgage, which he holds as a result of his dead brother's will.[76] Although Cooper says he hopes her plans will succeed so that she can make the mortgage payments, and also so that his nephew and surviving kin will not be reduced to poverty, he clearly deplores her "new way" and how she deals with the "nigresses" as racial equals. Cooper Main is an unreconstructed Confederate who swears a loyalty oath to the Union following the surrender only to maintain his family's land and status, and hopes to recover its wealth. He shudders when he admits his loyalty oath to Madeline, but he believes he needs to do what is necessary to restore his family's status, and the South more generally. One might imagine that he will embody the emasculated Southern planter like Ben Cameron in *The Birth of a Nation*, and who will use whatever necessary means to undermine Reconstruction, redeem the South, and restore white supremacy, championing a new politics of the Lost Cause by fighting to save white civilization. Undermining Reconstruction, creating a New South, and perhaps limiting black freedom is as far as Cooper Main will go, however. Not only does *North and South* recall *The Birth of a Nation* at this point, but *Gone with the Wind* as well, as Madeleine and Cooper embody the indomitable spirit of Scarlett O'Hara. However, it is at this point that *North and South: Book III* begins to critique these earlier texts. Scarlett may have embraced the new capitalistic spirit of the North as she schemes and shrewdly invests her money to participate in the construction and rebuilding of Atlanta, but she would never have embraced Madeline Main's outlook about black freedom and black historical agency.

Yet *North and South* goes further than this. While one could argue that the historical docudrama surrenders to "political correctness" by substituting the acceptable, though derogatory "nigressess" for the reprehensible "niggers," even though both terms are meant to be interchangeable as racial epithets, *North and South* is very attuned to the history of Reconstruction and recent historiography of the period, and works in this historiographic vein more than just adjusting its historical sensibility to post-civil rights America. While Cooper deplores the progress of freedmen and women and the institutions and legislation to protect and empower blacks in the South, he rejects joining the Ku Klux Klan when presented the opportunity. Shortly after Cooper leaves Madeline's home, he visits his white acquaintance, Gettys (Cliff De Young), who shares his antipathy about Madeline's "new way" and support for black empowerment, which also has caught the attention of many local whites who share their disgust.[77] Although the men share a drink, and clearly similar racial politics, when Cooper is invited to join a "political club" (which is clearly used as code for the Klan, and also recalls *Gone with the Wind*) because the sinister organization could use a reputable person of his stature, Cooper not only rejects joining the "political club" but also clearly rebukes it entirely. Despite his Lost Cause and Redemption politics, Cooper Main retains his honor by dishonoring and reproaching the Klan's activity. It is at this moment that *North and South* "redeems" the Lost Cause narrative by criticizing the Ku Klux Klan, thereby integrating it with the larger narrative discourse about reunion and national reconciliation. Indeed, in this constituent story between Gettys and Cooper Main, Gettys uses the racial epithet "nigger" and not "nigresses" like most white Southerners in this historical docudrama, signifying him and the Klan as morally reprehensible like the derogatory racial epithet, and unfit to be a part of the Reconstructed and reconciled nation moving forward towards human progress.

In contrast to earlier Lost Cause narratives, *North and South* portrays the Ku Klux Klan in profoundly negative ways. Despite the historical docudrama's admirable effort to reprimand the Klan's role during Southern Redemption, though, it was precisely Klan acts of terror against black freedmen and women as well as their supporters, lynching them and inflicting other forms of racial violence, that significantly undermined Reconstruction and black equality, empowering Redemption governments and reordering Southern society along white suprema- cist lines in the process.[78] While *The Birth of a Nation* and *Gone with the Wind* recognized and valorized the Klan for their instrumental role in restoring Southern "home rule," even when described as a "political club," these historical films nevertheless reflect historical arguments about the Ku Klux Klan shared by academic scholars, whether traditional historians like Woodrow Wilson and William Dunning who share these cinematic text's sympathies, or more recent historians who do not, and document the extensiveness of the Klan's racial violence and terror during Reconstruction.[79]

The 1988 television drama *Gore Vidal's Lincoln* similarly confronts the politics of the Civil War period as it tells the story of Abraham Lincoln's years as president. Where Civil War films at the beginning of the twentieth century presented the mythic Lincoln, this television miniseries illustrates the more human qualities of the president and describes the volatile political environment Lincoln (Sam Waterston) faced when he assumed the presidency. Rather than revered as a leader, *Gore Vidal's Lincoln* describes the ways the president was dismissed as a naive Western interloper who was ignorant about Washington politics, willing to push the country towards civil war when more experienced political leaders believed compromise with the Confederacy was in the nation's best interest. Furthermore,

Lincoln was ridiculed by Washington insiders for compromising his noble principles for the sake of political pragmatism. At the beginning of the miniseries, Lincoln is neither the "Man who saved the Union" nor the "Great Emancipator." Though the president believes raising volunteers to end the South's rebellion will preserve the nation, he apparently stands alone among congressional leaders and his own cabinet that this policy is in the country's best interest. The docudrama suggests that most of Washington, including the supreme commander of Union military forces, General Winfield Scott, accepts the legitimacy of the Confederacy, and seek reconciliation with the seceded states instead of confrontation. Even before the Civil War begins, President Lincoln faces a palace coup from members of his cabinet who believe he is provoking an unnecessary war.[80]

*Gore Vidal's Lincoln*, of course, does not reject the mythic Lincoln altogether as much as portray him as a more heroic president. The miniseries recalls a Shakespearian tragedy wherein an average American politician confronts the challenges of history as well as his own human shortcomings to redeem himself and his nation. Over the course of his presidency, Lincoln travels the hero's journey whereby he transforms from the pragmatic politician willing to preserve slavery in the existing states though not in the new Western territories, to the abolitionist who establishes a new nation based upon freedom and democracy for all Americans from the ashes of war and devastation. Though he finds himself alone in his quest and surrounded by people of lesser character who doubt him, Lincoln ultimately succeeds because he embraces eminent ideals above pragmatic solutions, saving the soul of the nation as much as the Union itself. Everywhere Lincoln turns, he faces tragedy and defeat: whether that be the death of his son Robert, the gradual insanity of his wife Mary Todd Lincoln (Mary Tyler Moore), anger and resistance from Northerners against his abolitionism, and repeated defeat on the battlefield. Nevertheless, his personal fortitude and indomitable strength of character enable him to overcome relentless crises to become a noble man.

Even though *Gore Vidal's Lincoln* is framed as a biography of the president, it is fundamentally about the ways Lincoln symbolized the nation, and his personal transformation reflects how the country evolved as well. Like the United States, Lincoln is a man with a diverse history. Born in slave-holding Kentucky, rising to prominence in the Midwest, and leading the North as president, Lincoln embodies the nation's three major geographic regions and their provincial cultures. At the outset of his presidency, he is as divided as the country, and seeks reconciliation though war appears inevitable. Initially, he is willing to accept slavery in the Southern states like most white Americans throughout the country, but gradually embraces emancipation in order for the country to extend its founding principles of freedom and equality to all Americans regardless of race.[81] In this regard, *Gore Vidal's Lincoln* comes closer to recent historical interpretations of the president than any of the films discussed in this chapter. The miniseries illustrates Lincoln's pragmatic politics at the beginning of his presidency, but shows how he later redefined the meaning of the Civil War to give it a more noble purpose.

Admittedly, the film minimizes the more controversial question that focuses upon whether Lincoln was ultimately responsible for emancipating slaves, although it seems to agree with this perspective as the miniseries primarily focuses upon the president. Moreover, it also minimizes the more conservative dimensions of the *Emancipation Proclamation*, namely that it actually protected slavery in the border states and emancipated slaves only in the Confederacy where, of course, he had no political authority. Nevertheless, *Gore Vidal's Lincoln* reinforces the argument articulated by historians such as James McPherson, who contend that Lincoln's election ultimately began the end of slavery as it ultimately provoked Southern secession, making the Civil War a war about slavery as much as one about preserving the Union. After all, the war disrupted and eventually destroyed the system of slavery and the South's way of life.[82]

Despite being the rare docudrama that confronts the politics of the Civil War, it nonetheless can avoid the more controversial historical interpretations because it ends before Reconstruction. Since *Gore Vidal's Lincoln* narrows its historical focus upon the president and those who closely surround him such as his family and fellow Washington leaders, it does not include the historical perspective of those Southerners who seceded from the United States and supported slavery (though it includes a scene where President-Elect Lincoln meets with Southern Congressmen prior to Virginia's secession to discuss how he plans to maintain slavery in the existing states), let alone those who fought for the Confederacy. Yes, the Southern point-of-view is represented by Mary Todd Lincoln, who admits her sympathies for slave-holding Kentucky, where she was raised like Lincoln, and continues to have relatives who hold slaves. Still, the president's wife does not have to fight a war to defend a way of life nor endure the tragedy of defeat (although her own family tragedies eventually lead to her insanity). In other words, this docudrama does not have to worry about the Lost Cause narrative competing with the emancipation narrative. Moreover, it can avoid the racial politics of this period in American history because the film does not have to discuss the racial violence of Reconstruction and the history of white supremacy in both North and South, which otherwise would have forced the miniseries to choose between the two competing historical narratives. Like John Jakes' *North and South*, *Gore Vidal's Lincoln* approximates recent trends in Civil War and Reconstruction historiography, but it still falls short of addressing the broader significance of this critical historical period, and the ways Lincoln's enduring vision of the United States as a racial democracy faced incredible challenges in the immediate years following his assassination. The Thirteenth Amendment, Lincoln's final dream before his tragic death (and which *Gore Vidal's Lincoln* includes as the docudrama concludes), only began the freedom struggles that African Americans and Radical Republicans continued during Reconstruction. As Eric Foner points out in his history of this era, telling their story demonstrates how free black people and progressive political leaders were instrumental in fulfilling the dream of racial equality that President Lincoln just began before his early death.[83] Disconnecting Reconstruction from the history of the Civil War as so many films and docudramas such as *The Blue and the Gray* and *Gore Vidal's Lincoln* do, only reifies Lincoln as the principal leader of black emancipation and denies freedmen and women their important historical role to make freedom a reality.

Still *North and South* and *Gore Vidal's Lincoln* are unique when juxtaposed to recent cinematic representations of the Civil War and Reconstruction. Films such as *Glory* (1989) and *Gettysburg* (1993) are transparently war films that correspond to themes of the war genre, focusing on soldier camaraderie and human endurance. But they minimize the political implications and historical interpretations of the Civil War, let alone explore Reconstruction. As the tagline of *Gettysburg* states, "Same Land. Same God. Different Dreams."[84] *Glory* engages the issues of slavery and racism in the Civil War, but they are meta-issues that frame the narrative discourse about racial equality and freedom rather than reflect specific historical problems defining the war itself, nor vexing the nation more generally. This does not take away from the film's powerful story of the Massachusetts' 54th Regiment and its important historical role as one of the initial black military units in the Civil War; but the film is ultimately about their heroics in the war, particularly their pivotal role leading the attack against Fort Wagner, and not about black freedom struggles beyond the unit itself.[85] Moreover, by focusing on the history of the Massachusetts regiment, *Glory* can avoid the more historically complicated issues regarding slavery's relationship to the Civil War and black emancipation during Reconstruction.

Anthony Minghella's *Cold Mountain* is an even more depoliticized film. Like Zwick's *Glory* it is a gripping narrative (and a great movie), but it defangs the politics of the Civil War. Perhaps *Cold Mountain* does not want to alienate viewers by portraying our protagonist Inman (Jude Law) as a Confederate soldier attached to pro-slavery ideology. Instead, Inman's politics are vague and ambiguous as a non-slaveholding white North Carolinian and reluctant Confederate soldier. By simply using his first name, Inman becomes the "white everyman" of the Confederate South: a generic type to absorb our sympathies, and to be the vehicle through which we can sympathize with the average white Confederate soldier who apparently seems to have shared Inman's ambiguous politics. In a classic intertextual moment, Inman joins the Confederate military out of "honor and duty," to preserve "a way of life," recalling Lost Cause films such as *Gone with the Wind*. Clearly, he does not state he is fighting to protect slavery despite the fact that this social, political, and economic "way of life" defined the secessionist movement. His politics remain nebulous as he apparently becomes disillusioned by the war, deserting the Confederate Army to return home to Cold Mountain and his love, Ada Monroe (Nicole Kidman), his true purpose in life.[86] While *Cold Mountain* is a powerful story about war and the human condition, it could be about any war, anywhere, and at any time, and completely avoids the history of the Civil War (let alone the "War Between the States," as Southerners describe the war), not to mention any attempt to illuminate historical meaning or understanding about this seminal historical event in American history.

As numerous scholars have pointed out, it was the support of Southerners like Inman who ultimately comprised the political and military backbone of the secessionist movement. Non-elite, non-slaveholding whites supported secession because they wanted to maintain their Jeffersonian dream of living life as independent yeoman farmers, knowing that this "way of life" was based upon a slaveholding society where black slaves worked plantations and performed the labor that was the necessary foundation of the South's wealth and power.[87] Yeoman Southerners and planters adhered to Jefferson's vision of an agrarian society, wanting to avoid industrialization and urbanization because they believed these aspects of modernity (and which they associated with the North) led to dependency and social decay.[88] White freedom and black slavery maintained this ideology of independence; and in this regard, secession and the establishment of the Confederacy were another moment of a Jeffersonian declaration of the independence. In the minds of white Southerners secession from the Union was much like colonial secession from the British Empire that established the United States as an independent republic during the American Revolution. Southern secessionists were willing to fight and die for their independence like earlier "Southerners" such as George Washington and Thomas Jefferson, even if the nineteenth-century secessionist movement may be a "lost cause." This historical interpretation about white yeomanry and Southern secessionism has revitalized scholarship about the American South in the Early Republic, offering new historical understanding for the reasons so many white non-slaveholders supported to preserve the power of the South's slaveocracy. But *Cold Mountain* avoids this historical argument altogether. Instead, history in this film is mostly a tragic back-drop for a movie that is really an engaging story of love and survival. Seemingly, *Cold Mountain* is an effort to present a more national narrative of reunion and reconciliation based on fated love, not the politics of Southern independence or freedom. As in *The Blue and the Gray*, the issue of slavery and emancipation are suggested whenever African Americans appear in the film. However, blacks and slavery are conspicuous by their notable absence or minimal presence, actually amplifying the issues of slavery and black freedom by the ways *Cold Mountain* wants to avoid these issues. Like *The Blue and the Gray*, blacks and the issue of slavery in *Cold Mountain* are present (and minimally at that) more as narrative furniture rather than people and issues central to the history of the Civil War.

Since Reconstruction remains a source of controversy for Americans, current filmmakers are probably hesitant to examine this period. By concentrating solely on the Civil War, however, historical dramas such as *The Blue and the Gray* and *Cold Mountain*, sustain a genre that perpetuates the national reconciliation narrative that dominated early-twentieth-century scholarship. Whereas historians and filmmakers once agreed upon the narrative of the Civil War and Reconstruction, they now disagree. Historians such as Eric Foner link the Civil War and Reconstruction, arguing that the constitutional controversy that led to the war became a larger struggle about black freedom by 1863.[89] Filmmakers and their continued efforts to separate the Civil War from Reconstruction (with the curious exception of *North and South*), in contrast, seek to avoid these interpretive debates, and arguably obfuscate the meaning of the conflict. Was the war about union or freedom? Among historians like Foner, Lincoln continues to play an important role in the emancipation debate.[90] Among filmmakers, his views about slavery are marginalized because they interfere with their division and reconciliation narrative (the television miniseries *Gore Vidal's Lincoln* being the notable exception). Not surprisingly, current films about the Civil War rarely include the president because of the controversies associated with the competing historical memories he signifies—is he the Great Emancipator or the Sympathetic Unionist?

As this chapter has examined the relationship between the historical profession and filmmakers, it has also raised the issue about the relationship between history and historical memory. Representations of President Lincoln and Reconstruction in historical scholarship and popular culture have long been areas where these two visions of history converged. Sometimes their perspectives have been similar, and most recently, different. In both cases they raise larger questions about how Americans identify themselves and the ideals to which they aspire. Michael Kammen has observed that Americans are a people of paradox—a people of celestial ideals who struggle to live up to them.[91] Efforts to understand Lincoln and the Civil War are exercises in this perpetual struggle. In historical memory, the American story is a biblical epic, with our Principled Puritans failing to live up to their religious vision of an American Eden. Like the Hebrew people of the ancient world, Americans desire to redeem the covenant the Puritans made with God to establish a city upon a hill. The Civil War, however, represents a virtual self-immolation that almost destroyed the American story. Like Noah who led his children through the Flood, Abraham Lincoln guided America through the carnage and destruction of the Civil War, only to renew the American covenant of freedom the founders of the nation envisioned. Indeed, Lincoln's *Gettysburg Address* redeemed this carnage by connecting the war to the meaning of the American Revolution and the American ideals embodied in the Declaration of Independence.[92]

D.W. Griffith understood this portrayal of Lincoln and the history of Reconstruction. He also recognized that the Civil War and Reconstruction created modern America, although one based upon white supremacy. Griffith encouraged his audience to engage with the past to understand a foundational and mythological narrative that informs them of the significant meanings defining American history and our national aspirations. Only Griffith's interpretation encouraged racial violence against African Americans. Ken Burns' much celebrated *The Civil War* documentary series recalls the mythos of this tragic conflict as well, understanding the ways in which personal narratives of contemporary Americans and the drama of the Civil War are rich with historical meaning.[93] Emphasizing Shelby Foote's narrative interpretation of the war with noted and respected academic historian Barbara Jean Fields only reinforces Ken Burns' documentary's

apparent belief: that the narrative of the Civil War illuminates historical interpretation and understanding as much as historical scholarship of this seminal
historical event. In other words, history and narrative are one and the same in
Burns' documentary; and judging by *The Civil War*'s incredible popularity, the
American people agree with this sentiment as well. However, like *The Blue and
the Gray*, Burns' *The Civil War* documentary series alludes to, but never explores
the visceral politics of Reconstruction: the real historical event that defines the
historical meaning of the Civil War, and also our national narrative of American
freedom. Today's historians have been able to reconcile the traditional vision of
Lincoln with the new social and political history of Reconstruction that includes
African Americans and the narrative of human emancipation. Like D.W. Griffith,
modern historians also encourage Americans to engage with their past, although
in a decidedly different political orientation. Today's historians want us to
understand the triumphs and tragedies of Reconstruction, suggesting how we need
to think about what it means for the United States to be a racial democracy. After
all, the subtitle of Eric Foner's monograph reminds us that Reconstruction was
"America's Unfinished Revolution." However, it remains to be seen if today's
filmmakers of movies, television docudramas, and even documentaries have the
boldness that Griffith once showed, and follow today's historians' encouragement:
to rewrite a cinematic narrative of the Civil War and Reconstruction connected
to recent historiographic trends, and write a revisionist history with lightning.

# 3

# ENVISIONING AND RE-VISIONING AMERICA

## Hollywood Westerns and Engaging the American Past

At the end of Michael Mann's *The Last of the Mohicans*, Chingachgook (Russell Means) laments to his white son Hawkeye (Daniel Day-Lewis) that Anglo-American expansion into the North American backcountry will one day bring the frontier to an end, populating the western boundaries of the British American colonies with white settlers. He says that the sun has set on the "Red Man" and the frontier now belongs to Hawkeye and his lover Cora Munro (Madeleine Stowe), but frontier pioneers like them will vanish as well once colonial settlers move west. Earlier in the film we learned that Hawkeye lived most of his life on the frontier, reared by his Mohawk father Chingachgook, largely removed from Anglo-American colonial settlements and their social conventions, even forgoing his anglicized birth name, Nathaniel.[1] Recognizing the tide of history, however, he decides to flee westward to Can-tuckee (that is, Kentucky territory) in order to remain free and independent of the social restrictions that he believes defines colonial life.[2]

As Hawkeye stands with Cora and Chingachgook staring westward in the film's closing scene, the sun sets upon them and the voluptuous wilderness that surrounds them, indicating the closing of the frontier, and the presence of Native Americans in the American historical landscape along with it. While Mann's *Last of the Mohicans* is set in 1757 as the French and Indian War (1754–1763) engulfs colonial America, it nevertheless reflects the same themes we associate with the history of the American West. Just as Americans would later move west of the Mississippi in the nineteenth century in search of land and freedom, Hawkeye intends to go west of the Appalachian Mountains with similar goals in mind. And just as white settlers confronted the dilemma of coexisting with Native Americans in the American West, Mann's film provokes us to think about the future of Indian peoples with the closing of the Appalachian frontier following British victory. Whether we are describing the Anglo–American frontier or the American West, the confluence of Indians, the landscape, and white settlement shaped the history of westward expansion and continues to define the Western film.

Like Chapter 2, this one expands upon the connections between cinematic history and academic historiography. Similar to the ways historians debate the significance of the American frontier and how we define the American West, Hollywood Westerns engage with these historical issues. As the historian Patricia Nelson Limerick has pointed out, Frederick Jackson Turner's Frontier Thesis has long dominated the historiography of the American West.[3] Turner's interpretive framework has attracted scores of historians and others because it told the history of westward expansion as the history of American democracy and individualism, taming the harsh, sometimes unforgiving Western landscape in the process. Armed with the tenacity of the American character, Western settlers ultimately succeeded civilizing the American West, bringing it into the broader scope of modern America by 1890, when all of the arable land west of the Mississippi had been settled according to the 1890 census of that year. For Turner, the long history of the American frontier that began with Anglo–American colonial settlement was over as Americans in the West became part of the larger history of industrial democracy with the rest of the United States at the dawn of the twentieth century.[4]

Since 1894, Turner's influential thesis has been seductive because it celebrates the triumph of American ideals and institutions as well as provided the kind of narrative closure in American history that mythologizes core American values. But as Limerick persuasively points out, this historical narrative presents the history of the American West from the settled, civilized American East, and privileges white settlement.[5] Rarely does Turner's thesis account for the presence of Native Americans, let alone other peoples such as the Spanish and Mexicans. Rather than telling the history of the American frontier, Limerick encourages us to understand the history of the American West; not the story of an imaginary line that bordered civilization and barbarity moving westward over time, but as one of a place that was contested and conquered, where the legacy of the past continues to shape life in the present.[6]

As such, the history of the American West is also the history of an idea, one that has shaped the American historical imagination ever since Thomas Jefferson encouraged the Louisiana Purchase in 1803. In fact, Limerick's definition of the American West encompasses those lands acquired from the Louisiana Purchase, as well as territory from the annexation of Texas, Oregon, and the Mexican–American War.[7] These lands west of the Mississippi stoked the dreams of Americans in the East willing to confront Native Americans and a hostile landscape to preserve the viability of Jefferson's idyllic yeoman farmer, hoping to remain free and independent. When we look at the history of the West from the vantage of those people already living there as white American settlers arrived, we see how these dreams confronted the realities of everyday life in the West, and the ways in which Americans—white, Indian, and Mexican—made a world together (sometimes violently, sometimes peacefully) that continues to define the American West today. However, we should not completely dismiss Turner's idea of the American frontier as it provides historical continuity with America's colonial past, a past that fueled Jefferson's ideas of history, and a vision for an independent United States in the years following the American Revolution. In the mind of Thomas Jefferson, the colonial frontier merged with the American West, manifesting in the Louisiana Purchase and reorienting the course of American history away from the Atlantic towards the West and Pacific. In *Last of the Mohicans*, Hawkeye's dream of being free and independent in Can-tuckee, then, is not a cinematic fabrication. It lies at the core of the history of the American West.

Beginning with Michael Mann's *Last of the Mohicans*, this chapter examines major themes in the history of the American frontier and the West, particularly the ways in which Hollywood films approach westward expansion and the legacy of Jeffersonian ideology. Furthermore, it looks at the ways these films engage Jefferson's views about Native Americans, and whether they approximate his ideals or that of his notable presidential successor, Andrew Jackson, the notorious Indian fighter. As this chapter explores the academic historiography about Jefferson's and Jackson's Indian policies, it will examine films such as John Ford's *The Searchers* and his (along with Henry Hathaway's and George Marshall's) *How The West Was Won* and the degree to which they approximate these respective presidents' vision of the American West.

## *The Last of the Mohicans* and the Historiography of the Early American Frontier

Whether they settled colonies in New England, the Chesapeake, or the Carolina Lowcountry, Anglo-Americans encountered Native American peoples, forging economic and diplomatic relationships that established boundaries among them. These boundaries emerged as the frontiers of Indian and settler societies, becoming "middle grounds" where social and economic encounters could lead to cultural exchanges. According to the historian Richard White, these "middle grounds" became entrepôts where economic trade could lead to cultural blending of Indian and colonial culture. Marriages between the two cultures were ways to solidify diplomatic or economic ties, sometimes producing children who were the literal embodiment of these "middle ground" communities.[8] Although violence periodically would erupt along the colonial frontier and threaten these communities, economic and social needs would force diplomatic negotiations, preserving the need for "middle grounds" as long as Indians and colonists continued to coexist. As much as Native Americans and settlers tried to live together, however, fundamental cultural differences inhibited lasting peace. Anglo-American desire for land, and their belief in private property conflicted with the Indians more communitarian values about land. As William Cronon notes, when Native Americans sold land to colonists they believed they still had the right to cultivate and hunt upon those lands, and did not understand why colonists would fence land in order to deprive others from using it.[9] Colonists would complain of natives trespassing upon their private property, and Indians in turn would complain that they were denied use of land they believed was held in common. In places such as New England, these differences manifested into violent conflicts such as King Philip's War, wars that were so devastating that they demolished middle ground communities as they became conflicts for cultural and social preservation.

One of the major issues in Early American history concerns the ways Anglo-Indian relations devolved from the promising First Thanksgiving of 1621 into violent conflicts like King Philip's War in 1675–76. Although some would argue that Puritanism and Anglo-American thirst for land prevented any hope for lasting peaceful coexistence between natives and settlers in New England, inevitably leading to conflict, others would maintain that the establishment of Praying Towns along the New England frontier suggests that they could have lived together. These Praying Towns were cultural middle grounds populated by converted Indian Christians and were established near Puritan communities in places such as western Massachusetts to facilitate trade and Puritan evangelism. Praying Indians in these towns became literate and could move between Indian and Puritan communities, serving the critical role as negotiators between them. Puritans such as John Eliot believed they should evangelize to Native Americans in the region, teaching them both Christianity and English culture. Working with Praying Indians, Eliot published a Bible in a local Indian dialect, and the future appeared promising for Puritans and the local Native American peoples of New England.[10]

However, land disputes eventually erupted and Praying Indians came under suspicion from both sides who questioned their fundamental loyalties. In fact, the murder of the Praying Indian John Sassamon was the catalyst for King Philip's War as he was accused of misrepresenting Algonquian land claims to English leaders. Massive slaughter between Native Americans and settlers led to what the historian Jill Lepore contends was the most violent war in American history.[11] The once harmonic relationship between Praying Indians and settlers vanished as colonists removed them from Praying Towns, doubting their loyalties because they fundamentally believed their racial allegiance lay with fellow Indians. The ultimate victory of the Anglo-American colonists led to the virtual extinction of Algonquians in New England, with many of them murdered or sent into slavery.[12] Without a sizable presence of Algonquians in the region, no more "middle grounds" were necessary between the English and local Native American peoples, and the New England frontier was practically closed.

However, other native peoples such as those that constituted the Iroquois nation remained along the New York frontier, and allied with the French in New France against the English settlers. During times of war, the French sometimes encouraged Indian raids to kidnap and hold English settlers ransom in exchange for French prisoners of war. The saga of John Williams' family during Queen Anne's War (1703–1713) tragically reflects the violent history of the Anglo-

American frontier and the persistence of middle ground communities along the colonial frontier. In 1703, John Williams' community of Deerfield, Massachusetts was attacked, and he, his daughters Esther and Eunice and sons Samuel and Stephen were kidnapped. His wife and other children were killed during the raid. The historian John Demos speculates that the Iroquois purposely raided this town to kidnap Williams as his value as a preacher would fetch a higher ransom or the release of French prisoners of equal value. Williams and the other kidnapped hostages were led through the Anglo-American backcountry into French Canada, where they remained until their release was secured. As the French surmised, the Massachusetts government wanted to release Williams as soon as they could, negotiating the terms of his release but not those of his children yet.[13]

As soon as Williams returned to his community he worked for the release of his children, or in his words, to "redeem the captives," but was only successful with having Esther, Samuel, and Stephen returned. Eunice remained behind, first living in a French Catholic community and then marrying an Indian husband. They later moved to a middle ground community of Indian and European settlers along the New York and French Canadian frontier. John Williams never gave up his effort to have his daughter returned, believing she remained a captive among the French and Indians. He died never seeing her again. Stephen continued his father's pursuit, only to learn that Eunice wanted to remain with her Indian husband and her children. She had fully become a member of the Indian-European middle ground, speaking French and converting to Catholicism, and dressing like the natives. Although she saw her brother a few times over the years and became a local celebrity in her former Massachusetts town whenever she visited, she eventually returned home to her adopted community, remaining an "unredeemed captive" in the eyes of her brother and former Massachusetts community.[14]

The stories of middle grounds, Indian–settler conflict, and Indian captivity along the colonial American frontier manifest in the history of the American West as well. They are also themes that emerge in Michael Mann's *The Last of the Mohicans* and John Ford's *The Searchers*. In both films, Indian captivity reflects broader questions about race, gender, and cultural exchange. However, where Mann's film recognizes captivity as a cultural middle ground that spawned an indigenous American culture and identity, Ford's film sees it as much more problematic, infused with American anxieties about race and miscegenation. In *The Last of the Mohicans*, Hawkeye is outwardly white, but his identity is a mixture of his Indian and Anglo-American upbringing. He continues to live among the Mohawks as an adult, but moves with ease (as do his Mohawk father and brother Uncas) among the colonial settlements along the frontier, speaking English and Mohawk and practicing Indian customs. As the colonists and English soldiers prepare to fight the French and their Huron allies, Hawkeye's Indian skills will become assets as he first saves Cora and her sister Alice (Jodhi May), the daughters of British colonel Edmund Munro (Maurice Roëves) from a Huron ambush and then later when they have been captured by the Huron, Magua. In contrast,

Debbie Edward's captivity in Ford's *The Searchers* is viewed by her uncle Ethan as a violation, and it is unclear for most of the film whether his obsession to find her is motivated by his desire to "redeem" her and bring her back to her Texas frontier settlement, or to kill her because she has been permanently corrupted by Indian culture. In both films, captivity is a racial middle ground, a space of cultural mixing and the possible future of the American character. They differ, however, whether cultural exchange and blending represents the promise of a new America or a sign of its decay.

Although Michael Mann's *The Last of the Mohicans* is based upon James Fenimore Cooper's classic novel of the same name, it nonetheless speaks to recent historiographic issues about the history of the Early American frontier. In the film's initial scenes, Native Americans maintain viable communities in North America, some peacefully coexisting with Anglo-American colonists, forging middle ground communities along the frontier of the Hudson River valley. In one of the film's early scenes, Hawkeye, Chingachgook, and Chingachgook's other son Uncas (Eric Schweig) visit a colonial family, where they enjoy each other's company and are clearly at ease with each other. Mann's movie actually sets up this scene like one we will also see in John Ford's *The Searchers* where white settlers are at first startled when they hear noises outside their cabin, reaching for their gun in the event of an Indian raid. Although Comanche Indians do raid the cabin and massacre its white inhabitants in Ford's film, initial settler fear turns into warm greetings and a convivial gathering among Mohawks and colonists in Mann's movie.

While some would maintain that this is a revisionist interpretation of colonial history and a cinematic fabrication, such amicable relations among Native Americans and Anglo-American settlers in the American frontier are historically accurate as earlier noted. When *The Last of the Mohicans* shows an Indian woman in colonial homespun garb moving through a town market and Indians playing along with white colonists in one of the film's early scenes, the movie reflects much of the recent scholarship about the social and cultural middle grounds native peoples and Anglo-American settlers forged along the frontier through the eighteenth century. Notably, the natives and settlers participate in an Indian sport that resembles field hockey, whooping an Indian war-cry and playing shirtless, activities that clearly suggest that Native Americans and colonists collectively play a game steeped in local Indian masculine traditions. In this town market scene we also learn that one of the local Indian leaders agrees along with white settlers in the colonial militia to support the English to fight the French and their Indian allies. Later, we discover that these Native American soldiers are just as afraid of their families and homes left unprotected by their absence as the white colonists, suggesting that Indian homes populate the frontier backcountry alongside those of the Anglo-American colonists.[15]

Mann's film also advances Frederick Jackson Turner's Frontier Thesis by illustrating the ways the American wilderness transformed Europeans into Americans. Here, *Last of the Mohicans* challenges recent arguments in Early American historiography about the degree to which Anglo-American colonists aspired to be more English and were proud to be part of the British Empire. Historians such as Jack Greene contend that British American colonists valued their connection to England and celebrated being subjects of what they believed to be the most progressive political system in Europe.[16] Only when the British Parliament began to abuse what the colonists believed to be protected English rights with a colonial taxation system to raise revenue following British victory of the French and Indian War did colonists begin to see differences between their American systems of government and that of the mother country. In *Last of the Mohicans*, however, the differences between the American colonists and the English were established as the colonists confronted the American wilderness and struggled to forge communities long before the imperial conflict that led to the American Revolution. Throughout the movie, the landscape is mysterious and powerful, beholding the beautiful and the violent; yet it is the source of the American character. The colonists and Native Americans connect with it and understand it, while it confuses and disorients the English. Americans stand in awe of the landscape, praising the bounty it provides while it terrifies the English.

Two particular scenes reflect this idea. In the opening scene, Hawkeye, Chingachgook and Uncas run through the forest hunting an elk. After Hawkeye shoots it, Chingachgook talks to their fallen prey, calling him brother and thanking him for providing them their food in an act of spiritual communion. Uncas stands near his father saluting the elk, likewise connecting with their victim in this religious ceremony. This scene demonstrates the way these three Mohawks (and at this point of the film, Hawkeye is viewed as much Mohawk as Chingachgook and Uncas) are part of a spiritual ecosystem shaped by the American landscape and Mohawk religious mysticism. In contrast, the wilderness is foreign to the English, pregnant with danger and something they fear. They travel through cleared areas of the forest, always on alert for whatever lurks behind the trees. For example, when English soldiers march through the forest to take their senior officer Duncan Heyward (Steven Waddington), Cora, and Alice to Colonel Munro at Fort William Henry, they become afraid and apprehensive as they hear noises emanating from the forest that surrounds them, standing confused and horrified when they are eventually ambushed by Huron Indians.[17] In this scene, the wilderness hides the unknowable, or at least the comprehensible, for the English. Yet its mysteries are not beyond their reach if they seek to understand it and the frontier communities its shapes, as Cora's experience illustrates.

Once the English are willing to adapt to the forest, recognizing its power and beauty, they can transform into Americans. This idea is best reflected in Cora Munro's evolution once she changes from the daughter of an English patriarch into an American woman. As Cora moves further into the wilderness guided by Hawkeye, Chingachgook, and Uncas, making their way towards Fort William Henry following the Huron massacre, she comes to understand the colonists and Native Americans. She learns to appreciate the way the wilderness defines the

American character and distinguishes the colonists from the English, especially as she falls in love with Hawkeye and sees the American frontier through his eyes. Following Hawkeye's arrest for abetting the desertion of men from the colonial militia (who want to return to the homes and families upon hearing that they have been left vulnerable to Indian and French war parties), she articulates her revelation to her father as she pleas for his release. Even as she confirms Hawkeye's earlier account of a massacred frontier settlement, her father refuses to set him free as commanding officer. Disgusted with her father's military priorities and denial of colonists' immediate needs for protection, she asserts that the English will never understand America and how different they are from the colonists over whom they rule. In anger, Cora states that English policies are not shaped with the colonists' interests in mind, and one day they will awake to discover how the Americans are an independent people, shaped by their struggles and the land upon which they live.[18]

In fact, the film's most direct affirmation of Turner's Frontier Thesis comes during scenes when we see English officers confronting the colonial militia. Throughout the film, the colonists are not portrayed as English men and women living on the edges of the British Empire. Rather they are Americans who happen to consider "England as their sovereign," as the colonist Jack Winthrop (Edward Blatchford) asserts as he raises the county levy (the quota of men) for colonial New York's militia. Whenever the English (who are always represented as the military, save for Cora and Alice) and colonists inhabit the same scenes, they stand at separate ends of the screen with significant space between them, and always looking at each other with palpable hostility and suspicion. Clearly Mann wants to illustrate how far apart the English and colonists are, and how independent the Americans already have become. Moreover, the English wear fine military or aristocratic dress throughout the film, while the colonists clearly wear homespun clothes, thereby further demarcating the cultural gap between them, and the independence of the colonists. Indeed, over the course of the film, Cora and Alice's aristocratic garb becomes crude and looks worn the longer they stay in America,[19] further illustrating how they are shedding their English identity. In this regard, Mann's film differs from recent historiography in Early American history that maintains that the colonists actually desired to be very English until the eve of independence. Historians such as Timothy Breen contend that one of the signs of colonial aspirations to be English was the significant degree they purchased English goods and fashions in the eighteenth century, particularly as the British Atlantic world become more connected as a result of Britain winning the French and Indian War.[20]

In contrast, *Last of the Mohicans* dismisses colonial efforts to consume English commodities or engage in the Atlantic marketplace. In one early scene, the camera pans over Americans walking through a town market populated by Indians and white settlers purchasing and selling one another's goods. Here, the film maintains that living along the frontier and disconnected from the mother country has made the colonists independent of the British, both geographically and culturally. Only as they fight alongside the English during the siege of Fort William Henry do they become conscious of how American they have become. During one of the film's most critical scenes, Hawkeye explains the massacre of his friend John Cameron's family and their homestead to white settlers and Native Americans in the colonial militia besieged at the fort, and how the English officers disregard the vulnerability of militiamen's farms and families. At this point, one white colonist states that if British tyranny rules the colonies, then he is not obliged to stay and fight what they begin to see as England's war with France, and one that has nothing to do with them.[21] Becoming fully conscious of American "rights" in the face of English "tyranny," some of these colonists "rebel" by deserting Fort William Henry to protect their families, with Hawkeye assisting them as they cross behind French and Indian enemy lines. According to *Last of the Mohicans*, the colonists were independent Americans even before the first shot at Lexington and Concord in 1775, a fact shaped by a long history of living along the frontier.

Much like Eunice Williams in John Demos's *The Unredeemed Captive*, the character Hawkeye reflects how white colonists adopted Indian customs and identified with Native American peoples with whom they settled. As earlier mentioned, *Last of the Mohicans* begins with Hawkeye running through the forest with his Mohawk father Chingachgook and his brother Uncas hunting an elk. As this scene unfolds, we notice Hawkeye chasing the animal shirtless while Chingachgook and Uncas remained fully clothed in colonial garb. Furthermore, we notice that his body is marked with Indian-style tattoos and he speaks Mohawk to his father and brother as they hunt the elk, and together the three of them participate in the spiritual ceremony that honors the elk as they prepare to eat it. Clearly, this opening scene establishes Hawkeye as much Mohawk as Chingachgook and Uncas and his later refusal to join the colonial militia only reinforces that he does not identify with white Anglo-American society. In fact, he speaks English only because Chingachgook sent him and Uncas to a school Eleazar Wheelock set up at Dartmouth College to proselytize English culture and Christianity to Native Americans.[22]

As much as Hawkeye believes he is Mohawk, his identity remains unstable throughout the film as most of the screen time takes place while he moves among either the English or the colonists, and we consistently hear people call him by his anglicized birth name, Nathaniel. Later in the film we learn that Nathaniel was rescued by Chingachgook after his mother and sister were killed, adopting him as his son and rearing him as Mohawk. In the film's initial scenes we learn that he is a fur trapper along with his father and brother, further suggesting that he lives in the middle ground world that defined the colonial American frontier. Although the film describes the fluidity of cultural exchange that defined the middle ground colonial settlements in the eighteenth century, *The Last of the Mohicans* presents race as a fixed social category, and denies the possibility of mixed-race relationships. The tragic deaths of Uncas and Alice illustrate this point. After Alice has been selected by the Huron sachem to be Magua's wife, Uncas attempts to save her. After confronting Magua and his war party, he is killed, and Magua summarily discards his body from a cliff. Alice then looks at Magua with tears in her eyes and jumps off the cliff,[23] plummeting to her death to lie next to her dead Uncas in the only way she can consummate their love. While the film presents Uncas and Alice's forlorn love as a tragedy, it also suggests that their mixed-race relationship has no place in the American future. In fact their attraction to each other is presented more as exotic desire encouraged by the savagery of the wilderness than a sincere emotional relationship: Uncas desires Alice because she is white, and she wants him because he is Indian.

In contrast, the relationship between Hawkeye and Cora can blossom because it is based upon a substantive emotional attachment that reflects how they have transformed into Americans. Over the course of the film, Hawkeye comes to embrace his identity as Nathaniel and life as Anglo-American, accepting this as the price he must pay in order to be with Cora. Cora has changed as well as she understands that Nathaniel's actions are based upon his knowledge of the frontier and not savagery, whether that means leaving massacred bodies unburied so as not to leave traces for Indian war parties pursuing them, or helping colonial militia men desert Fort William Henry. In turn, Nathaniel sees that she is no longer the aristocratic daughter of an English officer, and has emerged as an American woman shaped by the struggles of the frontier. As Nathaniel and Cora move closer to each other, they move further away from their original identities, forging a relationship that will shape the future of westward expansion. The final scenes of the film reinforce this transformation. Standing along a cliff, Nathaniel and Chingachgook pray to Indian gods to receive Uncas' spirit, spreading his ashes as they participate in an Indian burial ceremony together. Following this ceremony, however, Chingachgook notes that he is the last of the Mohicans and history is closing for the "Red Man." Where once Chingachgook embraced Nathaniel as his Mohawk son, now he no longer does. Instead, he sees him as part of a future of the frontier that belongs to "my white son and his woman,"[24] although one day they too will be a distant memory as white settlers move west and expand the boundaries of civilization. Affirming his conclusion, the final scene shows Chingachgook standing apart from Nathaniel and Cora, who have embraced each other as the three of them look towards the horizon, clearly signifying that their future will be one apart from his. As the film closes, the three of them collectively face westward towards the setting sun, suggesting that history will set upon all of them with the closing of the American frontier.

Chingachgook's poignant statement about the closing of the frontier and the demise of Native American peoples connects with historiographic arguments about the future of Indians in early America. Throughout most of *Last of the Mohicans*, we see the viable presence of native peoples from different nations along the American frontier. The character Magua reflects how Native Americans were still able to maintain positions of power by playing Europeans such as the English and

French against each other. The film also demonstrates some of the key themes in recent Native American historiography. Scholars such as James Merrell and Colin Calloway have demonstrated that the "new world" was as much a new world for Indians as it was for Europeans.[25] Death and disease of course decimated numerous Native American peoples upon European contact, but over time they were able to withstand these biological challenges, forming new Indian nations or blending existing ones.[26] Although Magua is clearly the film's villain, his life story connects with the history of many native peoples whose lives were transformed by the presence of English colonists. As we learn during the film, Magua was taken as a slave from his Huron community by Mohawks following an inter-Indian war. Eventually, he earned his freedom by demonstrating his loyalty to his Mohawk captors, and learned English and French as he became a powerful warrior. Yet, he maintained a vendetta against the English, and led a massacre against the English army and colonists after they surrendered Fort William Henry to the French. Magua's thirst for vengeance was satisfied only when he murdered Colonel Munro, cut out his heart, and captured his daughters.

To celebrate his victory, he returns to a Huron village with Cora, Alice, and Duncan (who was also captured following the massacre). In this powerful scene, Magua tells the Huron sachem that his victory demonstrates the power of the Huron people to the Europeans, and that they will remain a major diplomatic presence as they adapt to the economic and political practices of the English and French. As Magua announces his accomplishments to the approval of the sachem, Nathaniel enters the Huron village to exchange his life for Cora's. Asking Duncan to translate his English to French, Nathaniel denounces Magua's ideals by questioning the practices of the Europeans. Do the Hurons want to destroy their ecosystem, kill native peoples, and sell brandy to fellow Indians like the Europeans in their pursuit of power, actions which have led to the demise of native peoples throughout North America? As Nathaniel says, "These are the ways of the Yengeese (Yankees)."[27] Recognizing Nathaniel's wisdom, and to Magua's shame, the sachem frees Cora, and tells Magua to take Alice as his wife. Duncan, however, mistranslates Nathaniel's last statements so that he is taken as a Huron war trophy, and is burned alive.[28] This scene is significant in the ways it represents Native American customs and history. We see how this Huron village has been transformed by the presence of Europeans in North America. Some of the Huron wear colonial garb, but their clear understanding of French reflects how they have adapted to living among French settlers, whether through trade or as military allies. In this regard, this scene connects with earlier ones that show the Mohawks living among the English colonists, although describing the negative consequences European colonization has had upon Indian culture and society in this case.

Together, these Indian scenes in *Last of the Mohicans* accurately represent native customs such as Indian sport, religious ceremonies, and shaming rituals (as we see when the Huron humiliate Nathaniel as he enters their village by beating him and whooping their war-cry).[29] However, the Huron appear to be a weakened people as well, as Magua's speech illustrates. If they must demonstrate their power, then they must have lost a measure of it in the eyes of Europeans. As the historian Daniel Richter has shown, Iroquois peoples such as the Huron remained potent as long as multiple European powers vied for control of North America and needed them as allies.[30] In this way, Chingachgook's final speech reflects a measure of historical truth. As Richter notes, British victory in the French and Indian War removed the French military presence in North America, and thus the ability for native peoples to play a significant diplomatic and military role among the European powers.[31] The Revolutionary War and War of 1812 briefly enabled Indians to play these roles as Americans and the British needed them during these conflicts, but their importance again receded with the victory of the United States in both of these wars. As we will see, the future of Indians in the American republic hinged upon policies such as those of Thomas Jefferson and Andrew Jackson, presidents who tried to reconcile their presence among white Americans in the United States.

## The American West in the Age of Jefferson and Jackson

While the Appalachian Mountains and Mississippi River constituted the original boundaries of the American frontier, the Louisiana Purchase merged the history of the frontier with the American West as the border of the United States expanded to the Rocky Mountains in 1803. The Louisiana Purchase remains one of Thomas Jefferson's lasting legacies for the ways it shaped America's vision of itself as much as it increased the United States' geographic size. Worried that the United States was quickly becoming a manufacturing nation like those in Europe, Jefferson believed the Purchase would forestall the country from achieving this historical point in social development by maintaining itself as an agricultural republic for the foreseeable future by expanding through geographic space.[32] Jefferson always feared the consequences of industrialization and urbanization in the young United States, as they would lead to class inequalities, political tyranny, and social conflict as they did in Western Europe. As he stated in *The Notes on the State of Virginia*,

> Dependence begets subservience and venality, suffocates the germ of virtue, and prepares fit tools for the designs of ambition. This, [is] the natural progress and consequence of the arts [i.e. manufacturing] . . . While we have land to labor, then, let us never wish to see our citizens occupied at a work bench, or twirling distaff. Carpenters, masons, smiths, are wanting in husbandry; but for the general operations of manufacture, let our shops remain in Europe.[33]

To his dismay, Alexander Hamilton's tenure as Secretary of the Treasury under Presidents Washington and Adams propelled the United States in the direction of domestic commercial manufacturing with his economic policies that were designed to encourage the development of an internal financial infrastructure. With the establishment of the Bank of the United States and the circulation of credit, entrepreneurs could access the necessary capital to facilitate industrialization in the young republic.

To stem the tide of this historical trajectory, Jefferson hoped the American West would become the repository of yeoman farmers fleeing the congested East to preserve their independence and reject the prospect of lives as dreary factory workers. In Jefferson's mind, these yeoman farmers not only were "the chosen people of God," but also would constitute the nation's virtuous citizenry and protect the American republic's democratic institutions.[34] For Jefferson, the West would always offer possibilities for new beginnings and economic possibilities, opportunities to escape one's past and start life anew. In effect, the president laid the foundation for the West to offer the American Dream to those who needed to start over and leave their past behind. As we will shortly see, Hollywood Westerns reflect this Jeffersonian vision of the American West and demonstrate how this vision encountered the challenging natural environment and existing Native Americans. For his part, Jefferson hoped his dream of a yeoman's republic would be extended to Native American peoples now absorbed in the expanded United States, believing they too could be cultivators of the earth. However, his views about race and civilization sometimes contradicted his Indian policies, creating conditions for Indian and settler conflict in the new Louisiana Territory.

Thomas Jefferson believed in a biological definition of race that was a fixed social category, which in turn essentially shaped one's identity. However, he did not believe race necessarily determined one's culture or history. Jefferson saw many admirable qualities in native peoples, and believed they had the capacity to be civilized and assimilate into American society. Indeed, this was his hope as the United States expanded its boundaries westward. As he said in his letter to William Henry Harrison,

> Our system is to live in perpetual peace with the Indians, to cultivate an affectionate attachment from them, by everything just and liberal which we can do for them within the bounds of reason, and by giving them effectual protection against wrongs from our own people.[35]

He hoped that living near white settlers would encourage Indians to likewise become yeoman farmers. Jefferson believed that "our settlements will gradually circumscribe and approach the Indians, and they will in time either incorporate with us as citizens of the United States, or remove beyond the Mississippi." There would be a consequence for this, however, as assimilation into American society would certainly be "the termination of their history most happy for themselves," and as such "it is essential to cultivate their love."[36]

For most of *Last of the Mohicans*, the film reflects President Jefferson's perspective about the place of Native American peoples in the United States, and the possibilities for them to coexist with white settlers. In the movie's early scenes, we see Indians such as Chingachgook and Uncas speaking English, wearing colonial style clothing, and being familiar with colonial customs. During the town market-place scene, we observe a native woman in colonial garb as well as earlier noted, carrying goods that she will likely trade at this market.[37] In fact, we learn that Chingachgook once maintained views about the future of native peoples similar to Jefferson. As noted, he sent Hawkeye and Uncas to Eleazar Wheelock's Indian school. In the town market scene we also see Indians supporting the English war effort; they decide to fight alongside the British and American colonists at Fort William Henry. They too become concerned about the vulnerability of their homes like the American colonists, as their families populate the exposed frontier settlements as well.[38] In the end, however, *Last of the Mohicans* departs from its Jeffersonian view of Native American history. Beginning with the scene at the Huron village, we see native peoples question their future among the European settlers. As the Huron sachem notes, he has wondered since he was a young boy what policy would be best to follow in order to ensure Indian survival. Should the Huron become like the Europeans in order to adapt to their presence and power in North America (which would follow a Jeffersonian view of Native American history), or remove themselves to protect their nation from the corrupting influence of European trade and cultural exchange? This, of course, is the essence of the dialogue among the sachem, Magua, and Hawkeye. For his part, Magua believes that the Huron should become as powerful as the Europeans, and engage them on the Huron's terms. He states that his recent massacre of Colonel Munro, his soldiers, and Anglo-American colonists will demonstrate the mighty power of the Huron to Europeans and settlers alike. As a force to be reckoned with, Europeans and the colonists will respect them as equal partners in North American diplomacy.

Hawkeye, in turn, questions Magua's rationality as he tries to negotiate Cora's release. Do the Huron truly want to be like the "Yengeese?" Do they want to defile the ecosystem that provides them subsistence by despoiling it for profit? Do they want to sell alcohol to fellow indigenous peoples to trick them in order to secure better trading or diplomatic terms like the English do? In other words, the Huron way of life will be destroyed if they become like the Europeans and their colonists, and it would be best to remove one's nation from their corrupting influence. The Huron sachem, and by extension the film, apparently agrees with this sentiment as the sachem releases Cora from Magua's captivity. In the final scenes of *Last of the Mohicans*, the film increasingly takes the stand that regardless of whether Indians assimilate to Anglo-American society or remove themselves from it, the end of their race is imminent. In these closing scenes, we see the tragedy of native peoples fighting each other, first with Uncas' fatal attempt to save Alice, and then Chingachgook's confrontation with Magua. As he clobbers Magua to death with his weapons, the camera zooms out to show Chingachgook and Magua facing each other, poignantly staring as if they are asking one another whether this has become the tragic fate of their peoples—killing Indians to save Europeans. As the film closes, Chingachgook says that he is the last of the Mohicans and that the future will soon be over for the "Red Man" with the westward expansion of white settlers. Where Jefferson at least offered the possibility for native peoples to choose their fate, remaining historical agents who can set the course of their trajectory, the film concludes that extinction is inevitable for Native Americans.

In this regard, *Last of the Mohicans* ultimately affirms the views held by Andrew Jackson, the one-time Indian fighter and later American president responsible for the Cherokee Trail of Tears. Jackson also believed that the sun had set on the history of Native Americans. However, he intended to facilitate their demise by encouraging Indian removal in order to clear lands for white settlement. Following the end of the War of 1812, Native American peoples lost their significant diplomatic role in the American South once the British left the region and Indians could no longer ally with the British against the United States. In the aftermath of the war, General Jackson continued his military campaign against the Creek Indians, eventually achieving a victory that resulted with the Creeks ceding over twenty million acres of land to the United States.[39] During his first presidential administration, he also agreed to execute congressional legislation to remove native peoples to Indian Territory west of the Mississippi (in present day Oklahoma), believing it would be in their best interest. As Jackson stated in his second State of the Union speech,

> Rightly considered, the policy of the General Government toward the red man is not only liberal, but generous. He is unwilling to submit to the laws of the States and mingle with their population. To save him from the alternative, or perhaps utter annihilation, the General Government kindly offers him a new home, and proposes to pay their whole expense of his removal and settlement.[40]

Nevertheless, President Jackson maintained that Indian extinction was imminent. He said,

> Humanity has often wept over the fate of the aborigines of this country, and Philanthropy [sic] has been long busily employed in devising means to avert it, but its progress has never for a moment been arrested, and one by one have many powerful tribes disappeared from the earth.[41]

Chingachgook could not have said it any better. In fact, a number of American Western films take Jackson's perspective of Native American history. The question becomes whether these films see the extinction of Indian peoples as inevitable in the face of the westward expansion of white Americans, or if the federal government and American settlers actively pursued their extermination in order to make the United States a white person's country. As we examine *The Searchers* and *How the West Was Won*, we will see how these two films approach these questions differently.

John Ford's *The Searchers* is widely considered one of the best Westerns ever made. Although it seemingly tells the story of one man's obsession to pursue his niece taken captive by Comanche Indians, it probes the disturbing history of race in the West, and American anxieties about miscegenation. Where *Last of the Mohicans* presents Hawkeye's captivity as a positive experience that contributed to his frontier individualism, *The Searchers* portrays Debbie Edwards' (Natalie Wood) captivity as nothing short of racial defilement, necessitating her death in the eyes of her uncle Ethan Edwards (John Wayne). In the world of *The Searchers*, there is no middle ground between Indians and settlers, only a perpetual race war that will end in one or the other's extermination. Reflecting President Jackson's perspective of Indians, Ford's film presents a narrative where Native Americans do not have a place in the United States as an independent people. They either fully assimilate into American society and reject their Indian ties, like Ethan's eighth-blood nephew Martin Pawley (Jeffrey Hunter), or they remain beyond its boundaries fighting a war for cultural survival like the Comanche Indian chief Scar (Henry Brandon), a war they inevitably will lose. Where Thomas Jefferson held out hopes for Indian assimilation as yeoman farmers and participation in the settlement of the American West, Jackson believed native peoples needed to be removed in one way or another in order to make room for white settlers. As we will see, the narrative discourse of *The Searchers* closely mirrors Jackson's views about the future of Native American history.

As the film begins, we are introduced to a West Texas homestead and the barren land that surrounds it in 1868, three years following the end of the Civil War. Significantly, this scene opens from Martha Edwards' (Dorothy Jordan) point-of-view, where the darkness from inside the home fades into the color of the West Texas landscape as she opens the cabin door to see her brother-in-law and former Confederate officer, Ethan Edwards, who has been incognito since the Confederate surrender, riding up to the Edwards' homestead. Immediately, the film establishes the Edwards' home and surrounding landscape as symbols for safety and danger. Yet, Ford's movie complicates these symbols by signifying the homestead with darkness, a lighting technique that can be a motif for evil or menace, and the landscape with light, another lighting technique that can symbolize truth or righteousness. As Aaron Edwards (Walter Coy) and his wife Martha step onto the shaded porch, where the light and darkness meet, the film establishes its theme of moral ambiguity. Already the film alerts us that the ensuing narrative is a complicated story about white settlers and Indians in the American West, and one where moral and historical clarity will be elusive. Like Martha, Aaron looks to see Ethan arriving upon their homestead, although looking more reserved about his brother's return.[42]

While no one knows for certain where Ethan has been for the last three years, Mose Harper (Hank Worden), the local vagabond, has spread the rumor throughout this West Texas settlement that Ethan was seen in California.[43] While he is portrayed as crazed and mentally disturbed in *The Searchers*, Mose actually emerges as a central character, providing critical intelligence about Debbie Edwards' whereabouts after she has been captured by Comanche Indians. As he periodically appears in the film, it becomes evident that Mose Harpers is actually the literary Shakespearian fool whose superficial comic nonsense masks his intelligent perception of the racial boundaries and dangerous multicultural landscape of West Texas. As we will later see, the film suggests that Mose's lunacy is the result of his constant crossing of the racial boundaries that demarcate white, Mexican, and Indian settlements along the West Texas frontier.

Although Ethan dismisses Mose as "that old goat," he does not deny the rumor. As he gives Aaron freshly minted dollars, so new that Aaron marvels that they do not even have a mark, the film suggests that Ethan has robbed the United States mint in San Francisco. A disillusioned Confederate soldier who continues to wear his uniform because he refuses to put the war behind him, and who is a probable criminal, Ethan Edwards is a complicated man whose moral universe is just as vague as his recent past. Ethan is nevertheless welcomed as a war hero by the Edwards family, especially by Martha, whose gestures and care for Ethan's few belongings suggest a deep emotional past, one that appears to resurface with Ethan's return. Along with their children Lucy, Debbie, Ben and adopted son Martin "Marty" Pawley, Aaron and Martha receive Ethan into their family. However, Ethan's mysterious past and Martha's questionable fidelity threaten to undermine the bonds that hold this family together. Ethan's transparent racism further challenges the Edward's family structure as he denigrates Marty for being a half-breed.[44] Though Marty responds that he is only one-eighth Cherokee, in Ethan's eyes he is Indian nonetheless and refuses to be called his uncle. He calls Marty epithets such as "blanket head," and tells him not to "burn bonfires or bang drums" to alert him of the Comanche as they begin their search for Debbie.

While Ethan's vile racism becomes evident in these early scenes of the movie, we need to be careful not to associate his views about race and cultural exchange with the film's broader narrative discourse which sees race relations and cultural exchange as much more complex. Over the course of the film, the movie will provoke us to think about the definition of race and the degree to which it is biologically or culturally determined. In the early scenes of *The Searchers*, the film presents both these definitions of race from Ethan and Marty's perspectives. Ethan maintains the biological view of race, regarding Marty as Indian even though he has lived most of his life with the Edwards family and likely sees himself as white as much as them. However, we soon discover that Ethan is also quite familiar with Indian customs and apparently speaks "good Comanche" despite his race hatred.[45] Just as the moral universe in this film is ambiguous, so too is the racial landscape of the West Texas frontier. As *The Searchers* unfolds, clear definitions of whiteness and Indian are just as elusive as the meaning of good and evil. Once the Comanche people massacre the Edwards family and take Debbie captive, propelling Ethan and Marty to search for her over the next five years, Ford's film becomes a penetrating study about the meaning of race, nation, and the American character.

The day after Ethan returns, the captain of the local Texas Rangers Samuel Clayton (Ward Bond), who also happens to be the local preacher, arrives at the Edwards homestead to recruit more men for his posse of Rangers to pursue bandits believed to have rustled cattle belonging to the Jorgansen family. Ethan immediately suspects that the cattle were rustled to pull the men of this West Texas community away from their homes by Indians intending to attack the homesteads themselves. As such, he volunteers to go along with the Rangers along with Marty, but tells his brother Aaron to remain behind with Martha and the children in the event that the Indians do plan to attack the homes. Ethan's suspicion proves correct as we watch the Comanche and their chief Scar assault the Edwards homestead, killing Aaron, Martha, and Ben, setting fire to their home, and taking Lucy and Debbie captive. As viewers observe the Comanche raid from the settlers' perspective, we watch as they gradually sense the imminent Indian attack, recognizing their vulnerability and then the horror of their fate. *The Searchers* provides no motivation for the Comanche murder raid. We are not meant to understand Scar and his war party; only to see them as monsters for waging a race war against vulnerable white settlers. When Ethan and Marty return, we witness them survey the devastation of the massacre. Searching for survivors and finding Martha's sullied dress, Ethan tells Mose not to let Marty into the shed as it clearly holds Martha's defiled, dead body. Clearly enraged, both men are motivated to find the Comanche war party and liberate the captive girls. Although Ethan arrived at the Edwards homestead an aimless man, he is now driven with a purpose to avenge Martha's death and save his captive nieces. As they track Scar and his war party, Ethan discovers that Lucy has been defiled and murdered as well.[46] Vengeance has now turned to violent rage as he searches for his remaining surviving niece. Viewing the carnage from Ethan's point-of-view, we see that the Comanche have unleashed a race war, and they deserve nothing short of extermination. Moreover, it becomes evident that he believes this must be Debbie's fate as well if she is not quickly rescued.

Although the massacre of the Edwards family suggests a clear understanding of the film's racial and moral universe—white settlers are good and Indians are evil— *The Searchers* actually begins to complicate this universe as soon as Ethan and other settlers begin their initial search for Debbie and Lucy shortly after their family has been buried. The movie has already established that Ethan is intimately familiar with the local Indians, yet clearly despises them. He also revealed this race hatred with his treatment of Marty the evening he returned. He makes Marty feel uncomfortable by calling him a "half-breed" and refusing to take credit for actually rescuing him as child after his parents had been murdered by Indians. When Aaron reminds Marty that Ethan had "saved" him, Ethan flippantly says that "it just happened to be me."[47] Ethan begins to accept Marty only after he believes Marty has rejected his Indian identity. Although Marty had grown up with the Edwards family, he apparently remained connected to his Indian heritage. In fact, he struggles with his racial identity as he, Ethan, and the other Texas Rangers fight the Comanche following the Edwards family burial. As everyone around him shoot at the oncoming Comanche, Marty remains reluctant to fire his weapon. Interestingly, he is provoked by Mose to shoot, perhaps the one person who recognizes the racial conflict within him. Marty is immediately remorseful as he kills a Comanche Indian and Mose says, "You got one, Marty."[48] Burying his head into his arm, he realizes his racial transformation. When he killed his first Indian, he killed his Indian identity as well. No matter that he never had ties to the Comanche, in his mind he was killing a fellow Indian. With tears in his eyes, he maniacally shoots at the Comanche. According to the film, Marty has become white though Ethan has yet to accept him as such. He continues to regard Marty as Indian and in no way connected to the Edwards family, even though Marty asserts that he is. In his mind, Aaron and Martha took him in as an orphan and raised him, making him a part of their family. Marty pursues Debbie along with Ethan because he wants to save his sister—more so from Ethan than the Comanche once he realizes that Ethan wants to "put a bullet in her brain."[49]

Still, Ethan's race hatred and deep knowledge of Indian culture is difficult to reconcile. In perhaps one of the film's more startling scenes, Ethan shoots out the eyes of a buried Comanche Indian, saying to Brad Jorgansen, "Why don't you go ahead and finish the job." When Reverend Captain Clayton demands to know why Ethan just shot the eyes of this clearly dead man, Ethan explains that without his eyes, the dead Comanche is prohibited from entering the spirit world and must now wander the earth forever.[50] As the rest of this search party stares at him with confused astonishment that he knows this Comanche religious belief as much as for Ethan's brutality, only Mose reveals that he too knows this Comanche religious view of the dead. Ethan's further knowledge of Comanche customs reveals itself as the search party continues. As Clayton explains his plans for how their party will proceed to search for Debbie, Ethan replies that this plan is essentially pointless. They will never catch up with the Comanche like Clayton thinks they will. Ethan explains that the Comanche do not simply follow the same cultural rules as those in the party. Ethan knows that when the horses of white settlers tire, they leave their horses behind as they continue their search. Ethan explains that the Comanche will find those horses, ride them until they die, and proceed to eat them. Later, Clayton tells the search party that it will approach the Comanche camp in order to drive off their horses. Ethan, however, reminds him of the old Comanche custom whereby the Comanche sleep with their ponies. Most startling, Ethan understands what will happen to the captive girls if the party directly attacks the Indian camp. Both he and Clayton know that if the Rangers raid the camp, the girls will be killed, which is why Clayton wants to draw them away to possibly negotiate for the girls' release.[51] Astonishingly, Ethan's mute response reveals that not only does he know about this Comanche practice, but also he wants to actually encourage it—clearly hoping that they do murder the girls.

Ethan acquiesces to Clayton's plan even though it ultimately places the party in danger. Scar and his war party eventually find the Rangers, surrounding it and forcing the Rangers to cross a river in order to better defend themselves. As Clayton wonders aloud to Ethan whether the Comanche will attack, Ethan, again showing his familiarity with Comanche customs, answers that the chief must "in order to save face." The search party successfully repels their attack, but it becomes evident that they will be unable to force the Comanche to release Lucy and Debbie. As the party prepares to return to their West Texas community, Ethan reluctantly allows Marty and Brad Jorgensen (Harry Carey, Jr.), who has been courting Lucy, to accompany him to find the captured girls. Shortly thereafter, Ethan finds Lucy's defiled and naked dead body, burying her in his Confederate coat. Probably knowing how Lucy's condition will affect Brad, he refuses to tell him and Marty what he discovered. However, he is forced to explain Lucy's fate after Brad thinks he sees Lucy in the Comanche camp. Ethan furiously says to him that he does not see Lucy, but an Indian "buck" who is wearing her dress to bait them into an attack. Once Brad knows the truth, he becomes deranged with vengeance and storms into the Comanche camp, only to be summarily killed. As Ethan and Marty continue their search over the ensuing years, we further learn that Ethan can speak "good Comanche" as Scar notes. When Marty mistakenly trades goods for a Comanche Indian wife (he thought he was trading for a blanket), Ethan translates her Comanche in order for Marty to understand her. In turn, Ethan translates Marty's English for his new wife as they question her about Scar's location.[52]

As *The Searchers* unfolds, it becomes evident that Ethan's deep knowledge of the Comanche Indians has not led him to accept them as racial equals as one might have thought. In fact, it appears that the more he understands them, the more he believes that they should be segregated from whites. Indeed, it is his fear of miscegenation and Debbie's racial defilement that drives his obsession to find his niece. In perhaps the most provocative scene in the film, Ethan and Marty arrive at Fort Wingate to discover that the cavalry has rescued white captive girls and women after their attack of a Comanche camp, hoping that Debbie is among them. Significantly, the cavalry have placed these captives in the fort's chapel, perhaps believing that this icon of Western civilization will begin the process of their reassimilation into white America. However, we see that their experience living among the Comanche has driven them insane. When the officers, Ethan, and Marty approach them, one woman shrieks in horror, only to be soothed by an Indian rattle. In other words, this representation of Comanche culture soothes this hysterical woman. As Ethan and Marty look into the eyes of two captive girls, the girls stare back blankly, as if deranged. Marty shows them Debbie's doll hoping that if one of them is Debbie, she might recognize it. The girls, however, do not even see the doll but look crazed and confused about this American cultural artifact. The older captive woman again shrieks, grabbing the doll from Marty and caressing it as if it were an infant. The cavalry officer proceeds to say, "It's hard to

believe that they are white." To which Ethan responds, "They ain't white no more
. . . they're Comanche."[53] As he leaves the chapel, the film's lighting emits a
shadow over Ethan's face as he looks back upon the crazed girls and women with
a menacing stare as if to say that only death will save these captives from their
insanity. For Ethan, miscegenation and the mixing of races leads not only to
lunacy, but also to the corruption of white America as well.

As the film makes clear time and again, Ethan intends to save Debbie by killing
her once he catches up with Scar. In fact, when he and Marty finally reach the
Comanche chief and his people, his fears are confirmed as they see Debbie dressed
as a squaw sitting among Scar's other wives. Although Ethan and Scar act as if they
are conducting a business trade, they know the real reason why he and Marty are
there. Their mutual loathing is so palpable that the Mexican who led Ethan and
Marty to Scar senses the bad blood between them and wants to extract himself
from this awkward situation. Not only does Ethan identify Debbie among Scar's
wives, but also he notices the chief wearing his Confederate medal he gave Debbie
years ago when he arrived upon the Edwards' homestead, as well as a totem of
scalps that includes that extracted from Marty's mother. Though Scar is pure
monster, Ethan is here to fulfill his mission to kill Debbie and not avenge the
massacre of the Edwards family. Once he and Marty eventually leave Scar's tent
for their camp beyond the Comanche settlement, Debbie runs after them to
persuade them to leave her to be with her people. Speaking in Comanche, she
reveals that she sees herself belonging to Scar and his people. Only Marty believes
that Debbie can return and reassimilate into white society, perhaps because he sees
himself as an example of a former Indian who became a white American. Clearly
Ethan and Debbie disagree with him as Ethan draws his gun to shoot her, only to
be thwarted by Marty, who stands in front of Debbie before letting her escape
back to Scar. Ethan seethes with rage, returning to the white settlement in order
to prepare for another return to Scar's camp and to kill Debbie.[54]

Next time Ethan pursues Debbie, he is accompanied by the US Cavalry,
Reverend Captain Clayton and his Texas Rangers, and Marty. Before their
planned assault Marty is allowed to sneak into the Comanche camp to rescue
Debbie. Once inside Scar's tent, he implores Debbie to leave with him. This time
speaking English, she agrees. As Scar moves towards them, Marty shoots the
Comanche chief. Although dressed as a Comanche and clearly drawing upon his
Indian features to move through the Comanche camp, there is no doubt that
Marty has rejected his Indian identity. Killing Scar and rescuing Debbie completes
his identification with white America. Debbie's status remains unclear, however.
While the cavalry and Rangers essentially murder this entire nation of Noyaki
Comanche, Ethan again finds Marty and Debbie. As Ethan pursues them, Debbie
tries to flee, believing her uncle will kill her like he tried before. Surprisingly, Ethan
lifts her onto his horse, takes her into his arms, and says, "Let's go home, Debbie."
Together, they return to the West Texas white settlement where she, Marty,
Marty's girlfriend Laurie Jorgensen (Vera Miles), and Laurie's parents walk into

the Jorgensen homestead. Recalling the opening scene of the film, they walk into darkness as they all enter the home, while Ethan stands outside in the light, finally walking away as the door closes on him.[55] Does this mean that Ethan and the white Texacans now believe Debbie is white and redeemed? We will actually return to this question when we later examine *The Searchers* as a cultural text from the 1950s in Chapter 4. For now, though, it is important to note that the film concludes affirming the idea that there is no room for actual Native Americans in this West Texas community—and by extension, America. They will continue to remain outside of American society, and those that intend to survive by challenging white civilization like Scar and his band of Noyaki Comanche are fated for extermination.

Although technically an inferior film to *The Searchers*, *How The West Was Won* is nonetheless significant as a transition movie that stands between traditional Westerns like *The Searchers* that cast Native Americans as murderous savage villains and those revisionist Westerns that follow such as *Little Big Man* that portray native peoples as noble savages. Released in 1962, *How The West Was Won* is an epic star-driven Hollywood blockbuster that draws upon the efforts of three notable directors (Henry Hathaway, John Ford, and George Marshall) to tell the story of three generations of Americans moving westward to pursue their American Dream. The film's narrative discourse is conventional to the point of banality, but nevertheless reflects the optimism of Kennedy liberalism in the early 1960s. Although we will explore this film as a historical text that reflects Kennedy's America in Chapter 4, it is important to presently examine how it portrays Indians in the historical context of Jefferson's and Jackson's view of Native American history. *How The West Was Won* anticipates the noble savage motif of the revisionist Westerns as it attempts to rehabilitate the representation of Indians, going as far as to portray them as morally superior to white Americans. Yet, it differs from revisionist films like *Little Big Man* (that ironically are closer to Jackson's perspective that favors Indian removal despite their positive representations of Native Americans) as it maintains Jefferson's view that Indians should adapt to American civilization, or perish along with those Indians who refuse to assimilate.

*How The West Was Won* presents the historic American West in all its mythic glory. The film is a narrative about conquest, but one that focuses on conquering the land more so than Native Americans, although its overture suggests a different story. Significantly, the film's overture frames the narrative discourse with a musical score of popular traditional Western folk songs and with one specifically crafted for this movie entitled "The Promise Land." As the overture plays, the film presents a still shot of a painting that interestingly displays stagecoach riders who inhabit the western side of the painting charging oncoming Indians and buffalos, who are at the opposite end. Even before this film begins, white Americans already occupy the West. The movie itself begins with an incredible aerial shot that scans the majestic Rocky Mountains while Spencer Tracy's voice-over describes the Edenesque qualities of the American West.

In fact, once the actual narrative begins, we see that the movie is truly a biblical Genesis story about humanity's fall from grace and its ultimate redemption in the "promise land" that is the American West. However, in order for this history to begin, the movie must establish the ways the American West was once paradise. The opening sequence presents the West as bucolic and unspoiled. Only two kinds of people lived in this paradise, both of whom were noble savages who appreciated the bounty of the West and prospered from its riches without spoiling it—Indians and white trappers. This scene establishes the movie's revisionist tone by showing the white trapper Linus Rawlings (James Stewart) at peace with Native Americans. He easily moves through their village, and there is clear mutual respect between him and the people's chief. Nevertheless, this scene affirms that this is the white man's world even if is uncivilized. The camera remains focused upon Rawlings and he commands the center of the scene while the Indians inhabit the margins. The narrator tells us that mountain men and trappers like Rawlings were just as Indian except "in name and blood," and were in fact "more Indian than the Indians."[56] Apparently, Native Americans are barely significant even in the pre-history of the American West that evidently belongs to white men like Rawlings. Like the Eden of Genesis, the American West stands outside of human history, and Native Americans become part of this history only once they engage white American civilization. They are thus part of some primitive natural history just like the geography and animals of the West awaiting the arrival of white America. In this regard, *How The West Was Won* returns to a Jeffersonian perspective of Native Americans and their history. As early as his *Notes on the State of Virginia* in 1787, Thomas Jefferson connected Indians with the primitive American environment and believed them to be virtuous because they were closely tied to nature, much as they are portrayed in this film's opening sequence.[57]

The film actually strains to minimize the actual racial conflict between Native Americans and white settlers even though it illustrates the ways native peoples challenge the expansion of American civilization in order to survive. Likely the result of changing racial attitudes as a result of the civil rights movements of the 1950s and early 1960s, *How The West Was Won* portrays Native Americans positively even when they attack white pioneers. During one scene, a caravan of pioneers traveling along the California Trail is threatened by Indians. When the leader of the wagon train, Roger Morgan (Robert Preston) recognizes the Indian war party along a ridge and informs the caravan that they outnumber the pioneers, he tells them that the Indians actually want their livestock and supplies and are not interested in killing them. He recommends that the group release their lead horses for the Indians to seize, thereby facilitating their escape.[58] Though this scene replays a conventional cinematic Indian attack, Native Americans are not actually represented as murderous savages as they are in films like *The Searchers*. In *How The West Was Won*, Indians kill pioneers and vice versa, but the movie does not draw a moral boundary dividing good and evil like Ford's *Stagecoach*, a more traditional Western that presents a similar kind of Indian attack while vilifying and racializing native peoples.[59] *How The West Was Won* does not deny the historic conflict that arose whenever westward traveling pioneers encroached upon Indian territories, but it anesthetizes this history by rendering the Indian attack morally and racially neutral.

By the next scene, Native Americans actually become more virtuous than white Americans, particularly those whites who continually break negotiated treaties to advance their financial interests. As the Union Pacific and Central Pacific engage in their historic contest to lay railroad tracks over the landscape of the American West, they face resistance from native peoples who struggle to survive in the face of American modernity. In this sequence, the film primarily focuses upon the relationship between the Union Pacific and the Arapahoe people who fear the encroachment of the "Ironhorse," and how it will bring unwelcome white settlers and buffalo hunters. During this part of the movie, we further see the radical presentation of Native Americans that differs from *The Searchers*. Recall that Scar and his band of Noyaki Comanche were portrayed as evil bloodthirsty savages who massacre innocent white settlers without justification. As such, they are morally reprehensible and deserved virtual annihilation from the perspective of the film's protagonists. In contrast, the villain in *How The West Was Won*'s railroad sequence is Mike King (Richard Widmark), a man driven by the competition between his Union Pacific Railroad and the Central Pacific, and the profit-imperative to finance his railroad. Lacking ethics and honor, he easily breaks treaties and promises with the local Arapahoe nation in order to advance his pernicious interests. Acceptable buffalo hunters like Jethro Stuart (Henry Fonda) and cavalry officers like Zeb Rawlings (George Peppard) try to mediate between King and the Arapahoe chief, but to no avail. Though the film presents the Arapahoe as a primitive people, they are nonetheless noble savages trying to preserve their way of life in the face of technological progress. In *How The West Was Won*, actual Native Americans are cast to play the Arapahoe, and they speak an indigenous language that white men like Jethro Stuart also speak. Jethro Stuart and Zeb Rawlings are presented as honorable men because they respect the Arapahoe, and intend to keep their promises and abide by negotiated treaties.[60]

After King breaks yet another promise by rerouting the Union Pacific's rail lines through Arapahoe hunting grounds in order to save time, Rawlings renegotiates another treaty to prevent the Arapahoe from waging war against King and his railroad workers. King promises that in exchange for the agreement to the new railroad boundary, he will forestall the arrival of more threatening buffalo hunters and white settlers. Of course King breaks this promise as well, as he needs the money from the white settlers to finance the development of his railroad. The minute profit-seeking buffalo hunters and white settlers arrive, Arapahoe scouts working for Zeb quit, believing he has lied to their chief. Zeb then charges into King's office infuriated about King negating a treaty that he has made with the Arapahoe yet again, telling him that King can expect the Arapahoe to attack his railroad and the settlers. Here, the movie gives the Arapahoe just cause to wage war so they can preserve their honor and existence. Instead of attacking them directly, however, the Arapahoe lead a buffalo stampede against this railroad town. While we are horrified as the buffalo trample over workers and settlers, crush homes, and leave an orphan child crying over his dead mother, our anger is not directed at the Arapahoe but towards Mike King for provoking the Indians to attack. In fact, the Arapahoe are further portrayed as honorable people because they do not actually kill the settlers, but have the buffalos attack their settlement instead. Or as Zeb Rawlings points out, they are "sending an animal, to kill an animal (meaning the Ironhorse)."[61]

Yet, the movie does not completely align with the Arapahoe even as it portrays them as virtuous and honorable people. In the end, Mike King makes the profound statement that the Arapahoe must adapt to progress and history. Comparing them to the European immigrants coming on the train to settle this Western town, he notes that these new Americans will work and adapt to the modern world in order to survive. They are the future of American civilization, and he maintains that the Arapahoe must accept and adapt to modernity as well, or face extinction.[62] As vile as Mike King is, he nonetheless reflects Thomas Jefferson's view of Native American history. Like King, Jefferson believed history is on the side of white America, which embraces Indians as long as they assimilate to American civil-ization. With the end of Native America imminent, however, indigenous peoples need to embrace modern America, or die along with their way of life.[63] *How The West Was Won* may have revised the representation of Native Americans in the Hollywood Western, portraying them in a more positive light as an honorable people with a virtuous culture, but it nonetheless presents Indian people as endangered in the face of white American progress and civilization.

Ever since the colonial period, Americans dreamed of moving west in search of better opportunities and fresh beginnings. Initially, they looked to the American frontier beyond the Appalachian Mountains in the Ohio River Valley, and then lands west of the Mississippi once the United States secured the Louisiana Territory in 1803. Thomas Jefferson envisioned this territory to be a lasting repository of yeoman virtue for Americans to pursue their dreams of independence should they ever find themselves hemmed in by the rapidly industrializing and urbanizing American East. Jefferson believed Americans could forestall the history of social development that culminated with commercial manufacturing, the condition that currently plagued Western Europe and seemed to infect the East. He hoped the United States would remain a youthful nation arrested in the phase of commercial agriculture and avoid the class conflict and political corruption that he believed unavoidable once societies entered the final phase of social development. Scores of Americans migrated to the West sharing Jefferson's dreams of individual freedom, yeomanry, and personal redemption. Yet, these dreams encountered formidable challenges with the harsh natural environment and native peoples who already lived in the American West. Undeterred, Americans embraced these challenges, forging an American character defined by the hardy pioneer spirit that conquered the American West.

Films like Michael Mann's *The Last of the Mohicans* reflect the ways filmmakers interpret the history of the American frontier from this Jeffersonian perspective. Mann's film also illustrates another enduring legacy of the American frontier, namely the place of native peoples in the American social landscape. The movie initially takes a Jeffersonian view that Native Americans can become a part of American society, peacefully coexisting with white settlers as they adapt to their customs as well. Nevertheless, it ultimately sides with Andrew Jackson's vision of Indian history, maintaining that not only is there no place for Native Americans in the young American nation, but also they are fated to fade as a culture and race in the face of white American westward migration and the march of American civilization. The more vile racist implications of Jackson's view of Native Americans manifest in traditional American Westerns such as John Ford's *The Searchers*. Nonetheless, even more progressive Westerns such as *How The West Was Won* that represent native peoples more positively and recall Thomas Jefferson's interpretation of Indian history, affirm his more pessimistic view that recognizes the demise of Native Americans and their customs should they refuse to adapt to American progress. Yet, *The Searchers* and *How The West Was Won* also engage Native American history as a way to interrogate contemporary American race relations. As we will see in Chapter 4, these films use the American Western to examine the history of Indian–settler racial conflict to explore issues such as racial integration and institutional racism in light of the civil rights movements transforming post-World War II American society. The American Western has always been a way for Americans to engage their past to understand the American character. In the 1950s and 1960s, turbulent social and political events provoked them to question the direction of their cherished institutions and ideals. Hollywood Westerns emerged as powerful cultural texts that enabled Americans to look to the history of the American West and its sacred myths to help them navigate these tumultuous times.

# 4

# HISTORICIZING TRIUMPHS AND TRAGEDIES IN THE AMERICAN WEST

## The Hollywood Western as Cultural Text in Recent American History

This book has focused upon two major themes: first, the ways films illustrate the problematic relationship Americans have with their history, and second, how movies are living histories that provide insight into the connection between the American past and present. These two themes converge in the Hollywood Western. As Patricia Nelson Limerick has pointed out in *Legacy of Conquest*, all people espouse an origin myth, a "tale explaining where its members came from and why they are special, chosen by providence for a special destiny," and the western frontier has historically served this function for white Americans.[1] In the American historical imagination, the frontier and American West embody foundational values connected to the Jeffersonian principles of new beginnings, freedom, and pursuits of happiness. In this regard, the history of the American frontier is as much the history of an idea as much as it is the history of a place. Furthermore, whenever people look to the past to understand who they are and how they came to be, they read the past in terms of the present. In other words, the history they see says more about their contemporary world rather than the past as it actually happened.

Western films thrive upon this interpretive approach to the history of the American West. In turn, they can be read as cultural texts that engage the American past as a way to examine critical political, social, and cultural issues facing contemporary America. As much as *The Searchers* and *How The West Was Won* reflect historiographic interpretations about Native Americans in the American West, then, they also address post-World War II America, ranging from the civil rights movement to Cold War American foreign policy. Not only are these movies entertaining Westerns in their own right, but also they are a cinematic lens through which we can understand how Americans looked to their mythic past as a way to confront vexing issues in the United States during the 1950s and 1960s.

Collectively, these films use the tableaux of the American West to explore ideas about race relations, modernity, and the United States' role in international politics. As a genre steeped in American myth, history, and ideology, Hollywood Westerns also emerged as cultural texts that engaged major historical issues that shaped American society in the turbulent 1960s and 1970s. With movies like Arthur Penn's *Little Big Man*, Hollywood began to produce "revisionist" Westerns that challenged the United States' mythic past and its political institutions, especially in the aftermath of Vietnam and Watergate. However, with films like Clint Eastwood's *Unforgiven*, Hollywood Westerns assaulted the sacred mythos of the American West and the Jeffersonian ideology that defines it. Recent Westerns seem less about the history of the American West and more allegories about the modern United States. But as we will see, the endurance of the American West in the American imagination lies in its power as an idea; one that enables Americans to look towards their past in order to face their future.

## *The Searchers* and *How The West Was Won* as Post-World War II Cultural Texts

When *The Searchers* was released in 1956, Americans were beginning to process the ramifications of desegregation and integration following the two *Brown vs. Board of Education* Supreme Court cases that declared segregation unconstitutional, and demanded the desegregation of public institutions "with deliberate speed."[2] Thus the film's narrative discourse about race mixing and miscegenation reflects broader American anxieties about contemporary race relations. *The Searchers* takes us back to a time and place in the American past where the racial boundaries were also unclear. As the film follows Ethan Edwards' (John Wayne) and Martin "Marty" Pawley's (Jeffrey Hunter) search for Debbie Edwards (Natalie Wood), they cross racial and ethnic worlds occupied by white Texacans, Comanche, and Mexicans. Furthermore, Ethan and Marty embody the intersection of this multicultural frontier. Ethan speaks English, "Mexican" (as he calls Spanish), and Comanche while Marty is the product of miscegenation, albeit from an interracial relationship in his distant past. Ethan continues to view Marty as Indian for most of the film, and in the end Marty draws upon his Indian background to move through Scar's Comanche camp to rescue Debbie.[3]

As noted in Chapter 3, Ethan's multicultural awareness calcifies his race hatred, and Marty must choose between his white and Indian identities. Like Marty, Debbie must decide between her racial identities. Initially, she wants to "stay with my people" (meaning the Comanche) as she has lived with them for five years and is one of Scar's wives, although she later chooses to leave with Marty when he returns to rescue her again. Everyone in the West Texas community recognizes Debbie to be Noyaki Comanche despite her growing up white Texacan prior to her captivity. In the words of Laurie Jorgensen (Vera Miles), she has been "sold to the highest bidding buck . . . with savage brats of her own."[4] Still, Ethan decides not to kill her after Marty rescues her, and the Jorgensens receive her as family at the end of the film. Has Debbie become white again, or do the white Texacans accept her as Comanche? *The Searchers* never clearly answers these questions. In fact, it concludes with Debbie's racial identity remaining ambiguous, and perhaps requires one to think more carefully about the ways the movie's narrative discourse approaches the issue of race-mixing and racial integration.

*The Searchers* appears to suggest that the multicultural frontier of the American West produces confusion and lunacy as we see with the experience of Mose Harper (Hank Worden) and the white captive women rescued by the US Cavalry. Other than Ethan and Marty, Mose is the only character who occupies the film's three racial universes. We initially see him among the white Texacans, then with the Mexicans, and then finally among Scar's Noyaki Comanche. Without a racial or ethnic home, Mose roams the multicultural frontier "a crazy fool" as he later tells Ethan and the Jorgensens. Yet, Mose yearns for a home, and when Ethan offers him the sizable cash reward for finding Debbie, he tells Ethan that he would rather have a rocking chair. In fact, when we first see Mose at the Edwards home at the beginning of the film, he immediately seeks out Martha's rocking chair, telling her how he "is much obliged for the use of your rocking chair, ma'am" before he leaves with the Rangers to search for the Jorgensens' rustled cattle. Later Mose stumbles into the Jorgensen home deranged and physically feeble after nearly dying while living among the Noyaki Comanche, and is immediately taken to Mrs. Jorgensen's rocking chair to recuperate. He proceeds to tell everyone in the Jorgensen home that he told the Comanche that he was crazy, even eating grass "to fool them." When he asks Mrs. Jorgensen if she thinks he is crazy, she replies, "No, Mose, you're just old and sick."[5] But since he has brought information about Debbie and Scar, he has earned his reward. At the end of the film when Ethan rides up to the Jorgensen homestead with Debbie and Marty, Mose sways in his rocking chair rehabilitating from his "sickness." As *The Searchers* concludes, he enters the Jorgensen house along with everyone else except Ethan, finally finding his racial home.

The fate of the white female captives, however, remains unclear. The women and girls are obviously deranged and the cavalry officers believe placing in them in the chapel will begin their rehabilitation as white Americans. Housed in this iconic symbol of Christian civilization, perhaps there is hope that they will recover their whiteness. Although the cavalry officer states that it is "hard to believe that they are white," he nonetheless sees them as such, while Ethan believes "they ain't white." Ethan's menacing look suggests these female captives are beyond redemption and only death will save them from their lives as Comanche squaws. After all, this is the plan he has in mind for Debbie. Once she became one of Scar's wives, she no longer was Ethan's kin, or so he tells Marty. While Marty is not Debbie's blood kin, he nevertheless regards her as his sister. Ethan has disowned her the moment he learned "she has been living with a buck." Laurie Jorgensen surely agrees with Ethan. Marty says he has to go after Ethan as the Rangers and

US Calvary plan to attack Scar's camp "in a joint punitive action" against "known hostiles." To which Laurie replies, "fetch what home" as if she were not human. She knows that Ethan "will put a bullet in her brain . . . and Martha [Debbie's mother] would want him to." Reverend Captain Samuel Clayton (Ward Bond) appears to support Ethan's plan as he decides to directly confront the Comanche this second time, knowing the Indians will kill Debbie. In Ethan's mind, she is dead already as "living with Comanche is not being alive."[6] Much like white Southerners in D.W. Griffith's *The Birth of a Nation*, the white Texacans in John Ford's *The Searchers* believe protecting the virtue of white women is the paramount duty of white men as it essentially equates their protection with protecting white civilization as well. As mothers, white women sire the progeny of white men, and pass down to them a civilization's values. When white women marry outside their race, they corrupt white civilization itself. After all, miscegenation means just that—the biological disruption of the nation. If white men cannot preserve the virtue of their women by protecting them from racial intermarriage, then it becomes their obligation to protect white civilization by killing these defiled white women, or at least Ethan Edwards believes so.

In fact, one can even view *The Searchers* as a "birth of a nation" in the American West. Like Ben Cameron in Griffith's film, Ethan Edwards is a former Confederate officer who returns home to West Texas marginalized and emasculated. Ethan, at least, has retained a measure of dignity by refusing to attend the Confederate "surrender" as Reverend Captain Clayton notes, and remains an outlaw for not disavowing his loyalty to the Confederacy. Even though the Civil War has been over for three years, he continues to wear his Confederate uniform. His loyalty aside, he is clearly disillusioned as he gives his nephew Ben his military-issued sword and his medal of valor to Debbie.[7] Of course these are meaningful emotional gestures for Ethan and his nephew and niece, but they do not carry the military significance and honor they once held. In fact, there seems to be nothing honorable about Ethan at the beginning of the film. Not only is he a defeated soldier of a lost war, he is a suspected criminal as well. Still, he receives a hero's welcome from the Edwards family and is given the opportunity to remain with the family as long as he wants. Ethan's road to redemption, however, begins with the search for his captured nieces. Much like Ben Cameron's South Carolina, the West Texas white settlement is threatened by an external racial menace. Where unfit black politicians descended upon the vulnerable South to destroy white civilization according to *The Birth of a Nation*, so too have Scar and his band of Comanches waged their race war against white Texacans in *The Searchers*. Likewise, the virtue of white women and threat of miscegenation provoke the defeated former Confederate officers Ben Cameron and Ethan Edwards to "redeem" white civilization by saving endangered white women.[8]

Although virulently racist, Griffith's *The Birth of a Nation* accurately documents the Redemption movement during Reconstruction. Former Confederates and the Ku Klux Klan worked to restore white supremacy, terrorized emancipated black men and women, and enacted anti-miscegenation and anti-racial intermarriage legislation once they returned to power. Southern Redeemers believed they restored the honor of the Confederate "Lost Cause" by establishing a post-Reconstruction South based upon an ideological foundation dedicated to preserving the virtue of white womanhood and white civilization.[9] The defeated Confederate Ethan Edwards is motivated by a Redeemer movement of his own. He symbolically unites his "Lost Cause" and "Redemption movement" by burying his niece Lucy's defiled and murdered body in what Marty calls his "Johnny Reb" coat.[10] He is obsessively driven to search for Debbie over the next five years to save her from race-mixing with Indians. Once he realizes he is too late, he believes killing her will prevent any further corruption of white civilization. Laurie Jorgensen and other white Texacans apparently agree with him as the Rangers prepare their final assault on Scar's Comanche camp. Only Marty remains willing to rescue her. Reverend Captain Clayton wants to directly assault the Comanche because he knows that such an attack will provoke Scar to kill Debbie. Moreover, the Rangers, composed of former Confederate soldiers like Clayton, have been joined by Union soldiers for a "joint punitive action" against the Comanche. Like the former Confederate and Union soldiers who came together to fight black soldiers and dismantle black power in Griffith's *The Birth of a Nation*, one time Confederates like Clayton and Ethan Edwards join forces with "Yankee soldiers" to fight a race war against Comanche Indians in *The Searchers*.[11] They do not try to draw out Comanche warriors for a military engagement. They descend upon the camp shooting men, women, and children, driving away the horses so they cannot escape. This is evidently a war to establish a white nation in West Texas.

For Americans going to the movie theater to see John Ford's *The Searchers* in 1956, it seems they would leave the film believing it concludes that integration threatens social stability, and even American civilization itself. Yet, if we probe the film further, it appears to challenge this conclusion. From Ethan's point-of-view, this movie undoubtedly is about preserving the virtue of white women and white civilization, even if it means murdering his defiled niece. And though casting an American icon like John Wayne to play him might persuade viewers to see Ethan as heroic, the character's questionable ethics and racism make him hardly likeable. Over the course of the film, however, Ethan undergoes a personal transformation. He begins to accept Marty towards the end of the film after demeaning him for his scant Indian heritage, so much in fact that he intends to leave him his property should he die fighting Scar. Marty refuses to accept Ethan's gesture because Ethan rejects Debbie as blood kin and remains enraged at him for attempting to kill his niece. One could argue that Ethan now sees Marty as white or one could contend that Ethan has begun to accept him regardless of his Indian background. Either way the film has become an unstable text where we begin to question Ethan's true views regarding race.

Even more perplexing is his decision to rescue Debbie and return her to the Jorgensens alive. Everything in the movie's narrative to this point leads viewers to believe that Ethan will kill Debbie, so one finds it difficult to fathom that Ethan achieved racial enlightenment and now accepts Debbie given how he has been motivated to murder her and the Comanche Indians she regards as "my people." The quick answer to this dilemma of course is that it would be incomprehensible to believe an endearing American icon like Wayne would actually murder his niece and will eventually embrace her regardless of her race. But the film's views about race are further complicated with the concluding scene. As the movie ends, the Jorgensens, Marty, Laurie, Mose, and Debbie all enter the Jorgensen home, walking together offstage into darkness. Ethan initially remains outside in the brightly lit West Texas landscape, and then turns to leave as the movie's theme song hums "ride away." Arguably, this scene ultimately informs viewers of the film's actual view about American race relations. Inside the Jorgensen home walk the Jorgensens and their daughter Laurie, a multiethnic family of American and Swedish background; Mose, who embodies the multicultural world of the American frontier; Marty, who is of European and Indian ancestry; and Debbie, who everyone regards as Comanche at this point despite her white skin. The one person outside this multicultural America is Ethan, who eventually "rides away."[12]

Clearly, Ford's film has aligned Ethan Edwards with a racial view of America akin to that expressed in Griffith's *The Birth of a Nation* and those in contemporary American society who continue to adhere to similar perspectives about race. But in a more multicultural and racially integrated America, there is no place for people like Ethan Edwards and perhaps this explains why he refuses to enter the Jorgensen home, and why the door eventually closes on him—and by extension the America he represents. Of course this is only one interpretation of the film's narrative discourse, and this view may be difficult to reconcile for some viewers, given the way *The Searchers* reflects the conventions of traditional westerns where moral clarity align with classic racial boundaries drawn between whites and Indians. Nevertheless, Ford's film is actually a morally ambiguous movie, and racial boundaries are anything but clear. Perhaps Ford was working within the cinematic conventions of the Hollywood American Western in *The Searchers*, conventions he famously established with many of his earlier movies. But maybe he was beginning to undermine those conventions with *The Searchers* as he engaged our mythic past to challenge American institutions at a time when they were radically changing.

In fact, *The Searchers* satirizes American institutions time and again throughout the film. There is Reverend Captain Clayton's dual identity as local preacher and captain of the Texas Rangers. He humorously switches between these identities so many times people forget which one he is. Civility and manners are comically mocked during a savage fist-fight between Marty and Charlie McCorry (Ken Curtis), who try to remain polite as they brutally fight for honor and Laurie's affection. The film portrays the US Calvary as simultaneously barbaric as it mercilessly slaughters Indians in one sequence, and hilariously inept as it prepares to fight Scar's Comanche people at the end of the film.[13] Few things are as sacred in the American historical imagination as the American West. By complicating the racial universe of this mythic world and satirizing American civilization, *The Searchers* encourages us to think critically about American society in the 1950s. In subtle but important ways, Ford's classic and provocative film moves away from triumphalist traditional Westerns and anticipates the more iconoclastic revisionist Westerns that emerged in the late 1960s.

*How The West Was Won*, in contrast, is a celebratory traditional American Western despite its more progressive portrayal of Native Americans. It self-consciously embraces the mythos of the American frontier, and even narrates a biblical creation story of its own. Just as God miraculously creates Eden as a paradise unspoiled by humans and provides bountiful riches for Adam and Eve prior to their fall from grace, the American West likewise produced bountiful riches for primitive man—Indians and white trappers—who lived in harmony with this earthly paradise. In the film's opening sequence, an aerial shot pans the glorious Rocky Mountains and reveals a bucolic American West while Spencer Tracy's disembodied god-like voice describes the natural history of the West at "the beginning of its creation." In fact, *How The West Was Won* is an American Genesis story about paradise, humanity's fall from grace, and finding the "promise land." However, it is a Genesis story firmly rooted in Jeffersonian ideology. The film tells the story of three generations of Americans moving west to escape their past, finding redemption as they start life anew, and pursuing happiness living off the land. By connecting American history with Genesis and the history of the Hebrew people, *How The West Was Won* similarly describes Americans as God's chosen people bound to him by a covenant, and destined for greatness. The American pioneers in the movie are the cinematic embodiment of Jefferson's heralded yeoman farmer whom he believed to be chosen by providence for an exceptional destiny, and "whose breasts he has made his peculiar deposit for substantial and genuine virtue."[14]

Released in 1962, the *How The West Was Won* narrative discourse reflects President John F. Kennedy's "New Frontier" liberalism. Although it is a film that tells the story of Americans conquering the North American West, it also describes how this history of conquest shaped the American character and suggests this history will enable the United States to lead Western Civilization against the Soviet Union in the Cold War. President Kennedy self-consciously drew upon the legacy of the American frontier to craft his Cold War foreign policy. Whether it was his space program or diplomatic relations, Kennedy believed the indomitable spirit that won the American West would win the Cold War as well. Since the end of World War II, the United States assumed the role of Western superpower as war-torn Western European nations reeled from the devastation of war, and could no longer retain their position as international leaders. Furthermore, the United States secured its superpower status as the lone nation with the atomic bomb. Despite sustaining the most casualties during World War II, the Soviet Union nonetheless maintained the world's largest conventional military force, emerging as the United States' rival superpower.

The Cold War intensified once the Soviets detonated an atomic bomb and exerted its dominance over Eastern Europe with the Warsaw Pact, and China became a communist nation in 1949. Americans started to believe they were losing the Cold War to global communism, a sentiment further magnified by Sputnik and Soviet advances in the Space Race in the 1950s, as well as the Cuban Revolution and Missile Crisis in the latter part of the decade and into the beginning of Kennedy's presidential administration. Rather than despair, the optimistic Kennedy emboldened the American people to look towards their past when they also faced adversity and overcame immense challenges to settle the American West. The president reminded them that this history proved Americans were an exceptional people guided by providence, that they were the "city upon the hill" and model of a virtuous liberal democracy for the rest of the world. *How The West Was Won* turns Kennedy's vision of American exceptionalism into a compelling mythic narrative that also describes Americans as God's chosen people who will prosper as long as they fulfill their sacred covenant with him.

As noted, *How The West Was Won* initially presents the American West as a paradise inhabited by Indians and white trappers who roam free and take from the land only that which they need. In this regard, the movie recalls the story of Eden in Judeo-Christian theology where Adam and Eve similarly lived freely in a harmonic relationship with God and the natural world. Given the gift of free will, they nonetheless disobey God's order not to eat from the Tree of Knowledge, and were summarily banished. Though their sin resulted in their expulsion from paradise, this is the cataclysmic event that propelled human history in the Judaic and Christian cosmology. This history became an unfolding narrative about human redemption that told of God's promise to someday send a savior to redeem the sins of humanity and restore the harmonic relationship they once shared in paradise. In *How The West Was Won*, the West is portrayed as an American Eden free of human corruption, but similarly stood outside of human history. Like the Hebrews of the Old Testament, Americans were God's chosen people whom he would lead to the "promise land" of the American West, redeem them of their history, and restore paradise. As Spencer Tracy's voice-over informs us, Americans already proved they were an exceptional people since they settled Jamestown and Plymouth in the colonial period. As he says, "Where there was forest, they saw timber and houses, where there was land and rock, they saw farms."[15] Americans were hardworking, virtuous people who civilized the frontier. And even when the American landscape in the East restricted their ability to pursue their dreams, they made it yield to their demands with technological innovations, building canals for example to create infrastructure for travel and commerce. Blessed with dreams, a work ethic, and technological prowess, history and the hand of providence favored the Americans.

*How The West Was Won* weaves its Genesis mythology with Jeffersonian ideology as it tells the story of the Prescott and Rawlings families and their journey to the West to escape their pasts and start life anew. The patriarch of the Prescott family, Zebulon Prescott (Karl Malden), dreams of prosperity as a yeoman farmer and moves his family from upstate New York to the American Midwest to pursue his dream. However, the film's narrative discourse actually runs through his daughters Eve (Carroll Baker) and Lilith (Debbie Reynolds). With the Prescott daughters, the film again recalls the Genesis story as Eve and Lilith reflect the biblical women for whom they are named. Eve Prescott's dream is to marry and have a family while Lilith intends to remain a wandering independent spirit, much to her parents' dismay, though similar to the woman of Judaic legend who fled Eden to remain free rather than submit to Adam's patriarchy. As the Prescott family journeys westward, Eve meets her figurative Adam in Linus Rawlings (James Stewart). The film introduced Linus in the opening sequence living harmoniously with nature in the paradise of the American West free of sin as a white trapper. However, he readily admits to Eve when he initially meets her that life in the East has corrupted him, but he is reluctant to surrender his remaining independence to the institution of marriage.[16] Like Adam, Linus cannot resist Eve's temptations. Instead of returning to life as wild, natural man in the American West, he chooses to become civilized, marrying Eve, starting a family, and cultivating the soil in Illinois much as his biblical counterpart did once he left Eden.

Although Eve achieves her promise land as she establishes a family with Linus, her sister Lilith continues her journey west to remain free and escape the restricting social conventions she believes defines life in the civilized East. Drawing upon her singing talents, she lives independently in St. Louis as a vaudeville performer. Following her performance one evening, she learns that she has been left a gold claim by a former suitor, and immediately plans to head west to California to stake her claim. Unbeknownst to Lilith, Cleve Van Valen (Gregory Peck), a notorious gambler and con man, overhears the lawyer informing her about her inheritance and schemes to enrich himself by profiting from Lilith's claim as well. Apparently living independently in St. Louis has not been problematic for Lilith, but she encounters resistance to her lifestyle from Roger Morgan (Robert Preston), a man with traditional patriarchal views about gender relations, and whose caravan she wants to join as it journeys to California. Even though Lilith tells him that she can handle the challenges herself, including the harsh environment and potential Indian attacks, Morgan nonetheless sees her as a woman of ill repute who will tempt the virtue of the male pioneers in the wagon train. However, he will allow her to journey with the pioneers if she can find another traveler and suggests Agatha "Aggie" Clegg (Thelma Ritter), another single woman, but whose aspirations to find a husband out West he clearly finds unthreatening. Although initially reluctant, Aggie eventually allows Lilith to ride with her because she believes Lilith will attract men who might actually propose marriage to her instead.[17]

As they prepare to leave with the wagon caravan, Cleve attempts to ingratiate himself to Lilith and Aggie by offering his services as a man who can lead their wagon and protect them from Indians during the journey. Lillith, however, immediately recognizes that he is trying to con them and suspects that he knows about her claim. Morgan also can see that Cleve is a confidence man and gambler, someone with questionable virtues like Lilith. Aggie, however, is taken by his charm and agrees to let him join their group. As the pioneers set off from Independence, Missouri, the movie's narrator describes the Oregon and California trails that stem from this launching point for westward migration. As the narrator tells us, pioneers who traveled the Oregon Trail were virtuous, god-fearing farmers who dreamt of land and homesteads in the American West. Those who followed the California Trail, in contrast, were risk-takers like Lilith and Cleve, who dreamt of "quick riches" in booming mining towns and bustling cities.[18]

Although Cleve initially demonstrates his moral worth along the journey, Morgan becomes enraged when he sees him encouraging a poker game among the pioneers. Before he can expel him from the wagon train, however, the caravan is attacked by Indians. Morgan tells the men that the Indians are more interested in their livestock and supplies than killing them, and encourages them to cut the lead horse teams to satisfy the Indians. Cleve immediately returns to Lilith's and Aggie's wagon to free their lead horses, but leaves the women in order to save a couple of fallen pioneers. While the wagon train eventually escapes, Cleve remains missing. Morgan tells a despondent Lilith that he and some others will search for him in the morning. He also proposes marriage, having changed his mind about her character, and actually finding himself attracted to her independent spirit. Although flattered, Lilith does not want to be confined by his patriarchal views of marriage and declines his proposal. Shortly thereafter, Cleve returns with a wounded pioneer, barely alive himself. When Morgan sees Lilith's effusive efforts to help Cleve, he recognizes that she is actually in love with him and leaves them feeling demoralized.[19]

Lilith and Cleve eventually arrive at her mining claim, only to find that it no longer yields gold and Lilith actually owes money to those who have continued to work her claim while she was traveling west from Missouri. Emotionally crushed, Lilith leaves her claim as well as her dreams behind, starting over penniless in California. Soon thereafter, we discover with Roger Morgan that Lilith has become a bawdy showgirl in a predominantly male mining town, bitter and disillusioned. Morgan has come again to propose to Lilith, trying to convince her that he is the kind of wealthy man she has been looking for to marry. Lilith again declines his proposal, telling Morgan that she is still in love with Cleve even though he abandoned her once he discovered her mine was worthless. It turns out Cleve has returned to his career as a gambler, traveling the Sacramento riverboats making money playing poker. One evening he hears Lilith sing "Home in the Meadow," the song she once sang with her family before they journeyed west from upstate New York. She sings of a "wondrous land for the hopeful heart and the will-ing hand." Love-struck, Cleve proposes marriage to her even though he is "a no-good gambler . . . with only $1,200 in my pocket." He wants to take her to San Francisco where he believes they will become rich. It may be a small city and burns down every few years, he says, but it is always rebuilding and filled with unlimited opportunity. Lilith enthusiastically accepts, believing with the little money that they have, her singing talent, and his poker experience will be enough for them to establish a gambling house and become wealthy. Cleve, however, wants them to leave their compromising pasts behind them, and settle down as a married couple. He intends to use his entrepreneurial skills in more legitimate business enterprises such as the railroad industry.[20]

Later, the film returns to Lilith's narrative to show that she and Cleve achieved their dreams beyond measure living in San Francisco. Although Cleve has died and Lilith must sell her possessions including their mansion to pay their debt, she describes how they both made and spent their fortune three times over as Cleve became president of the San Francisco-Kansas City Railroad. Although Lilith's lawyer worries about her future, she tells him that she has everything she needs with her framed picture of Cleve and her ranch in Arizona. It turns out she has "Prescott blood" after all, she tells her lawyer. Like her parents, she too dreams of finding peace in her "home in the meadow" in the American West.[21]

Where Eve Prescott's narrative connected *How The West Was Won* to the biblical story of Adam and Eve and thus to the mythos of the Genesis creation story, Lilith's narrative is firmly grounded in Jeffersonian ideology. Lilith feels confined by civilization in the American East, and yearns to be free and independent out West. For Lilith, the West holds opportunities to achieve her American Dream and become wealthy. Moreover, she finds someone with similar dreams in Cleve. They are dreamers looking for opportunities around every corner. And though their initial hope to become rich with Lilith's gold claim failed to materialize, they did not abandon their dreams altogether. They realize they must start over and dream of going to San Francisco to take advantage of the unlimited opportunities that the future of this city appears to offer. And just as Jefferson envisioned, San Francisco also provides them the possibility to escape their morally questionable pasts and become respectable and upstanding citizens. As Lilith tells us, hers and Cleve's life was a series of "new beginnings" and now she plans to begin her life anew yet again, this time in true Jeffersonian fashion living close to nature with her "home in the meadow" in Arizona.[22]

The life of Zeb Rawlings (George Peppard) also reflects the redemptive nature of the American West. However, his narrative illustrates the ways the West redeemed American history more generally. The movie introduces Zeb as he enlists for the Union army during the Civil War, follows him as a US Calvary officer protecting the Union Pacific Railroad, and finally as a US Marshall fighting outlaws in the American West. As *How The West Was Won* begins Zeb's story, we immediately learn that he possesses his father's restless spirit. Although his mother resists Zeb's desire to join the army because Linus already has, she finally consents. Through Zeb, we witness the tragedy of the Civil War: first as it takes Linus' life and then Zeb's innocence. Like many young men who fought on both sides of the war, Zeb dreamed of joining the army to find honor and glory, only to encounter death and devastation instead.[23]

During the Civil War sequence, Zeb embodies a youthful American nation coming of age at a moment when the United States virtually self-destructed. Zeb, like President Lincoln, was reared in Illinois, Midwesterners drawn into a historic conflict that initially began between states in the northeast and southeast. Yet, the tide of the war turns in favor of the Union at key battles in the West. As we see, Generals Grant (Harry Morgan) and Sherman (John Wayne) win their major battles in the southwest, and plan their next strategies here before they turn towards the East to terminate the war. In their discussion, which we observe though Zeb's eyes, they lament how the war has devastated the American nation, but that one day a new nation will be forged through the crucible of this conflict.[24] In fact, the American West will redeem the country from this apocalyptic catastrophe as it will enable Americans disillusioned by war like Zeb Rawlings to begin life anew, and dream again of opportunity and happiness.

Zeb returns home at the end of the war to learn that his mother has died and his brother has cared for the family farm his parents left to him. Zeb turns the farm over to his brother as he never wanted to be a farmer, much as his father, and had returned home only to see his mother. With her dead, nothing ties him to Illinois and he now wants to begin his life over out West. As noted earlier in this chapter, Zeb is appointed as a US Calvary officer to protect the Union Pacific Railroad from hostile Indians. Though he strenuously works to maintain the peace between the railroad and Arapahoe Indians, the railroad's manager, Mike King (Richard Widmark), repeatedly breaks negotiated treaties. Zeb fulfills his obligation to protect railroad workers and white settlers when the Arapahoe lead a buffalo stampede to demolish the white settlement developing alongside the railroad, but resigns his commission once the stampede ends.[25] Once again history and modernity, symbolized with the railroad and the capitalist imperative that finances it, have corrupted the United States as the railroad integrates the nation, ensnaring Zeb along with the American West with its vicious tentacles.

Disgusted and disillusioned with the nation's future direction, Zeb retreats to the mountains of the American West where he becomes a mountain man, following in the footsteps of his father, who led a similar life years ago. Living as a trapper in the Rocky Mountains, Zeb once again starts his life over and believes in the redemptive nature of the American West. Rather than letting men like Mike King determine the course of American history, he wants to be among those who lead the civilizing of the West on different terms. Just as the West has forged the American character, it will define American history: it will tame both nature and the excess of civilization that corrupts the East. As he becomes a US Marshall, Zeb brings law and order to restless Western towns as the railroad further connects them into the American nation. And just as he defeats Charlie Gant (Eli Wallach) and his gang, the last of the West's notorious outlaws, in the final scenes of the film, he is ready to settle down with his family on his Aunt Lilith's ranch, now believing that the West has been won in the name of civilization and progress. However, this is a victory determined by the values of Jefferson and the American

West rather than the industrialized and modern East. As the film concludes, Zeb, his family, and Lilith once again sing "Home in the Meadow" even as they ride their buggy through the desolate and unforgiving Western desert.[26] Even though settling the impenetrable desert seems unimaginable, as they sing of their dreams to live in the peaceful meadow we know these three generations of Prescotts and Rawlings have the fortitude to tame the hostility of nature to establish their home, much as scores of Americans before them.

Indeed, as Lilith, Zeb and his family ride towards Lilith's ranch in Arizona, the movie transitions to the present day American West. While we first hear "Home in the Meadow" and then "The Promise Land" in the background, the narrator weaves the Western past with its present. He describes how the blood and toil of the pioneers yielded progress and prosperity in the American West. The film presents the Colorado River of the past and then its present, including a shot of the Hoover Dam, one of the technological marvels of the twentieth century as it brought water to deserts, creating farms and lawns where there was once sand and tumbleweeds. Here, the film recalls the technology that produced the Erie Canal described at the film's beginning, and enabled restless families like the Prescotts to move westward in search of their American Dream. We then see modern lumber yards, mines, and then cars driving Interstates 5 and 10 in Los Angeles. The film concludes with aerial shots of modern-day San Francisco and the Golden Gate Bridge, again recalling another scene earlier in the movie when this Bay Area city was more rustic.[27] Why has the movie concluded with the modern American West? As the narrator informs us, the legacy of those pioneers who initially settled the West continues to live. This is not a past disconnected from the present. Rather the film describes a living history wherein modern Americans perpetuate the values initially planted in the soil of the American West by our ancestors who settled the region. And just as American pioneers conquered the West, so too did they tame the corrupting influences of modernity. The American West has achieved progress and we are told that its once small, restless cities now rival the most sophisticated in the world. Yes the West was won, but it in turn shaped the American character defined by freedom, tenacity, and the courage to dream.[28] *How The West Was Won* is not a story about a lost Jeffersonian rural past destroyed by industrial capitalism, but the ways Jefferson's vision of rural America remains alive in the modern present, despite the fact that the majority of Americans are no longer yeoman farmers and we live in an industrialized and urbanized nation envisioned by Jefferson's arch-rival Alexander Hamilton.

Were it not for the concluding scenes of modern Los Angeles and San Francisco, *How The West Was Won* would have been a conventional, even trite Western movie. Yet its self-conscious reference to modernity provokes us to consider the relationship between history and myth, and its relevance to the modern United States. By weaving the Genesis creation story with actual events and people in American history, the film maintains that the American national identity was forged as Americans conquered the West. Yet, the West itself was defined by Jeffersonian ideology with its vision of human redemption, new beginnings apart from one's past, and pursuits of happiness. The movie argues that this Jeffersonian legacy did not recede with the advent of modernity because we are the inheritors of this vision of America. Moreover, as we face new challenges and frontiers in the modern era, whether that be international diplomacy or space, we can draw upon this legacy to triumph as a people much as our forefathers did as they conquered the West. As modern Americans have inherited the values of the pioneers of the past, we can be victorious in the face of present challenges. As the narrator and the song "The Promise Land" inform us, as long as Americans believe in freedom and their dreams, and "pull together as one," we can conquer the most insurmountable obstacle like the American pioneers of yore, perhaps even win the Cold War.

*How The West Was Won* remains a creature of Kennedy's America, with all its optimism and faith in American institutions and values. American pioneers embodied Kennedy's famous aphorism: they never "asked what their country could do" for them, but what they "could do for their country." This did not mean Americans were above reproach. After all, racism and labor exploitation were as much a part of the history of the American West as well, as the film demonstrates. But the nation's bedrock Jeffersonian principles, generated in the cauldron of westward expansion, always held the possibility for American salvation and renewal along with a promising future. As triumphant a vision of American civilization *How The West Was Won* presents, however, it reflects an interpretation of American history that would increasingly face challenges after President Kennedy's assassination and the turbulent events of the 1960s and 1970s. As we turn to American Westerns released after the critical year of 1968 when the president's brother, Robert Kennedy, and Martin Luther King Jr. were assassinated, war in Vietnam escalated, and the Democratic Party imploded at its Chicago Convention, Hollywood released films that looked to the American past and particularly Western history to probe American institutions and values more critically as a way to understand the tumultuous state of American society.

## *Little Big Man* and the Revisionist Western

As social and political movements transformed American society in the late 1960s, the American Western changed accordingly. The Western film has always been a cultural lens through which Americans looked to understand their history and national character, so we should not be surprised that revisionist Westerns released in the environment of civil rights struggles, the counterculture, Vietnam, and Watergate became a cultural space wherein Americans engaged their past to interrogate American institutions. Western movies released after 1968 ranged across the political spectrum, some of which self-consciously challenged traditional interpretations of Western history and corresponding cinematic representations, others of which were less revisionist but nevertheless reinterpreted the history of the American West in light of contemporary social and political issues. This chapter could have selected from an array of post-1968 Westerns such as Mel Brooks' hilarious satire, *Blazing Saddles* (Warner Bros., 1974), Clint Eastwood's conservative *The Outlaw Josey Wales* (Warner Bros., 1976), or Kevin Costner's liberal *Dances with Wolves* (Warner Bros., 1990). Instead, Arthur Penn's iconoclastic *Little Big Man* and Eastwood's anti-mythic *Unforgiven* were chosen for the ways they challenge the sacred mythos of the American West. Penn's revisionist film most clearly provokes viewers to think critically about contemporary America and the epistemological foundation upon which we have constructed American history. Less ambitious, though no less engaging, Eastwood's film confronts the Jeffersonian legacy of the American West, and the possibility for human redemption while escaping one's past. Although at different ends of the political spectrum, these films nonetheless reveal the loss of innocence, self-confidence, and optimistic ethos that characterized American society after 1968.

Released in 1970, Arthur Penn's *Little Big Man* assaults sacred institutions of American civilization such as the family, Christianity, capitalism, and the military. It tells the story of Jack Crabb (Dustin Hoffman), the sole white survivor of Custer's Last Stand, as he lived among the Cheyenne people and white settlers along the American frontier. After a band of Indians massacre a group of pioneers with whom Jack's family has traveled, the Cheyenne find Jack and his surviving sister Caroline (Carol Androsky). Caroline shortly flees thereafter believing she will be raped, leaving him behind to be adopted by the Cheyenne, who give him the name Little Big Man. Growing up with the Cheyenne, Jack says that he was not "playing Indian," but actually lived as a Cheyenne brave. As he reaches manhood, he is offered the chance not to fight a planned war against the US Calvary, but chooses to fight along with his people to demonstrate to himself and his nation that he is a Cheyenne warrior. During the battle, however, Jack is captured by white soldiers and is sent to live with Reverend Silas Pendrake (Thayer David) and his wife (Faye Dunaway) to be civilized into white America. Jack quickly becomes disillusioned with the Pendrakes when he discovers Mrs. Pendrake's infidelity, leaving them in order to start a life on his own among white Americans. He tries his hand as a traveling salesmen working with Mr. Merriweather (Martin Balsam), but his partner's corrupt business practices gets him into trouble with irate customers who discover they are selling poison instead of a healing tonic, a group of whom include his sister Caroline. He then briefly reunites with Caroline, who teaches him how to be a gunslinger. However, he leaves his life as the gunfighter Soda Pop Kid after he sees his friend Wild Bill Hickok (Jeff Corey) kill a man, then attempts to establish a new life and legitimate business after marrying his Swedish immigrant bride Olga (Kelly Jean Peters).[29]

Jack becomes bankrupt after his business partner swindles him, but is given new hope when encouraged to go west to find new opportunities by General George Armstrong Custer (Richard Mulligan). An arrogant narcissist, Custer assures Jack the West is safe with him and his soldiers protecting white settlers from Indians.

Of course Indians attack Jack and Olga's stagecoach and she is taken captive. Jack spends the next few years looking for Olga, living life as a trapper and sometime scout for General Custer. Following a war with the Cheyenne, Jack returns to his former people and marries Sunshine (Aimée Eccles), the daughter of his friend Shadow That Comes in Sight (Ruben Moreno) who died during this battle between the Cheyenne and US Calvary. Among the Indians, he has again found peace. His life, however, is disrupted when Custer and his soldiers massacre the Cheyenne, including Sunshine and their infant son. Jack tries to return to Custer's camp as a scout in order to assassinate Custer, but loses his will once he has the chance. As a scout, he tries to warn Custer against attacking Indians at Little Big Horn, but the arrogant general dismisses him, dying along with his soldiers at this iconic battle. Jack again is saved by Cheyenne Indians, and returns with them to spend time with his dying Indian grandfather, Old Lodge Skins (Chief Dan George).[30]

*Little Big Man* is a self-conscious revisionist Western that reflects the issues facing American society in 1970. Where the majority of Americans collectively believed their country was a model of democracy and freedom and supported a foreign policy to both protect its way of life and advance American civilization across the globe in the early 1960s, a sizable number vocally criticized this foreign policy at the height of the Vietnam conflict in the latter part of the decade. These critics maintained that the United States had become an arrogant imperialist superpower working on behalf of American business interests and the military industrial complex, and not its noble founding principles. *Little Big Man* creates a tableau of the American frontier to show the ways similar American institutions in the American past corrupted the nation with their hypocrisy, greed, and imperial ambitions. Although the white Americans in the film believe they are conquering the West to advance civilization, they are in fact defiling it as they destroy the more virtuous Indian way of life. It is they who are the "Human Beings" as Jack Crabb tells us, and the white Americans who are the savages. According to *Little Big Man*, the Cheyenne were apparently an early manifestation of the hippie counterculture, believing in free love and tolerance, and living communally and harmonically with the natural world. They have names like Sunshine and accept gay members. General Custer and his white soldiers, in contrast, are cold-blooded murderers masking as an army much as some Americans believed General Westmoreland and his American forces savagely killed the Vietnamese. As one watches Custer's massacre of innocent Cheyenne women and children in *Little Big Man*, it is difficult not to recall American soldiers similarly murdering innocent Vietnamese civilians during the My Lai massacre in March 1968.

Despite its revisionist representations of Native Americans, including casting actual Indians to portray them, the native peoples in *Little Big Man* remain "the white man's Indian." Undoubtedly, they are portrayed more positively than in more traditional Westerns and much more virtuous than the white Americans in the film. Nevertheless, they are one-dimensional characters whose people more

closely resemble a 1960s counterculture commune rather than an actual manifestation of the historical Cheyenne. True, the film illustrates some cultural
practices of the Plains Indians such as the warrior custom of "counting coup,"
whereby Indian warriors hit their enemies with the coup sticks to shame them
rather than killing them.[31] During the scene wherein we observe the Cheyenne
hitting US Cavalry soldiers with their coup sticks, Jack's voice-over informs us
how this Indian war custom placed them at a severe disadvantage against the
soldiers using guns. By Custer's Last Stand, however, the Plains Indians have
adjusted their war tactics to use rifles in order to defend themselves and attack their
foes. Nevertheless, *Little Big Man* largely portrays Cheyenne society as a counterculture to American civilization rather than one that is distinct and fundamentally
different. The film represents American society as unjust, individualistic, exploitive,
patriarchal, and sexually repressed, while showing the Cheyenne as the complete
opposite.

For example, the Cheyenne chief, Old Lodge Skins, accepts his white grandson
Little Big Man for who he is and even offers him the opportunity not to participate
in the nation's planned military engagement against the US Calvary so Little Big
Man does not have to feel conflicted between his white and Indian identities. In
contrast, Reverend Pendrake continuously beats Jack because he sees his
mischievous behavior connected to "heathen" and "savage" Indian customs. The
film presents Cheyenne polygamy in the context of hippie "free love" and natural
sexual behavior, viewed favorably in contrast to the Victorian and Christian sexual
repression of American society. Poor Mrs. Pendrake attempts to repress her sexual
desires with Christian female virtue, but her natural carnal desires overcome every
effort to control her temptations. When Jack is caught by Reverend Pendrake
rolling in barnyard hay kissing a young woman, he is mercilessly whipped by the
reverend for his "heathen" and "blasphemous" sexual behavior. Yet, Jack
ultimately becomes disillusioned with Christianity when he catches Mrs. Pendrake
having an adulterous affair.[32] Even when women want to free themselves from the
patriarchal and sexual repression of Christianity, they still cannot escape America's
broader Victorian sexual codes.

Later in the film, his dying friend Wild Bill Hickok asks Jack to give his
remaining fortune to Lulu, a woman he frequently sees at a local brothel. Jack is
surprised to see that Lulu is in fact Mrs. Pendrake, now a fallen woman of ill-
repute. Even when Mrs. Pendrake offers Jack the opportunity to finally act upon
the sexual impulse they both shared years ago when Jack lived with the Pendrakes,
Jack declines and drops Bill's money on her naked midriff in disgust. Clearly the
film comments upon the Victorian values of American society and the ways
they restrict women from exerting their natural sexual impulses, leading them
to disreputable behaviors either as hypocrites or whores. In contrast, Cheyenne
women are allowed to exhibit their sexual desires openly. Little Big Man's
Cheyenne wife Sunshine actually asks him to have sex with her three widowed
sisters. The film shows Sunshine's sisters accepting and enjoying their carnal desires

as Jack tries to have sex with all three women in one evening. The following morning Sunshine is a little emotionally distraught, but nonetheless thanks her tired and drained husband for being with the previously sexually deprived sisters.[33] Clearly the film embraces the countercultural value of free love and the ways sexual freedom leads to human freedom more generally.

The film adopts a similar attitude about gays and lesbians. Little Big Man describes the ways the Cheyenne nation accept homosexuals like Younger Bear (Cal Bellini), who does not want to participate in traditional masculine rites of passage as a young man, and later expresses his desire to dress like a woman and have a male spouse. Younger Bear openly displays his homosexuality, even flirting with Little Big Man and telling him he will be his wife after Little Big Man discovers that his captured wife Olga now lives with Little Big Man's mortal enemy, Little Horse (Robert Little Star). In contrast, Jack's sister Caroline Crabb represses her lesbian identity in American frontier society. Jack reunites with his sister after he and Mr. Merriweather sell Caroline and her male friends a tonic that is actually poison and are consequently tarred and feathered. Caroline is dressed in men's clothes as she slowly discovers that she has tarred and feathered her brother. Upon leaving Mr. Merriweather, Jack stays with his sister, who teaches him how to hold a gun and then become a gunfighter.[34] It is she who is confident holding and controlling this symbol of masculinity, not Jack. Although she wears a calico dress and imagines that she and Jack can stay together as a family, she clearly does not have a relationship with any other man. While the movie shows Caroline displaying her masculine tendencies as she openly dresses in men's clothes, she lives deep in the woods and clearly away from civilized society. Little Big Man suggests that homosexuality may exist in Victorian America, but requires gays and lesbians to remain hidden and live in its shadows.

Despite the movie's efforts to portray Native Americans and their culture more positively, it ultimately continues an established American tradition of "playing Indian" that goes back to the colonial period. Indian societies have always been viewed as the antithesis of American civilization, whether in the context of savagery or virtue. By the twentieth century, Americans critiquing the effects of modernity looked to Indians to remind themselves of a simpler and virtuous life free from the corruption of industrialization and civilization. As Patricia Nelson Limerick points out, rarely did they see Native Americans for who they actually were and how they established a society wholly separate from white America with a fundamentally different worldview. Patronizing whites who believed they had become like Indians themselves mostly viewed native peoples through a fragmented prism that was a counterculture to modernity. In other words, they saw Indians as a virtuous version of white America rather than a people with a worldview and culture completely different, and who rejected any political and cultural incursion upon their way of life by whites. Limerick describes how these well-meaning white Americans like George Catlin still wanted Indians to adopt particular aspects of American culture to civilize them to some degree, believing it would save them from a crueler fate, whether that be savagery or genocide. Later in the twentieth century, other left-leaning Americans wanted to introduce aspects of American civilization while protecting them from the more insidious effects of modernity.[35]

These more progressive white Americans may not have been advocating eliminating native peoples like Andrew Jackson, but their efforts to civilize them were a form of cultural extermination nonetheless. Whatever the case, those white Americans who lived among Indians rarely understood native peoples, and participated as members of their community to return to a virtuous way of life before returning back to white America. As Philip Deloria notes, "Playing Indian" has been a longstanding (white) American practice of performance where Americans embraced an oppositional identity that they imagined was freer and less encumbered than their constrained modern identities, but this act of "going native" was only temporary to expel the sins of modernity before returning to American society.[36] *Little Big Man*'s narrative discourse reflects yet another version of "Playing Indian." For Jack Crabb, Cheyenne society is a frontier version of a hippie community where he can practice Timothy Leary's counterculture aphorism to "turn on, tune in, and drop out." Ultimately the film portrays the Cheyenne as alternative Americans, not the real-life Plains Indians who actually exist. The film suggests that if Americans were to become more like the Cheyenne "Human Beings," they would be more virtuous American "Human Beings" not the Cheyenne people themselves.

Beyond interrogating contemporary social and political issues, Arthur Penn's film challenges the fundamental mythos of the American West and the epistemological foundation of historical knowledge. The movie begins with an historian (William Hickey) interviewing the geriatric Jack Crabb, hoping Jack will provide an ethnography of the Plains Indians. In order to have an accurate account of this oral history, he records the interview with a tape recorder. Evidently, this academic intends to conduct ethnographic research to present a factual history of the Plains Indians. As the elderly Jack tells him that he is the sole white survivor of Custer's Last Stand, the historians laughs before telling Jack he is not interested in his tall tales. Offended that he has been called a liar, Jack angrily demands the academic to turn on his tape recorder so that he can narrate how he "saw the Cheyenne for what they was" and "Custer for what he was."[37] In other words, Jack says he is going to tell the real truth about the history of the American West. Jack's story begins with the massacre of white pioneers, and appears to follow the conventions of traditional American history and the Western film: whites appear to be innocent victims of murdering bloodthirsty Indian savages. In fact, this scene immediately recalls Scar and his Comanche Indians murdering the Edwards family in John Ford's *The Searchers*.[38]

However, the movie begins to turn this historical interpretation upside down, and actually begins to directly engage the narrative discourse of Ford's film as well as the more triumphal history of the American West more generally. Like *The*

*Searchers*, *Little Big Man* is a captivity narrative. And Caroline Crabb believes that she will be raped by the Cheyenne, sharing the same fate of Martha and Lucy Edwards before they were murdered in Ford's movie. Yet we shortly learn that the Cheyenne are a peaceful people and it was not they who murdered the pioneers, only that they came upon Jack and his sister in the aftermath of the massacre, and took them into their nation for protection. Jack does not flee like his sister, and through his eyes we begin to observe a revisionist history that presents virtuous Indians in contrast to corrupt, villainous white Americans. In turn, the movie maintains that the history of the American West is not one of civilizing the frontier and ridding it from savage Indians, thereby challenging an interpretation advanced by films like *How The West Was Won*. Western History, in fact, is the insidious march westward of modernity and corruption, led by the narcissist General George Armstrong Custer and his murdering soldiers who killed a more virtuous people in the name of civilization. He clearly was not the honorable man who died at the Battle of Little Big Horn at the mercy of barbarous savages like his legend maintains.

*Little Big Man* thus overturns accepted historical truth, even celebrated American myth. However, it does not reject one historical truth in favor of a revised more accurate one. The film takes a more postmodern position that absolute truth about the American West does not actually exist. Should we stand on either side of the American frontier, one person's savage is another person's civilized "human being." In fact, the primary cinematic and narrative technique to advance this narrative discourse is to observe the history of the frontier through Jack's eyes and travel with him as he weaves in and out of Cheyenne and white American society. That Jack never remains in one society permanently, and is perpetually confused about the virtues and faults of either society correspondingly reflects the subjective nature of historical knowledge, especially concerning the history of the American West. And though Jack purports to tell the historical truth about the American frontier, he evidently embellishes and exaggerates that history as he incredibly survives one event after another without mortal consequence and slips through Indian and white American society with ease. Ultimately it becomes difficult to find historical truth in Jack's narrative, albeit it makes for an engaging and humorous story.

But are his tall tales without historical value? Are they much different than the legend and myths that grew around the historical General Custer and his Last Stand? In fact, the movie appears to suggest that in the absence of factual historical knowledge, a greater historical truth lies in the myths and legends we tell about the past. Indeed, the film seems to suggest that looking for a factual history of the American West is ludicrous. After all, the film concludes returning to the geriatric Jack Crabb holding his head in his hands, appearing distraught as if no one believes his story. In fact, as the camera zooms out and silence replaces the music score, it appears that the 110-year-old Jack Crabb is not in a convalescent home as one initially might have thought at the beginning of the film. Rather, we see him behind a fence, and it may be that he is actually in an asylum. Perhaps trying to find the historical truth of the American frontier has driven Jack insane.

Absent historical truth, the film nonetheless finds value in the mythic past of the West. In fact, it reinforces the West's Jeffersonian legacy in as much as it mocks it. Jack's constant new beginnings and pursuits of happiness border upon the ridiculous. On the one hand he is always trying to escape his past and invent new identities as he perpetually starts life anew, but notably this is always in the white American West. When he is among the Cheyenne, he maintains his identity as Little Big Man, and though he periodically leaves them, when he returns, it is as if he never left. And herein lies the mythic value of the American West, according to *Little Big Man*. The West still holds redemptive value for white America, but redemption requires confronting the corruption, hypocrisy, and racism of its institutions and values. Should it adopt the simpler, but more virtuous life of the Cheyenne "Human Beings" the sins of the past may be redeemed and they too may become "Human Beings" themselves. Arthur Penn's *Little Big Man* arguably falls short as an enduring classic of the Western genre like John Ford's *The Searchers* and Clint Eastwood's *Unforgiven* because it is so tied to the context of American society in 1970. Nonetheless, it remains a provocative film for humorously skewering the triumphant ethos and sacred myths that traditionally defined so many American Westerns. Moreover, it challenges Western epistemology and its certainty that we can find absolute historical knowledge in the past. However, it does not entirely jettison the mythic value of the American West and the Jeffersonian ideology upon which it rests. Although it satirizes the notions of new beginnings and escaping history, it still sees its redemptive value that the American people can become "Human Beings" if they better understand the complexity of their multicultural past and engage it from diverse perspectives.

## *Unforgiven* and the Anti-Myth Western

Where Arthur Penn's *Little Big Man* retains faith in the mythos of the American West and the possibility of human redemption (albeit from a radical multicultural perspective), Clint Eastwood's *Unforgiven* rejects this mythos and the Jeffersonian ideology that scaffolds it. *Unforgiven* tells the story of William Munny (Clint Eastwood), a one-time infamous killer known for his "notoriously vicious and intemperate disposition," who initially put this past behind him when he married Claudia Feathers. As Will tells his friend Ned Logan (Morgan Freeman), his wife cured him of drinking, swearing, and everything associated with his sinful past. Once married, Will and Claudia began to live the Jeffersonian dream in Kansas, wherein he became a yeoman farmer and began his life anew, evidently escaping his past, at least in his mind. Whenever people remind Will of his notorious past in the film, he tells them "I ain't like that no more." However, Will's Jeffersonian dream begins to unravel once Claudia dies from smallpox in 1878, and an epidemic of the "fever" begins to kill his hogs, putting him in desperate straits. When a young man calling himself the Schofield Kid (Jaimz Woolvett) familiar with Will's past rides up to his farm inviting him to be his partner to kill two men for whom a $1,000 bounty has been placed, Will initially rejects this opportunity because he wants nothing to do with his past and sends the Kid on his way. However, once two more hogs become infected with the "fever," he changes his mind, re-embraces his past as a murderer, and rides out to join the Kid. We see that Will has successfully distanced himself from his past when he has difficulty using his pistol to shoot targets and mounting his horse even before he leaves his farm. However, his skills gradually come back to him and he decides to enlist his former partner Ned Logan to join him. Apparently Ned has been able to escape his outlaw past as he too has settled down with his Indian wife Sally Two Trees (Cherrilene Cardinal) and has similarly become a yeoman farmer. When Will rides up to Ned's farm, Sally knows that Will's past has come along as well once she sees his shotgun and begins to worry for her husband. Initially, Ned declines to join Will, only to finally agree when he hears about the reward and that the bounty has been placed on two cowboys for "cuttin' up a lady."[39]

In actuality, only one of the cowboys sliced Delilah Fitzgerald (Anna Levine), a prostitute whom he attacked with his knife for laughing at the diminutive size of his penis. Both the senior prostitute, Strawberry Alice (Frances Fisher), and the saloon owner/pimp Skinny DuBois (Anthony James) seek justice from Sheriff Little Bill Daggett (Gene Hackman), she for the cowboy defacing Delilah and he for the disfigurement of his property. Immediately we realize these women are categorically dismissed as whores and property by Little Bill, socially dead and without civil rights. Little Bill recognizes that Skinny has lost property and his investment after Skinny shows the sheriff the contract he made with Delilah that denotes their agreement for him having brought her from Boston and providing room and board at his saloon in Big Whiskey, Wyoming. Skinny argues that no one will want to have sex with a "cut up whore," and demands restitution for his business loss. Without trial or punishment, Little Bill settles the matter by having the cowboys give Skinny five of their ponies as compensation, damages which Skinny accepts. Strawberry Alice is horrified that the cowboys are released without "as much as a whippin'" and the callousness with which Delilah (and by extension all the prostitutes who work for Skinny) are dehumanized as property—apparently whores are just like horses. But just because "they ride us like horses, that don't mean we are" as Strawberry Alice tells her fellow prostitutes, and so they pull together their capital as bounty for whomever will kill both cowboys (despite the fact it was only one of them that defaced Delilah).[40]

In these opening sequences, Eastwood's film has already demonstrated that this is not Jefferson's redemptive American West full of opportunity and potential happiness. Neither Will nor Ned have been able to escape their past as infamous murderers as they embrace it in order to pursue the bounty that Strawberry Alice and the other prostitutes have issued. Though Will's life as a yeoman farmer may have made him more virtuous (though the film makes a better case that this was Claudia's influence), it has produced neither prosperity nor happiness. Will thought he had been redeemed from his past sins once he married Claudia, and as Ned tells him, he would not intend to kill the hunted cowboys were Claudia still alive. But he is a failed farmer, and he needs to find a way to give his kids a better life, as Will replies. Although he refrains from swearing, alcohol, and sex for most of the film, he nonetheless knows killing the cowboys for money damns him, even if he rationalizes that their murder is justified because they dishonored a woman. And though the prostitutes seek justice, in actuality they want vengeance with the murder of the two cowboys. They are enraged that they are treated as exploited property. In all likelihood they had their American Dream as well. Delilah journeyed west from Boston hoping for a better life even if it meant temporarily working as a prostitute. That these women have been saving their capital before they ultimately use it for the bounty reveals that they had hoped that one day they would escape their current predicament and start over as more honorable women. Even Little Bill dreams of building his modest home with a porch to enjoy smoking his pipe. Yet this dream is frustrated by the persistent bad weather and his poor skills as a carpenter, about which his fellow sheriffs constantly tease him. Moreover, it is a dream left unfulfilled as he dies at the hand of Will Munny for unjustly murdering Ned.[41]

*Unforgiven* not only undermines the Jeffersonian myth of the American West, but also challenges the very nature of historical knowledge just like Arthur Penn's *Little Big Man*. Eastwood's film does not adhere to a postmodern interpretation of history like Penn's film, but it questions the epistemology of history nevertheless. The movie interrogates the relationship between history and myth with the constituent story of English Bob. English Bob (Richard Harris) is the first notorious gunfighter to arrive in Big Whiskey to pursue the prostitutes' bounty. He travels by train with his biographer W.W. Beauchamp (Saul Rubinek) who has come to observe and record Bob's exploits for his book, *The Duke of Death*. At first English Bob lives up to his notoriety as he insults American travelers with his English ethnocentrism and haughtiness. However, we quickly learn that the image he has crafted for Mr. Beauchamp is a fabrication. Much of English Bob's notoriety is based on his ruthless killing of Chinese laborers, and his fabricated image begins to unravel when he is unable to defend himself against Little Bill once his guns have been seized (due to Little Bill's issued ordinance that demands visitors to Big Whiskey must turn over their guns while they remain in the town) and imprisoned. Bill laughs at the narrative Mr. Beauchamp has constructed, mocking English Bob as the "Duck of Death" and indicting him for advancing lies rather than the truth. In turns out that Little Bill was at the incident in Kansas that English Bob claims established his reputation as a skilled gunfighter, though one he has embellished to enhance his notoriety. To further undermine the veracity of his history, Little Bill points out that Mr. Beauchamp was not at this event in a Kansas saloon, and therefore did not witness the actual event.[42]

In other words, Mr. Beauchamp is inventing and peddling a myth instead of writing history as it actually happened. Further shamed, English Bob admits that Little Bill's version of the story is accurate. In turn, Mr. Beauchamp begins to write Little Bill's history for his likely readers in the American East, believing he will publish a history of the American West from the Sheriff's vantage that still retains its mythic qualities. By the end of the film, this history and myth of the American West crumbles as well, as Little Bill dies at the hands of Will Munny. As Will leaves Big Whiskey with dead men in his wake, Mr. Beauchamp looks upon him with awe as if Will may be a better story to tell his readers in the East than either English Bob or Little Bill. But there is nothing redeeming about Will as he is nothing more than a ruthless killer who reflects the dark side of the American West. Does he want to valorize a man like Will Munny, who has a reputation for shooting men, women and children for fun? Do we want to believe that the American West creates people like Will Munny? Do Americans want to see him as heroic? To do so would require Americans—including us as the film's audience—to turn their backs on the Jeffersonian legacy of the American West, and the sacred mythos they have constructed around Western history as well.

As we see, Jefferson's vision of a redemptive American West that offers new beginnings and opportunities is summarily dismissed in *Unforgiven*. The West in *Unforgiven* is a world of failed and frustrated yeoman farmers, dehumanized prostitutes, corrupt civic institutions, and injustice everywhere one looks. In fact, this world is Jefferson's nightmare. Money, like Will Munny, corrupts everything it touches, while guns and vengeance determine justice, not the rule of law. The American West in *Unforgiven* is morally ambiguous, where good and evil, corruption and justice, are difficult to discern with clarity. The film often projects the moral tone of the film with low-level lighting. Natural lighting emits shadows while people have conversations, sometimes covering the faces of actors to illustrate their psychological and ethical conflicts. The concluding scenes are shot at night in pouring rain, lit by kerosene lamps. In these scenes the lighting and simulated weather are most appropriate because this sequence illustrates that Will is ultimately damned and "unforgiven." As he rides into the town of Big Whiskey to avenge Ned's unjust death, Will has descended into hell. By this point, he and the Schofield Kid have shot the cowboys and received their bounty. Ned had actually left them earlier because he realized he could not kill them after all, even when given the chance. But on his way home to Kansas, he was captured, tortured, and then killed by Little Bill, before his body is publicly displayed to deter other people from pursuing the bounty. One of the prostitutes tells Will about Ned's death as she gives him the reward, and immediately he knows what he will do. Picking up the bottle of whiskey he has been refusing for most of the film, he takes a drink as he hears the prostitute describe how Little Bill has been telling everyone about Will Munny's notorious reputation for killing innocent people, even women and children. Will does not deny this past as he has been to this point of the film. In fact, he embraces it as he tells the Schofield Kid to take his share of the money.

Horrified, the Schofield Kid looks upon Will as if he is a monster and wants nothing to do with him or the reward money.[43] To him, taking the money will damn him like Will as it equates the life of a man with property and cash value.

The film ends with Will killing Little Bill and other members of his posse, and threatening those who attempt to get in his way as he leaves. The mere aura of Will's past scares those who remain alive, who quickly hide as Will leaves Big Whiskey. He further threatens to kill everyone and his family if they try to follow him, and promises to return to kill again if Ned is not properly buried. Alive in hell, Will is ultimately unredeemed and "unforgiven" despite all his efforts to escape his past. The film finally concludes with Will standing over Claudia's grave once more as the sun sets. The film titles then scroll and inform us that Will has left his farm in Kansas, rumored to have traveled to San Francisco and started a successful business.[44] Yet, this is only a rumor. Just as it began, the film ends on this ambiguous note. Perhaps Will has actually fulfilled a Jeffersonian dream of beginning life anew in this Western city, becoming a prosperous businessman while escaping his past. But we are told that this is mere speculation, and maybe he has not gone to San Francisco after all, and his past still continues to haunt him. Whatever the case, the American West in Eastwood's *Unforgiven* remains morally ambivalent and unredeemed, and reflects an American society that is equally ambivalent about its future. By 1992, the United States had won the Cold War, but its future remained uncertain as it groped for a new identity as the world's lone superpower. During the Cold War, the boundaries between good and evil were clearly drawn. Without the Soviet Union and before the emergence of Islamist terrorism following the events of September 11, 2001, those ethical boundaries were less clear. One can thus read *Unforgiven* as a cultural text of post-Cold War America. However its lasting value as a modern classic remains its cinematic power as the anti-mythic Western that challenges the foundational Jeffersonian principles that traditionally defined the history of the American West.

From the time pioneers ventured west, Americans valorized a sacred mythos connecting the American national identity to the history of the American frontier, one that was reified in mass culture, initially with popular fiction and nickelodeons, and eventually with film. Movies such as Michael Mann's *Last of the Mohicans*, John Ford's *The Searchers*, and especially Henry Hathaway's, John Ford's, and George Marshall's *How The West Was Won* reflect this optimistic vision of the American frontier and its relationship to our national character. However, this celebratory interpretation of the history of the American West crumbled in the face of vocal criticism of American institutions and policies that were viewed as undermining the founding cherished ideals that many Americans maintained made them a noble people and civilization for others to emulate. Revisionist Westerns like *Little Big Man* interrogated our national sacred mythos in the turbulent era after 1968 to challenge contemporary American society, but nevertheless remained hopeful of historical redemption if Americans examined their past more honestly, embracing its sins as well as its triumphs. By 1992, however, the American Western reflected a society that was more ambivalent about the redemptive possibilities of American history, and thus the American character. The American Western has always been a way in which Americans engaged their past to understand their present condition and future possibilities. With films like Clint Eastwood's *Unforgiven*, however, the Western may have achieved its apex as a defining historical and cultural text. In the end, Eastwood's film remains ambivalent about the mythic nature of the American West and illustrates how Americans cannot escape their history nor avoid the corrupting influences of modernity. If anything, *Unforgiven* demonstrates that the history of the American West is Jefferson's nightmare rather than an achievement of his dream.

# 5

# IMMIGRATION, THE AMERICAN DREAM, AND THE PROBLEM OF THE IRISH AMERICAN EXPERIENCE

Ron Howard's *Far and Away* begins with drunken Irish men telling folk tales in a tavern before we see peasants confront their landlord Daniel Christie (Robert Prosky) and his family as they ride through the local village in late-nineteenth-century Ireland. Although the film adheres to the traditional American immigration story whereby immigrants leave the old country for the United States searching for better opportunities, it spends significant time in Ireland to illustrate historic class and gender conflicts and how they limited the dreams of its principal characters, Joseph Donnelly (Tom Cruise) and Shannon Christie (Nicole Kidman). Yet, the film diverges from the traditional immigration narrative in two significant ways even as it reinforces it: firstly, Joseph and Shannon are not propelled to leave Ireland because of the devastating famine that forced the first major wave of Irish emigration in the 1840s; second, it is not the story of Europeans becoming American as much as Europeans already possessing American values in the old country ultimately able to practice them once they move to the United States. In Ireland, Joseph already exhibits a spirit of Jeffersonian individualism even though he is a frustrated renter dependent upon the mercy and good graces of his landlord, and Shannon has adopted habits of a modern American woman as she tries to free herself from the patriarchal traditions of her Irish aristocratic family.

Furthermore, the termination of this immigration narrative concludes in the American West with the historical Oklahoma Land Rush, where Joseph and Shannon are finally able to shed their Irish ethnicity and truly achieve their American Dream as Jeffersonian farmers. According to the film, Joseph and Shannon could fulfill their dreams in the American West because European immigrants maintained ethnic social and cultural ties in the urbanized and industrialized East. In Oklahoma, however, Joseph finally escapes his past as a poor Irish renter and Shannon hers as a privileged Irish aristocratic woman imprisoned by its patriarchy. Together, they envision starting their lives anew in Oklahoma completely disconnected from their European past, living a life as independent, equal farmers and free Americans.[1] More than an American immigration story, *Far and Away* is a traditional American Western whereby the Jeffersonian legacy of the American West ultimately transformed ethnic immigrants into white Americans.

Released in 1992, Howard's film recalls a historical interpretation of the American immigration experience and westward migration at odds with recent immigration historiography. Yet, it nonetheless reflects an interpretation of this experience of immigration that Americans continue to reify. Moreover, this is an interpretation that a small number of academics continue to contend in their scholarship despite recent trends in immigration scholarship. Like *Far and Away*, conservative scholars such as Thomas Sowell maintain that the Irish ultimately fell into the American social landscape after initial generations endured struggles, becoming a model for others to emulate in their stories of immigrant Americanization.[2] Thus, one may want to criticize *Far and Away* for its celebratory and arguably superficial interpretation of the American immigration experience, but it connects with an established myth Americans believe about their national history and collective identity, and one that is reinforced by academics like Sowell and even eminent American historians such as Oscar Handlin and Bernard Bailyn.

Yet, other scholars see the history of Irish immigration tinged with much more conflict and violence, and demonstrate how the process of Americanization was not widely embraced by the Irish themselves, and especially not by Anglo-Saxon nativists who despised their presence in the United States. Scholars such as Matthew Frye Jacobson have argued that the Irish were racialized by these nativists like other subaltern peoples living in the urbanized and industrialized North from the mid-nineteenth century until the civil rights struggles following World War II.[3] In fact, filmmakers such as Martin Scorsese have presented this interpretation of the Irish American experience in movies like *Gangs of New York*. As different as these interpretations of the American immigration story may appear, however, they nonetheless reinforce a similar theme: namely, that the Irish American historical trajectory fundamentally remains the model for all immigrants coming to the United States. While it is not the purpose of this book to agree or disagree with this contention, it does examine films about the Irish experience in the United States in order to show how they reflect major themes in American immigration historiography, and the ways these movies provide a lens through which we can interrogate the mythos of the American national identity. This particular chapter thus explores arguments in immigration historiography and two films about the Irish experience, the previously mentioned *Far and Away* and *Gangs of New York*. Chapter 6 will further examine academic and cinematic historiographic interpretations of the American immigration experience as they connect to Italian Americans, recent European immigrants, and particularly Mexican Americans.[4]

## The American Dream and the Enduring Themes in Immigration Historiography

Despite recent academic trends that stress the critical role of gender, race, and ethnicity in American history, American exceptionalism and the American Dream remain the central interpretive frameworks animating immigration historiography, whether or not historians agree with these ideologies. Ever since its colonial beginnings, Americans and European commentators have marveled at the unique American experiment, and what Alexis de Tocqueville described as the "equality of social conditions" that enabled native-born Americans and recent (predominantly western European) immigrants alike to widely participate in democratic politics, and pursue their collective socio-economic dreams, making it an exceptional nation in the Western world.[5] As Hector St. Jean de Crèvecoeur stated,

> In this great American asylum, the poor of Europe have by some means met together, and in consequence of various causes; to what purpose should they ask one another what countrymen they arc? Alas, two thirds of them had no country. Can a wretch who wanders about, who works and starves, whose life is a continual scene of sore reflection of pinching penury; can that man call England or any other kingdom his country? A country that had no bread for him, whose fields procured no harvest, who met with nothing but the frowns of the rich, the severity of the laws, with jails and punishments, who owned not a single foot of the extensive surface of this planet? No! urged [sic] by the a variety of motives, here they came. Every thing has tended to regenerate them; new laws, a new mode of living, a new social system; here they become men: [sic] in Europe they were as so many useless plants, wanting vegetative mould, and refreshing showers; they withered, and were mowed down by want, hunger, and war; but now by the power of transplantation, like all other plants they have taken root and flourished! Formerly they were not numbered in any civil lists of their country, except those of the poor; here they rank as citizens.[6]

Well before the French people presented their gift of the Statue of Liberty to the United States with its moniker of "give me your poor, your tired, and your hungry," European travelers such as St. Jean de Crèvecoeur, and de Tocqueville articulated a similar vision of the American social landscape beginning in the late eighteenth century.

Moreover, Dorothy Ross has contended that this idea of exceptionalism has defined the American social sciences since the emergence of the university system in the late nineteenth century, even in academic scholarship that criticizes this fundamental American worldview.[7] Thus, while race, gender, and ethnicity have been significant analytical modalities that have provided important revisions of the American experience, these interpretive social categories ultimately connect particular immigrant histories to the dominant and traditional beliefs about American exceptionalism and the American Dream. In part, the elasticity of the Dream and the ways in which individuals have defined its meaning throughout time enable us to understand the reasons why generations of immigrants have been willing to uproot themselves from traditional social ties to begin life anew in a foreign land. Whether the United States has ever been a "land of opportunity" remains debatable, but this idea nonetheless has been the prevailing historiographic interpretation of our national story. Undoubtedly, this historical narrative continues to be powerful because it celebrates American cultural values of individualism, labor discipline, rebirth, and perennial optimism. More profoundly, this interpretation enables many Americans to internalize and understand American history because it connects a relatively remote past and people with more immediate family histories.

However, in our retelling of family stories, myth, memory, and history collide to frame a historical perception of the American immigration experience that fundamentally emphasizes historical progress. Indeed, for many Americans their real engagement with our national story is in the history of their family's collective migration experience (whether coming to, or moving within America) to pursue all manners of opportunity, a vision of the past that affirms a historical narrative about the ways American institutions and values created the social, economic and political conditions for their families to achieve the American Dream. Although critical events, issues and the ways they have shaped the course of human history may animate our study of the past, for most Americans the more genuine connection to, and real understanding of our national historical narrative is based upon personal migration stories, as the popularity of genealogical research at local and state archives perpetually remind us. And herein lies the real power of social history: the ability for the average American to acquire information about their personal past by practicing "history" as they research their familial "roots," tracing generations of kin who have shaped the course of American history. This social experience reinforces Jeffersonian ideas of independence, freedom, and pursuits of happiness, and provides the semblance of a shared national heritage which functions as a cultural adhesive that nominally and loosely defines a common American narrative. As we will see, historical scholarship and American films mutually reinforce these powerful ideas, whether or not we want to argue that this is history or myth.

Beginning in the 1940s, Oscar Handlin examined a number of the historical issues that continue to define immigration historiography. In monographs such as *Boston's Immigrants* (1941), *Race and Nationality in American Life* (1948), and *The Uprooted* (1952), Handlin explored ideas such as the push-and-pull factors that motivated people to come to the United States, immigrant community formation and cultural retention, and the conflict between ethnic identity and Americanization. In *The Uprooted*, his Pulitzer Prize winning book, he went so far as to say, "Once I thought to write a history of the immigrants in America. Then

I discovered that the immigrants *were* American history."[8] In general, Handlin's career reflects broader trends in American history and historiography. In *Boston's Immigrants*, Handlin describes the challenges the Irish encountered as they migrated to Boston, and the socio-political conflicts that ensued between them and nativist Americans (primarily of Anglo-American heritage). Over the course of the nineteenth century, the Irish strengthened their ethnic identity as they developed socio-cultural institutions,[9] and in the process illustrated a communitarian approach to local and national politics that challenged an American political culture based upon Lockean liberal ideals of possessive individualism.[10] The conflict among nativist and Irish Bostonians would intensify during election cycles, and significantly abated only once Irish immigrants and their children became more attached to their new homeland during the Civil War, when many declared their allegiance to the United States and joined the military to preserve the Union, demonstrating a commitment to the American idea of nation in what many considered the ultimate act of citizenship as they fought in the armed forces. While Handlin notes this important shift in nativist and Irish relations in Boston, he nevertheless refuses to end his narrative on a progressive or optimistic note in this book, pointing out how ethnic conflict would continue, rising or subsiding depending upon broader historical events, although ethnic tensions would never become as intense as they were before the Civil War.[11]

Handlin's methodological approach in *Boston's Immigrants* stresses social tension and affirms difference in American history, a modality that also informs *Race and Nationality in American Life*, his other monograph written in the 1940s. In this provocative book that anticipates later scholarship about race, ethnicity, and class in American history, Handlin demonstrates how African American slavery interconnected with the American ethnic and working-class experience, a complicated narrative that also included immigration and Americanization.[12] Although he never uses academic argot such as "the social construction of race," Handlin nonetheless illustrates the ways in which race has indeed been a historical and social construction throughout American history in *Race and Nationality in American Life*: that is, how definitions of race change at particular moments in time depending upon social and historical circumstances. Handlin further shows how European immigrants have been just as invested in the ideology of race as native-born Americans, as this ideology collectively accelerated the ability of ethnic white workers to climb the social ladder and achieve the American Dream. Rather than accepting contemporary Marxist scholarship that indicted industrial capitalism for driving a racial wedge among different racial and ethnic groups in the American working class, Handlin contends that race is a protean ideology grounded in particular historical contexts—that is, it is as much an historical construction as it is an ideological one. As we will see, this vision of modern capitalism, "whiteness," and ethnic racism informs recent scholarship by historians such as Barbara Jean Fields, David Roediger, and Matthew Frye Jacobson whose collective works provide significant insight into the history of race in America, but whose research actually elaborates upon Handlin's historiographic interpretations formulated over half a century ago.[13]

By the 1950s, however, Handlin began to emphasize consensus and "sameness" in American society, highlighting its exceptional nature and the ability of immigrants to surmount incredible challenges to achieve prosperity for themselves and their children. While he accounts for the social and cultural costs for immigrants as they arrived to the United States, their sacrifice nonetheless enabled their children to acquire a better quality of life than they would otherwise have had in either the old country or in the United States.[14] Readers may sense the immigrants' feelings of alienation and disconnection in America while reading Handlin's rendering of their historical experience in *The Uprooted*, but may also finish the monograph believing American immigrants made incredible social, cultural, and especially emotional sacrifices in order that they, and especially their children, could have a better life. Yet, one cannot read *The Uprooted* without considering the intellectual and historical contexts framing Handlin's interpretation of the American immigration experience in the 1950s. In his study of the American historical profession, Peter Novick suggests that World War II and the Cold War were critical historical events that account for this historiographic transformation in Handlin's later works.[15] As Handlin stated, "The focal point of history's concern is continuity, and continuity implies that elements of sameness persist."[16] Like his professional contemporaries, Handlin shifted from a methodological approach inherited from Progressive historians such as Charles Beard and Carl Becker that examined class and ethnic conflict in American history, to one that emphasized cultural and political consensus in the history of the American liberal tradition.[17] In this regard, Handlin affirmed the powerful hold of American exceptionalism upon social science disciplines that Dorothy Ross has described in her study of the American academy, particularly as the liberal West became locked in an ideological war with the Marxist-Leninist (and later Maoist) East during the Cold War.

Monographs by scholars such as Thomas Sowell and Bernard Bailyn affirm Handlin's optimistic interpretation of the American immigrant experience reflected in his *The Uprooted*. Collectively, Sowell and Bailyn's scholarship describe the exceptional nature of American society and the ways it has provided the social, economic, and political conditions for American immigrants to achieve prosperity once they have surmounted the initial challenges of social dislocation, poverty, and even bigotry. Perhaps Sowell's work is the most optimistic as he celebrates the unique achievements of ethnic immigrants who triumphed over various forms of discrimination to enjoy the panoply of benefits in American society as citizens of the United States, if not within their lifetime, then eventually in that of their descendants.[18] For Sowell, the history of the Irish in America is the template for the history of most ethnic and racial groups in America, including Jewish Americans and Asian Americans. Interestingly, Sowell draws upon Handlin's *Boston's Immigrants* in his chapter about the history of Irish Americans, but notably differs from Handlin's conclusions. Where Handlin believed social tensions remained palpable between Irish and nativist Bostonians, although less so after the Civil War, Sowell sees a historical trajectory of progress for Irish Americans, having overcome bigotry and socio-economic discrimination since their initial mass immigration in the 1840s.[19] As Sowell states,

> The Irish have in fact become so Americanized that some lament that they have lost their distinctive qualities. But becoming American can hardly be regarded as failure. It remains the dream of many around the world. And was the dream of millions who first embarked on the perilous journey from Ireland.[20]

In his study of immigration in colonial British America, Bernard Bailyn also argues that the exceptional nature of American society enabled Europeans to achieve a level of prosperity unequal to their peers in the old world. Where some scholars such as Nicholas Canny have argued that the Anglo-American colonies were just another destination for migrants in the British Empire to seek economic opportunity in the seventeenth and eighteenth centuries, Bailyn contends that socio-economic conditions in the British American colonies, primarily access to land and private property, uniquely created conditions for European immigrants to succeed in ways unheard of among their contemporaries in the British Isles.[21] Scholars may agree that the British Empire was a "world in motion" throughout the eighteenth century, but the years following the Seven Years War (1756–1763) provided unparalleled peace in the Atlantic world once the British emerged as the primary European military and political power following their victory over the French in 1763. Furthermore, British security of the Atlantic Ocean enabled safer passage of ships transporting Europeans to British North America. The Anglo-American colonies may have been on the "periphery of civilization," according to Bailyn, but the demographic growth of England's urban centers and the enclosure of pastoral land throughout the British Isles made the land-rich Anglo-American colonies increasingly attractive as a prime destination for struggling Europeans.

While Bailyn does not sufficiently examine the manifold ways violent encounters among Native Americans, European Americans, and African American slaves contributed to the emergence of a unique colonial American culture and society, he does account for the ways violence on the Anglo-American periphery produced an exceptional world that provided European Americans a variety of opportunities for socio-economic success and the possibility to start "new beginnings" as they fled their troubled past.[22] In many ways, the critical ingredients to what would characterize the "American Dream" existed during the colonial period. Ideas such as risk, an entrepreneurial culture, and the belief in rebirth and redemption found fertile ground in the British American colonies, influencing men like Thomas Jefferson to imagine the new United States as a place for European Americans to envision lives as independent and free people, and enable them to imagine the possibility to "pursue happiness," no matter how they defined this idea.

## *Far and Away, Gangs of New York,* and the Irish American Experience: Establishing and Contesting the American Immigrant Narrative

Collectively, these historiographic interpretations of American exceptionalism and the American Dream are reflected in films such as Ron Howard's *Far and Away* and Martin Scorsese's *Gangs of New York*. Howard's *Far and Away* most approximates Handlin's *The Uprooted* as well as Sowell's and Bailyn's works. *Far and Away* follows the lives of Joseph Donnelly and Shannon Christie whose lives are constricted by Old World traditional values of class and gender in Ireland, and who dream of freedom in America unavailable to them in their homeland. The film's initial scenes in Ireland may depict Irish stereotypes about drunkenness, folk beliefs, and pugilism, but they also present a world defined by landholding, communitarianism, and violent class conflict. Land and community are the defining values in the movie's representation of Irish culture. The film opens with bucolic vistas of the Irish landscape and we see the local village's shared folk traditions in the early scenes at the local tavern. But *Far and Away* also notes how the beauty of the Irish countryside is fraught with violence and class tension. As the opening titles state, "The tenant farmers, after generations of oppression and poverty, have begun to rebel [around 1892] against the unfair rents and cruel evictions imposed upon them by their wealthy landlords."[23] Provocatively, landholding and freedom will drive the film's narrative discourse about Irish American immigration rather than the Great Famine of the 1840s, typically the cataclysmic historic event that propelled so many Irish men, women, and children to come to the United States. Contrary to most historiographic interpretations of Irish immigration (though not entirely fictional), *Far and Away* will emphasize Joseph's pursuit to become an independent landholder in America rather than present a narrative about poverty, starvation and survival that prompted so many of the Irish to come to America. Indeed, Joseph flees Ireland mostly to avoid a duel for dishonoring an Irish gentleman and escape his eventual trial for the attempted murder of Shannon's father, the wealthy landlord from whom the Donnelly family rents land and whom Joseph holds responsible for his father's death. Had these "events" not happened, one doubts whether Joseph would have left Ireland.

Joseph is thus a product of traditional Irish values even as he seeks to escape them. He has grown up in late-nineteenth-century Ireland where most of the land is controlled by wealthy gentlemen who rent their land to the majority of local villagers, holding the awesome power to revoke rented land, and even capriciously burning the homes of families like Joseph's when they challenge the landed gentry. The film clearly shows these tensions between renters and landholders in the opening scene depicting villagers shouting and harassing the landlord Daniel

Christie. Joseph, however, is not presented as part of this world as the following scenes show him seemingly alone on his family's rented farm struggling to till the land, far removed from the violent chaos enveloping the village. In these initial scenes, we see that Joseph is an oddity in his family and community as he holds values and ambitions different from his brothers and fellow villagers. The movie depicts Joseph as a sober, independent, hard-working peasant while his brothers are portrayed as drunken parasites living off of his labor. In a scene when they mock his work habits, they provoke him into a fight only for him to defeat both brothers and return to his work. In part, this scene illustrates Joseph's pugilistic skills to provide the audience with a character attribute that will enable him to survive and succeed in Boston as a boxer; but the film suggests that his pugilistic abilities are only deployed in order to protect himself, rather than demonstrate an inherent attribute stereotypically associated with the Irish.

The death of Joseph's father as a consequence of the local gentry setting fire to the Donnelly home prompts Joseph to leave the family farm to exact revenge. In the subsequent scenes, we observe Joseph moving through the luscious countryside as he pursues Mr. Christie. The film affirms Joseph's class status by juxtaposing the green, bucolic landscape with Joseph's drab, gray clothes. Despite years of laboring in the fields, Joseph is nonetheless disconnected from the bounty and fertility of the Irish soil, land that is systematically controlled by Irish landlords who hold power beyond his reach. The movie further reinforces class status by contrasting character costume between the gentry and peasant villagers. As Joseph journeys through the countryside seeking Mr. Christie, he enters a tavern where peasants are likewise dressed in gray. As the villagers interrogate Joseph, Mr. Christie enters the tavern wearing colorful, garish clothing. Despite the clear class differences between Mr. Christie and the peasants, he easily moves among these villagers, connecting with them by buying a round of drinks. As Mr. Christie imbibes with them, they gratefully accept his noblesse oblige, and happily listen to him as he jocularly recounts his marital troubles, offering a moment of collective masculine commiseration. Again, the film shows Joseph removed from this episode of a traditional harmonious patrician–plebeian relationship lubricated by liquor, and further demonstrating how he is a stranger in his homeland.

Joseph quickly discovers that the local landlord carousing with the village peasants is Mr. Christie, and begins to plot his murder. Although Mr. Christie did not set the Donnelly home on fire, Joseph emphatically holds him responsible for his father's death. Yet, Joseph soon discovers that Mr. Christie is not a monochromatic monster invested in the oppression of Irish peasants. In fact, it turns out that he is oblivious to the death of Joseph's father, and understands his vendetta. While camaraderie, alcohol, masculinity, and honor apparently cross class lines in *Far and Away*'s Ireland, history and tradition drive a wedge among the Irish rather than true class identities (English conquest and colonialism are curiously absent from this narrative about Irish oppression). Class tensions exist, but not class consciousness. Indeed, *Far and Away* needs to promote this idea in order to demonstrate the possibility for Joseph and Shannon to have a romantic relationship and why they can share an American Dream of land and freedom. Although this is a simplistic representation of traditional Irish class conflict, presenting this as a superficial, historical construction rather than a structural one with a long, deep past will ultimately enable Joseph and Shannon to bond in America once they are emancipated from Irish history and the indigenous traditions that have corrupted class relations.

Joseph follows Mr. Christie to his estate and attempts to shoot him, only for his gun to malfunction and injure him, thwarting his pursuit of vengeance. Although exposed, the Christie family take Joseph into their home, tending his wounds before he faces a duel with Stephen Chase (Thomas Gibson), Mr. Christie's aristocratic overseer and his daughter Shannon's suitor. At this moment, the film introduces Shannon as a precocious young woman chafed by traditional gender conventions, and who yearns to go to America where she believes she can be "modern." During these scenes at the Christie estate, Shannon challenges her mother's efforts to have her adhere to Victorian customs during a tea party with guests. When Shannon is asked to play the piano, she launches into an American ragtime tune, astonishing her mother and friends, who expected more classical music. In these scenes, we observe the ways Shannon is just as alienated from her world as Joseph and is frustrated by the ways traditional Irish customs restrict her from being her true self and fulfill her dreams. As she tells Joseph, she wants to sail for America where land is free and she can be an independent landholder. More than Joseph, she believes in an American Dream, and wants to escape her history in order to fulfill it. Although Joseph initially refuses to go with her, his disastrous attempt to duel Stephen provokes him to flee with Shannon where he assumes the role of her servant as she pays for his passage to America.[24]

Once they arrive in Boston, Shannon's dream goes awry. She has been swindled, has her valuable family silverware stolen (the sale of which was to pay for hers and Joseph's trip west), and finds herself destitute. She and Joseph are encouraged to go to the Irish community where they are told they will find shelter and jobs. Here they meet Mike Kelly (Colm Meaney), the ward boss, who directs them to the local brothel for shelter and informs them that they will find jobs with a local poultry factory. Moving among Irish working-class immigrants Joseph tells Shannon that they are among his people now and that she should follow his lead to remain safe now that she has been stripped of her class status. To protect her, Joseph tells everyone that Shannon is his sister, and together they share a room, work in the poultry factory plucking chickens, saving their meager earnings so they can still make their way west to the promised free land in Oklahoma Territory.[25] In this regard, Howard's *Far and Away* follows much of the immigration historiography that describes the immigrant experience between the 1880s and 1920s. Many immigrants arriving in America came in this period hoping to be independent landholders, with some like the Swedes, Norwegians, and a few Germans succeeding as they made their way to the American Midwest, where they found ethnic communities willing to help them to make their start in America as yeoman farmers. Most, however, headed to urban centers like Boston, New York City, Chicago, Milwaukee among other places. Some like Joseph and Shannon had dreams of becoming landholders and worked in factories hoping to save capital so they could buy land in the American West. These immigrants also headed to ethnic communities where they could find ward bosses or other local leaders who could help them find shelter and work.[26]

However, not all these immigrants came to America planning to make it their home, hoping to work in factories, save money, and eventually return to their homeland. Historical events such as World War I, the Johnson-Reed Act (1924), and the Great Depression inhibited immigrants from going back to the old country. Whatever their dream, most European immigrants settled within their respective ethnic communities, retaining many of their traditional customs. Whether because of Anglo-Saxon prejudice or collective choice, many immigrants remained Europeans (be they Irish, Italian, Poles, Jews, etc.) in America, resisting acculturation as well as assimilation.[27] Ron Howard's film reflects how the Irish in Boston maintained old world customs and found support in the strength of the community's social and cultural institutions. Although we will explore this theme in other films about the European American experience in Chapter 6, it is most reflected in the relationship between Mike Kelly and Joseph in *Far and Away*. As Joseph sees that his path to success and respect in the Irish American community lies in his pugilistic skills, his ties with Mike Kelly and his patrician on the City Council, Darcy Bourke (Wayne Grace) strengthen. During the movie's boxing scenes, we watch Joseph rapidly move up the Irish community's social and economic ladder as he wins fight after fight. Joseph can quit his job in the poultry factory because he can make more money in one night of prize fighting than he can in one month working in the factory. Shannon is astonished at Joseph's rapid rise and conspicuous consumption (especially of suits and hats), and reminds him that his spending prevents him from saving money to buy the material necessities to travel to Oklahoma. In part, scolding Joseph reflects her frustration with working in the poultry factory, where she despises the foreman who barks orders at her and deducts her wages when she openly challenges him on the factory floor in plain sight of her fellow workers.[28]

Despite the film's connection to these particular themes in immigration historiography about cultural retention, it also shows the ways Joseph and Shannon rebel against the social and political institutions that sustain the Irish American community in Boston. Just as Shannon challenges the authority of her boss, Joseph similarly confronts the authority of the community's political bosses. Joseph believes he has earned his reputation and wealth from his own merit, independent of Mike Kelly and Darcy Bourke's support. Yet, when they demand the undefeated Joseph to fight his equal in the Italian American community, Joseph says he chooses when and whom he will fight. Insulting Councilman Burke prompts Kelly to pull Joseph aside and remind him about the patrician patronage politics that control the Irish community, pointing out the hierarchical lines of authority and how Joseph's success depends upon respecting them. Kelly says that just as he made Joseph successful, he can take everything away. Recognizing Kelly's points, he agrees to the boxing match. Here *Far and Away* illustrates that the Irish immigrants may be living in America, but they continue to practice old world patrician–plebeian politics. The Irish living in Boston are not hyphenated "Irish-Americans," but Irish living in America. Because Joseph and Shannon desire the American Dream, they resist assimilating into Boston's Irish community. To this point, the film has demonstrated the ways Joseph and Shannon maintain an independent spirit and want to control their own destiny, traits we associate with American possessive individualism. If they are going to live out their American Dream, it cannot happen as long as they live in Boston's Irish community.

Moreover, since we associate the American Dream with hard work and sacrifice, Joseph's wealth and success as a prize-fighter is elusive and superficial. Even Shannon recognizes that. But she is nonetheless jealous at the ease with which Joseph makes money. Though material wealth and becoming rich has been the American Dream for many, the film demonstrably asserts that money is actually a corrupting force and the success one achieves through it is an illusion. Land is the path to independence and freedom, and the true measure of success. In Irish Boston, Joseph has lost sight of that, and so too does Shannon as she envies his wealth. Frustrated with her menial job and meager wages, Shannon decides to become a saloon dancer, and potentially a prostitute, in order to access the fast road to wealth. However, Joseph saves her from the latter possibility when he sees Burke accost Shannon at the major prize-fight pitting him against the reigning Italian boxer. Wearing sashes to mark their national affiliations and with men in the crowds waving Irish and Italian flags, Joseph is the standard bearer fighting for the honor and pride of the entire Irish masculine community. Joseph begins to win the fight, only to become distracted by Burke's lascivious behavior towards Shannon, ultimately losing the fight—and everything he has gained as a result. Shortly thereafter, Mike Kelly storms into Joseph and Shannon's apartment, taking all their savings. Though Joseph declares they have earned the money, Kelly vehemently points out that it was he who gave them all their opportunities, including their jobs and the roof over their head. As Kelly has his henchmen throw Joseph and Shannon into the street, he says that he will ensure that no one will provide any support to them, thereby banishing them from Boston's Irish community.[29]

In the following days, Joseph and Shannon struggle to survive, encountering anti-Irish bigotry as they look for food and shelter in the snow-filled streets of Boston. Finally, they come upon what appears to be a vacant house, entering and then burgling food. Though filmed in minimal lighting, this scene recalls Shannon's aristocratic lifestyle in Ireland as she touches dining room crystal and Christmas tree ornaments. Joseph senses her longing, and offers to serve her so she can reimagine a time when her life was filled with so much promise. But Shannon wants them to pretend that this is their house that they share as man and wife. Although this poignant scene is critical to advance the love story between Joseph and Shannon that has been developing to this point, it is also significant for the film's narrative discourse about the exceptional nature of American society where an aristocratic woman can imagine a peasant husband, clearly a relationship that would never have developed in Ireland. In this scene, the camera focuses upon how Shannon and Joseph are equals. As they discuss their dreams and share a momentary kiss, they sit side-by-side at the dining table. Where Shannon was Joseph's superior in Ireland, and he hers in Boston's Irish community, they now share a common life as paupers, brought down from their respective elevated social standings. But just as they affirm their love for each other, the homeowner shoots Shannon. Joseph escapes carrying her, wandering the streets looking for help, only for people to close their window shutters and ignore these desperate Irish vagrants. Remembering that Shannon's family and former suitor Stephen have come to Boston looking for Shannon, Joseph takes her to their apartment, leaving her so she can receive critical medical attention. As Joseph flees Stephen and the Christies, the film score plays Irish folk music as if to affirm that Shannon has returned to her Irish past while Joseph heads into an unknown future.[30]

However, Joseph has gone west to work building railroad lines, laboring alongside other immigrants, African Americans, and Native Americans. Though the railroad symbolizes a promising American future as it connects the East and West, Joseph appears to have reached a dead end, especially as he looks longingly upon pioneers in their Conestoga wagons heading towards Oklahoma Territory. Viewers are meant to remember that this was once Joseph's dream, but now he has lost his moorings, seemingly having given up on his American Dream. But just as he has reached his nadir, Joseph has a dream where he and his father talk about their hopes of one day becoming landholders, free and independent. Once he awakes, Joseph is inspired to pursue his American Dream once more, leaving the train of fellow laborers, joining the pioneers, walking along their wagon train as they head towards Oklahoma Territory.

Instantly, *Far and Away* shifts genres, becoming a Western as Joseph's immigrant narrative falls into the broader American historical landscape about westward expansion and Jeffersonian visions of landholding, independence, and freedom. Although we sense that this is where the film was heading all along, the movie's cinematic style changes as it focuses upon Western themes such as the prominence of the Western landscape and the ways it frames the film's narrative discourse. The open skies and broad vistas dwarf Joseph and his fellow pioneers, signifying that they are leaving a world behind as they march westward. The smile on Joseph's face and determination in his gait (as he will apparently walk all the way to Oklahoma Territory) reflect how his particular immigrant American Dream has converged with other pioneers looking to escape their past in the East (and Europe in his case) to start life anew as Americans. Perhaps the film best affirms its Western motif when Americans in the West call Joseph by his name without any suggestion of bigotry, unlike in the East where he was always identified as Irish, even called the epithet Mick in the railroad labor camps.[31] In Oklahoma, Joseph has escaped history and is no longer an Irishman living in America: he is Irish-American. In fact, the film maintains that the West holds this promise for all Americans regardless of race or ethnicity as it shows an African American man receiving his land marker after Joseph, suggesting he will have equal opportunity to stake a homestead in the historic Oklahoma land race.[32] Of course, in order to tell this history it must dismiss that of those Native Americans who occupied most of Oklahoma Territory, but whose land was ceded to the United States government. The stoic Native Americans distantly observing the American settlers as they make fools of themselves jockeying for premier position at the starting line is the only suggestion that *Far and Away* is aware of their history.[33]

Unfortunately, just as Joseph believes he has totally left his past behind him, he hears Shannon's voice as he prepares for the land race. It turns out that Shannon, her parents, and Stephen have all come to participate in the Oklahoma land race as well. However, Shannon has not been able to escape her past as Joseph has. In fact, Stephen reminds her that he and her parents are here only to satisfy her desire, as if they are in Oklahoma to satisfy a childish whim. Shannon may be in the West, but she is still shackled by Old World patriarchy, and only she and her father appear to hope that they can start new lives with their Western homesteads. Mr. Christie, in fact, appears to truly be a renewed and redeemed man. Gone is his patrician class identity and alcoholic behavior, now intoxicated by the prospect of leaving his Irish past behind him. Mr. Christie tells his wife Laura that they have a chance to start over and not be circumscribed to the life they were born into. Instead of an Irish history defining him, he welcomes the chance to start over and make his own history, on his terms. Just as Joseph, Mr. Christie pursues an American Dream disconnected from his traditional past and has him in control of his own destiny. As Mr. Christie says to Laura, "The Wild West suits me."[34]

The American West, however, does not suit Stephen as he only reluctantly participates in Shannon's adventure because he wants to marry her. Stephen has no desire to change, and probably intends to maintain his patriarchal view of the world once he and Shannon establish their homestead. When he sees Joseph, Stephen moves to thwart whatever romantic intentions Joseph may have, obliquely telling him that he might be shot in the confusion of the race if he does not stay clear of Shannon. Even as Joseph maintains his distance, the film provides symbolic reminders that Joseph and Shannon maintain romantic feelings for each other. In one particular scene, they wish each other well in the land race, separated by a clothesline. Here, the film recalls a similar scene in Boston when a clothesline in their apartment served as not only a dividing line to provide privacy, but also the line through which the other peered as they watched each other change clothes. Despite their persistent bickering, these are moments when Joseph and Shannon could not deny that they are attracted to one another. Yet, now in the West and at the moment when each has the opportunity to fulfill the dream that inspired them to leave Ireland and enabled them to endure their struggles in Boston, they realize that their dream will not be complete without the other one as part of it. As if still chained to Irish conventions of honor and class, they sublimate these feelings in these scenes leading up to the race. Only after Joseph, Stephen, and Shannon spot the stake that marks the land that Shannon and Joseph had always envisioned, complete with tall golden grass and a stream, do their sublimated feelings surface. As they did at a critical moment in Ireland, Stephen and Joseph duel, this time in the Oklahoma landscape for the right to claim their land. During their fight, Joseph is crushed underneath his horse, becoming unconscious as his head hits a rock. At this point, Shannon relinquishes her dream to have this land so that Joseph can have it and fulfill his, telling Stephen to leave. With Stephen gone, Shannon tries to resuscitate Joseph, imploring him to open his eyes to behold his land. Although Joseph has drifted near death, he awakens, and together he and Shannon take hold of the stake, claiming the land as theirs.[35]

*Far and Away* obviously portrays an optimistic American immigrant narrative, even as it admits the struggles, sacrifice, and discrimination immigrants faced before they could achieve their American Dream. However, this historical interpretation of the European immigration experience is not too different than the one advanced by scholars such as Thomas Sowell, Bernard Bailyn, and to some degree Oscar Handlin. The film actually most approximates Sowell's interpretation that ethnic Americans endured numerous challenges when they immigrated, but the exceptional nature of America as a nation without class enabled them to eventually share the bounty of a prosperous America. As earlier noted, Sowell acknowledges that immigrants like the Irish endured discrimination, but hard work and struggle ultimately earned them a place in America's social and political landscape.[36] For Sowell the benefits of becoming American outweighed any costs to remaining European ethnics, even if this meant disconnecting one's ties to culture, tradition, and history. Oscar Handlin is much more stoic about the European American experience. Although he shares Sowell's optimism about the assimilation of European Americans into American society and how they eventually became citizens who can participate in American democracy, he remains more circumspect about the price Americanization exacted. For him, emancipating oneself from history, culture, and tradition has been a tragic experience, perhaps most reflected in the gulf between immigrant parents and their children. As he concludes his *The Uprooted*, Handlin wonders whether the sacrifice immigrants made for their children was worth the cultural chasm that now existed between them. For Handlin, these immigrants remained tied to Old World customs, living adrift in their new homeland, and alien to their Americanized children.[37]

Martin Scorsese's *Gangs of New York* addresses some of the historical issues Oscar Handlin examined about the European immigration experience, particularly the role the Civil War played in the Americanization of the Irish. Like Handlin's *The Uprooted*, Scorsese's film sees immigration history as the lens through which to understand American history, and even supports Thomas Sowell's contention that the Irish immigration experience is the template for the broader American immigration experience.[38] However, *Gangs of New York* demonstrates how violence and conflict shaped this history, dividing the nation in a civil war as much as the war fought between the North and the South, issues which Handlin and Sowell significantly minimize (although Handlin accounts for this to some degree in his *Boston's Immigrants*).[39] Where Handlin's *Boston Immigrants* describes the ways the Irish became American citizens as they fought for the Union army, Scorsese's movie illustrates the ways they were used as cannon fodder to fight an unpopular war, and ultimately earned their rights as Americans by controlling the streets and asserting their potent demographic presence to control local politics. The film also demonstrates how immigration history reflects the major themes of American history.[40] In *Gangs of New York*, Scorsese uses the Civil War as the backdrop of his narrative to probe historic tensions between American nativists and ethnic immigrants,[41] and their fight to determine the future of New York City. Rather than telling a narrative about immigrants gradually adapting to American society by adopting the dominant culture of white Anglo-Saxon Protestants, *Gangs of New York* demonstrates how they were active historical agents who challenged Americanization and struggled to define theirs and their children's American experience on their terms.

Gangs are often viewed as the violent refuge of thugs fighting to control street turf, battling to uphold masculine codes of honor. Scorsese's film, however, provokes viewers to consider gangs in a more sociological context. In his movie, gangs serve their traditional roles for marginalized men in ghettoized communities; but they are also institutions of extralegal justice, a street manifestation of the legal system for marginalized peoples. According to *Gangs of New York*, subalterns like immigrants and ethnic Americans could theoretically turn to municipal authorities to seek justice, but they doubted their fairness because they were controlled by nativists. In Scorsese's film, gangs are like other vital immigrant institutions such as the church, protecting the safety of immigrant communities from nativist violence. Perhaps this is best reflected in the movie's opening scene when Priest Vallon (Liam Neeson) dons a clerical collar and carries a Catholic cross as he prepares to battle Bill "The Butcher" Cutting (Daniel Day-Lewis) and his band of nativists.[42] Much as Catholic clerics would march into battle alongside medieval crusaders to sanctify battles and protect them in God's name, Priest Vallon transforms this gang fight into a holy war for the survival of God's immigrant children. Vallon's Catholic cross and the communion which he and his gang the Dead Rabbits receive as they march towards their street battle signify that this gang fight is as much about the preservation of ethnic customs and traditions as it is about who controls the streets of the Five Points district. Later in the movie, *Gangs of New York* draws further comparisons between local gangs and civic institutions when it shows amateur fire brigades battling in the streets of the Five Points. As flames engulf a couple of buildings in the district, different brigades converge on the scene and compete to extinguish the fires. Rather than pulling their resources together, they literally fight each other in the street for the right put out the flames.[43] Much like street gangs, these fire brigades identify with tribal loyalties and battle turf wars to determine which brigade can extinguish the fire, thereby earning honor and respect from the community. By drawing this connection between the brigades and local gangs, the film illustrates how they both are manifestations of the various social and civic institutions that govern this "city of tribes."

Priest Vallon's death during the street battle between his Dead Rabbits and Bill Cutting's Natives proves critically important to the film's narrative discourse. As *Gangs of New York* unfolds, Vallon's legacy as an immigrant leader respected in the Irish community haunts his son Amsterdam (Leonardo DiCaprio) who tries to come to terms with his identity as an Irish American in nineteenth-century New York City. Upon Vallon's death, Bill sends Amsterdam to the Hell's Gate orphan asylum. Here, the asylum directors rear him as an American Protestant for the next sixteen years. Standing in front of a Protestant cross as he prepares to leave, Amsterdam is handed a Bible and encouraged to perform his religious and patriotic duty by enlisting in the Union army to serve God's mission to end the scourge of slavery in America. However, Amsterdam ignores their plea, tossing the Bible into a river as he crosses a bridge, heading towards the Five Points district and his old Irish community. He enters the underground caves that serve as homes for many immigrants and ethnic Americans, returning to the one he and his father once occupied. Before he was taken to Hell's Gate, he had buried the knife that Bill used to kill his father along with the necklace of St. Michael his father had given him. Returning home, he digs up these mementos and prays for guidance as he plans to avenge his father's death.[44] Despite his years at the orphan asylum, Amsterdam never surrendered his tribal ethnic loyalties, and he now intends to affirm them by honoring his father and kill Bill "The Butcher." In order to execute his plan, he quickly immerses himself in the Five Points integrated community, moving among European ethnics, African Americans, and Chinese immigrants. He soon learns that his old community has changed radically since he left. Where his father was able to use his gang the Dead Rabbits as an extralegal institution to protect the ethnic communities in the Five Points from the nativists, Bill "The Butcher" now controls the district and local gangs pay him tribute in order to operate, which now exist only as petty crime organizations for hoodlums. Amsterdam joins one of these gangs, quickly learning that the local police officers are corrupt, and are as much under Bill's control as the gangs.[45]

As he runs with a local gang, Amsterdam sees that Bill emerged as a legitimate political force while he was at Hell's Gate, using municipal institutions such as the police, fire brigades, and the electoral process to ensure that he and his fellow nativists dominate the Five Points. Wearing tailored suits and a gentleman's hat, Bill lords over Lower Manhattan with such power that the eminent party boss William "Boss" Tweed (Jim Broadbent) of Tammany Hall turns to him to help develop a political base in the Five Points and win local elections. Both "The Butcher" and Boss Tweed recognize the demographic power of the growing ethnic and racial communities in the district but maintain different perspectives about how best to deal with it. As Bill and Tweed walk along the city's docks observing the vast number of Irish immigrants disembarking anchored ships, Tweed tells Bill that this is the future of America. He says, "This is the image of our country. Americans are borning [sic]." Bill replies, "I don't see Americans, I see trespassers. Irish harps that will do the work a nigger does for a dime for a nickel . . . what have they contributed?" When Tweed says they provide votes, Bill states, "They vote how the archbishop tells them." Tweed tells Bill that "there is a handsome price if you deliver these people to the polls and they go Tammany's way." Spitting in disgust, Bill says,

> My father gave his life to make this country what it is. He was murdered by the British on the 25th of July in 1814 . . . do you think I am going to help you befoul his legacy by giving this country over to them that has had no effort in the fighting of it because they come off the boat crawling with lice and begging you for soup.

Tweed then says, "You are a great one for the fighting Bill, but you can't fight forever . . . you are turning your back on the future."[46] Though Scorsese's film veers from historical fact at times, its representation of Bill "The Butcher" accurately reflects historiographic interpretations of American nativism in the late nineteenth century.[47]

After Tweed states his point about immigration and the American future, Bill replies, "Not our future" and walks away with his minions, including Amsterdam, who now works for him.[48] As Bill and Amsterdam leave the docks, they move off-screen and the camera remains to follow a group of emaciated Irish men disembarking a ship to first receive food, and then sign (or mark) a series of documents that grant them citizenship for enlisting in the Union army. During this sustained sequence the camera marches along with these men from the moment they disembark, sign these papers, dress into their uniforms, and then re-embark upon another ship making its way towards the battlefield in Tennessee. As we hear a woman singing an Irish song lamenting how "Paddy has come to fight Lincoln's war," the camera zooms out to show coffins unloaded while the men ascend the ship, placed next to what seems to be endless rows of other coffins.[49] Among the more significant scenes in *Gangs of New York*, this sequence powerfully contradicts everything Bill has just said about the Irish, while questioning the meaning of Irish participation in the Civil War. In this scene, Irish men do not volunteer for the Union army to prove their allegiance to the United States as they become citizens as Handlin argues. Rather, we see disoriented and starving immigrants bamboozled into fighting an incomprehensible war, used as cannon fodder by the desperate Union army. The film does not deny the historiographic argument that the Civil War Americanized numerous Irish men as they were granted citizenship for military service, but it challenges the meaning of the term "American" when Irish men are oblivious to the war's purpose and nativists dismiss that their enlistment transforms them into Americans. In this scene, the film provokes us to think beyond the conflict between nativists and ethnic immigrants in the Five Points district: it demands that we think about the broader issue of what it means to be an American.

In this regard, the film's narrative tension focuses upon Amsterdam's internal struggle to honor his father or remain loyal to Bill. As Amsterdam moves within Bill's inner circle, he comes "under the wing of the dragon," as he says, earning Bill's respect and even saving his life after an attempted assassination by an Irishman.[50] Bill admires Amsterdam's cleverness and ingenuity, overlooking his ethnic identity and accepting him into his group of "native" Americans, all the while becoming a father-figure to Amsterdam. But following the assassination attempt, Amsterdam runs away, bursting into tears, confused about his identity. Though his name connects Amsterdam with New York's Dutch ethnic past and his brogue reveals his more immediate Irish identity, nativists such as Bill accept him as one of them while people within the Irish community such as Walter "Monk" McGinn (Brendan Gleeson) question his allegiance. Monk once fought alongside Priest Vallon and his Dead Rabbits, and recognizes Amsterdam despite his best efforts to conceal his past. Amsterdam eventually attempts to kill "The Butcher" and resurrects the Dead Rabbits, emerging as a leader of the integrated Five Points community. Following a series of confrontations with Bill and his natives, he emerges as a viable representative of the multicultural Five Points neighborhood, attracting the support of Boss Tweed and threatening Bill's power in the process.[51]

*Gangs of New York* climaxes with a street fight between Bill's gang of "Natives" and Amsterdam's trans-ethnic, trans-racial gang, clearly a battle that will determine which one will control the future of the Five Points. However, just as the fight begins, cannon bombs from naval ships explode in the streets of the district, disrupting the gangs, who now find themselves battling Union soldiers. The troops and ships had actually arrived to put down the mob fomenting the draft riots that erupted days earlier, but they attacked the gangs along with the rioters while they tried to take control of the city. Up to this point in the film, *Gangs of New York* has told two narratives of civil war: one connected to the war between North and South, and one between nativists and American immigrants. At various moments, the two narratives converged, particularly the scene where Bill and his minions protest the *Emancipation Proclamation* with other New Yorkers, and another where an audience (that includes Bill and Amsterdam) throws tomatoes at the actor portraying Lincoln during a theatrical presentation of *Uncle Tom's Cabin*. The draft riots sequence, however, weaves the two civil war narratives for a sustained period in order to resolve the film's major themes about the American immigration experience.

In this sequence, *Gangs of New York* connects with historiographic arguments that see the New York City draft riots as a pivotal moment in Civil War and immigration history. The film describes the class tensions connected with the riots, particularly the issue concerning the ability for men with $300 to avoid the draft. As Amsterdam says, "for the poor, it might as well have been three million dollars."[52] When the draft riots erupt, the movie shows the mob attacking wealthy uptown Manhattanites and vandalizing their homes. However, the film also shows the racial dimension of the riots, revealing the palpable racism in New York City. As we hear a voice-over of a man reading the newswire describing the mob attacking a black orphanage, we watch the crowd attack African Americans, even lynching one man before they hang and burn him from a lamppost. In this regard, the film reflects Civil War historiography about resistance to Lincoln's draft policy as well as fighting a war to free black slaves.[53] It further connects to recent immigration scholarship that contends that the draft riots reveal the persistent racism among ethnic Americans as well as how they were still marginalized in American society despite their participation in the American Civil War.[54]

However, *Gangs of New York* advances its own historiographic argument about the ways the New York City draft riots changed the course of the city's history, and arguably American history more generally. As Union soldiers attack gang members, American history intersects with the city's history. During the melee Bill is mortally wounded by cannon shrapnel, and then stabbed by Amsterdam, stating, "I die a true American."[55] As he closes his eyes, so too does history close on this history of American nativism and ethnic tribalism. In the final scenes of the movie, Amsterdam notes that New York City truly became a city in the days following the draft riots. Political leaders such as Boss Tweed made concerted efforts to meet the needs of immigrants and ethnic Americans, and worked to integrate them into urban life. American nativists would undoubtedly remain, but the future belonged to Amsterdam and his integrated, multicultural community.

While *Gangs of New York* powerfully and viscerally presents this historiographic argument, this conclusion is debatable. In fact, the entire premise that the Five Points was an integrated, multicultural community challenges much of the historical scholarship about immigrant communities in mid-nineteenth-century American history. In their scholarship, historians such as David Roediger and Matthew Frye Jacobson describe more self-contained immigrant communities that generally were hostile to one another, and especially to African Americans.[56] While Roediger points out that Irish immigrants and African Americans lived in integrated communities early in the nineteenth-century urban North, by the mid-1840s (when *Gangs of New York* begins), the Irish became more race conscious, denigrating African Americans as they became protective of their whiteness.[57] In fact, the film does show examples of Irish racism towards blacks, particularly with Bill's minion McGloin (Gary Lewis), but we mostly see Irish acceptance of African Americans. They are shown either as members of local gangs or as inhabitants of the Five Points community. The latter is most powerfully illustrated in scenes where they coexist with ethnic Americans in the neighborhood's underground caves beating African drums before Priest Vallon's street fight with the nativists,

or performing African dances.[58] Perhaps this is representative of New York City—
but in the twentieth century. The film reflects the ethnic and racial diversity of
the city in the mid-nineteenth century, but minimizes the ethnic and racial conflict
among blacks and ethnic Americans. Otherwise, the draft riots of 1863 would not
have materialized as violent attacks against African Americans. There is a powerful
disconnect between the film's historical argument about multicultural New York
and the racial terrorism of the draft riots it portrays.

However, *Gangs of New York* is not ultimately concerned with representing the
historical accuracy of the racial landscape of New York City in the 1860s. As a
historical film about the Civil War it may be engaging with another historical epic
about the same period with similar cinematic ambitions in mind—namely D.W.
Griffith's *The Birth of a Nation*. In both films, the American Civil War provides the
narrative vehicle to tell stories about blood, kin, race, and nation. Amsterdam
Vallon speaks for both movies when he describes how New York City was "born
of blood and tribulation" in the Civil War era. Just as Griffith's *The Birth of a Nation*
focuses on families torn apart by war and civil strife, so too does Scorsese's *Gangs
of New York*, albeit manifesting in the streets of New York City instead of
American battlefields. And in both films Lincoln and race play prominent roles in
the respective films' narrative discourses.

In *The Birth of a Nation*, Lincoln's calling for 75,000 volunteers formally
provokes war between North and South and his assassination transforms the nature
of Reconstruction, necessitating the Ku Klux Klan to redeem his memory and the
nation. In *Gangs of New York*, Lincoln's *Emancipation Proclamation* and draft policy
divide New York City. Although Lincoln is not physically present in the film as
in *The Birth of a Nation*, he is represented on poster bills and by an actor during
the theatrical dramatization of *Uncle Tom's Cabin*.[59] These representations receive
the violent vitriol from those like Bill "The Butcher," who throws a knife at a
poster drawing of Lincoln during the *Emancipation Proclamation* parade; by those
who throw tomatoes at the actor playing Lincoln during the *Uncle Tom's Cabin*
play; and by those who set fire to a poster picturing Lincoln with Frederick
Douglass. In both films, racial terror against African Americans connects to their
broader narratives about the meaning of the American nation. Where *The Birth of
a Nation* maintains that racial violence and the triumph of white supremacy birthed
a new American nation, *Gangs of New York* contends that the racial terror and
urban violence connected to the draft riots ultimately led to the emergence of a
multicultural New York City.

In this regard, *The Birth of a Nation* and *Gangs of New York* want to be taken
seriously as history. Throughout Griffith's film, primary and secondary sources are
cited to validate the historical accuracy of particular scenes in the film. In his movie,
Griffith advances an historical interpretation about the Civil War and
Reconstruction. Though the film's particular narrative about the Stoneman and
Cameron families provides dramatic tension, its broader intention is to present
a cinematic history about the ways the Ku Klux Klan redeemed American

civilization from black misrule and racial integration. *Gangs of New York* is less ambitious historiographically, but nonetheless practices history as it tells the story of the conflict between nativists and immigrants in the Five Points. To validate its historical accuracy, the movie often shows still shots of contemporary newspapers or poster bills that display historical facts, either preceding or following a dramatization of those facts. Just as historians cite sources in footnotes to substantiate their arguments, Scorsese presents these still shots of newspapers, poster bills, and lithographic pictures to verify the film's historical claims. Perhaps the most dramatic use of this cinematic technique comes during the draft riot sequence and a lithographic representation of a mob lynching and burning an African American man precedes a reenactment of the same event in the movie.[60] Sometimes a movie is just a movie, a story on the screen to immerse us within its narrative, and escape reality for a few hours. However, a movie is more than simply a story, wanting us to engage our past and challenge us to think about the meaning of American history. *Gangs of New York* is such a movie. It takes us to a moment in our past where the United States stood at a historical crossroads, and shows us how the immigration experience says so much about what it means to be American.

When Oscar Handlin claimed that immigration history *is* American history in his iconic work *The Uprooted*, he simultaneously turned years of racist, nativist American views of immigrants and corresponding interpretations of American history on its head, and reordered the mythos of the American national identity. As discussed in previous chapters, the American frontier traditionally has been the source of the American mythos whereby the frontier absorbed Europeans beginning in the colonial period, and provided them with land so scarce in Europe, freeing them from class restrictions, and enabling them to become virtuous independent yeoman farmers, Jefferson's "chosen people of God." Where their brethren in Europe continued to face a life of class struggle because they were denied economic opportunity and freedom, the American frontier and its seemingly endless supply of available land emancipated the United States from the history of violent class conflict plaguing Europe. Handlin's immigration narrative reconfigured this mythos by turning all of the United States into a cultural frontier whereby its democratic institutions and limitless economic opportunities transformed European ethnic immigrants into virtuous American citizens. Previously, the dominant Anglo-Saxon American elite defined and shaped the course of American history. Handlin demanded that we understand the origins of American history and the American national identity from those subaltern peoples who lived at America's margins. Although Handlin's aphorism was an American cultural revolution of sorts, it consequently enabled Americans to do what they do best— escape their history. Gone is the history of American immigration as one of violence and institutional racism. Of course, immigrants endured significant challenges, even oppression according to Handlin and his more recent academic followers such as Thomas Sowell. But this history of oppression, no doubt sad and not inconsequential, ultimately receded as the United States embraced the contribution of immigrants and even some of their culture into the so-called American "melting pot," including national celebrations like St. Patrick's Day and incorporating ethnic foods such as pizza and tacos into our national diet. Ron Howard's *Far and Away* and the scholarship of academics like Handlin and Sowell point to the Irish as the historical exemplars who overcame initial ethnic persecution to achieve American success. If the Irish could surmount these challenges, why cannot other immigrants coming to America searching for freedom and opportunity follow them?

Recent immigration historiography and films like Martin Scorsese's *Gangs of New York* remind Americans that the Irish American experience was much more formidable and violent than the story as told by Handlin in *The Uprooted* and *Far and Away*. Moreover, it was not one whereby dominant Anglo-American society eventually embraced the Irish after years of struggle and discrimination, as much as a history whereby immigrants wrested control of their destiny, and American history in general, from Anglo-Saxon Americans intent upon keeping them at the margins of American society. In fact, Handlin described this version of Irish history years ago in his *Boston's Immigrants*. More recently, Mathew Frye Jacobson powerfully argues in his *Whiteness of a Different Color* that American immigration history, especially the Irish American experience, is a racial history and not simply one of "ethnicity," a term he actually rejects because it negates how European immigrants were racialized for most of their history, and have only recently been accepted as white Americans once World War II overturned years of racial discrimination. Likewise, Scorsese's *Gangs of New York* reminds us of this racialized history of American immigration, and similarly worries that white Americans will run away from it as they continue to reify the immigrant myth articulated by Handlin in his celebrated *The Uprooted* and (in the words of Jacobson) expressed in the Ellis Island version of history that so many Americans cherish. But is the Irish American narrative, whichever version one chooses to accept, the template for all immigrants coming to the United States? As Chapter 6 turns to the histories of Italian Americans, recent Europeans, and particularly Mexican Americans, we will see how academics and filmmakers approach American immigration and the American Dream, and the degree to which their narratives adhere to the Irish American experience.

# 6

# THE EUROPEAN AMERICAN AND MEXICAN AMERICAN IMMIGRATION EXPERIENCE

## The Problem of Narrative in American Social History

As Francis Ford Coppola's *The Godfather* begins, the audience hears a disembodied accented voice declare, "I believe in America." Although this appears to be a simple statement celebrating the possibilities of the American Dream, we shortly see this phrase connected to the political universe of the mafia and the Italian American community in post–World War II New York. While this declaration will become specific to the constituent story about Amerigo Bonasera (Salvatore Corsitto), an ambitious undertaker, and his relationship with Don Vito Corleone (Marlon Brando), it also defines the movie's broader narrative discourse about the complexities and limitations of the American immigrant experience. In this opening sequence, Bonasera announces his belief in America while turning to the world of organized crime. The undertaker has come to Don Vito's home "on the day of [the don's] daughter's wedding," seeking the don's services to avenge his daughter. Bonasera describes how she was assaulted by "American boys" who "tried to take advantage of her," and was beaten severely for resisting their sexual advances. While the undertaker trumpets how "America has made my fortune," it is clear that he has lost faith in its institutions. He initially sought justice through the American legal system, only to be astonished that the perpetrators received a "suspended sentence." Following the trial, Bonasera was further humiliated when the boys "laughed in my face." Enraged and dishonored, he told his wife that "for justice I will go to Don Corleone." Bonasera's proud declaration actually reveals the major theme about the relationship between ethnic identity and the American Dream that drives the narrative tension in *The Godfather*. Bonasera had hoped to distance himself from the Italian culture and traditions reflected in Don Vito's ethnic community, pursuing his American Dream by disconnecting from this world because he "did not want to get into trouble," a decision Don Vito clearly understands. But now he has returned to the protective social networks of the

Italian American community and the ethical system administered by the don, realizing that these ethnic institutions and its values ultimately provide the form of "justice" that will restore his family honor.[1] As we quickly learn, Bonasera's ethical and cultural dilemma will also trouble Don Vito's youngest son Michael (Al Pacino) who, like Bonasera, has distanced himself from his father's ethnic traditions, only to eventually accept the mafia's moral philosophy in order to avenge the don's attempted murder.

From the beginning of *The Godfather*, we are confronted with the incredible pressure American immigrants and their children historically faced while negotiating Old World traditions and social ties as they aspired to become American in their new homeland. Yet, this film also describes the morally ambiguous consequences of embracing American values when they try to reject or deny their ethnic communities and the deep history tied to its institutions and values. Although the opening scene of *The Godfather* immediately introduces us to Don Vito Corleone and the magnitude of the respect and power he commands within his ethnic universe, the film eventually becomes the story about his youngest son, Michael. As the only son with an anglicized name, Michael also struggles to live in the hyphenated "Italian-American" world. At the beginning of the film, Michael has clearly attempted to amputate himself from his family and his Italian heritage, going so far as to attend an Ivy League college, serve in the Marines during World War II (he actually arrives at his sister's wedding in his military uniform to distinguish himself from his family), and date Kay Adams (Diane Keaton), a white woman completely ignorant of the customs and traditions of his Italian American community. After describing his father's violent tactics to help the singer Johnny Fontane (Al Martino), and the don's godson, become a celebrity, Michael says, "That's my family Kay . . . That's not me." Nevertheless, Michael will later embrace his family, and by extension his ethnic heritage, eventually succeeding his father to become the don of the Corleone crime organization. In giving his son the anglicized name, Vito initiated Michael's Americanization process, and hoped that Michael would avoid the "family business." In a critical scene that is ostensibly about Michael's anticipated assassination, the narrative tone shifts as Vito describes his aspirations for his son. He tells Michael that he "makes no excuses" for the life he has led, and how he had expected his older son Santino (Sonny) to become involved in the family business. But he had hoped Michael would avoid his family's criminal connections, knowing how its lethal tentacles would limit Michael's ambitions. He wanted Michael to have a "legitimate" American Dream: to be "Governor Corleone, Senator Corleone . . . the person holding the strings."[2]

Initially, Michael adhered to his father's plans, even severing his ties with the family's nuclear ethnic world when he joined the Marines following the Japanese attack on Pearl Harbor, which his brother Sonny (James Caan), recognizes. In fact, Sonny is enraged by Michael's enlistment as it declares to the entire Corleone clan that his brother's ultimate allegiance lies with the American nation—and not his family. In an elliptical scene at the end of the second *Godfather* film that is a coda to this movie and prologue to the first *Godfather*, Sonny denigrates people who would fight for a cause unrelated to their family (including extended ethnic relations). As he says, "Your country ain't your blood."[3] As this scene and the one of the wedding in the first *Godfather* film reveal, Michael's original American Dream was to escape this ethnic past, embracing an American identity defined by his military service and a relationship with a white woman who was totally removed from the world of his family. Eventually, however, it becomes Michael's ambition, or perhaps conceit, that he can redeem his family's history by transforming its criminal organization into a legitimate American business. This is his renewed American Dream, and one that significantly has roots in a Jeffersonian view of history.[4] Much as Thomas Jefferson envisioned the redemptive possibilities of the Louisiana Purchase for Americans living east of the Mississippi in the early nineteenth century, Michael plans to move the family's business operations from New York to Nevada, where the Corleone family can begin a new history free from its Old World, criminal past. In the West, the family will continue to be engaged in the "vice industry," although now in an America where it can practice its business legally, becoming the vehicle to achieve a legitimate American Dream for the Corleones.

Throughout the three *Godfather* movies, Michael struggles with living in the hyphenated world inhabited by American immigrants and their children, negotiating his identity, loyalty, and aspirations as he comes to terms with his ethnic heritage while pursuing his ambitions. In this regard, the *Godfather* films reflect a few of the themes about the American immigrant experience that animates academic scholarship: the conflicted life immigrants and their children confront while living between cultures; and the ways choosing to become American also demonstrates how a person defines "history." Whether the films are about European Americans or Mexican Americans, these movies collectively reveal how negotiating one's ethnic or racial heritage corresponds with the ways they view the past, and whether they can escape it as they become "American." In this way, their histories parallel that of the Irish as described in Chapter 5. However, these films more approximate the cultural challenges and racialized history reflected in Martin Scorsese's *Gangs of New York* than Ron Howard's more optimistic and mythic *Far and Away*.

Earlier chapters have described the various ways cinematic histories and historical scholarship have sometimes converged on historiographic issues in the past, but how they have diverged more recently, particularly where historical questions focus upon the Civil War, Reconstruction, race, and slavery. As Chapter 5 demonstrated, however, films about the immigration experience closely reflect current debates within immigration historiography, a factor we can attribute to the driving force of the American Dream mythos, and the powerful ways it continues to frame the American immigration narrative. Even as recent historical scholarship has illuminated the centrality of race, ethnicity, and the history of "whiteness" in the history of American immigration, films that were made in the 1970s such as the first two *Godfather* movies can be re-examined in light of this newer scholarship. After all, the history of Americanization has always been interconnected with issues of race and citizenship, especially in the ways the process of becoming American is entangled with becoming "white."[5] Additionally, immigration movies and historical scholarship reflect the ways social history has matured since the 1970s, and maintains narrative power despite the fulmination of its critics.

As social history superseded more traditional methodological approaches to historical scholarship (such as that which defined political and intellectual history) in the 1980s, it has been criticized, particularly by American conservatives out-side the historical profession, for privileging, even fetishizing the "ordinary" or "everyday" life of people in the past. In American historiography, social history produced a profound revision of the American national narrative as it sought to include previously marginal, illiterate, and minority peoples. The political controversy over the National History Standards curricula in the 1990s was the most public manifestation of this debate. Social history announced that mar ginalized Americans had a history, possessing a narrative connected to our collective national story, and have had the agency to shape its historical trajectory throughout our past. Perhaps because Oscar Handlin's *The Uprooted* reinforced, even reified, the open nature of American society and the virtue of its democratic institutions, it was a social history that many American could embrace. The history of American minorities and women challenges Handlin's version of American history as it reveals how these opportunities and institutions was closed to minority peoples until the recent era (and some would maintain that it remains closed). Critics lament that this social history of American minorities and women has fractured the teaching of American history, creating a chasm between the American historical profession and the American public in the process.[6] However, historical films actually belie this claim, illustrating how the American public connects with stories about ordinary people who have faced extraordinary historical events.

Whether they watch movies like *Gone with the Wind* or *Gangs of New York*, the American people have found a way to engage with nondescript, historically fictional protagonists who actively influence the course of history. In this regard, historical movies actually advance the political project of social history: to demonstrate how common folk are agents of historical change. For scholars of queer, feminist, and racial minority histories, this has been an empowering academic movement. One of the animating philosophies of history and theoretical purposes for studying it has been the idea that we should recover the past in order to address the politics of the present, and to provide critical knowledge in order to change the future.[7] Where this vision of historical scholarship has emboldened the social histories of American women, gays, and minorities, leading to important social and cultural achievements, the gains of immigration historiography have been more problematic by comparison, even though it has some academic connections with these historiographies. Much of the academic scholarship about the European American experience describes a process that has largely reached its termination, in terms of European immigrants "becoming American." As much as immigration historiography addresses provocative issues about Americanization, the academic trajectory of this history inevitably ends with a narrative closure, even historical catharsis, about the moment when those immigrants shed their old world ties and embrace American values (i.e. the story of the Irish, Italians, Poles, etc., who were once ethnic immigrants in the past, but whose descendants are now "mainstream" Americans). However, we should not be so quick to accept this historiographic interpretation. Even though this academic argument attempts to provide closure and catharsis, films such as *My Big Fat Greek Wedding* suggest how the complexities that historically defined the European American immigration experience persists in contemporary America.

Moreover, the immigration historiography about racial and ethnic minorities such as Mexican Americans reveals how their historical experience also reflects recent immigration policies, rendering narrative closure and historical catharsis unclear. As we will see, some monographs such as George Sanchez's *Becoming Mexican American* brilliantly connect the immigrant narratives of Mexican Americans with the European American experience, albeit within the context of historic Anglo-Mexican relations and racial prejudice. While accounting for the particular historical relationship between the United States and Mexico (including the contiguous border that remains politically charged), Sanchez's book nonetheless suggests the kind of closure and catharsis associated with the European immigration historiography as he concludes his historical narrative in post-war America when Mexican Americans made political efforts to identify with their home in the United States. Similar to histories about European Americans in cities like Chicago during the early twentieth century, Sanchez describes the complex historical challenges facing Mexican immigrants, their children, and their ethnic community in Los Angeles during the same period. Sanchez's book ultimately celebrates their triumph to establish a hybridized culture in their new homeland as they become citizens of the United States, presenting a narrative that affirms the mythos of the American Dream.[8]

In contrast, monographs such as Douglas Monroy's *Rebirth* deny the reader this kind of narrative closure. In fact, Monroy offers two possible historical endings to his story of Mexicans in Los Angeles from the Great Migration to the Great Depression from which his readers can choose.[9] While one may be confused by, and even frustrated with the way Monroy presents different "conclusions" to his historical narrative, perhaps the larger purpose is for the reader to choose the ending he or she desires. In this regard, Monroy's book offers an empowering history that forces the reader to confront different possible historical outcomes of the Mexican American immigration experience based upon the political choices we presently make as Americans. *Rebirth* arguably challenges us to understand and empathize with the history of Mexican Americans in Los Angeles over the course of the twentieth century to connect their past to our current political climate. Monroy's text immerses us in a particular immigrant experience in order for Americans to consider contemporary issues regarding immigration policy, and potentially affect the course of future national politics and history. *Rebirth* may be an unsatisfying narrative, but it nevertheless provokes us to engage with our past so that we can shape our national future, a political philosophy that actually recalls the fundamental mission of social history.

## *The Godfather* and Italian American Experience: Ethnicity, Whiteness and the American Dream

Although Irish people were the primary European immigrants during the first main wave of migration to the United States in the mid-nineteenth century, the next major influx of immigrants came from much more diverse European backgrounds, with many coming from Italy and Eastern Europe. Between 1880 and 1924, this second wave of European immigration coincided with rapid American industrialization, attracting many immigrants hoping to work in factories as a way to secure the social and financial stability that eluded them in their home countries. Yet, their American dreams were circumscribed by the nativism that continued to prevail in the United States. While Scorsese's *Gangs of New York* suggests that nativism declined in the Civil War era, it actually remained a powerful movement. This next wave of European immigrants faced similar prejudices the Irish experienced earlier, but now they had to contend with new cultural forces that challenged their ability to integrate into American society.

The advent of Social Darwinism and scientific racism in the late nineteenth century together became an ideological weapon for nativists to justify discrimination, who maintained that racial inferiority of these recent European immigrants made them "unfit" for American citizenship. As Matthew Frye Jacobson notes, whiteness remained an unstable racial category in late-nineteenth- and early-twentieth-century America. Although the Naturalization Act 1790 stipulated that "white persons" living in the United States for five years could become naturalized Americans and could apply for citizenship, nativists argued that undesirable European immigrants were in fact not "white."[10] Marginalized from American society, these European immigrants developed social institutions within their ethnic communities to support one another in their new homeland, and from the pernicious forces of American racism. However, these institutions reinforced ties to the old country and traditional customs, including language. In the end, historical events such as the Johnson-Reed Act 1924 (which set quotas and restrictions for immigration), the Great Depression, World War II, and the civil rights movement transformed the history of European immigration. As the American racial landscape became a bipolar world divided by black and white in the maelstrom of the civil rights movement, European immigrants and their descendants emerged as white Americans.[11]

Yet, the transformation of European ethnics into white Americans remained contested throughout this period, especially as whiteness and Americanization required one to disconnect from their ethnic past and the communities that reinforced traditional customs. Often this historical dynamic played out between parents and their children, where the latter would sever their ethnic ties in order to become American and pursue the American Dream. Francis Ford Coppola's *Godfather* probes this generational struggle in powerful ways, revealing the complicated history of Italian immigration and the process of becoming American. Coppola's *Godfather* films follow the trajectory of the European immigration experience over the course of the twentieth century, telling the narrative of Michael Corleone and his pursuit of the American Dream. Although the films initially follow the rise of his father Vito Corleone from an orphaned Italian immigrant to the most powerful man in the mafia underworld, they eventually focus upon Michael's struggles to live within the hyphenated world of "Italian-American." As we see from the early scenes of the first *Godfather* film, Michael is ambivalent about his Italian heritage. While he comes to his sister's wedding and is willing to be in the family's wedding photograph, he arrives wearing his Marine uniform with his white girlfriend Kay Adams, symbols that clearly affirm his Americanization. At the wedding, he describes his father's business to the naive Kay, explaining that Don Vito once threatened to have a man killed in order to help his godson. As he finishes relating the story to the stunned Kay, Michael says, "That's my family Kay, that's not me."[12] As we will see, the first *Godfather* film is about Michael moving away from his avowed identity as an American towards accepting himself as a hyphenated "Italian-American." This psychological and cultural journey will require him to reject his initial American Dream that would have him disconnect from his ethnic past, and craft a new one that will enable him to Americanize the Corleone family by connecting its ethnic history to the broader American experience.

The story of Americanization in the *Godfather* films, however, is a tragic one, as it forces people to make choices between competing sets of loyalties and worldviews. As such, the process of becoming American is not easy, often exacting a powerful price, and the movie presents life in the hyphenated world as confusing and disorienting. Perhaps this explains why Michael initially attempts to completely assimilate into American society, and why Vito Corleone completely rejects it, remaining an Italian in America. As either Italian or American, one can see the world and their place within it with moral clarity. For those who try to live in the in-between world of the hyphen, such clarity is elusive, and one can find himself ethically compromised trying to choose between conflicting cultural systems. Amerigo Bonasera's meeting with Don Vito at the beginning of the film reflects this dilemma. As described earlier in this chapter, Bonasera tells the don that he initially pursued justice for his daughter's attempted rape through the American judicial system. When that failed him, he decided to come to Don Corleone with the request that the don punish the attempted rapists. However, rather than using traditional ethnic customs of honor, respect, and obligation to earn the don's favor, he attempts to pay him with cash.[13] Not only does Bonasera dismiss the traditions of the Italian community with this gesture, but also he insults the don and the moral universe within which he operates. In this exchange between Bonasera and Don Corleone, we see the competing cultural systems of the Italian community and American capitalism. As Bonasera tells Don Vito, American capitalism "has made my fortune."[14] Yet, it becomes evident that capitalism has corrupted him in the eyes of Don Vito.

Beyond material wealth, the don sees American capitalism as a pernicious cultural system that devalues and dehumanizes social relationships, relationships that men like him believe are vital to sustain and protect the Italian American community. The cash nexus is an impersonal system of exchange, allowing one to walk away from the transaction once it is completed without any further connection or obligation. This is likely what Bonasera wants when he offers to pay the don for his favor in cash. By denominating the don's services with a cash value, the transaction will be complete once he provides it, enabling him to maintain ethical distance from the likely criminal act he wants the don to perform. Although Bonasera has bought into the American system, the don refuses to negotiate on these terms. For Don Vito, the currency of exchange for favors is denominated in honor, respect, and obligation, a currency that will forever bond Bonasera to the don until the don calls upon him for a favor of his own. In other words, Bonasera will not be able to walk away from the act the don will have done to the men who beat his daughter like the cash nexus would allow him, keeping him obliged to Don Vito and personally connected to the don's criminal action. Once he negotiates this transaction on the don's terms, he is pulled back into the Italian American community which he thought he escaped while pursuing the American Dream.

With the narratives of Vito and Michael Corleone, the *Godfather* films juxtapose the differences between being an Italian in America and becoming Italian American. The first two *Godfather* films illustrate how Vito is an Italian living in America, initially growing up in New York City's Italian community and then as the most powerful mafia leader in the United States. Born Vito Andolini, Vito immigrated to America as a young boy to escape the wrath of Don Ciccio, a Sicilian mafioso who already killed his father, brother, and mother. As Vito arrives at Ellis Island, we watch him and other immigrants stare with awe at the Statue of Liberty as their ship passes by this iconic symbol that welcomed scores of immigrants coming to America seeking opportunities for a better life.[15] In these opening scenes of the second *Godfather* film, the movie clearly connects Vito's immigration narrative with the broader American immigration experience, where his new homeland will offer better prospects and possibilities than he otherwise would have had in the old country.

Upon arriving at Ellis Island, Vito must endure the bureaucratic immigration process like his fellow migrants, waiting in long lines in order to officially enter the country. As we observe young Vito endure this process alone, we see his vulnerability, first when his name is changed by the immigration officer, who renames him Vito Corleone (giving him the last name associated from the Sicilian city from where he came originally), then when he is quarantined by the doctor for having smallpox, and finally when he is placed in a cell by himself. Standing in this sterile room with only his small suitcase, Vito stares through the window at the Statue of Liberty, singing a Sicilian folk song.[16] As this scene fades, we can only sympathize with this young boy who must make a life in America without his family, braving the new world alone and vulnerable. As we later learn, though, Vito has grown up in New York City's Italian American community, taken in by the Abbandando family. We next see an adult Vito Corleone (Robert De Niro), now married and with his first son Santino (Sonny), and working for Mr. Abbandando at his grocery store. In the De Niro sequence, we also see the contours of the Italian American community in which he lives. Here, people continue to speak Italian and identify as much by their region of origin (that is Sicilian, Calabresi, Napolese, etc.) as much as Italy itself. We are clearly observing Italians living in America rather than Italians becoming American.

In fact, the theater scene in this sequence first introduces viewers to the crime boss Don Fanucci (Gaston Moschin), a man who illustrates the divide between those Italians who retain their cultural connections to the old country, and those like him who have begun to acculturate to American society and values. Vito's friend Genco Abbandando (Frank Sivero) has invited him to the theater to see his fiancée perform. Significantly, the majority of the dialogue in the De Niro sequence is spoken in Italian. As Genco and Vito sit in the audience, Genco raves about his fiancée's beauty and talent. During the performance, however, Don Fanucci, wearing his characteristic white suit and hat, stands to leave. Genco shouts at Fanucci to sit, only to cower in apology once he recognizes the don. As Fanucci walks out of the performance, Vito wants to know more about the don, sensing his power and marveling at his ability to provoke fear in men like Genco. Genco tells him that Fanucci is with the "Black Hand" crime organization and extorts a percentage of the profits from Italian American businesses.[17] Although brief, this conversation is nonetheless significant as it informs viewers about Vito's values, ones that will later shape him as he rises through the mafia criminal underworld. First, this dialogue reveals Vito's astonishment that Fanucci would exploit Italian American businesses for personal profit, suggesting that he finds capitalizing upon the vulnerabilities of fellow Italians immoral and criminal. Second, it illustrates how Vito values his family, telling Genco how important his wife and family are to him and wants Genco to be happy with his fiancée as well. In fact, Vito's values about family and community are interconnected, as he sees the Italian American community as an extended family, in all probability because it embraced and supported him when he arrived to America alone.

Vito's values stand in marked contrast to Don Fanucci's. Like Bonasera, America has made Fanucci's fortune, and he is driven by American capitalism as much as the mafia traditions that enable him to rule over the Italian American community. Fanucci has become Italian American where everyone else around him in his ethnic community retains cultural ties to the old country. Indeed, this is likely why he leaves the theater performance. On stage, Italian actors dramatize a play about a man who immigrated to America and has started a family, but now awaits letters from his mother with longing. Once he finally receives a letter, he learns that his mother has died. The actor then begins singing "Pensa Mama" (Thinking about Mother) while holding a gun to his head. Behind him the scenery shows the Statue of Liberty and New York City on one side, Italy on the other, and the Atlantic Ocean dividing the two places.[18] This performance likely speaks to many in the audience anguishing about their families back in Italy whom they have left behind while they forged a new life in America. For Fanucci, however, this is rubbish. He is not thinking about the mother country; he could not care less now that he has become prosperous in New York. As his garish white suit illustrates, he is a self-made man in America, standing apart from those around him who retain strong ties to the Old World. In this regard, the De Niro sequences in the second *Godfather* film connect to recent immigration historiography. As Liz Cohen and Douglas Monroy have illustrated, immigrant communities in places such as Chicago and Los Angeles retained their native cultures, sometimes using mass media such as radio and the victrola to perpetuate traditional customs.[19] As long as immigrants continued to arrive from Europe and Mexico, they revitalized ethnic culture in urban communities during the early twentieth century. Only when the flow of immigration ceased as a result of the Johnson-Reed Act (1924) and the Great Depression did this continual rebirth of ethnic culture whither.

Vito's life is changed forever when Fanucci comes to Abbandando's grocery store to ask Genco's father to employ Fanucci's recently immigrated nephew. Knowing he cannot refuse Fanucci, Mr. Abbandando employs his nephew, but must release Vito because he cannot afford to keep them both. Although this is financially devastating for Vito, he nonetheless tells Mr. Abbandando that he has appreciated everything he has done to help him since he arrived to America, and will always remember this favor.[20] Here, we see an example early in Vito's life wherein a favor becomes a profound emotional gesture that ties people to each other in an economic web of honor, respect, obligation, appreciation. Vito feels indebted to Mr. Abbandando for taking him in and providing him with a job, a debt that will not be repaid until Vito returns the favor. For Vito, the moral economy of favors is grounded in a pre-modern worldview that values human relationships, protecting people and communities from the indifference and exploitation of modern industrial capitalism. At this point, the film begins to draw comparisons between Vito and Fanucci to illustrate the complicated ways immigrants adapted to their new life in America. Driven by the profit motive, Fanucci extorts from his fellow Italians and exploits their vulnerability, disregarding the consequences this will have upon people in the community as he pursues his American Dream. Although American capitalism has made him wealthy and powerful, it has corrupted him as well. No ethical system binds him to the Italian community he lords over, and his power rests only upon his ability to instill fear.

As Vito becomes entangled in the criminal underworld, he begins to see Fanucci's tenuous hold on power. Shortly after he leaves Abbandando's grocery store, Vito joins with Peter Clemenza and Sal Tessio to form a criminal organization selling stolen merchandise. When Fanucci demands a substantial cut from their profits, Clemenza and Tessio intend to concede. Vito, however, says he will give Fanucci only half of what he demands when he meets him. Although the two are wary about Vito's plan, they go along with it. Vito then tells them to remember that he has done them a favor, again reminding viewers how Vito values this system of economic exchange. As Vito performs more favors, he gradually accumulates power over people who are indebted to him. Instead of cash, Vito accumulates favors that become a source of human capital that further empowers him the more he accumulates. By not "cashing in" on the favors others owe him, he continues to maintain power over those who remain indebted and obliged to his services. In this exchange between Vito, Clemenza, and Tessio we see the ways Vito amasses personal debts that will enable him to rise to power, initially over his business partners, and eventually the entire criminal underworld. When Clemenza and Tessio ask Vito how he plans to get Fanucci to take less, Vito says in English, "I'll make him an offer he won't refuse."[21]

Significantly, this is the first time we hear Vito speak English, signifying that the cold and violent world of business is conducted in the language of America, as if to avoid corrupting the mother tongue. At their meeting, Fanucci is initially outraged with the reduced payment, but then admits his admiration for Vito's moxie. Before Fanucci leaves, he says that he sees a promising future for Vito with his organization. Vito, however, already has plans for himself. During a religious ceremony celebrated in the streets, Vito assassinates Don Fanucci and replaces him as the leading mafia boss in the Italian American community.[22] Where Fanucci was driven by the capitalist imperative, Don Vito now develops a political structure based on a traditional Sicilian system of favors and obligations to extend his power and legitimacy throughout the Italian American community. Don Fanucci embraced America and its corrupt path to prosperity, to his eventual demise. Don Vito, in contrast, remains firmly tied to his Italian traditions and its values of honor, respect, and family, values that enable him to become one of the heads of the five mafia families who control the American criminal underworld.

In fact, the specter of American capitalism and its system of cash exchange are central issues in the first *Godfather* film as well, as Don Corleone must choose whether or not to participate in the embryonic drug trade. Virgil "The Turk" Sollozzo (Al Lettieri) meets with the Corleone family offering to include the don in the local trade, hoping their business relationship will provide the needed political connections that the don has cultivated to protect Sollozzo's drug trafficking. While this choice could lead to further material wealth for the Corleone family, it would require the don to compromise his ethical system and likely result in the loss of his influential political relationships. As Don Vito points out, the politicians and judges with whom he works consider gambling, prostitution and his other criminal activities as petty vices. Drugs, however, are a much more serious criminal enterprise that neither he nor his political and legal connections want a part of. Don Vito's decision leads to his attempted assassination and a bloody war between his family and those who support Sollozzo. Although, the don eventually recuperates, he is too physically weak to assume his once powerful position. His oldest son Sonny initially takes over as head of the Corleone family, but his rash temper leads to imprudent decisions as he "goes to the mattresses" to avenge his father's attempted assassination. Eventually Michael assumes control of the family business (discussed in more detail below) becoming don of the Corleone family. Michael appoints his father as conciliari, turning to him as advisor and mentor.

Despite his ethnic ties Vito Corleone nonetheless has an American Dream. As noted earlier, he did not want his youngest son to be part of the family business. Vito maintains no regrets for the life he has lived, despite his connections to the criminal underworld; but he had hoped Michael might become a legitimate political leader as a governor or senator. As Vito's only son with an anglicized name, educated at an Ivy League college, and distinguishing himself as a Marine in World War II, Michael appeared destined to fulfill his father's dream. But as Michael pursues his American Dream, he alienates himself from his family. As mentioned earlier in this chapter, this process begins with his enlistment in the Marines following the Japanese attack on Pearl Harbor, angering his brother Sonny. Sonny sees his enlistment as a betrayal to the family, stating that only "saps" fight for something other than their family.[23] When Michael responds "That's Pop talking," we see the divide between him and his family.

Sitting at the table with his other brothers Fredo Corleone (John Cazale) and Tom Hagen (Sonny's friend whom the don adopted when he was orphaned) and sister Connie Corleone (Talia Shire) as they prepare their father's surprise birthday party, we even see the distance between Michael and his siblings. He sits alone across the table from them, dressed fashionably in a bright sport coat and open collar while his brothers wear more conservative suits with ties, save Fredo, who dresses in a similar style as Michael but whose clothes are much darker colors.[24] As Sonny seethes because he believes Michael has "broken Pop's heart" and "ruined Pop's birthday," Tom (Robert Duvall) sternly asks him why did he not consult him and their father before he enlisted. Tom points out that Vito worked hard for Michael's deferment, telling him that "Your father and I have talked about plans for your future." Visibly angry, Michael responds, "You have discussed plans for my future?"[25] Michael is clearly agitated that Tom and his father intend to control him, stripping whatever agency he may have to determine his future. When the children hear Vito enter into the house, all of them rush to the living room to surprise him save Michael, who remains at the table with his hand against his face in a gesture intended to mentally separate himself from the rest of his family. As this scene fades, the camera and lighting stay with Michael while darkness shrouds his family in the other room, accentuating how he is going to face his American future alone.[26]

Following the end of the war, Michael appears to have every intention to continue down the path of Americanization. As he courts Kay, he no doubt believes he has become American, perhaps even white, living independently in New York City, away from the Corleone family compound in Long Island. Once he learns about his father's assassination attempt, however, he slowly finds himself returning to his family and their Italian customs. In fact, this process begins almost as soon as Michael reads about his father's attempted murder and after he immediately calls his brother Sonny from a nearby telephone booth, closing the booth doors on Kay while he talks to his brother. Considering how open he was with Kay about the nefarious side of his father's business earlier at his sister's wedding, and telling her that he wants nothing to do with his family, this gesture to talk to Sonny privately begins the process of embracing his Italian heritage and turning away from Kay and the white American world she embodies. This process accelerates at the hospital when Michael suspects another attack against his father after he discovers that Vito has been left alone and vulnerable in his hospital room. After moving his father into a more secure room, he goes outside with Enzo, a former Italian soldier who has come to pay respects to Don Vito, who used his political connections to help Enzo avoid deportation and marry his Italian American girlfriend. Both Michael and Enzo stand outside and pretend they are mafia bodyguards as the would-be assassins drive by. Shortly thereafter the police arrive to arrest Michael and Enzo. After an officer tells Captain McCluskey (Sterling Hayden) that they are "clean" and even notes that Michael is a war hero, the flustered captain hits Michael, breaking his jaw. Whatever illusions Michael had about being white and American are shattered, just like his jaw, as the police— and by extension the American state—see him as another "guinea whop," in the words of Captain McCluskey.[27]

Michael's ambition to become part of the white American racial landscape connects with recent immigration historiography. Scholars such as Liz Cohen and Matthew Frye Jacobson note that a constellation of historical events factored into the ways European immigrants and their children transitioned from ethnic Americans (although Jacobson resists using the term ethnic as he sees the history of immigration as racial rather than cultural) into white Americans. Beginning with the Johnson–Reed Act 1924, the tide of European immigration abated when strict quotas limited the number of people entering the United States. Without the persistent influx of immigrants to refresh cultural ties to the old country, ethnic Americans built social institutions to help them adapt to life in the United States. The receding immigration of Europeans came to a halt with the Great Depression as jobs that once attracted laborers practically ceased to exist. Furthermore, the

Depression devastated ethnic institutions such as banks, grocery stores, mutual aid societies and to some degree parochial schools, all of which had sustained cultural and social ties within ethnic communities.[28]

The absence of these cultural institutions prompted ethnic Americans to turn to New Deal programs and labor organizations such as the CIO (Congress of Industrial Organizations) for survival, gradually bringing them into the New Deal coalition as they participated in the democratic political process as American citizens. When World War II broke out, ethnic Americans, particularly Italian and German Americans enlisted or were drafted, declaring their allegiance to the United States and fighting for American ideals, much like Michael Corleone in the *Godfather* films. Once they returned, veterans took advantage of government programs that enabled them to pursue a college degree or buy a home, programs that took many of them out of their ethnic neighborhoods to suburbs where they became immersed into the world of white America. The transformation of ethnic Europeans into white Americans accelerated with the advent of the civil rights movement following World War II as the racial landscape was defined in terms of black and white. Finally, the election of John F. Kennedy demonstrated that a considerable number of white Protestants had come to accept ethnic Irish Catholics as white Americans, closing the contentious history of the Irish American experience. Although we will see that the historical events between the Johnson-Reed Act 1924 and Kennedy's election did not completely end the history of ethnic America, collectively they did accelerate the process of Americanization for European immigrants and their descendants.[29]

Michael's rise in the mafia underworld begins in the scenes following his encounter with Captain McCluskey as he plots with his brothers Sonny and Tom to protect their father and avenge his assassination attempt. With Don Vito in hospital, Sonny has taken over the reins of the family business and wants to wage war against those responsible for his attempted murder, namely the Tatalia family and the drug trafficker Sollozzo. While Sonny believes fighting the Tatalias and killing Sollozzo will protect Don Vito, Tom worries that Sonny's "all out war" will turn the other underworld families against the Corleones in order to preserve the peace. Tom says that Sonny is taking the attack against his father personally and ignores the implications that escalating violence will have on the family business. As the brothers heatedly argue in their father's study, the camera slowly turns to Michael, who sits calmly in a chair in the corner of the room. With the lighting shadowing Michael's face to signify his descent into the morally ambiguous world of the mafia, he rationally argues that as long as Sollozzo remains alive, their father's life remains in jeopardy. Someone must kill Sollozzo and his bodyguard Captain McCluskey before they make another attempt on the don's life.

Sonny and Tom look at their younger brother "who did not want to get mixed up in the family business" with astonishment. Sonny jokingly tells Tom that Michael takes their father's attack personally, pointing out that he wants to kill Captain McCluskey for breaking his jaw. Michael retorts that McCluskey is a corrupt cop mixed up in the drug business, and reminds Tom and Sonny that they have newspaper reporters on the family payroll. They could use these contacts to plant stories about McCluskey's corrupt relationship with Sollozzo, suggesting that his death was the likely outcome for his involvement in the criminal underworld. Since Sollozzo wants to arrange a meeting with the Corleone family to negotiate a truce, Michael offers himself as the family's ambassador since everyone believes that he is removed from the Corleone's mafia ties and will likely negotiate peacefully. His intention to go along with this plan at this arranged meeting is a ruse, as he plans to kill both Sollozzo and McCluskey. However, he also recognizes that he will have to live in exile to avoid retaliation, returning at a later time when this mafia war is over. Everyone in the room (Sonny, Tom, and Don Vito's closest advisors Peter Clemenza and Sal Tessio) stare at Michael with awe as they recognize his brilliance. Tom agrees that the plan might work and will start contacting reporters, while Clemenza talks about ways to plant a gun at the restaurant where Michael will meet Sollozzo and McCluskey. Sonny again teases his brother about getting involved in the family business, jesting how Michael will "get blood on your Ivy League suit."[30]

During this meeting in the don's study and the following restaurant scene, we watch Michael's transformation from an Americanized Italian to an Italian American. As already noted, Michael's war service and relationship with Kay at the beginning of the film illustrate how Michael saw himself as an American who happened to have an Italian heritage. As he includes himself in the plot to eliminate Sollozzo and McCluskey, Michael embraces his family, the mafia, and the Italian traditions that define both of these institutions. Yet, he does not wholly reject himself as an American. In fact, he considers his Americanization a cultural and social asset that enables him to see the best interests of the family and its business. His brother Sonny is so immersed in mafia customs that he sees only a war among the families in the criminal underworld as the resolution. While Tom counsels Sonny about the foolishness of "going to the mattresses," in terms of the human and financial costs to the family business, he does not see another way out other than a negotiated truce. As Sonny notes, Michael draws upon his Ivy League education to concoct an ingenious plan to which his brothers and father's advisors marvel. Where Sonny is governed by stereotypical ethnic passions, reason and objectivity, an epistemology connected with modernity and the Enlightenment define Michael and likely the result of his education. During his meeting with Sollozzo and McCluskey, we witness Michael's internal conflict between his American and Italian loyalties. As Sollozzo tries to talk to Michael in Italian to separate Italian business from the American world the police captain embodies, Michael stumbles while trying to speak Italian, demonstrating how removed he has become from his ethnic heritage. In order to negotiate with Sollozzo he must speak English because he is so unfamiliar with his Italian culture, to his frustration. However, his once American ambition to amputate himself from his family and its Italian customs vanishes once he assassinates Sollozzo and McCluskey. Although a war hero who clearly knows how to use a gun, Michael nonetheless fumbles as he tries to kill both men, illustrating how conflicted and confused he is about his identity.[31]

Once he follows through with their murder, he completely aligns himself with the criminal underworld that historically defined his family. As an exile in Italy he immerses himself with his Sicilian past and its customs. Speaking Italian fluently and then marrying an Italian woman, Appollonia Vitelli (Simonetta Stefanelli), Michael has every intention to embrace his Italian heritage. Yet, he does not wholly become Italian. He is clever enough to know when to draw upon his American background when it advances his personal and business interests. In Italy we watch Michael comfortably move within the Sicilian community. However, when he wants to win the approval of the father of Apollonia, Michael has his bodyguard Fabrizio translate his requests from English. Of course, Michael could have negotiated with Apollonia's father in Italian, but speaking English and describing his family's prominence in the United States is designed to impress her father. As he woos Apollonia, Michael respects conservative Italian courting customs, accepting chaperoning traditions and eventually marital customs that include her family and community. Juxtaposed to earlier scenes where he and Kay attend a movie alone as a couple and even play around in bed at a hotel room (they laugh as they fall between the twin beds they put together), the scenes between Michael and Apollonia reflect the degree to which Michael moves ever closer to becoming Italian.

Although Apollonia jests Michael about her broken English vocabulary and nascent driving skills, it becomes apparent that Michael has the intention of eventually returning to America with his Sicilian bride to establish an Italian American family. Shortly after Michael is told that Apollonia will "make a good American wife," however, she is tragically murdered by a car bomb planted by Fabrizio, which was intended for Michael in retaliation for Sollozzo's murder.[32] With his Italian life over, Michael returns to the United States, taking over the family business after Sonny is murdered. Two years later, he decides again to begin a family. However, this time he chooses Kay for his wife, clearly signaling that he wants an Italian American family that has legitimate connections to his new wife's white American world. As Michael resumes his relationship with Kay, though, he approaches it with the rationality and objective distance that characterized his decision to murder Sollozzo and McCluskey, clearly disconnected from the passion that characterized his and Kay's love affair at the beginning of the film. His eventual marriage to Kay becomes closely linked with his business ambitions and new American Dream, one that will legitimize the Corleone family by disassociating it from its criminal past.

Indeed, Michael's reconstituted American Dream secures his identity as Italian American. Where his mafia connections and its Sicilian customs tie him to his Italian heritage, his pursuit to legitimize his family's name by moving to Nevada is profoundly American as it is grounded in Jeffersonian ideology. As noted in previous chapters, this ideology maintained that migrating west would allow constrained Americans to start life anew, escape their past, and pursue possibilities that would enable them to achieve the American Dream. By moving the Corleone family to Nevada, Michael can legitimately practice his business enterprises as he legally purchases casinos for his gambling operations. In Michael's mind, the Corleone family will not be tied to the mafia criminal underworld nor its notorious past in Nevada as it is in New York. In Nevada, he can escape this past and imagine the possibility for the Corleones to become a leading family, perhaps no different than the nineteenth-century robber barons such as the Stanfords and Huntingtons who legitimately amassed a fortune in California's railroad industry despite questionable business practices.

Nevertheless, to achieve his American Dream, Michael must maintain his connections to the mafia, as the final scenes of the first *Godfather* film illustrate. After Michael and Tom propose a deal to the Las Vegas casino magnate Moe Greene (who resolutely rejects Michael's offer to sell his stake in the Corleone casinos), Michael proceeds to have Greene (Alex Rocco) and the heads of the major mafia families assassinated, as well as his brother-in-law Carlo Rizzi (Gianni Russo), whom he holds responsible for Sonny's murder. These assassinations take place simultaneously with Michael's godson's baptism. As this religious ceremony takes place and Michael takes his sacred vows as godfather, the murders he ordered occur. Clearly the film juxtaposes the sacred and the profane to illustrate how Michael now moves in the same ambiguous moral universe as his father. Evidently, Michael is baptized into the mafia faith as his godson is baptized into Catholicism. Though his godson's Original Sin is absolved, we are left to wonder if Michael's sins have been absolved as well. As the film closes, Michael blatantly lies to Kay that he did not kill Carlo (which technically he did not, as he issued the order rather than commit the crime himself). The film ends from Kay's point-of-view where she and the audience watch as the door to Michael's study (where his mafia business is conducted just like his father's) shuts her, and us, out of this Sicilian defined universe.[33]

Michael's dream to escape his past in Nevada proves elusive, however. Initially, his narrative in *Godfather, Part II* suggests that he has achieved his American Dream. Like the first *Godfather* film, Michael's story begins with a religious ceremony and Catholic sacrament, this time with his son's First Communion. Now living in Lake Tahoe, Michael celebrates his son's religious ritual with a grand party, much as his father did with his sister Connie's wedding in the first *Godfather* film. Where his sister's wedding was grounded in Italian customs, the party for Michael's son is very American. So much so, that when a family friend, Frankie Pentangeli (Michael V. Gazzo) tries to encourage the orchestra to play an Italian folk song, it ends up playing "Yankee Doodle" even as they try to follow Pentangeli's direction, much to the humor of the members of the party. In frustration, Pentangeli leaves the stage, clearly feeling out of place at this very American gathering. Moreover, it appears Michael may have become American himself as he receives a certificate of appreciation from the Nevada politician, Senator Pat Geary (G.D. Spradlin) on behalf of his son. However, this very American celebration shortly becomes shadowed by Michael's business dealings much as those conducted by his father at Connie's wedding.[34] In fact, these scenes recall Don Vito's meetings and demonstrate that Michael has actually not escaped his mafia past.

During his private meeting with Senator Geary, we witness how much the established white power structure continues to see Michael in terms of his ethnic past, particularly as the senator spews epithets at him that recall those stated by Captain McCluskey in the first *Godfather* film. It turns out that Michael has not achieved his American Dream, and the rest of the film narrates the gradual demise of Michael's empire, particularly the destruction of his family. Following the party, assassins attempt to murder Michael in his bedroom, provoking him to alienate himself from even the closest members of his family as he searches for those responsible for his attempted assassination. He doubts his brother Tom's loyalty and becomes estranged from his wife Kay, who aborts their unborn child because she refuses to bring another child into the morally corrupt Corleone family. Once Michael discovers that it was his brother Fredo who was responsible for his attempted murder, he has his brother killed. At the end of the film, Michael sits alone contemplating the ruins of his family, ruminating over his relationship with his father and the significance with which Don Vito regarded his family.[35]

Arguably, Michael's pursuit of his American Dream and efforts to escape his ethnic past provoke him to lose sight of the foundational Italian values that enabled his father to establish the Corleones as the leading mafia family in the United States. In fact, Michael has forgotten the values of honor, respect, and family, values that his father considered paramount. One can criticize the second *Godfather* film as too ambitious for trying to simultaneously narrate Vito's rise to become the eminent don of the mafia world and Michael's demise from his powerful position. However, the film perhaps wants the audience to consider the price for pursuing the American Dream and fleeing one's ethnic past. Michael becomes corrupted as he pursues his American ambitions, unable to redeem neither himself nor his family's name as a result, the primary purpose for moving his family west to Nevada. Though Michael attempted to emulate his father at the end of the first *Godfather* film, he actually becomes more like Don Fanucci in the second *Godfather* movie. Similar to Fanucci, Michael tries to disassociate from his ethnic past in Nevada, turning his back on those Italian customs that sustained the Corleone family in America even as he maintains mafia connections to secure power. In *The Godfather, Part II*, Michael's mafia is less "La Cosa Nostra" to the Italian American community (as it was for his father) and more of an ethnic business enterprise he uses as a vehicle to achieve his American Dream to legitimize his family's name.[36] The *Godfather* films have been popular with Americans for a variety of reasons, among them for telling a powerful story about the American immigrant experience. Yet these films are morality narratives of the American Dream, celebrating our nation for embracing the poor and meek from the Old World while providing them opportunities for social and economic advancement in the United States. But these films also caution us about the price of Americanization and escaping our histories as we try to start life anew. The *Godfather* films provoke us to consider the value of our ethnic pasts and the rich traditions that sustain and protect our families while providing them hope as they try to achieve the American Dream.

## *My Big Fat Greek Wedding* and Recent European Immigration History

While Matthew Frye Jacobson suggests that the civil rights movement and election of John F. Kennedy closed the racial history of the European immigration experience as Europeans, and that their descendants were absorbed into white America, recent films about European immigration such as Joel Zwick's *My Big Fat Greek Wedding* challenge this claim. This humorous film tells the story of Toula Portokalos (Nia Vardalos) and the tensions between her loyalties to her Greek American family and her desire to become American. For Toula, becoming American involves acquiring an education and marrying her white middle-class boyfriend Ian Miller (John Corbett). As in the *Godfather* films, the family embodies ethnic traditions and one's allegiance towards their family reflects one's loyalty to their ethnic past. In both films the marriage between an ethnic European and a white American reflects the critical step for the ethnic European to become American. More than the *Godfather* films, however, *My Big Fat Greek Wedding* illustrates the ways Americanization equates with whiteness and disconnecting from one's ethnic history. As Toula aspires to achieve her American Dream, she wants to be like the white blonde girls at school, eat white food, and maintain a relationship with her white boyfriend, all while separating herself from her very large, very ethnic Greek American family. Unlike the previous films discussed, *My Big Fat Greek Wedding* demonstrates the burdens that ethnic American women encounter as they pursue the American Dream. As we will see, women like Toula Portokalos face greater challenges from their family to remain connected to their ethnic families, marry men within their ethnic communities, and bear children in order to pass down ethnic traditions.

When *My Big Fat Greek Wedding* begins, Toula and her father Constantine/Gus (Michael Constantine) are driving to the family restaurant "Dancing Zorbas" in the dark hours of the early morning. Not only is Toula very tired, but also she is demoralized, telling us through her narrative voice-over her shame of being Greek American. As she recounts various moments of humiliation during her childhood, she says that Greek women are expected to do three things in life: marry Greek men, have Greek babies, and make Greek food. Her father is clearly disappointed in her because she "looks old" as she approaches thirty and has yet to marry a Greek husband. All her life, Toula wanted to be like the white girls at school, and her parents' strenuous efforts to preserve Greek culture make her an outcast. As she sits alone during lunch time, she is teased by blonde girls sitting together at another table for eating Greek food: when she tells them she is eating moussaka, the girls giggle by calling it "moose caca." Her father makes things worse by celebrating Greek contributions to world civilization to white girls who carpool with Toula, further shaming his daughter. Moreover, she is marginalized within her own family. Her older sister Athena (Stavroula Logothettis) has fulfilled the dreams of her parents by marrying a Greek man and having children, and her brother Nick (Louis Mandylor) is the favorite by virtue of being male. Working as a waitress in her family restaurant, Toula feels that her life has reached a dead end, suffocated by her parents' expectations and the Greek traditions that do not offer the kind of life she wants to lead.[37]

Her life begins to change, however, as she convinces her mother Maria (Lainie Kazan) that she could contribute more to the family if she could take courses at a local community college. Together, Toula and her mother con her father by letting him believe he thinks it is in the family's best interests for Toula to attend school. Attending the junior college has immediate effects on Toula. Although her confidence in the classroom reflects her intellectual potential and the ways her education will enable her to achieve her American Dream as a working woman, her cosmetic changes better illustrate her growing independence and self-esteem, demonstrating how she has taken more control of her life. She replaces her eyeglasses with contact lenses. She exercises, sheds weight, and wears make-up. As she becomes more physically attractive, she is invited to sit among the blonde white girls in the college cafeteria. She joyously joins them for lunch, and takes out her sandwich made with white bread as if to affirm that she is just as white as them. The gleaming smile on Toula's face demonstrates that she is beginning to live her American Dream, one that allows her to be American while still remaining a part of her Greek community. As she begins to work at her Aunt Voula's (Andrea Martin) travel agency, she feels she has arrived as a Greek American woman. However, her new life encounters challenges when she meets Ian Miller. Her infatuation and budding love affair with Ian strain her loyalties to her family. Knowing how much her parents will disapprove of her relationship with Ian, she lies about her evening activities.[38] Telling them about Ian would only confirm their original suspicions about going to college: a girl with an education becomes too independent, putting herself before her family, and eventually pursuing a life as an American apart from them. Still, Toula's relationship with Ian represents the ultimate threat. To Constantine, he is the "Xeno"—the foreigner who challenges Greek traditions, particularly the sacred value of marriage. If Toula were to marry this American Xeno, not only would he lose his daughter, but also Toula would lose her ability to pass down Greek culture.

In this regard, Toula is only too happy to escape her family and her Greek past. Nevertheless, as she and Ian decide to marry, she begins to realize the value of her family and Greek heritage. For his part, Ian is infatuated with the idea of her Greek family. As the only son of white upper-middle-class parents, Ian felt suffocated as well by their high expectations and white antiseptic lifestyle. He moderately rebels by becoming a teacher instead of a lawyer like his father, and wears long hair. As he looks at Toula and her family, he sees warmth in her extended family and pride in their ethnic traditions. In his mind, Toula has history while he does not, and he wants to be a part of it. He is willing to convert to the Greek Orthodox faith, play along with the jokes Niko makes at his expense, and adopt peculiar Greek customs such as spraying Windex on cold sores, one of Constantine's idiosyncrasies.[39]

In fact, Ian's narrative is part of the film's larger discussion about whiteness and Americanization. As much as these were Toula's ambitions, *My Big Fat Greek Wedding* ultimately views them as sacrifices not worth making, celebrating ethnicity and history instead. Ian's parents are a people without culture and a past. As Constantine says, they are "toast." Throughout the film, bread is a profound metaphor for culture. Like culture, when bread is ingested, it becomes a part of a person, providing nutrition and sustenance. When Toula wants to eat white bread she is telling us how much she wants to become white. Accordingly, when Constantine calls the Millers "toast," he alludes that they are bland and devoid of culture. After all, when Toula meets the Millers for the first time, they cannot distinguish Greeks from Gautemalans, and when they visit the Portokalos family, they bring a bland undecorated bundt cake. Although this humorous scene is meant to juxtapose the very large Portokalos family (which includes a huge extended family) with the very small Miller family (just Ian and his parents), the bundt cake takes on its own life as Maria cannot fathom what it is and has difficulty pronouncing it. Later on, she finds the bundt cake so lifeless that she puts a plant in the cake's center to give it character. However, the film holds out hope for the Millers, and by extension white America. Like the bundt cake, white Americans can have character if they become part of ethnic America. In fact, in the film's final scenes, they are invited to dance along with the Portokalos family at Toula and Ian's wedding reception, thereby being invited to become part of the large Portokalos family as well.[40]

But it is Toula's transformation that reinforces the film's narrative discourse. Despite her desire to become American and white, these goals are ultimately not worth achieving. Instead, one should pursue the dream of becoming the hyphenated American, which in the end both Toula and to some degree Ian do. And if it means he can remain connected to his daughter, Constantine can accept this as well. In fact, to encourage Toula to remain a part of her Greek family and its ethnic past, he provides a house as Toula and Ian's wedding gift—but a house next door to his. It is not a house with Greek columns and a Greek flag painted on the garage like her father's, but it is one where Greek traditions can live alongside American customs. In fact, Toula embraces her hyphenated identity and wants to pass it on to her and Ian's daughter. Their daughter will go to Greek school like Toula did when she was a young girl, but she will also be able to participate in Brownies as well, a rite-of-passage for many young American girls to which Toula was denied.[41] As the film concludes, we are meant to ponder the significance of history and our collective ethnic and racial pasts that are rich with customs. Our connection to these pasts enable ethnic and racial traditions to persist, providing a source of meaning in the customs we share. Perhaps the film wants us to consider how white America once was connected to these pasts, but became disconnected from them over time as they achieved the American Dream, looking towards the future as it pursued opportunities. By reconnecting with our ethnic and racial traditions, in effect becoming a constellation of hyphenated Americans, we can recover our histories.

*My Big Fat Greek Wedding*'s ideas about hyphenated America stand in contrast to the *Godfather* films that tell narratives about the ways the ambiguous world of the hyphen is often confusing and disorienting. It also challenges recent scholarship about immigration and ethnic America. In his thought-provoking book about post-ethnic America, David Hollinger cautions against a multicultural United States comprised of a panoply of hyphenated Americans. Ties to our ethnic and racial pasts often promote a nationalism that vies for our allegiance as citizens of the United States. In contrast, Hollinger wants Americans to have a "postethnic perspective [that] emphasizes the civic character of the American nation-state, in contrast to the ethnic character of most nationalisms." As a civic nation the United States can transcend the particularism of ethnic nationalism, tying Americans as a national community with a common experience and work towards common endeavors that benefit the collective above ethnic particularisms.[42] In other words, we signify and celebrate the unum in our national motto "e pluribus unum" (out of many, one).

In *Roots Too*, Matthew Frye Jacobson remains critical of the resurgence in ethnic affiliation among European Americans. First of all, it remaps the history of whiteness from that which defined the WASP-oriented Plymouth Rock narrative to the Ellis Island immigration experience. Not only does this interpretive shift minimize the intense ethno-racial struggles that European immigrants and their descendants faced (which films such as *Gangs of New York* and the *Godfather* films document), but also it suggests that the triumphant narrative of Americanization is possible for numerous Americans from various ethnic and racial backgrounds, overlooking how persistent racial intolerance impede the ability for non-white immigrants and their descendants from achieving the American Dream.[43] In other words, it reinforces the story of ethnic America celebrated by Thomas Sowell, whereby the initial struggles, even discriminations, that immigrants endured ultimately will vanish over time as they assimilate into American society and adopt culture. According to Sowell, once people disconnect their ties to their ethnic and racial pasts and traditions they can benefit from the exceptional social, economic, and political possibilities in America.[44] Apparently, if only other ethnic and racial groups such as Mexicans, Latinos, and African Americans would follow the history of European Americans, then they too will experience the fruits of the American Dream, as have the Irish, Italian, and numerous other groups of European immigrants. As we now turn towards the ways cinematic and academic historians have examined the Mexican American experience, we will see how the history of Mexicans in America is much more complicated than Sowell maintains.

## *Mi Familia, Real Women Have Curves,* and the Mexican American Experience

The major issues animating Mexican American historiography center upon whether Mexican immigration history adheres to the European American experience or if it follows more closely to the racially defined history of African Americans. In the first interpretation, Mexican immigration parallels other narratives of the Latino experience such as the Cuban and Puerto Rican, where immigrants and their descendants encountered challenges, even prejudice as they tried to carve out a life in America, conditions very similar to that which Europeans encountered in the late nineteenth and early twentieth centuries. Like European immigrants and their descendants, as Latinos assimilated into American society and adopted American culture, they too became American citizens, and gradually left their ethnic past behind. Among Latinos, Cubans are often held up as the model minority group as they quickly assimilated in the years since the Cuban Revolution, emerging as a powerful political constituency in places like Florida. True, Cuban ethnic communities continue to survive, sustaining traditional customs and the Spanish language. Nevertheless, the Cuban community does not define itself in opposition to the dominant white American power structure. In fact, it supports it and finds ways to work within the American political system to advance its interests. However, we must remember the uniqueness of the Cuban American experience. The Cuban community in the United States grew exponentially after Fidel Castro took over the Cuban government, a historical event that propelled numerous Cuban exiles to immigrate to places like Miami. Here, they worked with the United States government who shared similar interests to depose Castro from power. Once it became increasingly evident that these exiles would not return to Cuba in the immediate future, they began to make home in the United States and acculturated into American society, all the while still trying to undermine the Castro regime. As such, the Cuban experience did parallel the European American experience, and arguably Cuban Americans were more successful more quickly than European immigrants and their descendants precisely because the conditions of the Cold War favored their rapid integration into American society.

The distinctiveness of the Cuban American experience must be noted because it also reflects how different it is from the history of Mexicans in the United States. Two factors quickly become evident when we compare Mexicans to other immigrant groups. First of all, the first generation of Mexican Americans were not immigrants at all, as substantial portions of the western United States were once part of Mexico, becoming part of the United States after the annexation of Texas and the Mexican–American War in the mid-nineteenth century. As a consequence of the Treaty of Guadalupe Hidalgo in 1848, many former Mexicans were immediately granted rights as American citizens. Even though a number of these Mexican American citizens assimilated into American society, especially elite Mexicans who tried to retain power in the new political environment, these rights could not protect them from white American racism. Newly arrived white Americans used political institutions to seize prime land from wealthy Mexican Americans and use the poor as laborers. Much of the history of early California is the history of Mexican Americans marginalized in their homeland.[45] Second, although the history of Mexican settlement in the American West receded with time, it nonetheless shaped lasting race relations between Mexicans and Anglos (as white Americans were referred). And though these former Mexican territories became part of the United States, Mexico and the United States continued to share a border. This, more than any other factor, defines the Mexican American experience and informs every interpretation of Mexican immigration.

Much as industrialization and the prospect of a better life attracted countless Europeans to America, so too did they attract numerous Mexicans. And just as political turmoil and limited chances to become productive farmers propelled Europeans to the United States, events like the Mexican Revolution and diminishing prospects to own land in Mexico provoked marginalized Mexicans to immigrate to America.[46] Comparisons to the European American experience do not end there. As many European immigrants imagined they would return home after accumulating enough capital working in the United States, Mexicans immigrated in the early twentieth century with similar aspirations. Moreover, the same historical events that affected European immigration and Americanization, namely stricter immigration laws, the Great Depression and New Deal, and World War II, also influenced the history of Mexicans in America over the course of the twentieth century. Much as early generations of European ethnics faced discrimination, so too did Mexicans. Like their European counterparts, Mexican immigrants fought the forces of Americanization, even as it manifested within their homes as their children embraced American customs such as fashion and popular culture.

In many respects, these early generations of immigrants were Mexicans living in America much as those Europeans who resisted American assimilation. Yet, we cannot forget the border. For as congressional legislation sought to restrict immigration with the Johnson-Reed Act (1924), enforcing this law along the United States–Mexico border was much more difficult than along the Pacific and Atlantic coasts, where immigration officers were more successful keeping out unwanted migrants from Asia and Europe. Uneven border control enabled Mexicans to come to the United States illegally; they revived Mexican culture in the American southwest at times when Europeans became more American. The question in Mexican American historiography then becomes whether the Mexican immigration narrative is a history of remaining Mexican or becoming Mexican American.

The films *My Family/Mi Familia* and *Real Women Have Curves* effectively address this question, though offering different answers. Gregory Nava's *My Family/Mi Familia* tells the story of the Sanchez family and their struggles to make a life in Los Angeles over the course of the twentieth century. At times it draws parallels to the European immigration experience, but it also notes how the Mexican and European narratives diverge, particularly in the ways racism and the border defined Mexican American history. In many ways it is a unique film as it examines the meaning of history and the function of stories as ways to engage the past. While history often equates with fact and truth while stories are fiction, *My Family/Mi Familia* explores the significance of the latter and questions the value of the former. As we will see, *My Family/Mi Familia* asks us whether passing down an emotionally engaging living past through family stories is more valuable than the objective and disconnected history that purports to be the true narrative. Patricia Cardoso's *Real Women Have Curves* is a less ambitious film, but nonetheless a poignant story of Ana Garcia (America Ferrera) who wants to live her American Dream and pursue a college education. Her story closely parallels that of Toula Portokalos in *My Big Fat Greek Wedding* as she finds her mother to be a major roadblock on her path to achieve her dream, much as Toula's father initially stymied hers. As with *My Big Fat Greek Wedding, Real Women Have Curves* is a movie about generational conflict and parental fears that their children will severe ties as a result of the latter's Americanization. However, where *My Big Fat Greek Wedding* resolves this narrative and generational tension, the relationship between Ana and her mother in *Real Women Have Curves* remains ambivalent as Ana leaves home to attend Columbia University.

Gregory Nava's *My Family/Mi Familia* begins with a voice-over by Paco Sanchez (Edward James Olmos) describing two different cities of Los Angeles: the one where he grew up with his family in a predominantly Mexican American community, and the other inhabited by Anglos. These two versions of Los Angeles are divided by the Los Angeles River, connected by a bridge Mexican Americans cross in order to work for Anglos, though rarely, if ever, crossed by Anglos. As Paco tells us about these two cities, the camera shows the immense skyline of downtown Los Angeles from the vantage of the Mexican community on the other side of the river.[47] Though this camera shot illustrates the geographic gulf separating downtown LA and Mexican LA, it also demonstrates the deep cultural divide as well. While the magnificent skyscrapers symbolize the white Anglo power structure that dominates most of Los Angeles, they are nonetheless sterile and removed from Mexican Los Angeles. These skyscrapers may dwarf the small homes of the Mexican barrio, but these homes are colorful and closely connected, symbolizing the vibrancy and interconnectedness of this ethnic world. Already the film establishes Mexican Los Angeles as a place steeped with history and culture while Anglo Los Angeles is devoid of them. Viewers are also provoked to consider the multiple meaning of bridges. Though the bridge connects two places together, sometimes bringing different peoples together, it also reinforces the differences between those places, as the it enables Anglo LA and Mexican LA to remain separate. As we see later in the film, the Anglos who mostly cross the bridge are police officers (themselves the embodiment of the white power structure), and Memo (Bill) Sanchez's future in-laws, who appear completely alien in this Mexican American community.

As *My Family/Mi Familia* unfolds, the metaphor of the bridge reflects not only the wide gulf between Anglo and Mexican Angelenos, but also their two different histories. In this context, Nava's film immediately prompts viewers to think about whether or not the Mexican experience in America connects with the broader American historical narrative. Furthermore, it reflects scholarly debates within Chicano historiography as well. Although some immigrant historians place the Mexican American experience within the broader American immigration narrative that emphasizes inevitable assimilation, Chicano scholars debate whether Mexicans in the United States largely remained Mexican or adapted to American society and forged a hybridized culture.[48] In this regard those scholars who argue for cultural retention in Mexican Los Angeles see the "bridge" as connecting two separate and culturally distinctive peoples in the city. Scholars who maintained that a dynamic syncretic Mexican American culture emerged in twentieth-century Los Angeles see the "bridge" as bringing Mexican and American culture together. In both cases, however, neither group of scholars hyphenate Mexican American, reflecting how they see Mexican immigrants as balancing life as Mexicans and Americans rather than living betwixt and between these two worlds in a cultural borderland. The title of *My Family/Mi Familia* reinforces this perspective. Nava's film is neither the Americanized "My Family" nor the strictly Mexican "Mi Familia." It is a movie about the life of the Sanchez family, who are both Mexican and American. As we will shortly see, the two members of the Sanchez family who try either to live in the borderlands of the hyphen or to assimilate into the dominant Anglo culture, namely the brothers Chucho and Memo (Bill), discover the tragedies of Americanization.

As the movie begins with Jose Sanchez's journey from Mexico, Paco informs us that he is relating the story passed down from his father. His father's version of the journey starts with the exciting passionate story about Jose's brother Roberto's infidelity and violent death at the hands of his aggrieved wife, events that led to Jose's flight to Alta California. Though a humorous and arresting narrative, Paco immediately informs us that Jose's version of his immigration narrative did not actually happen, and that his father was a simple peasant who came to Los Angeles looking for better opportunity. Beginning with Jose's story, viewers understand that we will be watching two versions of the past, the accurate history and the tall-tale family legend. Although sometimes we are informed which version we are watching, often we are not. *My Family/Mi Familia* weaves history and myth, but it privileges the latter as these are the stories passed down from one generation to another, and is the emotionally engaging and lived experience that connects each to the other. The past as myth is alive, an oral history that is imbued with greater significance because it combines the past with the present. Whether the events in the past actually happened is less important than the way these myths impart meaning to a family's understanding of its origins and experience over time. Although Paco tells us that the humorous story about Jose's brother is fictional, he does not entirely dismiss his father's tall-tales about coming to Alta California fighting wild animals and bandits.[49] It is apparent that Paco does not exactly believe the veracity of Jose's stories, but he relishes telling viewers because they make for an exciting story designed to draw us into his family's narrative. By telling us the same stories he was told as a child, Paco includes viewers into the Sanchez American saga. Rather than outsiders objectively learning the Sanchez family as a subject in American immigration history, we become part of an extended family reliving the past to understand the Sanchez American experience. To understand the Sanchez family, then, is to have intimate knowledge that connects us with their living history as it unfolds over time.

As the young Jose (Jacob Vargas) eventually arrives in Los Angeles, seeking a distant family member known as El Californio (Leon Singer), a name he earned because he was alive when California was still a part of Mexico and emphatically maintains that he continues to live in Mexico even though Los Angeles is now part of the United States. As Jose settles down in Los Angeles he finds a job as a gardener, crossing the bridge daily to work for Anglo Angelenos. One day, he meets Maria (Jennifer Lopez), also a Mexican immigrant; they marry and start a family, living with El Californio in the barrio of East Los Angeles. Shortly thereafter, El Californio dies, and according to family legend is buried in the yard because he wanted his remains to stay within Mexican California. In the yard, Jose grows corn, a staple Mexican food, beginning an annual family tradition that perpetuates an Old World custom in his new world. But just as Jose and Maria believe they have achieved the good life, their American Dream of family and happiness, Maria is deported by La Migra (US Immigration), who conduct a raid of the barrio to send back illegals. Despite Maria's protestations that she is actually a legal American immigrant, La Migra dismiss her claims as she tries to show them her papers, and send her back to Mexico, pregnant with her second child Chucho.

Here, *My Family/Mi Familia* begins to describe one of the unique dimensions of the Mexican American experience that fundamentally demarcates it from that of the European immigration. The perpetual presence of La Migra and the threat of deportation made the lives of Mexican immigrants precarious, fomenting distrust and suspicion of the American state. In this environment, Mexicans were less likely to acculturate to American society as they were viewed as Mexicans regardless of whether Mexican immigrants became naturalized Americans like Maria, or even citizens born in the United States. In Mexico, Maria bears her child, and begins the long journey back to Los Angeles, dreaming of one day reuniting with Jose and their children. She and Chucho endure a perilous river crossing when they travel towards California. As a white owl watches Chucho practically drown, Maria is barely able to save her child and make it to shore. Still, as Paco tells us, the river gods wanted to claim his younger brother that day, and cheated death by denying them their sacrifice. In fact, Chucho will be haunted by the owl and river gods throughout his life; his fate forever tied to this event. In this sequence, viewers are apprised of not only a significant moment in the film's plot development, but also how Mexican folk beliefs define the Sanchez American experience as the family carries them to Los Angeles. Maria and Chucho ultimately find their way to Los Angeles and to Jose. As she introduces her son to her husband, they feel they have been fortunate and blessed as their family is now reunited and they can resume their American life.

It seems that Jose and Maria continue to live their American Dream of family and happiness as the film transitions to the wedding of their eldest daughter Irene (Maria Canals). By this point, Jose and Maria have had three more children: Toni, Guillermo (Memo), and Jimmy. As Paco tells us, with each family addition, the house has enlarged. In fact, the Sanchez home becomes a metaphor for the family itself. Every room seems to be painted a different bright color and the rooms are added organically. While there is clearly no architectural order or coherence to the house, nonetheless it is alive with warmth and exudes comfort as it conforms to the needs of the Sanchez family. As the family prepares for the grand wedding, the family hustles and bustles throughout the house, teasing each other as they nervously get ready for this significant family event. And though this will be a wedding steeped in Mexican traditions, we also see the ways American culture has affected the Sanchez family, particularly Chucho. Now much older, Chucho (Esai Morales) listens to American pop music and has become a Pachuco, the leader of a gang in the barrio. In fact, his gang life intrudes upon Irene's wedding as the leader of a rival gang taunts him during the reception. As we learn, Chucho's gang life enables him to pursue his American Dream by profiting as a drug dealer, a materialistic one that entails nice cars, clothes, and money. As a vato (barrio slang for bad-ass), Chucho does not want to follow in the footsteps of his father. Jose continues to work hard as a gardener, and is proud of the way he provides for his family despite the menial and degrading labor involved. Chucho finds his father's work demeaning and emasculating and tells him he will never stoop to his kind of work.[50] As a gang leader and drug dealer, he commands respect in the barrio and makes his money quickly, refusing to conform to the racial and labor hierarchy controlled by the Anglos. As a Mexican American, Chucho has bought into the American system of capitalism, but turns to crime in order to profit and buy American commodities. American culture has corrupted Chucho, but it enables him to live his American Dream.

During a powerful scene, Jose confronts Chucho about selling drugs and prohibits him from further dealing marijuana while he lives under his roof. As they fight, Chucho denounces his father's way of life, showing the significant cash he has made from the drug trade and telling Jose that this is all Anglo-Americans care about anyway, not the hard work Jose performs at his menial job. Jose then evicts Chucho from his house, though regretting his decision immediately. Chucho proceeds to attend a dance, where he is provoked into a knife-fight with his rival gang leader. The fight ends with Chucho wounded and fatally stabbing his foe, forcing him to live in hiding. His younger brother Jimmy secretly brings him food and tells him news about his family. But with the police hunting him, he cannot see his parents, and his persistent questions about his father suggest that he too regrets his fight with Jose. The river gods have finally caught up with the wounded Chucho as the white owl from the Mexican river looks upon him and he hears the white police officers closing in.[51] As the sergeant has told his police force that Chucho is a noted criminal who is armed, lethal force will be required to capture him. Chucho's fate has thus been sealed. Once they catch him, Jimmy looks on with horror as the police brutally beat Chucho to death. As with La Migra, when either Mexicans or Mexican Americans confront the American state in *My Family/Mi Familia*, they encounter institutional racism, and in the case of Chucho, with lethal consequences.

If capitalism is the means by which Chucho pursues his American Dream, education and whiteness are the paths by which his brother Memo (Enrique Castillo) achieves his goals to become an American. As Paco tells us in the narrative voice-over, Memo is the pride of the family. As a young boy, viewers see him always reading or studying, and it is clear his hard work and diligence as a student will be the keys for his economic and social mobility. More than all his other sons Memo has internalized Jose's work ethic. Eventually he crosses the bridge to attend UCLA and law school, sometimes visiting his family in the barrio and remaining connected to them even as he becomes successful. However, once Memo begins to practice law and anglicizes his name to Bill, it is clear he wants to disconnect with his ethnic past as he now apparently equates Americanization with whiteness. He consummates his identity as a white American with his marriage to a white woman, Karen Gillespie (Dedee Pfeiffer). Bill brings Karen and her parents to the Sanchez home for the families to meet one another, but he begins to start making excuses for his family's ethnic customs, even going as far as to explain to his puzzled future in-laws why his family calls him by his pet name, Memo, which he says is the "Spanish diminutive for Bill." Bill has gone so far to imagine himself as Anglo that he has rejected his family name. He drives up to his parents' home in his Mercedes-Benz wearing a suit, clearly illustrating his wealth and status that tower above his family's very modest lifestyle. During this scene, he proceeds to shame his father for telling the family legend about El Californio being buried in the yard, forcing Jose to retract the legend and say that it is only a fictional story. Even as the family exude their pride for Memo to the Gillespies, it becomes clear that Bill is ashamed of his family. He has even lied about his brother Jimmy, having told his future in-laws that his brother has been away at school, although he has actually been in prison.[52]

Even though the family supports Memo's "stories," they can see that he has disassociated from his parents and siblings as he has moved into the white world of the Gillespies. The meeting between the families grows awkward and uncomfortable, finally exploding as Jimmy's son runs into the gathering naked and wearing an Aztec headdress, shocking Bill and the Gillespies. Bill shouts at his brother Jimmy to control his son as he ushers his fiancée and future in-laws out of the house, taking them back across the bridge to their comfortable white world and away from this traditional Mexican ethnic community. We never see Bill again for the rest of the movie, suggesting that he has completely disconnected from his family and ethnic history. Although the various films examined in this chapter have presented different ideas about education, Americanization, and whiteness, *My Family/Mi Familia* clearly sees these aspirations very negatively, even tragic as Memo's ambitions provoke him to turn his back on his family and past. Although Nava's film does not explicitly state that the children of Mexican parents who pursue a higher education and have goals to succeed in the Anglo-American world reject their family and ethnic heritage, it does suggest this conclusion by not providing an alternative to Memo nor showing another character who is similarly successful while maintaining ties to their ethnicity. Much like his brother Chucho, Bill has become corrupted by American values. But where Chucho was an actual criminal, he never lost his ties to his family and community despite his bitter disagreements with his father. Indeed, he is remorseful about their dispute and appears to want to reconcile before he is brutally murdered by the white Los Angeles police officers. Chucho thus achieves a measure of redemption from the film's perspective despite his criminal past. Alternatively, *My Family/Mi Familia* suggests that Bill's Americanization is in fact a more criminal act than his brother's drug dealing as in the end he disavows his family and ethnic history.

Of all Jose and Maria's children, Jimmy (Jimmy Smits) reflects the Mexican American experience. As Paco tells us, Jimmy is the soul of the family. Like Michael Corleone, he is the last child and the only one with an anglicized name. When we first see Jimmy as a young boy, he is an innocent kid who idolizes his older brother Chucho. He asks Chucho to teach him to mambo, but he also enjoys playing the quintessential American game of baseball in the streets with his friends. However, when he is torn between helping his embattled brother and playing baseball, he chooses to assist Chucho. He loses his innocence as he watches the white police officers brutally murder his brother, a cataclysmic moment that forever scars and haunts him. Jose and Maria choose to believe that Chucho's death was connected to that fated day when he was supposed to be taken by the river gods as an infant, and who now returned to reclaim what was taken from them— in other words, they shroud his death in Mexican folk religion. Jimmy, however, knows that which others in the family likely remain unaware, and details Jimmy chooses not to divulge to them.

Consequently, Jimmy internalizes his rage, which festers as he ages. For him, America embodies unjust institutional racism rather than hope and opportunity. He grows up to be a vato Pachuco like Chucho, spending much of his young life in jail. Though his life appears to have reached a dead end once he is released from prison, he meets Isabel (Elpidia Carrillo), a young Guatemalan immigrant who recently received political asylum with his sister Toni's assistance. Jimmy discovers that Isabel has witnessed the kind of injustice and brutal violence against family relatives like him, and develops a close emotional bond with her. In Isabel, Jimmy has found his soul mate, and begins to give life another chance. They eventually marry and their life together begins promisingly. Tragically, Isabel dies at a public hospital giving birth to their son Carlitos, which Jimmy sees as another example of unjust institutional racism. Although the doctors tell Jimmy that they have tried everything possible to save her, Jimmy believes otherwise, noting that if she were white and wealthy rather than ethnic and poor, they would have worked harder to prevent her death. Emotionally crushed by this perceived American racial barrier, Jimmy senselessly robs a jewelry store (arguably a symbolic attack against wealthy America) and consequently spends the next five years in prison.[53]

His parents in turn raise his son Carlitos, teaching their grandson many of the same Mexican traditions they imparted to their own children. When Jimmy returns, he finds his father harvesting the corn in the yard and they share a moment of family tradition as Jimmy ponders whether he should become Carlitos's father. Jimmy's instinct is to run from fatherhood as it embodies his hurt and anger as a result of Isabel's death. Jose and Maria nevertheless want him to embrace this role even though Carlitos has rejected him. Jimmy's transformation as a father is also his transformation as an American. Like Chucho, Jimmy believes at this point in his life that America is the sum of its materialism and cultural commodities. Consequently, he tries to buy Carlitos's affection with a trip to Disneyland and then with a *Star Wars* toy (the Millennium Falcon), iconic symbols of American pop culture. Carlitos summarily rejects these gestures and continues to dismiss Jimmy.

But just as Jimmy is ready to give up, his parents encourage him to persist and work hard for Carlitos's affection. Slowly Jimmy begins anew with his life and dedicates himself to fatherhood. Simultaneously, Carlitos begins to accept him for the person that he is as he was never interested in the things that Jimmy could buy. Eventually, Jimmy tells his father that he and Carlitos need to leave for Texas to have a chance as a family apart from his criminal past. Like so many American sagas, Jimmy wants a new life steeped in a Jeffersonian tradition of personal redemption and new beginnings. If Jimmy stays in East Los Angeles he will be haunted by his past. Going to Texas enables him and Carlitos to start life anew with opportunities of future happiness that Jimmy knows he will never find in LA. Yet, we sense that he will continue the family's Mexican traditions as he stands in the cornfield with his father while telling Jose of his plans to go to the southwest with Carlitos. As Jimmy and Carlitos head for Texas and their promising future, Mexican customs will unite with American values as they start over as a family.

*My Family/Mi Familia* concludes with Jose and Maria sitting at the table ruminating over their life, surrounded by pictures of their family and their very Mexican home. And though they live in a quintessential Mexican neighborhood in East Los Angeles, they describe how they have achieved their American Dream. As we watch them sip coffee at the kitchen table in their modest house, we can see that material wealth, so often the symbol of the American Dream, was never their aspiration. Rather their dream was a good life based upon traditional Mexican family values and the American work ethic. They came to East Los Angeles as Mexicans but have become Mexican Americans over time. In many respects their story parallels that which George Sanchez documents in his book *Becoming Mexican American*. Sanchez demonstrates that Mexicans maintained their cultural ties as they acculturated to life in America. Assimilation into Anglo-American society was not the aspiration for most Mexican immigrants in Los Angeles, although they could not ignore the forces of Americanization dividing them and their American-born children,[54] much as it did between Jose and Chucho and Memo/Bill and his family. Nevertheless, the terminus of the Mexican American experience was never to shed their ethnic past as it was for European Americans. Over time Mexican Americans internalized Jeffersonian values of life, liberty, and the pursuit of happiness, but the meaning of happiness was to retain a measure of their ethnic past and traditions as they forged a life in America. Gregory Nava's film embodies this sentiment. Indeed, perhaps that is why the film begins with Paco sitting at the typewriter to document his family history.[55] While legends and stories are the lived Mexican experience in America, to become a true American history it needs to be a printed narrative as that is how American culture validates history. By printing his family's narrative in order to publish it as a book, then, he brings together his family's Mexican and American experience.

Much like Joel Zwick's *My Big Fat Greek Wedding*, Patricia Cardoso's *Real Women Have Curves* tells the story of the daughter of recently immigrated parents, and who aspires to attend college, while carving out a measure of personal independence for herself. In both films, the marriage of their daughters reflects parental concerns about familial loyalties and ties to ethnic traditions. Where Toula Portokalos is able to reconcile her relationship with her parents, however, Ana Garcia is unable to resolve the tension between her and her mother. More than any of the films discussed in this chapter, *Real Women Have Curves* illustrates how the forces of Americanization divide immigrant parents and their children. As in the case of Toula and Memo/Bill from *My Family/Mi Familia*, education drives a wedge between Ana and her parents, though in different ways. In the case of all three, education is tied to social mobility and the possibility of disassociating from one's ethnic past. However, Ana's parents recognize, and to some degree embrace education as a means for their daughter to have more opportunities and become successful. For Ana's mother Carmen (Lupe Ontiveros), though, her daughter's American education has inculcated her with corrupt American values that contradict and undermine traditional ethnic values, especially those regarding gender. While Carmen has imparted Mexican values about femininity and womanhood upon Ana and her sister Estela (Ingrid Oliu), Ana rejects them, having adopted more American feminist ideas of independence, equality, and beauty. The conflict between them, then, is as much about who controls Ana's body as much as her future. In other words, Ana's educational ambitions are only the surface of the tension between her and her mother. Much deeper is that Ana's education has taught her (and will likely continue to teach her) to be an independent American woman.

*Real Women Have Curves* begins with Ana's mother feigning illness as she tells Ana that she believes she is pregnant. By the exasperated look on Ana's face, we know that this is not the first time Carmen has tried to convince her daughter that she is pregnant. From this scene, we already see that Carmen and Ana have a tense relationship, one that is likely connected to Ana growing up and no longer dependent upon her mother. Just as Ana is about to graduate from high school and move onto a new phase in her life, Carmen is likewise moving onto a different phase of motherhood, one that she is not ready to embrace. As Ana leaves the house, we see her incredible daily journey to attend Beverly Hills High School. Ana and her family live in downtown Los Angeles, and Ana must take multiple bus trips just to get to school. Later we learn from her teacher Mr. Guzman (George Lopez) that Ana is an exceptionally brilliant young woman who was selected to attend an elite public high school. Nevertheless, the cultural and social distance between Ana and her predominantly white privileged classmates is as vast as the geography that separates her home from her high school. This is apparently the last day of school, and Ana's classmates tell one another of their postgraduate plans; many of them will attend elite American universities. When it is Ana's turn to divulge her plans, she lies as she has yet to apply to college, and tells her peers that she intends to backpack through Europe. After class, Mr. Guzman asks Ana what happened to her plans to apply to Columbia University. Ana honestly tells him that she never completed the application. Trying to reassure her, Mr. Guzman tells Ana that he knows someone at Columbia's admissions office, and will try to help her out.[56]

On her way home, Ana picks up her last check from her fast-food job. The palpable disgust between her and her manager clearly illustrates that Ana resented this job, but likely worked here to contribute to her family's income. Ana knows that she will have to find another job, but her obvious ambitions and apparent fierce independence require that it be one that is not a dead-end menial food service job like the one she had. Ana comes home to her graduation celebration that includes her parents, sister, cousins, grandfather, and neighbor. At her celebration, we see how Ana's Mexican heritage is a vital part of her life. As her cousins play their guitars and sing in Spanish, Ana holds conversations with her grandfather and neighbor who apparently understand fluent English but only speak Spanish (much as Ana understands fluent Spanish but only speaks English). Mexican culture so defines Ana's graduation party that Mr. Guzman immediately speaks Spanish when he arrives to discuss Ana's college plans with her parents.[57] Mr. Guzman is clearly concerned that a gifted young woman like Ana will be discouraged from attending college.

Perhaps to demonstrate that he has acclimated to American society and understands its values, Ana's father Raúl (Jorge Cervera, Jr.) tells Mr. Guzman that he speaks English, and proceeds to explain that he and his wife want Ana to attend college, but not immediately as she needs to work to help the family. He further says that when it is time for Ana to apply for college, she is expected to enroll at a local university so she will be close to home. Here, Ana's parents express values that align with those held by many Mexican immigrants who want their children to work in order to contribute to the family income. However, they differ from those who hold traditional values that restricted the education of women in order to encourage their roles as wives and mothers.[58] For many Mexican immigrants the American educational system and its policies of compulsory attendance for all children was their first encounter with Americanization and its intrusion into the Mexican family.[59] Though Carmen appears to accept that Ana will eventually attend college, she is adamant that the family's needs supersede those of Ana's individual ambitions. Mr. Guzman implores Ana's parents to reconsider as their daughter has the intellectual talent to attend a premier American university. But the defeated look on his face reveals that he knows he is up against a wall of Mexican tradition that stands in the way of Ana's academic possibilities. Following Mr. Guzman's conversation with her parents, Ana thanks him for coming to her celebration and trying to convince them to let her apply to Columbia, but she is resigned to the future her parents have planned for her.[60]

Ana's immediate summer plans include working at her sister Estela's garment factory now that she quit her food service job. Although Estela worries whether she can afford to pay Ana, her mother convinces her to employ her sister, and Ana soon joins her mother and the group of Mexican American seamstresses who also work for Estela. As a Mexican mother, Carmen perpetually worries that her daughters remain unmarried, and daily prays to the patron saint of marriage that they will find husbands. Still, she most worries about Ana because she exhibits behaviors and an attitude that she finds unfeminine and will discourage potential suitors—in other words she does not conform to the ideal type of the Mexican woman. Carmen tells her daughter that she is overweight, too assertive and independent, and does not even walk like a woman should. For her part, Ana is proud of the woman she has become. She is comfortable with her body, and even is willing to undress down to her basic undergarments on one particularly hot day at work, to her mother's disapproval. As they argue about Ana immodestly displaying what Carmen sees as an overweight body at work, Ana maintains that her mother's notions of ideal femininity are literally suffocating, and exclaims to her and her coworkers that she is going to free herself from her mother's cultural restrictions. Embolden by Ana's assertiveness, Estela and her fellow coworkers proceed to also strip down to their undergarments, to Carmen's abject horror.[61] In this critical scene, we see that Ana's body has become a cultural battleground between her and her mother, where Mexican and American notions of femininity vie for control.

Like Toula in *My Big Fat Greek Wedding*, Ana pursues an emotional relationship with someone who is white. Yet Jimmy's whiteness is more symbolic of his

American privilege than the imposing cultural threat that Ian's whiteness reflects. But like Toula, Ana must sneak out at night and lead a deceitful life in order to maintain her relationship with Jimmy (Brian Sites), a friend since their days at Beverly Hills High School. However, it becomes clear that she wants to be with Jimmy because he accepts her for who she is and does not find her body unattractive, unlike her mother. Eventually, she loses her virginity to Jimmy, and sees herself as a new woman as a result. In fact, as she looks at her nude body in the mirror with appreciation the day after having sex, her mother walks by and immediately knows that Ana is no longer a virgin, looking upon her daughter with disgust and shame.[62] The cultural divide between Ana and Carmen has become so vast that Carmen effectively disowns her daughter, a tragedy that becomes evident to Ana when she leaves home for college.

As it turns out, Ana completed and submitted her application to Columbia earlier that summer while working for her sister. When she is accepted, she remains undecided about whether to attend until she receives her father's blessing. Until the last moment before she leaves for New York City, she hopes she will receive her mother's as well. As she leaves for the airport, she pleads for her mother's acceptance only to be met with silence. Emotionally crushed, we wonder if Ana and her mother will ever be reconciled as Ana starts her new life at Columbia. Nevertheless, Ana has come to terms with her mother's cultural values and her identity as an American woman. As the film concludes, Ana walks the streets of New York City confident and independent, but in the feminine manner that her mother once showed her on the streets of Los Angeles.[63]

*My Family/Mi Familia* and *Real Women Have Curves* are films about the Mexican American experience that emphasize becoming Mexican American rather than remaining Mexican in the United States. These films illustrate the ways Mexicans adapted to life in America and adopted core American values such as pursuits of happiness and redemptive new beginnings while retaining essential Mexican traditions based upon family and heritage. Whether these films accurately reflect the historical Mexican American experience remains debatable, however. Conservative critics maintain that as long as Mexicans continue to speak Spanish as their primary language, and immigration (both legal and illegal) is not restricted, Mexicans will be a distinct subculture apart from American society. Although coming from a different political perspective, historians such as Douglas Monroy see the history of Mexicans in America as one of continual cultural rebirth throughout much of the twentieth century precisely because Mexican traditions are revitalized as immigrants consistently arrive from the old country. Monroy sees the US–Mexican border as fluid despite strenuous political and legal efforts to control it. Consequently, families are able to sustain ties across the border as Mexicans living in America, and perpetually connected to the old country.[64] In this regard, Monroy's view is reflected in *My Family/Mi Familia* with Jose's journey to California, believing he migrated only to northern Mexico, and El Californio maintaining he still lived in Mexico despite the fact California was now in the United States. Maria's deportation and eventual return to Los Angeles with Chucho likewise corresponds with Monroy's argument about the fluidity of the border. The film also illustrates that La Migra's deportation of Mexicans in America immigrants is never permanent, as Maria and Chucho's experience also demonstrates. As Nava's movie suggests, Mexicans can always find a way to get back to the United States.

To be Mexican American is as much a state of mind as a lived experience, enabling Mexicans to retain allegiance to their ancestral home precisely because the cultural and social conditions exist in places like Los Angeles to allow Mexicans in America to remain Mexican. *My Family/Mi Familia* and *Real Women Have Curves*, however, stop short of supporting this conclusion. In this regard, Douglas Monroy may be closer to the historical accuracy of the Mexican American experience than both of these films. In fact, one of the virtues of Monroy's book is that he argues that the Mexican American experience is fundamentally too diverse to have a singular historical trajectory. Monroy argues that the ways in which these two films narrate the Mexican American experience is just one historical trajectory while there is another that accounts for continued Mexican cultural rebirth that is equally valid. Whichever one chooses to see, or wants to continue, depends on what kind of America one wants to envision. Whatever the case, Monroy's ethnic America (and for that matter George Sanchez's) is not Thomas Sowell's ethnic America where the trajectory of immigration history ends with assimilation into American society and disconnecting from one's ethnic traditions and past. Sowell's story of ethnic America might define the historical trajectory of European Americans (and there are still those historians who would disagree with his interpretation of the European immigration experience), but it is not a historical template that can be grafted upon the Mexican American experience.

While Douglas Monroy's *Rebirth* is an engaging interpretation about Mexican cultural retention in mid-twentieth-century Los Angeles, it also provokes us to think about the American immigrant experience and the purpose of social history more generally. *Rebirth* refuses to provide narrative closure to the history of Mexican immigration, in large measure because this experience continues to unfold into the present. Consequently, his monograph presents two possible conclusions, one where Mexicans become Mexican Americans as a result of serving in World War II, participation in Los Angeles politics, and stricter immigration laws.[65] This historical trajectory clearly parallels the history George Sanchez narrates in his book *Becoming Mexican American*. But Monroy says there is an equally valid historical conclusion that tells the story of continued rebirth of Mexican culture in post-World War II Los Angeles. In this narrative Operation Wetback (which deported over 1 million Mexicans by 1953) and the Bracero Program (which brought selective Mexican workers to labor in California's agriculture industry), continued turbulence in Mexico and limited opportunities (factors that propelled Mexican migration at the beginning of the twentieth century) provoked further migration to the United States legally and illegally after World War II.[66]

Ultimately, whichever historical trajectory concludes the Mexican American experience depends upon how we choose to end it with contemporary immigration policy, according to Monroy. In some ways, Sanchez's *Becoming Mexican American* is a much more satisfying history because it provides the kind of narrative closure to the Mexican American experience that parallels the European American immigration narrative that so many Americans celebrate, and one that Monroy's *Rebirth* clearly lacks. Of course Sanchez would agree that the history of Mexican American immigration continues into our present time, but he argues that this recent history is tied to different political circumstances and economic imperatives than those that unfolded from the early twentieth century through World War II.[67] In this regard, Sanchez's book better connects his history to broader currents in American immigration historiography that also maintain that the immigration experience terminates with Americanization to some degree or other.

Yet we should not be seduced to accept narrative closure to a dimension of American history that will probably never end. The danger of academic history remains its reification of historical context. While there is obvious virtue to understanding the past as something discrete from the present, it also tempts us to think that what happened in the past is over, when actually it is very much alive. The Mexican American experience is only the most obvious example of this kind of living history. The emergence of American social history has been one of the most significant scholarly developments in the history of the American historical profession. It has shown how people previously rendered marginal or considered unimportant because they did not occupy the powerful corridors of government and finance nonetheless shaped the currents of American history. And immigration historiography has been among the major contributors to the social history project. Yet, we need to resist the desire for narrative closure to historical experiences that continue to be a part of our contemporary life. However one finds multiple endings to Mexican American history frustrating, this approach appreciates the ways the Mexican American experience is a living history. As we will see in the following chapters, there are times when narrative closures are necessary, particularly in the case of national historical trauma. But we should remember that the attraction of recent immigration films like the *Godfather* films, *My Big Fat Greek Wedding*, *My Family/Mi Familia*, and *Real Women Have Curves* lie in their ability to tell living histories. Similar to Monroy's *Rebirth* and recalling one of the original purposes of social history, these films remind us that we can become active historical agents when our pasts engage our present in an ongoing conversation, helping us to understand our collective historical experience while enabling us to shape our nation's future.

# 7

# BEYOND DALLAS

## History, Narrative, and the Struggle for Meaning in the Kennedy Assassination

At a critical moment in Oliver Stone's *JFK*, Jim Garrison (Kevin Costner) travels to Washington DC to meet Mr. X (Donald Sutherland), a shadowy former figure in the government's intelligence community, hoping to gather more evidence to strengthen his fragile case for uncovering the conspiracy to assassinate President Kennedy.[1] Garrison has been stymied by multiple sources while preparing his case to prosecute Clay Shaw/Bertram (Tommy Lee Jones), a local New Orleans businessman whom he believes is the link that will unravel the complex web of people and organizations involved in the plot to kill the president. During his meeting with Mr. X, however, Garrison discovers that his pursuit of justice in a provincial New Orleans case has actually drawn him into a much more corrupt and sinister conspiracy that includes intelligence agencies, major military leaders, and President Johnson. While searching for a small nugget of evidence to convict Shaw, Garrison instead receives a conspiracy narrative from Mr. X that implicates the current president in the Kennedy assassination. As Garrison listens in astonishment, Mr. X unravels a gargantuan conspiracy theory that indicts (nay, convicts) national leaders for conspiring to assassinate the former president as part of a coup d'état to install Johnson as president and escalate American involvement in Vietnam. Having heard Mr. X's revelations, Garrison is no longer a mere provincial attorney. Exposed to the "truth" behind the Kennedy assassination, he becomes the iconic, betrayed American who accepts what was once considered unthinkable: that the US government will murder and lie at will in order to advance its interests. To this point in the film, the narrative has privileged Garrison's noble, if naive pursuit to expose the conspiracy, wanting us to sympathize with his quixotic prosecution. But in this film sequence, the film requires that we adopt his perspective. We observe Garrison visiting historic memorials of slain leaders in the national capital, with an especially evocative camera shot of him at Kennedy's gravestone. As Garrison looks longingly at the memorial and its eternal flame, we watch an African American father and his daughter pay homage to Kennedy's memory.[2] Clearly, this scene provokes us to remember Kennedy's short tenure as president and the ways he inspired Americans to greatness, including advancing black civil rights (although historically this is questionable). In feeling Garrison's pathos, we too listen to Mr. X's recounting of events, and it is we who also feel betrayed by our government for shattering our American innocence.

The Washington DC sequence demands that we confront our history. While this sequence is an important constituent story in and of itself, it is also critical to the film's narrative discourse about the historical significance of President Kennedy's assassination and our modern epistemological understanding of history. The capital sequence intends to answer longstanding historical questions about those involved in the conspiracy to kill the president. The mise-en-scène juxtaposes light and darkness, color and black-and-white film, documentary footage with historical reenactment, while accelerating time and history, all in an effort to indict the shadowy and sinister forces within the government for the president's murder. The effect is disorienting and disturbing. Although this sequence includes a camera shot of the phrase "Study The Past" etched upon a federal building, history has been refracted, and like Jim Garrison we have trouble discerning fact from fiction. Whether we like it or not, the film has brought us into Garrison's disturbing world, and we see history as he sees it. Along with Garrison we tour great monuments of American history. Although we visit monuments to American triumphs, we linger at those signifying American tragedy, particularly those honoring Kennedy and Lincoln. With Garrison, we mourn the loss of leaders who inspired American greatness, but whose tragic deaths altered the course of American history. The film's focus on these memorials contrasts sharply with the sinister narrative of power and the dark side of American politics Mr. X tells. While more than propelling the film's narrative, the Mr. X scenes present a counter-historical narrative documenting how our national leaders eliminated President Kennedy because he wanted to end the Cold War and withdraw American soldiers from Vietnam.[3]

At its core, *JFK* is American history as tragedy. Later, Garrison presents a variation of Mr. X's counter-history as "evidence" of a conspiracy to kill President Kennedy at Shaw's trial. After submitting ballistic tests, medical reports, and testimonies during the trial to support his case, he asks the jury in his closing statement to "remember their dying king" and convict Clay Shaw. Critically, the camera angles shift from Garrison's perspective to that of the jury throughout the trial. With this cinematic technique, we have been implored to dismiss the *Warren Report* and convict Shaw (and by extension his co-conspirators). This sequence attempts to provide the narrative closure and historical catharsis that Americans have yearned for since President Kennedy's assassination. It is also a cinematic device to negate the jury's quick deliberation. Where the jury returned with a verdict of "not guilty" within hours, effectively pronouncing Garrison's case a farce, the film treats the verdict as a tragedy, emphasized by the final scene where Garrison walks into the light (of truth?) with his family, while darkness shrouds Shaw, the jury, and reporters (i.e. the rest of America). The New Orleans jury represented in the film may have dismissed the truth of Garrison's case, but the film has effectively retried the case, and a much different American jury— the viewing American public—has been asked to render a new verdict on the conspiracy to assassinate President Kennedy. Whether the film succeeds in effectively presenting this revisionist history is one of the major issues this chapter addresses.

*JFK*'s counter-narrative may appear outrageous, but the film deftly crafts this history with black-and-white documentary footage, interlaced with black-and-white film reenactment, while citing documents to support its conspiracy theories. In effect, the film practices history. These cinematic devices have been utilized throughout the film, most notably in the opening sequence, but while its mix of historical fact and reenactment advanced the film's plot to this point, in the Mr. X scenes, the film uses these cinematic techniques to advance an historical argument, analyzing and interpreting historical data in order to demonstrate the significance of President Kennedy's assassination. Unlike reading printed text, however, we do not stand detached from the film's historical argument because we have become engaged in the movie's narrative. Throughout the Mr. X sequence we are in a state of disequilibrium and disbelief like Jim Garrison, unable to discern fact from fiction. We have now become ensnared in the film's revisionist historiography, and from this point forward we have to take the film seriously as history (whether we dismiss it as bad history is another issue) as much as cinematic narrative. That is, we have to recognize and engage *JFK* as a work of historical scholarship as much as a film.

The Washington DC constituent story stands at the center of the film for a number of reasons. Garrison's visit to the capital is emotionally engaging, and viewers, like Garrison, yearn for truth to the JFK assassination, and accountability for the murder of our "dying king." Since the film has provoked sympathy and nostalgia, viewers are prepared for Mr. X's explosive and damning conspiracy theory. Yet, the film apparently recognizes pathos and nostalgia alone will not persuade the audience. Using black-and-white film, historical footage, and referencing government documents, the movie demonstrates its acumen as cinematic history, provocatively interconnecting rumor, innuendo, and fact to construct a historical narrative that interprets events surrounding the Kennedy assassination. More significant than the conspiracy theory itself, though, the film's historical interpretation provides the kind of narrative closure that the *Warren Report* (the official document relating the government's investigation of the assassination) never could, thereby producing a historical catharsis for viewers that shrouds the Kennedy assassination with greater historical meaning. Herein lays *JFK*'s power as history. Whatever we may think of its revisionist history and manipulation of facts to advance its conspiracy theory, the film's ability to offer viewers narrative closure and the possibility of historical catharsis overpowers criticisms of the movie, although whether it is successful achieving closure and catharsis will be examined later in this chapter. *JFK* presents viewers with a historical narrative of American innocence lost, a trust betrayed by national leaders, and a narrative catharsis that enshrines the JFK assassination as an "historical event" that explains the ensuing socio-political chaos and disintegration of American society following President Kennedy's death.[4]

Despite the controversy surrounding the JFK assassination and widespread acceptance that it was a major "historical event" for numerous Americans alive at the time of President Kennedy's death, the assassination remains woefully neglected by the historical academic community. Indeed, Max Holland has pointed out that academic scholarship on the Kennedy assassination has been written largely by non-historians. Although Holland wrote a literature review in the historical journal *Reviews in American History*, his review critiques a monograph written by an English professor, and other "histories" written by non-historians. In reviewing Peter Dale Scott's *Deep Politics and the Death of JFK*, Holland is astonished by the ways some conspiracy theories have been accepted by academics, cloaking their conspiracy theories as scholar-ship, that in turn have been published by reputable university presses.[5] Holland points out that conspiracy theories are nothing new in American history, but where historians have been able to put most of these theories to rest (such as President Roosevelt's advance knowledge that the Japanese were going to attack Pearl Harbor), historians have largely abandoned scholarly inquiry into the JFK assassination. As Holland states,

> In stark contrast [to the Roosevelt-Pearl Harbor conspiracy] historians have forged nothing close to a consensus on the assassination; in fact their voice is rarely raised. Very few of the more than 450 books and tens of thousands of articles that compose the vast assassination literature published since 1964 have been written by historians.[6]

Whether historians have abandoned this significant event in post-World War II American history is debatable, but Holland accurately demonstrates that historical interpretations of the assassination have been mostly shaped by non-historians, many of whom write their books outside peer-reviewed journals.

Why academic historians have avoided writing scholarship about the JFK assassination remains a mystery. But the way the historical discipline has traditionally defined its craft, its methodologies, and its purposes largely inhibits a scholarly approach to the assassination. Although the historical profession has moved beyond the positivist tradition, the pursuit of objectivity, and Leopold Van Ranke's mantra to write history "as it actually happened," these formative ideas continue to shape how historians approach their craft.[7] If history is partly the activity of conducting historical research to recover data to tell a story "as it actually happened" and as accurately as possible, Kennedy's assassination resists this kind of historical treatment. The sheer mass of information, and much of it contradictory, (as well as government documents still concealed from the public) continue to challenge the historian's effort to reconstruct a narrative of "what actually happened" in order to find historical truth in the assassination. In this regard, the Kennedy assassination questions what we mean by "history." On the one hand history is the collection of events, actions, ideas and the constellation of happenings that have occurred in the past, what the historian Charles Beard calls "past actualities."[8] But history is also the scholarship historians produce, where they have assembled their research and given coherence to these "past actualities," constructing an analytical narrative in the process that provides either an explanation or interpretation of historical phenomena. Some scholars maintain that this production of historical scholarship is the very definition of history.[9] But given the problematic nature of the historical evidence in the Kennedy assassination and how difficult it is to verify and scrutinize it, attempting to reconstruct an historical narrative of this recognized "historical event" is complicated, rendering a scholarly interpretation of the assassination nearly impossible.

Does this mean that history does not exist unless historians say it exists? Of course not, but the professionalization process, especially peer review, ensures that certain professional standards and rules are met, and that there is a method used to evaluate and determine what stands for "good" history. However, it is the historians' commitment to these standards and to the ethos of writing an accurate history of "what actually happened" that may prevent them from swimming in the shark-infested waters that characterize the current literature on the JFK assassination. In part, the dilemma of the Kennedy assassination is a methodological one. Although historians have embraced non-traditional approaches to recovering the past, the historical profession nonetheless still privileges and grounds research in documentary evidence. After all, the historical discipline relies upon written and documentary sources for its methodological approach, differentiating it from other disciplines such as archeology, anthropology, and geology that use artifacts, ethnography, and soil-sampling among other forms of evidence to study the past. But in the case of the Kennedy assassination, the official government documents, including the *Warren Report*, are not wholly recognized as legitimate. How can we know "what actually happened" in Dallas on that fateful day in November 1963 if historians question the legitimacy of the official documents and if other empirical evidence such as the Zapruder film and ballistic tests, among others, cast doubt on the *Warren Report?* How can we get the details of the assassination straight and achieve a historical consensus of who actually murdered President Kennedy if the empirical evidence is contradictory or contrived?

In actuality, the JFK assassination is more than a matter of finding conclusive evidence that will tell us "what actually happened." After all, most Americans believed the Warren Commission after the release of its report in 1964, whereas, according to a more recent study, about 80 percent currently do not.[10] The issue is why have Americans shifted from believing the *Warren Report* to disbelieving it. Conspiracies theories such as those postulated by Jim Garrison after his infamous trial abounded in the wake of the initial release of the *Warren Report*, and Max Holland persuasively argues that the confidential documents that were initially shielded from the American public but are now available for review do not fundamentally challenge the report's original conclusion that Oswald acted alone.[11] In fact, the persistence of conspiracy theories reflects how the Kennedy assassination is as much an epistemological dilemma as it is a historical one. The assassination provokes us to think about whether it is possible to "know" the historical details of the president's murder, and what this knowledge is supposed to reveal to us in terms of historical significance and meaning. And herein lies the possibility for fictional narratives to provide the historical knowing and explanation that we yearn for and that academic scholarship fails to offer. Historical fiction, such as Don DeLillo's *Libra*, minimizes the significance of historical detail while highlighting broader epistemological issues confronting recent American history. Because the focus of DeLillo's historical novel is the relationship between history and modernity in post-World War II America and not "who shot Kennedy," DeLillo can interpret the greater meaning in the JFK assassination. DeLillo offers a different kind of narrative closure than Oliver Stone as he tells the story of the dark side of the American Dream, modernity, and the limits of the Enlightenment Project.

Jürgen Habermas has articulated the phrase the Enlightenment Project to describe particular ideals valorized by Enlightenment thinkers that continue to characterize modernity, most notably the reification of historical subjectivity (sometimes also referred to as possessive individualism and individual agency), individual freedom, and human progress.[12] While there are other characteristics of modernity (such as the promises of empirical science and technology to produce human progress, issues that DeLillo's novel also addresses) the ideals of historical subjectivity and progress figure prominently in American visions of individual independence and pursuits of happiness. That DeLillo chooses Lee Harvey Oswald as his protagonist wrestling with these American ideals and the Enlightenment Project illustrates the book's fundamental irony and its critique of modernity and American history.

According to DeLillo, the Kennedy assassination, and particularly the pathetic life of Lee Harvey Oswald, signifies and amplifies a recurring theme in modern American life: the tension between our cherished vision of individual agency and pursuits of happiness, and the greater historical forces that push and pull us through time in ways that seem beyond our control. In his rendering of President Kennedy's murder, DeLillo finds understanding and meaning in American history. Although *Libra* provides narrative closure, arguably it is questionable whether it provides historical catharsis, a process of working through our collective historical trauma to integrate our traumatic past with our contemporary condition. The ability to achieve integration simultaneously respects our tragic past, but reconciles it with our present. History, then, is not a disconnected or repressed past, but an enveloping, integrated past-present rich with meaning and significance that enables us to comprehend our world and also shapes the way we imagine our present-future. Interestingly, Stone's *JFK* suggests catharsis but it remains debatable whether it provides satisfactory narrative closure. The film does not fundamentally resolve all the historical questions it raises even as it convincingly demonstrates that the *Warren Report* is problematic and unreliable.

Perhaps the limitation of Oliver Stone's film, ironically, is that the film constructs a docudrama whose purpose is decidedly scholarly, trying to recover the historical details of Kennedy's assassination. In the spirit of Leopold Von Ranke, the film wants to reconstruct the past "as it actually happened," asking us to take it seriously as a history, presenting facts, events, and documents to inform us, at the very least, that the *Warren Report* was not only wrong, but also fabricated to delude Americans into believing Lee Harvey Oswald acted alone. And though Stone's film provides an enigmatic narrative closure, there is a measure of historical catharsis as the film balances the scales of a powerful traumatic event in American history. The film signifies one American tragedy with another, where the murder of our "dying king" is equated with a powerful conspiracy theory of a coup d'état. The film recognizes that something so horrific as President Kennedy's assassination and America's lost innocence necessitates an evil so grand that a coup d'état becomes believable: it substantiates and legitimizes our trauma. The *Warren Report*'s conclusion that a deranged, insignificant, Marxist sympathizer could murder a beloved, treasured American president does not measure up to this American tragedy,[13] and actually demeans the extensive trauma Americans endured in the wake of the Kennedy assassination. In actuality, whether the *Warren Report* is correct or a fabrication is immaterial. Fundamentally, Americans continue to look for a historical catharsis to reconcile President Kennedy's assassination. Historical narratives present opportunities for Americans to work through their collective historical trauma, enabling them to integrate this traumatic moment with recent history, and finding historical meaning in tragic events. While it seems evident that academic historians have failed to write scholarship that achieves this historical integration, we will see whether Oliver Stone's and Don DeLillo's historical narratives succeed in working through the Kennedy assassination, the historical trauma that continues to haunt Americans.

## History, Narrative, and Reconciling Historical Trauma

As numerous scholars have demonstrated, narrative is more than a representative style to relate "how things happened" or "how things are." Narrativity is also a methodological and interpretive approach that recounts or sequences events and data, examining the philosophical and intellectual issues that have animated particular cultures throughout human history. Across space and time, people have constructed and told stories to illuminate what they believe to be meaningful, valuable, beautiful, and worth knowing, no matter whether these narratives are represented in the forms of myth, literature, or history.[14] As Edward Branigan notes, "Making narratives is a strategy for making our world of experiences and desires intelligible. It is a fundamental way of organizing data."[15] Moreover, narratives are fundamentally historical. H. Porter Abbott writes that "narrative is the principal way in which our species organizes its understanding of time."[16] That history and literature have overlapped for millennia demonstrate how narrative is ultimately epistemological: it is an intrinsic construction for people to know their universe through stories, whether they are fictive or real.

Emplotted with beginnings, event sequences, and endings, narratives are allegories that reveal what a narrator or author considers substantively and culturally significant, an explanation or interpretation of the contemporary world around us, as well as the human condition.[17] In this regard, historical narratives, whether they are literary or historiographic,[18] emplot real-time people and events to tell stories about the past, and with the larger purpose of signifying our past-present.[19] While definitions of history are as manifold as fish in the sea, those articulated by G.W.F. Hegel, Walter Benjamin, Michael Oakeshott, Hayden White, and Dominick LaCapra (despite their contrasting political subjectivities) are quite helpful in order to understand the epistemological and ontological function of historical narratives and their relationship to historical trauma such as the Kennedy assassination.[20] Collectively these scholars define history as more than the "past as it actually happened," recognizing a past-present (to use Oakeshott's term) where the past and present mutually define each other, and are enveloped in a relationship in such a way that their fusion shapes our contemporary epistemology and ontology.[21] History in this regard is the philosophical and interpretive framework that sequences and emplots past actualities, to use Charles Beard's term for the collection of all that has happened in the past,[22] signifying and amplifying (more so for Benjamin than others) that which has occurred in the past, but rendered meaningful to us in relation to our present condition. For Hegel, history is animated by our historical subjectivities and the pursuit of human emancipation. As "historical events" present themselves, particularly as dialectical confrontations between absolutist/totalitarian structures and freedom, people encounter this phenomenological spirit of emancipation and determine the course of their histories. Because the fundamental goal of all human societies is freedom, according to Hegel, it will ultimately triumph and end the dialectical struggle of history.[23] History, then, is a chronology of progress, driving towards the philosophical realization and political actualization of human emancipation. For Hegel, there is a past, present, and future, which collectively define a history that is threaded and interlocked by this pursuit of individual freedom.[24]

Oakeshott shares Hegel's liberal vision of history, but disputes that there is a disjuncture between past and present, minimizing history as a movement of progress. For Oakeshott, we look to the past through the lens of our present historical subjectivities, and consider that which is historically significant only in relation to our present condition (individual freedom, free-market capitalism and liberal democracy in the case of Western civilization), a condition that informs our present-future as well.[25] Hegel and Oakeshott are thoroughly grounded in modernity and the Enlightenment Project, although Oakeshott was less optimistic than Hegel about the history of human emancipation. Benjamin's philosophy of history is also rooted in modernity, but critiques the Enlightenment vision of human progress, historical subjectivity, and the possibility of emancipation. In his "Paris, Capital of the Nineteenth Century," Benjamin denies history as progress, and maintains that our present is an intensification of the past, where we fetishize artifacts from the past, rendering them significant, in terms of their present exchange value. History is phantasmagoria, an optical illusion that accentuates or diminishes the objects of the past based upon the currency of the present.[26] Much like walking through a Paris arcade, we wander through history's corridors, amazed at its structural aesthetics; but we are on the outside looking in, peering through the arcade store windows separated and disconnected from what we want. This disconnection only amplifies our desires to behold the artifact on the other side of the window. Connecting with the historical artifact only increases its value for us; for we believe that beholding this object will unlock the mysteries of the present as much as the past, communicating historical meaning to our present condition. History, then, is commerce, and historians are rarified merchants and antique collectors, signifying the baubles of the past by telling us how their accumulated historical worth has important exchange value in the cultural marketplace.

Oliver Stone's *JFK* and Don DeLillo's *Libra*, to different degrees, reflect these philosophies of history. Despite its cynicism, *JFK* maintains that we are historical agents that can achieve progress once we discover the historical truth behind the Kennedy assassination, emancipating ourselves and American history from the lies propagated by the government. Like Benjamin, *Libra* critiques modernity, particularly the ideas of historical subjectivity, technological progress, and the relationship between empirical truth and knowledge. While these themes and motifs characterize the book generally, they particularly manifest in the characters of Lee Harvey Oswald and Nicholas Branch. Where Oswald struggles with agency and his "rendezvous" with history, Branch, the CIA historian, searches in vain to find the truth embedded within the history of the Kennedy assassination. Throughout the novel, Branch struggles with his project to write the "secret history" of the assassination, deploying historical methodologies and technologies to sift through the morass of information, hoping his research will enable him to know "what actually happened." For Branch, the assassination resists historicism and narrativity, and not for lack of information; rather for its abundance. Sitting in his isolated room,

> Branch must study everything. He is in too deep to be selective. He sits under a lap robe and worries. The truth is he hasn't written all that much. He has extensive and overlapping notes—notes in three-foot drifts, all these

years of notes. But of actual finished prose, there is precious little. The stuff keeps on coming. There are theories to evaluate, lives to ponder and mourn.[27]

It is precisely at the nexus of historiography and literature where Hayden White sees the potential for narrativity to address the problem of historical meaning. Throughout his scholarship, White has called for a rethinking of historiography. Instead of working in the tradition of social science, a modality that locates its analytical research methodologies in explanations and truth claims, themselves legacies of nineteenth-century positivism, White provokes the historical profession to think about their historical practice as a literary construction.[28] In this context, historical narrative represents the past as it draws upon literary tropes and figurations to analyze and interpret how and why things happened in the past the way they did. For White, this form of historical narrativity is fictive, imaginative, and literary. Nonetheless, it pursues the historically significant and meaningful, reaching towards the philosophical, and recalling the tradition of Hegel and other major figures of the Western historiographic tradition.[29] In "The Question of Narrative in Contemporary Historical Theory," White pushes his argument further, proposing narrativity as a theoretical and methodological approach to reconstructing the past. Narrative is more than a way to represent history, it can inform how we read it and interpret historical significance. In White's view, historiography is fundamentally fictive: historians imagine and construct a logic to historical data that are not necessarily self-evident.[30] By signifying the "historical event," constructing a plot structure and event sequence to amplify historical significance, historians in effect practice a form of narrativity. As White points out, historiography is fundamentally allegorical. When historians magnify a historical moment, person, or idea, they are pointing out that it is more than what it is.[31] The year 1776 is not just a date, as it may have been for numerous people in the Anglo-American Atlantic world at that time. John Adams may have declared that this date should be remembered and celebrated with fireworks and pageantry, but his contemporaries were more circumspect. Over time, however, it has become a meaningful date for Americans (but of course not for the British) because of their national independence, even though independence was never assured at this point in time. Thus, 1776 has allegorical meaning for us precisely because of how we signify it to our present condition. With narrative theory, as Hayden White points out, historians can free themselves from the fiction that they practice objective social science, a methodology that results in the writing of austere and limiting historiography. Instead, historians should see the potential of narrativity and the ways it better achieves the project of historiography. Historians need to tell stories and narrate allegories whose purpose is to interpret meaningful history.[32]

From this perspective, we can examine *JFK* and *Libra* as works of history, even though we may disagree with their historical methodologies or conclusions. As narratives, they seek to illuminate the significance of President Kennedy's assassination, particularly in the ways it shaped the course of post-war American history. However, both the film and novel treat this "historical event" differently. In *JFK*, the assassination is the "event" that altered American politics and society in fundamental ways, particularly in terms of our military escalation in the Vietnam War. In *Libra*, President Kennedy's assassination is a historical allegory, the dark side of the American Dream and the problematic relationship between history and modernity. However, the film and novel recognize that this "historical event" is signified by the national trauma it engendered: how this trauma lingers; how it has become part of our collective cultural and historical memory; and how it has been passed down through generations. Younger Americans may not feel the visceral trauma as those who witnessed the assassination and endured its aftermath, but stories have been passed down to them as cultural artifacts signifying its importance. So much so, in fact, that Kennedy's assassination has coded our language and historical memory, framing the discourse of historical trauma. Perhaps a simple question at the time, the phrase "Where were you when you heard Kennedy was shot?" has nonetheless become a signifier and historical mantra of collective engagement with our historical experience, and has shaped how we have confronted other national traumas ever since. Following the September 11th terrorist attacks, the question morphed from "Where were you when Kennedy was shot?" to "Where were you when the planes hit the two towers?" As Dominick LaCapra has demonstrated, looking at moments of collective trauma and the ways people "work-through" their experience reveals how they utilize this historical experience to construct personal identity. Moreover, the ways in which they retell and reconstruct their historical narrative frames the way they interpret the past and transmit it as a cultural artifact to succeeding generations.[33]

Here, Walter Benjamin's view of history as the present's intensification and magnification of the past is instructive. Especially in *JFK*, the assassination is amplified precisely because the film intends to explain the chaos and deterioration of American society following President Kennedy's death. The film is not alone in this interpretation of American history. Younger generations (to whom Oliver Stone dedicates this film) are familiar with this view of history precisely because this event has been narrated and transmitted as historical trauma. In order for collective historical trauma to be passed down to later generations successively, descendants need to either identify or empathize with the traumatic experience, two different methods of "understanding" this past.[34] Whether younger Americans identify or empathize with those who experienced the Kennedy assassination is questionable. But Oliver Stone's *JFK* demands that viewers identify with those who experienced it. By staging historical reenactments, shooting film sequences in black-and-white, and inserting documentary footage, the film wants viewers to relive the trauma of the assassination, particularly in the trial sequence at the end of the film. That the film successfully allows viewers to "work-through" this trauma, achieve historical catharsis and integration, however, remains debatable. Nevertheless, narrative approaches to the past offer an opportunity to confront historical trauma and the possibility of achieving historical resolution and meaning. Historiography of the assassination, however, mired as it is in the debates over "what actually happened," obfuscates historical resolution precisely because the search for historical answers to "who shot the president" overlooks the broader historical narrative for which Americans yearn.

## Academic Scholarship and the Kennedy Assassination

As Max Holland has pointed out in his literature review, "After Thirty Years: Making Sense of the Assassination," the historical profession has largely "abdicated" writing scholarship about President Kennedy's assassination.[35] While Holland does not sufficiently explain the reasons for his conclusion, academic historians, like *Libra*'s Nicholas Branch, may find themselves confused by the volume of information, conflicting evidence, and the problematic nature of the major primary source document, the Warren Commission's report, which conceals more information than it reveals. Holland attributes the *Warren Report*'s failings to omissions that were later exposed by additional government investigations as well as revelations that the Federal Bureau of Investigation (FBI) and CIA withheld information from the Warren Commission, further discrediting the report. Holland believes that the exigencies of Cold War politics and the history of the intelligence agencies' culture of compartmentalization explain why information was withheld from the Warren Commission, but ultimately these data (as they have come to light in recent years by the release of government documents under the Freedom of Information Act 1992) do not undermine the *Warren Report*'s fundamental conclusion that Oswald acted alone. Rather, this information has revealed, according to Holland, only the FBI and CIA methods of covert operations during this heightened period of the Cold War, and how these agencies acted as they did in the interests of national security.[36] Holland ultimately agrees with the *Warren Report*'s conclusion, and believes that it is possible to historicize the Kennedy assassination in the broader history of post-war American foreign policy. The larger historical significance of the president's murder, according to Holland, lies not in the specificities of the assassination itself but in its connection to the frenzied politics of the Cold War, and the United States' paranoid policies towards Fidel Castro and Cuba.[37] In this respect, Holland's arguments provide an important academic interpretation that offers a way to understand historical meaning in the president's assassination. However, before we further explore Holland's interpretation, we need to briefly examine the major book he critiques in his literature review, Peter Dale Scott's *Deep Politics and the Death of JFK*.

Peter Dale Scott's book is not simply a lengthy conspiracy theory about the plot to kill President Kennedy disguised as academic scholarship, despite Max Holland's claims.[38] While professional historians may challenge Scott's use of evidence and conclusions, Scott, a professor of English at the University of California, Berkeley, follows historical practices, such as utilizing a scientific method to present his research and analysis. For Scott, National Security Agency Memoranda 263 and 273 are explicit evidence that President Kennedy planned to withdraw from Vietnam and his death enabled the Johnson administration to escalate American military involvement in South East Asia.[39] These documents, of course, are those referenced by Mr. X in Oliver Stone's *JFK*, and for both the film and Scott, they reflect a historical and political disjuncture that allude to a high-level government plot to eliminate President Kennedy. Although it is unclear whether Stone drew upon Scott's earlier research about the relationship between the CIA and the mafia while writing the screenplay for *JFK*, there are startling similarities between the film and Scott's books, particularly the conclusions regarding Kennedy's attitudes about the Vietnam War and the curious escalation of the conflict following Kennedy's death.[40] The publisher of Scott's book evidently sees the connection between *Deep Politics* and *JFK* as Stone is quoted on the cover of Scott's reissued and updated book, stating that it "will become part of our alternate history—to be read and studied by future generations."[41] Scott's prodigious research aside, his conclusions about the assassination and the calibrated efforts to murder President Kennedy are more innuendo than proof, raising questions and suspicions, rather than providing evidence of a high-level plot to assassinate Kennedy.

Nevertheless, as scholarship, Scott's book theoretically advances the idea of "deep politics" as a way to understand the labyrinthine, compartmentalized, and secretive culture of the American government, especially its intelligence agencies. Scott describes the way this covert, arguably corrupt culture is tolerated by legitimate public authorities because the interests and covert methodologies of these intelligence agencies reinforce legitimate politics and broader institutional and public interest.[42] Much like the ways local authorities tolerate the existence of the mafia or gangs (that is "organized" crime) because of their mutual interests (after all, without the criminal element why would local authorities need extensive police powers over its citizens, according to Scott), so too the rogue covert operations of intelligence authorities advance greater government interests, whether that is working to undermine Castro's regime in Cuba during the Kennedy Administration or fighting Nicaraguan Marxists in the Iran-Contra episode during the Reagan Administration.[43] In many respects, Scott's theoretical concept of "deep politics" contributes to understanding Holland's interpretation of US intelligence operations during the Cold War, as well as these agencies' activities in Stone's *JFK* and DeLillo's *Libra*. Sadly, Holland summarily dismisses Scott's book based on his view that the book is a lengthy conspiracy theory masquerading as academic scholarship.[44] While Holland impugns the University of California Press for publishing Scott's book,[45] perhaps the editors and peer-reviewers recognized the scholarly contribution Scott's book makes in terms of understanding the political culture of modern bureaucratic organizations. Moreover, for Scott his book is not the indictment of American politics as some have claimed; rather his history of the plot to kill President Kennedy is a call to citizenship to make America's political institutions accountable to its history and people, a rallying cry for readers to reclaim what is best in the American political tradition. In this regard, Scott's book is an effort to recover historical significance in the Kennedy assassination and the sinister practices of the American government. As he states,

> This book is written in an age of declining belief in the Enlightenment, when grandiose designs for political change, such as socialism and communism, have in most cases been thrust aside . . . Deep political analysis is one specific attempt at enmindment [the respect for truth in darkness] in the political area. It grounds the process for political change in a larger context less amenable to control, not to reject the inspiring vision of change, but to render it more possible . . . Just as there is more to life than logic, there is more to America than its shadows. I believe that America, for all its shortcomings and present difficulties, is still an unusually open society, where it is still possible to strive for even greater openness and justice. This is an appeal to America's residue of humanity, an appeal based on faith more than on logic.[46]

Readers like Max Holland may find Peter Dale Scott's *Deep Politics and the Death of JFK* an exercise in political paranoia, but as we will see with Stone's *JFK*, sometimes paranoia can be an alternative form of active citizenship and historical subjectivity, where suspecting and questioning political institutions are efforts to make them accountable to its citizens for their alleged corrupt activities.[47]

Ostensibly, Max Holland's "After Thirty Years" is a literature review assessing recent publications about President Kennedy's assassination. In actuality, very limited time is focused on these works, and much of the essay is Holland's effort to redeem the Warren Commission's report, and contextualize the president's death in the history of the Cold War's heightened politics following the Cuban Revolution. In contrast to Scott and Stone, Holland argues that Kennedy was actively engaged in destabilizing the Castro regime, and not working for some sort of political détente with the Soviet Union, or lessening the intensity of the Cold War (let alone removing American forces from Vietnam) as Scott's *Deep Politics* and Stone's *JFK* maintain.[48] Arguably, Holland conveniently overlooks the National Security Agency Memoranda 263 and 273 that Peter Dale Scott and the film *JFK* cite to demonstrate Kennedy's intent to "end the Cold War."[49] Yet, Holland persuasively illustrates how President Kennedy and Attorney General Robert Kennedy were active "Cold Warriors" who wanted to undermine Castro's Cuban Revolution. After the Bay of Pigs disaster, President Kennedy may have wanted to publicly distance himself from his administration's Cuban operations, but he also wanted his brother to be intimately involved with covert efforts such as Operation Mongoose to destabilize Castro's regime so the president could feign "plausible deniability."[50] According to Holland, the US government's covert operations, including the numerous attempts to assassinate Fidel Castro, intensified the Cold War during the Kennedy Administration, and Castro publicly announced that these efforts to undermine the Cuban Revolution might have similar repercussions for the United States. Holland points out that these statements could not have been lost upon a publicly avowed Marxist and Castro sympathizer like Lee Oswald, who probably read Castro's pronouncements in a local New Orleans newspaper, and decided to act upon them.[51]

According to Holland, Oswald was a deranged loner in whose mind acting on Castro's insinuations was an act of support for the Cuban Revolution and perhaps would present an opportunity for him to defect to the Caribbean island.[52] From this view, the Warren Commission ultimately got the story right, although it had to work with a deliberately secretive intelligence culture to advance its case. In the end, though, revelations of these agencies' dissembling further undermined the legitimacy of its report. The faults of the *Warren Report* aside, the fundamental significance of President Kennedy's assassination for Holland lies in the ways in which the death of the beloved president was a tragic casualty of the Cold War. The Cold War had produced a bureaucratic culture that justified murder, assassination, and other morally questionable activities, defining a compartmentalized political culture in the American intelligence community and making it a cornerstone of American foreign policy in order to protect and advance American interests. In this way, Holland believes he has balanced the scales of an American tragedy, finding historical meaning in President Kennedy's assassination. The president's death traumatized the American people, but it may have been the price, according to Holland, they paid for their government's feverish pursuit to undermine Castro's Cuban Revolution and win the Cold War.[53] Holland makes a compelling case for understanding the Kennedy assassination in the broader history of Cold War America; it is debatable, however, that his interpretation can provide the necessary resolution Americans seek in order to "make sense of the assassination." As Holland readily admits, about 80 percent of Americans continue to disbelieve the *Warren Report*, and believe there was a wider conspiracy to kill the president that extends beyond Oswald as the lone gunman.[54] Holland may want to attribute this phenomenon to the spurious conspiracy theories advanced by Peter Dale Scott and the film *JFK*, but it may also be that Americans seek a kind of closure to this traumatic "historical event" that only conspiracy narratives provide. As we turn to Oliver Stone's *JFK* and Don DeLillo's *Libra* we need to examine how the conspiracy theories surrounding the Kennedy assassination operate as stories with a particular logic and resolution that address the tension, complexities, and emotionality inherent in this historical tragedy.

## *JFK* and the Tension between History and Narrativity

Not since *The Birth of a Nation* has a movie provoked so much controversy about the relationship between film and history as Oliver Stone's *JFK*. While the film engendered wide-ranging discussions among the American public at the time of its release in 1991, academics from a variety of disciplines have also participated in these dialogues, and continue to engage the film from multiple perspectives.[55] In fact, one of the central issues remains the positionality and subjectivity of Oliver Stone as the primary filmmaker and author of this historical film. Where historians may be quick to identify him as the principal author and therefore putative historian of this cinematic text, narrative theory reminds us that such overt identification between author and narrative is misleading. Even if we recognize Stone as the *implied author* (as some narrative theorists would suggest) we still have to account for the collaborative nature involved in film production.[56] Films reflect numerous authorial voices, from directors, screenwriters, producers, cinematographers, to studio executives, among others, and determining any principal authorial intentionality in the narrative remains elusive. Thus, we should resist identifying Oliver Stone as the "historian" representing and interpreting the history of the Kennedy assassination in the film. Nevertheless, we can still interrogate the movie as an historical text with a narrative sensibility influenced by multiple authors, and examine how it represents history in the ways academics traditionally associate with the practice of historical scholarship. Indeed, the film provokes us to consider it in this vein. While some scholars contend that *JFK* reflects postmodern history, the film is actually grounded in a modernist epistemology, recalling the positivist tradition in American historiography. As a film, *JFK* choreographs a pastiche of fact and fiction through its cinematic historical reenactments; but it is not a conventional docudrama where history is a plot device to advance narrative discourse. The film, in fact, asserts that it practices history: it advances an historical interpretation based upon documentary evidence, claims to represent the Kennedy assassination "as it actually happened," and postulates a knowable truth-claim concluded from the evidence presented throughout the movie.

Scholars who maintain that *JFK* represents a postmodern history focus upon the ways the film mixes fact and fiction, questions epistemological assumptions about modern "historical events" containing knowable historical truths, and the complicated and provocative ways images structure our reality and inform our historical subjectivity.[57] From a postmodern perspective, that the film interweaves fact and fiction to the point where they are indistinguishable, is not problematic. All historiography, viewed in this light, is fictive anyway since writing history entails imagining and constructing a historical narrative while assembling research data, filling in the interpretive gaps, and providing an architectonic argument about the subject's broader historical significance.[58] Cinematic history like *JFK* is only more transparent about its literary and scholarly attributes than an opaque scholarly monograph. As compelling as these arguments about the postmodern nature of *JFK* are, they nevertheless overlook how rhetorical and academic the film actually is. The film does not present the history of the Kennedy assassination as an epistemological quandary that questions the possibility of historical knowledge and knowable truth (even though I am sympathetic to this argument). In fact, the film maintains that there is a historical truth that will expose those involved in the president's murder once all the evidence is presented honestly to the American public. Much like its contemporary television sibling *The X-Files*, with which it shares its paranoid political and historical sensibilities,[59] *JFK* contends that powerful figures within our government continue to shield us from the historical facts; but the film maintains that the "truth is out there" to discover nonetheless. *JFK*, in fact, draws upon the historical profession's tradition of positivism to present a counter-historical narrative, evidences its historical arguments with verifiable data via a scientific method, and advances its own historical interpretations.

Positivism informed American historiography in the late nineteenth and early twentieth centuries. Drawing upon the legacy of the German historian Leopold Von Ranke, American historians embraced his mantra to write history "as it actually happened."[60] Although American academics selectively chose the methodologies Von Ranke actually employed, they nevertheless took his maxim to frame their scientific method to scrutinize historical data objectively, believing they were letting the facts speak for themselves as they assembled data.[61] Once the history was collected and written with these objectives in mind, historical scholarship was subjected to peer review and the judgment of the historical academic community. Heavily influenced by natural scientists and their scientific methodologies, positivist historians believed that their empirical approach to research, and writing dispassionately, would produce good history.[62] According to this perspective, historians should avoid interpreting history, otherwise their histories become about them as an historian, and less about the recovered truth in their retelling of the past. Of course Oliver Stone's film is not dispassionate in the least, but it recalls this positivist tradition by framing its historical narrative as a truer history than the one propagated by the *Warren Report*, presenting documentary evidence and scientific data to support its historical arguments.

Over the course of the twentieth century, positivism lost its central position in the professional historical community. As Charles Beard points out, increasingly professional historians recognized that the pursuit of historical objectivity and practicing a neutral "scientific" historiography was a fallacy.[63] For Beard, professional historians should surrender their quest to practice history as a science, believing they can discover historical truths (for they are unknowable according to Beard), recognize that history is not simply the retelling of historical facts, and that historiography fundamentally entails analysis and interpretation (which the positivist historians adamantly disdained). In this regard, historians, according to Beard, should maintain their commitment to the empiricism of the scientific method as they approach their research, but take the historical interpretation itself not as a truth, but as an "act of faith."[64] Contemporary academic historians approximate Beard's aspiration by engaging history as an "act of faith" and resist the idea that the past holds historical truths. In contrast, Stone's *JFK* recalls the positivist approach to historiography as the film aspires to let the facts speak for themselves, to retell history "as it actually happened," all in an effort to reveal historical truths about President Kennedy's assassination.

The film's opening sequence, Garrison's encounter with Mr. X, and Clay Shaw's trial are particular moments when the movie adheres to a scholarly methodology as it narrates the history of the JFK assassination. The opening sequence is especially provocative in the ways it presents historical data and documentary footage, as well as stage historical reenactments to fill in interpretive gaps, all collective efforts that are necessary to support the broader interpretive arguments that frame the film. This opening sequence effectively narrates Cold War history in a matter of minutes, from President Eisenhower's Farewell Address through the history of the Kennedy Administration, until the fateful day of the president's assassination in November, 1963. The Martin Sheen voice-over is rhetorically critical as he narrates the event-sequences in the film's introduction. As narrator, Sheen manipulates how we read the cinematic texts that are a montage of documentary footage and historical reenactments. Eisenhower's Address warning of the power of the "military industrial complex" is one of the rare moments where a text speaks for itself, obviously because it reinforces the film's interpretive arc about the influential role of sinister forces in the government and their probable role in the president's murder. Other times we hear President Kennedy speak about diminishing international tension produced by the Cold War and against American involvement in the Vietnam conflict. Again, these moments of selective textual utterances are to support the film's broader arguments about Kennedy's intent to end the Cold War and withdraw American forces from Vietnam, political actions the movie argues that "made Kennedy so dangerous to the establishment," as Jim Garrison will later say to Mr. X.[65]

Aside from these moments where the presidents speak for themselves, the narrator's voice-over historicizes Cold War events as it assembles and interprets historical data. In fact, these episodes of textual utterances by Eisenhower and Kennedy act as evidence for the historical argument about Kennedy's vulnerability presented by the narrator. The film further frames our historical perspective with its music track and selection of documentary footage. The soundtrack simulates drum and trumpet marches to reinforce the regal and presidential aura of John F. Kennedy throughout the opening sequence. Brilliantly, these march tunes morph into staccato drum beats that escalate dramatic tension while leading up to the moment of Kennedy's assassination. Before we hear gunshots fire, however, the soundtrack plays a lone trumpet, signifying an isolated Kennedy and the melancholia surrounding his death. The film has actually been manipulating our emotional and historical sensibilities to this moment with powerful images of President Kennedy as inspirational leader and devoted father and husband. Whatever later historical information we have learned that challenges these views of Kennedy (such as his questionable leadership and decisions during the Cuban Missile Crisis or his extramarital affairs), the film wants us to dismiss this later history in order to relive and reencounter Kennedy's mythic Camelot. Arguably, the film is narrating a national myth and not history, but the film asserts that this myth is our collective national history.[66] We feel the melancholia at the end of this opening sequence precisely because the film has demanded that we relive history and become intimately connected with the Kennedy family. Kennedy's assassination was at once the death of our king of Camelot and our paternal figure. By showing home-movie footage of the Kennedy family, the film immerses us in the Kennedy clan, and like his children Caroline and John, we mourn the death of our national father-figure, taken from us at such a young age, ours as well as his, and shattering our youthful innocence. The film eerily wants us to revisit this moment in American history precisely to relive historical trauma. Once we have become emotionally destabilized and traumatized, we are ready to hear the film's explanation for our psychological state and help us work through our melancholia to achieve historical catharsis.

The historical sequencing and deployment of documentary film footage in the movie's opening sequence has a larger rhetorical purpose as well. As the film jump-cuts between various representations of historical film footage, it also begins to present historical reenactments, sometimes inserted between those representations of factual documentary footage, making it difficult for the viewer to discern between these real and fictive representations. Initially, the viewer can determine the historical footage with those moments of historical reenactment. One of the first reenacted scenes involves a woman who has been tossed from a moving car and tries to inform authorities that there is a plot to kill the president. Of course the authorities dismiss the woman's claims as hysterical, and this reenacted episode provides dramatic tension to accelerate the film's narrative. But it also acts as a cinematic device to integrate the "historical events" just narrated by Martin Sheen with the film's broader narrative discourse about the extensive conspiracy to assassinate President Kennedy. Significantly, this reenacted scene is shot in black-and-white, a rhetorical and cinematic device that will be used often throughout the film to historically authenticate the ideas and events presented in these scenes. Over the course of the opening sequence, the film has slowly presented these historical reenactments, but accelerates their integration along with the staccato drumbeats, disorienting the viewer and his ability to critically differentiate what is historically accurate and what is not.

Significantly, as the film's narrative pace quickens towards the assassination, the movie begins to integrate scenes from the Zapruder film, splicing and lengthening this amateur movie while synchronizing the grainy reenacted scenes that are shot to look like the Zapruder film footage. As Marita Sturken points out, this distortion of the Zapruder home movie is significant. Zapruder's film has become as much a cultural and historical icon as it has an authoritative historical document.[67] In fact, it is the film's status as an historical document that arguably disproves the Oswald as lone gunman theory, as Zapruder's film suggests that a gunshot may have come from the notorious grassy knoll. The integration of the Zapruder film with the movie's broader narrative discourse is an important moment that signifies *JFK*'s intertextuality.[68] The movie draws upon a preexisting and culturally significant text, in this case the Zapruder film, that has already been encoded with historical meaning and with which audiences are already familiar. Viewers know the Zapruder film quite well, at the very least, because of its widespread deployment to scaffold arguments about Kennedy's assassination. Indeed, the Zapruder film *is* the assassination, having taken on such cultural (more so than historical) significance because it suggests a wider conspiracy beyond Oswald and the desire for Americans to know the truth about Kennedy's murder. By presenting Zapruder's film and integrating it into the cinematic narrative along with reenactments, *JFK* viscerally does what Americans have long hoped the Zapruder home movie would do: it explains the mysteries locked in Zapruder's film by filling in the interpretive gaps suggested in this iconic film. This cinematic synchronization reminds viewers of the alternative and by now authoritative historical text that questions the *Warren Report*. Moreover, it historically authenticates *JFK*'s historical narrative of an extensive conspiracy to murder President Kennedy. The introduction of the distorted Zapruder sequence at the beginning of the film also establishes a historical dialogue between the movie and viewer that will become more evident in the film's trial scenes that take place later in the movie. In the trial sequence, the Zapruder film moves from its status as cultural and historical icon to one that signifies it as the ultimate source of historical evidence that Jim Garrison argues discredits the *Warren Report*. We will return to the Zapruder film as we examine the film's trial scene, but it is important to illuminate the film's manipulation of this historical icon in the opening sequence. *JFK* splices Zapruder's home movie and extends its twenty-six seconds, documenting Kennedy's assassination by adding reenactments shot similarly to that of footage in Zapruder's film, all in an effort to legitimize the film's interpretation, explaining the Zapruder film's historical gaps and advancing a historical argument about the extensive conspiracy to kill President Kennedy.

This chapter earlier examined the Washington DC and Mr. X sequence in *JFK*, but it is worth reviewing briefly to note how it connects with the film's broader narrative discourse about the historical significance of President Kennedy's assassination. The role of Mr. X as an informant is critical to the film not only for the information he conveys to Garrison, but also because his mysterious identity reinforces the shadow government and compartmentalized political culture that defined intelligence agencies during the Cold War. Mr. X. is factually based upon Fletcher Prouty, a "Deep Throat" informant who brought National Security Agency Memoranda 263 and 273 to the public's attention.[69] *JFK*'s 2003 DVD edition now includes a documentary about Prouty and his knowledge of the high-level government plot to assassinate President Kennedy, provided in the DVD package to further evidence and substantiate Oliver Stone's movie. Nevertheless, the mystery informant identified as Mr. X is also a clever narrative device to illuminate the sinister culture operating within the government, a figurative "Deep Throat" character common to mystery or "who dunnit?" movies, the film genre that fundamentally defines *JFK*. The Mr. X constituent story is another moment of *JFK*'s intertextuality that recalls and references similar genre films such as Alan

J. Pakula's *All the President's Men* (1976), where a similar elusive (although literally called)"Deep Throat" character provides information about the Watergate scandal and high-level government corruption.

To review, Jim Garrison has come to the capital at Mr. X's invitation because Garrison's investigation "is very close" to uncovering how far into the highest reaches of the government his case involves. Mr. X informs Garrison that people within the government have taken notice of his case, and are working to undermine Garrison's investigation.[70] Mr. X, now retired from the intelligence community, wants to help Garrison with his case (although he refuses to identify people who would have supported Garrison's ill-fated case) because he now believes that the government has become controlled by irrational forces, and exerts its sinister power to advance the interests of an elite few who are invested in the Vietnam War. Coming at the midway point of the film, the conversation with Mr. X has less to do with the narrative of Garrison's case against Clay Shaw/Bertram to this point of the film (although it will connect to the way Garrison presents his evidence against Shaw); but as a constituent story within the film, it significantly advances the movie's narrative discourse. It is at this point of the film where historical significance is less about the details of the Kennedy assassination (which had seemed to be the initial thrust of the film's narrative), and is now about the ways in which the president's death is an allegory or signifier for a larger, more corrupt history of American politics.

From the Mr. X sequence forward, *JFK* transitions from a narrative about a particular conspiracy to kill the president to one about the metaconspiracy to escalate US involvement in Vietnam. In other words, the Kennedy murder is a smaller story of a broader narrative about political corruption reaching beyond the assassination itself and demonstrates the abusive power of hidden forces within our national government. As Mr. X points out, the murder of the president was the easy part. Assassinations of political leaders were a standard method of covert operations for "black ops" organizations within the government, according to Mr. X, and were deployed numerous times during the Cold War, with the Bay of Pigs and Operation Mongoose being just a few examples.[71] It was the selling of the Vietnam War to a shaken and traumatized American public that was the greater challenge. And significantly, it is at this moment in Mr. X's conversation with Garrison that the film actually moves away from its principal narrators (Garrison and Mr. X) to a black-and-white scene reenacting a dramatic moment where President Johnson informs military and government officials that if they can handle Kennedy, he will give them "their damn war."[72] Not since the opening sequence of the film have we been taken outside the film's narrative universe that principally focuses on Jim Garrison and his struggle to discover who killed President Kennedy.

Yet, much like the opening sequence, Mr. X's monologue and his corresponding constituent story dramatize the narrative by mixing documentary film footage and reenactments. Moreover, it is at this point where the film recalls the opening sequence (which was largely factual but to some degree interpretive) to further evidence Mr. X's metaconspiracy. When Mr. X describes the role of "black ops" and covert operations in the Kennedy murder, we have been made aware already of such events from the historical footage presented in the opening sequence, especially those images referencing the Bay of Pigs fiasco.[73] Together these two sequences represent one of the movie's major themes: that our government will unscrupulously remove political leaders and overthrow regimes considered inimical to American interests. Thus, the purpose of the opening sequence is partly to prepare us for Mr. X's more powerful yet politically charged narrative of a metaconspiracy. The narrative about the hidden evil forces at work in our national government, only hinted at the beginning of the film, becomes a full-throttle hypernarrative of political intrigue, conspiracy, and massive corruption in Mr. X's dramatized narrative. Critically, it is in the Mr. X sequence where the movie synchronizes the film's detective narrative story with this metaconspiracy constituent story to articulate the movie's broader narrative discourse about the ways in which Kennedy's murder was the signifying "historical event" that tragically altered American history.[74]

The Mr. X constituent story is also the moment when the film is most historiographic. Where the opening sequence reflects a more chronological review of major events of the Cold War and the history of the Kennedy Administration (such as one could find in a standard history textbook), the trial sequence reflects the film's positivist methodologies to dispute the *Warren Report* and argue that Kennedy's assassination was a coup d'état. However, it is during the Mr. X sequence where *JFK* presents historical questions, analyzes factual and docu-mentary evidence presented, and interprets the broader historical significance of Kennedy's murder. In fact, during the rolling of the credits at the film's beginning, *JFK* cites two authors and their publications referenced for the movie: Jim Garrison's *On the Trail of the Assassins* (1988) and Jim Marrs' *Crossfire: The Plot that Killed Kennedy* (1989). Although these books are perhaps not works of academic scholarship, the point is that the film is citing its sources and providing a bibliography with the intent to present a scholarly argument. Indeed the film most practices a historical method when it cites National Security Agency Memoranda 263 and 273. Not only does Mr. X reference these government documents, but also the film snapshots (with an audible track that simulates a moving camera shutter) of the National Security Agency memoranda as if presenting the evidence to the viewer. Yes, these snapshots are fabrications and arguably they reinforce the critical characterization that Mr. X's historical argument is simply fantastic and counterfeit. But the film's point is that by presenting these simulated documents the movie signifies that the National Security Agency memoranda actually exist, and are available for public scrutiny.

For all intents and purposes, the film is presenting a scholarly notation at this moment in the movie, a cinematic version of a footnote for viewers to verify. The movie suggests to viewers to test its hypothesis and conclusion if they challenge the historical argument the film is presenting. In sum, the film is practicing the scientific method of historical scholarship that Beard maintained needs to be at the foundation of the historical discipline, and recalls the sine qui non of positivist historiography: to let the facts present themselves in order to be scrutinized and challenged via peer review. Of course the film is working outside the historical academy, but it is playing by its rules. We may disagree with *JFK*'s arguments and perhaps its historical methodologies, not to mention how the film asserts and supports its historical arguments in such clumsy and verbose ways. Nevertheless, *JFK* adheres to scholarly methods and wants to be identified as historical scholarship. We may consider it bad, perhaps even dangerous historiography; but its widespread release for public consumption and scrutiny also subjects the film to a version of peer review. The great degree to which *JFK* has been challenged, critiqued, and praised is a measure of how precisely the film practices or malpractices historiography. But the film knows that the historiographic arguments presented in the Mr. X sequence alone are not sufficient. It recognizes that more than historical explanation for the president's murder is necessary. The film needs to provide narrative closure and historical catharsis to achieve historiographic impact. As the trial sequence reveals, a case needs to be made and evidence needs to be presented to prove that there was an extensive, high-level government conspiracy to kill President Kennedy. In this regard, the purpose of the trial sequence is to provide the answers the American public has been searching for since President Kennedy's assassination, presenting an opportunity to work through the historical trauma his untimely death provoked.

As *JFK* recalls the narrative devices of the detective-mystery genre throughout the film, especially while Garrison discovers clues to uncover the plot to kill President Kennedy, the trial sequence represents the key cinematic moment where all the questions raised by the film's narrative discourse will ostensibly be answered in the climactic trial scene, especially the resolution to the question, "Who dunnit?" In detective-mystery films those answers may sometimes be alluded to over the course of the film (as in the case with the Mr. X constituent story in *JFK*) but the proverbial dots still need to be connected with an elaborate and dramatic display of evidence to satisfactorily prove the prosecutor's (and in some films the defendant's) case, if not for the viewers, then for the film's characters, particularly the judge and jury hearing the case. However, in *JFK* the stakes are actually higher. The trial sequence's (and by extension the film's) ambition is not only to achieve closure to the film's narrative discourse by answering the internal narrative questions, but also closure, if not catharsis, to our historical trauma. In the trial sequence, Jim Garrison has to prove "without reasonable doubt" that Clay Shaw is connected to a government conspiracy to assassinate President Kennedy, and in the process that the *Warren Report* was a fabrication, a ruse put over the American people to hide the sinister power of a shadow government. For viewers sitting in judgment of the film's historical arguments and narrative discourse, those seeds of doubt already have been laid in the Mr. X constituent story, and the function of the trial sequence is to demonstrate "what actually happened" on November 22,

1963, and the "truth" behind who assassinated the president. Precisely because the film has decided it needs to examine these issues, it turns to the positivist tradition of American historiography that reifies factual evidence, drawing upon scientific methods and empiricism to prove its historical case.

Perhaps the most powerful moments during the trial scene are not the testimonies of witnesses like Willie O'Keefe, who testify Shaw was connected to the assassination plot, but from scientists and doctors who testify about powerful political, military, and police forces interfering with their work, either to perform an autopsy or investigate forensic evidence connected to the president's murder. The film provocatively reenacts these testimonies showing how powerless these scientists and doctors are in the face of those working to cover up the conspiracy. But it is here where the reenactments assault our historical sensibilities and recall our trauma by displaying a cadaver of President Kennedy, including a replica of Kennedy's visage with the back of his head shattered, and blood matted in his hair. In one of these reenactments doctors are shown putting fingers in the cadaver's bullet wounds, as well as weighing the president's brain (which we also learn was lost during the Warren Commission's investigation). More than recalling our national trauma, these reenactments further traumatize us as they graphically, and arguably viscerally, assault us psychologically, horrifically requiring us to relive Kennedy's death. If viewers did not need to achieve historical catharsis before watching *JFK*, after these scenes of horror and violence, they probably want, perhaps demand, resolution for the president's murder, as well as proof to questions raised by Garrison (and the film's narrative discourse) about the murder conspiracy.

Provocatively, the answers are presented when Garrison shows the Zapruder film which he notes is shown for the "first time to the American public" during Shaw's trial.[75] Here, *JFK*'s intertextuality is significant. Narrative theory regarding intertextuality points to the ways texts are always in conversation with other texts, sometimes simultaneously or historically.[76] In this regard, the narrative discourse of *JFK* has an intertextual relationship with the Zapruder film, in the ways it references and cites it in the film to advance its historical argument. But more significantly, *JFK* is an actual narrativization of the Zapruder film itself, filling in the interpretive gaps by providing answers to the questions Zapruder's home movie raises. This is the movie's stunningly rhetorical and technical achievement. Replaying the Zapruder film during Shaw's trial situates Garrison's arguments with *JFK*'s opening sequence. During this introductory sequence we are reminded of the powerful camera and gunshots that Zapruder's film reveals. In point of fact, part of *JFK*'s intertextuality relies upon the movie tapping into the audience's knowledge of Zapruder's film and the ways it has become a signifying cultural and historical icon. As noted earlier, *JFK* relies on the Zapruder film as an icon, and how it informs our prior knowledge of the assassination. It also draws upon the ways we believe, almost ironically, that its brief twenty-six seconds simultaneously illuminate the mysteries while holding the answers to President Kennedy's murder, whether we actually have or have not seen the Zapruder film. We are thus not surprised to see Garrison replaying the film though it is presented as something "new" for the judge and jury. We are also not surprised to hear Garrison claim that the film is irrefutable evidence that a shot came from the grassy knoll. Finally, we agree with Garrison that the Warren Commission's conclusion about the singular "magic bullet" that pierced Kennedy and Governor John Connally is bogus. Thus *JFK* actually reminds rather than persuades us that we have already dismissed the *Warren Report*. For viewers, replaying Zapruder's home movie during the trial scene is a reminder of what we already know, not providing evidence to support a new theory. Though not intellectually persuasive, the Zapruder film is nonetheless deployed in the trial sequence to intensify our emotional connection to the Kennedy assassination, an intensity magnified by Garrison repeatedly showing the "kill shot" and repeatedly stating "back and to the left, back and to the left . . ." This short sequence, then, demands that we accept the "grassy knoll theory" and more importantly amplifies our trauma by continuously replaying the horror and violence of the "kill shot."

In the generic courtroom drama formula, the movie's closing arguments typically provide an eloquent resolution to the constituent trial story, and closure to the broader narrative discourse. Does Jim Garrison's closing statement do this? In part it does, as Garrison's soliloquy eloquently summarizes the arguments discrediting the *Warren Report* and elaborates upon the ways Kennedy's murder was part of a metaconspiracy to launch a coup d'état. However, Garrison's closing arguments become problematic once he asks the members of the jury (as well as the viewers) to remember "your dying king" as they (and we) deliberate upon the evidence to convict Clay Shaw. Such a conviction, Garrison argues, will begin to unravel "the house of cards" protecting those within the government covering up the president's murder. However, neither the film's narrative discourse nor the constituent trial story has adequately connected Clay Shaw to this metaconspiracy. Thus, we are not surprised that the jury quickly deliberates and acquits Shaw. So how should we treat the film's closing scenes, and do they provide narrative closure and historical catharsis? The film has raised a variety of questions about those involved in the Kennedy assassination, implicating, nay accusing, numerous powerful political, military, and intelligence leaders in the president's murder, and has made these issues the cornerstone of Garrison's legal case. But the jury categorically dismisses Garrison's case, even treating it as a farce. Nevertheless, the film's narrative discourse has been choreographed through the film's various constituent stories to fundamentally demonstrate that Garrison knows the truth behind the Kennedy assassination, even though practically everyone else rejects his conspiracy theory.

The ostensible narrative closure revolves around Garrison's personal victory despite his legal defeat. Rather than laugh and mock Garrison's effort like Clay Shaw, the jury, and reporters following the end of the trial, the film wants us to sympathize with Garrison and his noble search for the truth. In his closing arguments, Garrison tells the jury of donations from supporters, mostly small cash, who believe in his cause and yearn to uncover the truth behind those responsible for killing the president. The film ends with Garrison vowing to continue his pursuit to bring those involved in the conspiracy to trial despite his recent legal defeat. This final episode constructs a mise-en-scène that conveys this message. As the film closes, Garrison walks towards the light shining into the courthouse while Shaw, reporters, and the jury stand in darkened shadows. The film's point is as clear as it is predictable: recalling Plato's image of the cave, Garrison advances towards the light, emancipated that he knows the truth about Kennedy's murder and the sinister government forces at work, while others remained enslaved to the illusions—perhaps delusions that the government is not culpable in the plot to kill President Kennedy—produced by the cave's shadows.[77]

While this final scene may be unsatisfying as narrative closure, let alone historical catharsis, perhaps the film wants to leave these issues unresolved. Actually, an unresolved closure and lack of catharsis would maintain the spirit of the film and its idea of history. Firmly rooted in modernity and the Enlightenment Project, the film asserts that there is a knowable truth to the Kennedy assassination and Garrison has exposed it. Now armed with this knowledge, the film practically implores us to become agents of history like Jim Garrison, and make our government accountable for its lies and corruption. The film, in this regard, champions the ideas of historical subjectivity and possessive individualism. From the film's perspective, our nation will be better served if we were to take political action as citizens to ensure that justice is resolved. Herein lies the film's promise of emancipation, human progress, and especially historical catharsis. We will finally work through our collective national trauma and integrate our history with our present condition by becoming historical agents like Jim Garrison, learning the truth about the Kennedy assassination and living our lives according to the idea of America envisioned by President Kennedy. In other words, *JFK* fundamentally demands that we rewrite our national history, one that is currently shaped by a corrupt government. Such an act of historical agency will change our present world and our future as well. In effect, we can take back our country and truly make it the democracy we envision it to be. In this vein, the film requires us to shape American history and society according to John F. Kennedy's New Frontier liberalism: we are not asked what our country can do for us, but what we can do for our country. According to *JFK*, taking control of our historical narrative in order to expose the truth about Kennedy's assassination is the promise of a better future and a path towards human progress.

Although the focus of *American History Goes to the Movies* is the relationship between film and history, it is necessary to briefly explore Don DeLillo's historical novel *Libra*, and juxtapose it to Oliver Stone's *JFK*. Examining these historical narratives together will enable us to gain a deeper understanding about the ways the Kennedy assassination is a modern "historical event" that signifies larger issues about recent American history and modernity's philosophy of history. In this regard, both the film and novel allow us to see the critical function historical narratives play in our efforts to achieve historical meaning in the Kennedy assassination. If historical agency and exposing the truth about President Kennedy's assassination are the themes of *JFK*, they are the themes of Don DeLillo's *Libra* as well. However, in DeLillo's historical novel these ideals and much of the philosophy and history of modernity are challenged and critiqued. *Libra* is a narrative about the dark side of the American Dream and the ways in which our pursuits of happiness, individual freedom, and our efforts to shape history can have deadly consequences. By taking the point-of-view of Lee Oswald (arguably even making him the book's protagonist) we observe the tensions between fate and free will, wondering whether history moves us along its trajectory or whether we have the ability to determine the historical course of our lives. As in the movie *JFK*, *Libra* recognizes the Kennedy assassination in the ways Hayden White describes the "historical event."[78] Throughout the book, the president's murder not only is a historical moment in itself, but also represents the crushing weight of history, and questions the possibility of history to contain knowable truth. In this regard, the book, as we will see, more closely approximates a postmodern view of history rather than the film *JFK*, as scholars contend.[79] As *Libra* critiques modernity's reification of historical subjectivity, it also challenges modernity's historical and scientific epistemologies.

Don DeLillo's *Libra* reflects this postmodern sensibility in the ways David Harvey theoretically defines and uses the term: the postmodern references and alludes to the modern while critiquing it, sometimes highlighting the absurdity of its epistemological order of knowledge, often framed in playful and ironic discourses.[80] In addition to its critique of modernity, the novel is a bricolage and pastiche of constituent stories involving Oswald, covert intelligence operatives, and the CIA historian Nicholas Branch, all of which collectively connect to a narrative discourse about the absurdity and irony of history. Like the film *JFK*, *Libra* mixes fact and fiction; but in contrast to the film, DeLillo's historical novel blends the real and fictive partly to point out the absurdity of knowing the truth of the assassination itself. Nevertheless, *Libra* recognizes the assassination as a "historical event" signifying greater historical meaning. As a narrative about modernity, the novel examines the relationship between the feelings of alienation and the desire for belonging, looking at the complicated ways history addresses this relationship. Over the course of the book, we become aware that the referenced "little rooms" that the principal characters frequently find themselves enclosed in represent a common motif about alienation, individualism and modern bureaucratic compartmentalized culture. History, as we learn, is the means by which these characters escape these small, isolating spaces, and to connect to something larger themselves.

The life of Lee Oswald is the central narrative that reflects the tension between modernity and the American Dream. The book begins with Oswald as a young boy enthralled with riding the New York subway system, feeling the thrill of moving in darkness, not knowing where it may take him, winding and propelling him through underground tunnels. By introducing us to Oswald in his youth and while living in New York City, *Libra* highlights the ways this metropolis is the capital of the twentieth century and modernity, much as Walter Benjamin saw Paris as the capital of the nineteenth century. Where the Parisian arcade symbolizes modernity and its discontents for Benjamin, so too does the subway represent these ideas in DeLillo's historical novel. Moreover, New York is the capital of the American century, a century dominated by American technological ingenuity, finance capitalism, and military weapons, all in the service of advancing, even "spreading" its American Dream across the world.[81] The American century promised human progress: advanced scientific knowledge to cure human ailments; liberal democracy to protect individual freedom; and liberal economics to promote individual prosperity. But if this was the promise of the American century, somehow Oswald missed the "train" that will enable him to enjoy the fruits of the American Dream. In the novel, the subway reflects the progress and efficiency of modern technology, but it also contributes to mass alienation:

> This was the year he [Oswald] rode the subway to the ends of the city, two hundred miles of track. He liked to stand at the front of the first car, hands flat against the glass. The train smashed through the dark. People stood on local platforms staring nowhere, a look they had been practicing for years. He kind of wondered, speeding past, who they really were . . . They went so fast sometimes he thought they were on the edge of no-control . . . Another crazy-ass curve. There was so much iron in the sound of those curves he could almost taste it, like a toy, you put in your mouth when you are little . . . A tenth of a second was all it took to see a thing complete. Then the express stations, the creaky brakes, people bunched like refugees. They came wagging through the doors, banged against rubber edges, inched their way in, were quickly pinned looking out past the nearest heads into that practiced oblivion.[82]

The people on the subway are isolated individuals, faceless and disconnected, devoid of their humanity, hurtling in the underground darkness as they go off to their destinations. But the subway episode also reflects the historical novel's idea of history. The subway, like history, winds, twists, and collectively propels people in darkness, towards a known, yet desolate destination. In this passage, the book suggests that although we "share" this historical moment collectively, our myopic individualistic concerns alienate us from one another. In other words, we may share time and space en masse, but we do not engage each other as our solipsism and individual pursuits of the American Dream disconnect us from one another as a national community. The subway constituent story reflects Walter Benjamin's philosophy of history as much as it contributes to the book's narrative discourse about history and modernity. In the *Arcades Project*, Benjamin articulated history and the "historical event" as the accumulation and intensification of the past. In

*Libra*, the subway represents the accumulated history of technological "progress," the intensified historical artifact that is part of a longer history of the locomotive. The train initially carried commercial commodities to far-flung destinations over the course of the nineteenth century, and now carries people in the underground subway to various destinations that make up their dysfunctional lives. As a "historical event" the train is not the signifier of modern scientific progress where the train and its tracks act as sinews of the body politic, creating a national community. Rather it has done the opposite. The subway, according to *Libra*, actually intensifies and amplifies people's alienation as it places them in "small spaces" imprisoned by the iron train, history, and modernity:

> People crowded in, every shape in the book of faces. They pushed through the doors, they hung from the porcelain straps. He was riding just to ride. The noise had a power and a human force. The dark had a power. He stood at the front of the first car, hands flat against the glass. The view down the tracks was a form of power. It was a secret and a power. The beams picked out secret things. The noise was pitched to a fury he located in the mind, a satisfying wave of rage and pain . . . Never again in his short life, never in the world, would he feel the inner power, rising to a shriek, this secret force of the soul in the tunnels of New York.[83]

The presence of the television throughout *Libra* signifies it as a "historical event" of the twentieth century as well, but it is also critiqued as another example of modern technological progress. Although television has been celebrated for creating a national community, connecting people as a nation across a mammoth and expansive geographic space such as the United States, in DeLillo's novel it is also a destructive atomizing force. Televisions are a common motif in a variety of DeLillo's novels (particularly *White Noise*), reflecting the ways that technologies control us and shape our worldview rather than acting as mere instruments used by people to acquire information, knowledge, and to be entertained. That the novel quickly moves from young Oswald riding the subway to him watching television demonstrates how these twin technologies, supposedly created to make our lives better, efficient, and enhance our sense of community, actually are sinister projects contributing to our alienation in modern America, (de)constructing our sense of self and society. In the case of television, our history and our reality, and by extension our epistemologies, are structured by its technological force. For example, as Oswald ponders his role in the plot to assassinate President Kennedy, he watches a double feature on late night television:

> The first movie was *Suddenly*. Frank Sinatra is a combat veteran who comes to a small town and takes over a house that overlooks the railroad depot. He is here to assassinate the President. Lee felt the stillness around him. He had an eerie sense he was being watched for his reaction . . . He felt connected

to the events on the screen. It was like secret instructions entering the network of signals and broadcast bands, the whole busy air of transmission . . . They were running a message through the night into his skin . . . Lee knew [Sinatra] would fail. It was, in the end, a movie. They had to fix it so he failed and died . . . Then we watched *We Were Strangers*. John Garfield is an American revolutionary in Cuba in the 1930s. He plots to assassinate the dictator and blow up his entire Cabinet . . . Lee felt he was in the middle of his own movie. They were running this thing just for him. He didn't have to make the picture come and go . . . John Garfield dies a hero. He has to die. This is what feeds a revolution.[84]

As the passage illustrates, the television represents a larger theme about historical agency and historical destiny connecting this constituent story about Oswald watching television before assassinating the president to the book's broader narrative discourse about history and modernity. The book's title, *Libra*, of course reflects this theme most clearly. DeLillo's historical novel poses the question of whether we are in control of our historical agency or whether the patterns and broader forces of history, like our astrological signs, determine our fate, twisting and propelling us in a direction which has an end, but one of which we are fundamentally unaware. The book also poses the question of whether history is the sum total of patterns and connections, or whether it is a series of coincidences. Oswald ruminates over this frequently throughout the book, and is reminded, especially by David Ferrie, that history is more than the sum of coincidences, that it has patterns and directions: it reveals signs and omens that we can interpret to know our fate, but despite our best intentions, it sets our course with a predestined trajectory. Ferrie points out to Oswald that his astrological sign is the Libran, how his fate hangs in the balance, and the direction he chooses to tip the scales will determine the outcome of the conspiracy to kill President Kennedy. Ferrie tells Lee, "You're a quirk of history. You're a coincidence. They devise a plan, you fit it perfectly. They lose you, here you are. There's a pattern in things."[85] Everywhere Oswald looks, he sees signs and omens about history's plan for him. At times he thinks he is the master of his own fate, yet the signs, such as the television movies about assassination plots that he watches, tell him that his life has already been determined by the fates of history.

Presenting the life of Lee Oswald as the central story in *Libra* is more than an ironic gesture to narrativize the Kennedy assassination. Humanizing Kennedy's assassin, by telling his life story mixed as fact and fiction, enables this historical novel to interrogate the meaning of the American Dream and its philosophy of history. The American Dream posits that if people work hard, play by the rules, acquire an education, nothing will limit them in their aspirations, nor inhibit them from achieving success. According to this ideology, the only thing that prevents people from acquiring material prosperity and their pursuits of happiness are the constraints they put upon themselves. *Libra*, however, twists, inverts, and summarily critiques this foundational American philosophy, demonstrating how vacuous it is and how it is not as easily attainable as Americans are led to believe. As Lee's mother repeatedly states in her statements to the Warren Commission, she has faced numerous challenges as a single mother, but her American Dream is to have a decent home for Lee, and provide him with his material needs as much as she possibly can. Despite a broken marriage and frequently moving from home to home, she believes she did the best she could for Lee. As she states in her testimony to the Warren Commission, "How on God's earth, and I am a Christian, does a neglectful mother make such a decent home, which I am willing to show as evidence, with bright touches and not a thing out of place."[86] Although Lee's mother wants to excuse her culpability in his psychological history, she actually believes they were a decent American family. They may have fallen on hard times, but they did what they could to make ends meet, pursuing, if elusively, an American Dream.

Oswald's educational and military career are presented in the novel as examples of the ways democratic American institutions were not vehicles through which Lee could succeed, but contributed to his history of abject failure. As the book begins, Lee is frequently truant or simply does not attend school. He has learning disabilities, but school authorities do not attempt to work with his academic low achievement. He is simply written off as a loser, an identity which is reinforced by kids at school and in the neighborhood. Yet, in the book, Lee assumes this identity with pride and dreams of an alternative identity that imagines him as successful. Indeed, Lee lives a perverted, nightmarish American Dream. Rather than give up on the institutions and people that have given up on him, he maintains a faith and belief there is a better tomorrow. The future holds promises of a better life, whether that is in the army, defecting to Russia, returning to the United States, or fighting for the Cuban Revolution and hoping to immigrate to Cuba. *Libra* presents Oswald as profoundly American, perhaps more so than the celebrated president he assassinates. And even if America has given up on him, he has not given up on its values. Schools and the military are fundamentally democratic institutions in the United States, defined by an ideology of meritocracy and offer the possibility of success based upon achievement tied to merit. While these institutions fail Oswald, he continues to believe that success is just "around the corner," moving his family around to live out his dreams. Oswald struggles with the forces of history and his individual agency, but he fundamentally believes he is a part of history. History is the solution to Oswald's misery. It will provide him with the celebrated individual notoriety he has been hoping for all his life. And it is the television that provides him with his historic celebrity. When he assassinates President Kennedy, he no longer is the loner and isolated Lee Oswald, the American failure. He is repeatedly identified as Lee Harvey Oswald, his full name magnified by the media as if to signify greater importance to the man accused of assassinating a beloved, celebrated president. Oswald achieves his American Dream by killing the American president. And herein lies the irony of history:

People will come to see him, the lawyers first, then psychologists, historians, biographers. His life had a single clear subject now, called Lee Harvey Oswald . . . He and Kennedy were partners. The figure of the gunman in the window was inextricable from the victim and his history. This sustained Oswald in his cell. It gave him what he needed to live.[87]

Like Oliver Stone's *JFK*, Don DeLillo's *Libra* mixes fact and fiction to emplot constituent stories as well as the book's narrative discourse. However, *Libra* does not provoke the same controversy about its narrative methodologies as *JFK*. Perhaps because DeLillo writes a disclaimer at the end of the novel that states his book is fundamentally a work of fiction, *Libra* has not produced the same outcry as Oliver Stone's film. But it should also be noted that *Libra* does not attempt to reveal the historical truth about who assassinated President Kennedy. DeLillo's book does address certain historical truths, but its historical objectives are more Aristotelian. The book's narrative discourse maintains that we can achieve historical meaning from the Kennedy assassination, but its historical significance does not revolve around the historical details concerning the question "Who shot JFK?" The book's historical goals are more literary, focusing more upon the ways in which President Kennedy's death is an allegory about modernity and the American Dream. The *Warren Report* and the numerous historical documents cited in the book are employed to advance *Libra*'s narrative discourse that questions modernity's epistemology of history and our ability to know historical truth, not to engage with the historical minutiae within the *Warren Report* itself. True, by weaving a narrative about a broader conspiracy to assassinate the president, including many of the same figures Oliver Stone's *JFK* references, DeLillo's *Libra* challenges the Warren Commission's conclusions. However, disputing the findings in the *Warren Report* is not the objective of the novel's narrative discourse as much as examining broader historical issues about modern American life. Nevertheless, when the book weaves fact and faction, such as drawing upon the *Warren Report* to recount the life of Oswald while fictionally elaborating upon the report to fill in the interpretive gaps, it is "reenacting" history similarly to the ways Oliver Stone's *JFK* reenacts scenes throughout the film. Yet, since the narrative discourse examines the epistemological dimensions of history rather than offer answers to more detailed historical questions, *Libra*'s deployment of historical documents compliment rather than undermine the book's narrative.

Nicholas Branch and his struggle to write "the secret history" of the Kennedy assassination is the constituent story that reflects the book's broader themes about modernity and the epistemological dilemma of knowing the history of the Kennedy murder. Branch's historical project and his life in his isolated "little room" symbolizes the irrationality of modern bureaucratic institutional culture, rather than one reflective of Weberian rationalism. Max Weber argues that the compartmentalization of modern bureaucracies promote an empirical and rational culture that stresses industry and efficiency.[88] However, as Weber describes this industrial and rational approach to bureaucratic productivity, he also maintains that modern bureaucratic rationalism produces isolation and alienation, among bureaucrats themselves, but more importantly between bureaucrats and the subject of their compartmentalized work. Bureaucratic culture reifies the objectivity of the task at hand, and not the subjects that define the nature of the work, whether those are economic figures or everyday people. *Libra* critiques this modern bureaucratic culture in the constituent story about the former and current CIA operatives such as Winn Everett, who conspire to stage an assassination attempt of President Kennedy. Their objective to destabilize Fidel Castro's regime and the Cuban Revolution, however, leads to the objectification of President Kennedy himself in their efforts to achieve their political goal. Although they may be caught up in the frenzy of the Cold War and their plot is to make a strategic miss of the president, the compartmentalized institutional culture that has defined their lives for so many years has led Winn Everett, Larry Parmenter, T.J. Mackey, among others to disregard the human cost involved in their plan, which they believe will escalate hostility between the United States and Cuba and produce a more aggressive foreign policy against Castro.[89] The unraveling of this conspiracy and the actual murder of the president is one of *Libra*'s critiques of modern bureaucratic rational culture, as well as one of the book's central tragic ironies.

Nicholas Branch's constituent story is also about the futility of our historical epistemology and possibility of recovering "historical truth." Isolated in his small room in a CIA compound, Branch sifts through the massive information collected about the president's assassination. In addition to the data he has collected, the unnamed Archivist continues to deluge Branch with more information. The Archivist sends scientific data about ballistic tests, autopsy reports, information that the Warren Commission never received. He has information regarding CIA operatives and other intelligence personnel who may or may not have been involved in the conspiracy. Although Branch has tried to write his "secret history," he is simply overwhelmed and buried under files, notes, and reports:

> Paper is beginning to slide out of the room and across the doorway to the house proper. The floor is covered with books and papers. The closet is stuffed with material he has yet to read . . . This is the room of lonely facts. The stuff keeps coming.[90]

Branch's frustration with his research and writing reflects more than his dilemma to write a neo-positivist history of the president's assassination "as it actually happened," it also represents the futility of writing such a history altogether. Despite the massive evidence available to him, Branch cannot write his secret history. He knows he can assemble the data, but he does not know how to emplot it. In other words, Branch cannot write a historical narrative that provides an explanation of the Kennedy assassination, let alone one that offers historical meaning. In other words, not only can we never know the historical answer to who was involved in the president's murder, and how widespread was this conspiracy, but also we cannot even tell the story of the president's assassination because we do not know the story we want to tell:

> Branch has become wary of these cases of cheap coincidence. He's beginning to think someone is trying to sway him toward superstition. He wants a thing to be what it is. Can't a man die without the ensuing ritual of a search for patterns and links?[91]

Of course the "search for patterns" to illuminate historical causality is precisely the nature of practicing history, and that this eludes Nicholas Branch reflects our epistemological quandary. We want to "know the historical truth" but apparently we do not know the historical story we want to tell. We know we do not fully accept the findings of the Warren Commission, but what else is there? We understand and empathize with Nicholas Branch's dilemma, because it is our dilemma as well:

> You have lost me, Chief Justice Warren . . . [Branch] begins to merge with Oswald. He can't tell the difference between them. All he knows for sure is that there is a missing element here, a word that they have canceled completely . . . Oswald is inside him now. How can he fight the knowledge of what he is? The truth of the world is exhausting. He lowers his head and runs into the concrete wall . . . He reads into the night. He sleeps in the armchair. There are times when he thinks he can't go on . . . He knows he can't get out. The case will haunt him to the end. Of course they've known it all along. That's why they built this room for him, the room of growing old, the room of history and dreams.[92]

While we, like Branch, search to know the history of the assassination, traditional efforts to historicize this "historical event" will continue to elude us. *Libra* leaves Branch's constituent story without narrative closure, where he is left alone in his little room befuddled, frustrated, "left to die," without ever writing the "secret history" of the assassination. However, *Libra* nonetheless does offer narrative closure, to the book's narrative discourse about modernity and the American Dream, and perhaps a measure of historical catharsis. The Kennedy assassination signifies a major "historical event," but one that is pregnant with irony. Not only did Kennedy's death end the optimism of the American century, but also it arguably ushered American society into the postmodern age: where images not facts represent reality; historical truth is unknowable; historical subjectivity remains elusive; and the American Dream is attainable for some, but it is also an American illusion and nightmare for others.

Oliver Stone's *JFK* and Don DeLillo's *Libra* reveal the limitations of academic history and its ability to recover an historical explanation and understanding of

President Kennedy's assassination. But they also illuminate that achieving historical meaning in this "historical event" is achievable through historical narrativity. By emplotting "historical events" and people in a series of stories, connected to a broader narrative discourse, *JFK* and *Libra* are works of history that attempt to provide historical closure to a traumatic national event in American history. Whether the film and historical novel achieve this successfully remains debatable, but they illustrate the significance of narrativity as a historical methodology and as historiography, particularly in the history of the Kennedy assassination. Narrativity is not simply a way to tell or represent history; it is also a way to articulate historical interpretation. Ultimately, we seek historical interpretation when we study the past in order to understand the past's broader historical significance and meaning. Although Oliver Stone's *JFK* arguably undermines its narrative discourse by trying to retell the Kennedy assassination in a neo-positivistic manner, that is to narrate the facts "as they actually happened," it nonetheless reflects the critical ways narrativity as a historical methodology is instrumental in the historiography of the Kennedy assassination. The film's narrative closure remains problematic, and it is debatable we achieve historical catharsis once the film ends. But perhaps this is intentional. It may be that the film's intent is to encourage viewers to integrate the historical trauma produced by President Kennedy's death by becoming historical agents themselves, making their political institutions accountable for their questionable, even dubious role in the investigation of the president's murder.

Don DeLillo's *Libra* more successfully provides narrative closure in resolving the book's narrative discourse, but remains questionable whether the novel sufficiently provides historical catharsis. Perhaps this is not the book's intent as much as it is for Oliver Stone's film. But *Libra* nonetheless signifies President Kennedy's assassination as a "historical event." In the book, the president's murder is an allegory about the limits of the Enlightenment Project, a critique of modernity's claims of historical subjectivity, the promise of scientific empiricism, and the possibility for human progress. Furthermore, the novel's postmodern sensibility illuminates the ironies of history (such as Oswald asserting historical agency and achieving his American Dream by assassinating President Kennedy), as well as modernity's epistemological claim that historical truth is knowable. Nevertheless, *Libra*, like *JFK*, reflects how narrativity as historical methodology can reveal historical understanding and meaning even in an "historical event" such as President Kennedy's assassination, an American tragedy whose specific historical details and answers continue to elude us.

# 8

## "WE ARE ALIVE IN HELL"

### Finding Historical Meaning and Significance in 9/11

The film *United 93* begins with the men who would become the hijackers of this airplane seemingly performing their ordinary morning routines. Some are dressing while others are praying and reading religious texts. Yet, mixed into these apparent displays of their daily tasks are suggestions that something ominous is about to happen, beginning with the pulsating soundtrack that establishes the film's dramatic tension. In this opening scene, we view one of the men palpably anxious and another shaving his entire body. Initiating the film from the hijackers' point-of-view profoundly establishes the tone of the film, particularly in the ways it weaves the ordinary and extraordinary, attributes that will also define the course of events on September 11, 2001. Moreover, this scene reinforces our historical knowledge about what happened on 9/11, namely that Islamist extremists hijacked American commercial aircraft, and turned them into weapons of mass destruction directed towards American landmarks such as the Twin Towers of the World Trade Center and the Pentagon. This historical knowledge will predicate the way viewers engage the movie, powerfully reinforcing the cinematic sensibility of fear that unfolds over the course of the film. Precisely because we know what happened on that day in September 2001, the film's narrative tension intensifies as the events move towards the hijacking of United Airlines Flight 93, emotionally enveloping us in the movie's terror. Yet, the opening moments of *United 93* do not portray these men as menacing terrorists even though we know their malevolent plan. In fact, we become acutely aware in this scene, as well as in those that follow, that the movie is about the ways people transcend the banality of everyday life to perform the heroic.

Despite the opening scene's narrative power, whether the hijackers actually enacted these morning activities on September 11th is purely speculative and interpretive. Nevertheless, the scene provokes viewers to take the hijackers' perspective, and Ziad Jarrah in particular, the character who is identified as the group's leader and who will pilot the plane once the hijackers seize control of the aircraft.[1] As the narrative of *United 93* proceeds, we observe his anxiety and his hesitation to actually follow through with the planned suicide mission. Moreover, we also watch him call someone on his cell-phone before boarding the plane, stating "I love you" in German (although it is unclear if he is speaking to an answering machine or to a person on the other line). In *United 93*, Ziad Jarrah is not a monster, an embodiment of evil; rather he emerges as a scared, perhaps misguided human being who exhibits similar emotions as the other passengers on the plane. After all, these passengers are also talking into their cell-phones like Jarrah before boarding the plane, further connecting him with his fellow passengers. A sense of dread falls over Jarrah's phone call, as we know that he knows this will be the last one he will place.

In fact, the film will later recall this early scene of people placing pre-boarding phone calls with another one when passengers make frantic calls as the hijacked plane plummets towards earth, contacting their loved ones to say their last farewells. These are arresting and wrenching scenes that illuminate the ways a most basic act we take for granted becomes a precious solemn gesture weighted with emotional significance for the passengers of United 93. Sadly, some passengers will say goodbye to answering machines or whomever they can reach, hoping the person at the other end of the phone call will relay their last message to family members. These scenes that focus on the final phone calls reflect the film's powerful narrative discourse about the ways we revere human relationships when we face catastrophe. *United 93* is not a jingoistic film about the indomitable American spirit against jihadist al Qaeda terrorists; it is a story about the ways in which we signify and cherish personal relationships, and how these relationships help us endure life's tragic moments. Significantly, though, the film also includes Jarrah as part of this narrative discourse and encourages us to empathize with him, perhaps even understand him, although we are never meant to (nor would want to) sympathize with them.

In this respect the film attempts to do something that the *9/11 Commission Report* had hoped to achieve as well: that is, provide Americans with answers to questions about the terrorists' motivation to perform such incredibly malevolent acts on September 11th and from their point-of-view. It is questionable whether the film or the 9/11 National Commission's report adequately succeed in this regard, but *United 93*'s narrative discourse and initial empathetic treatment of Jarrah provide a level of catharsis to the historical trauma produced by the events on September 11th that the *9/11 Commission Report* has yet to resolve. It also offers a level of psychological meaning to a national tragedy where other narratives about the terrorist attacks arguably have failed. However, it is less clear whether *United 93* or the *9/11 Commission Report* provide "historical" understanding of the September 11th terrorist attacks nor how these narratives consider the events of 9/11 collectively to be a significant "event" that has shaped American history.

Drawing upon academic and cinematic representations of the September 11th terrorist attacks, this chapter examines the ways in which these representations portray these attacks as an "historical event." By signifying particular moments in the American past as "historical events" we acknowledge that these moments represent qualitatively different, perhaps more important episodes than others in American history, profoundly imbued with greater meaning. In the pantheon of epic American historical events, the American Revolution, the Civil War, the Great Depression and World War II stand apart and typically receive widespread recognition as transformative moments in our history that have shaped the American character. Where other historical episodes stand in relation to these major events reflects the degree to which we regard them as important, and how they also have influenced the course of American history. But this perspective is partly determined by our position in time as well. For example, we arguably recognize the Mexican–American and the Spanish–American wars as more significant historical events today than we might have a generation ago because of recent trends in American foreign policy, including the 2003 Iraq War. For many Americans who came of age in the post-World War II era, President Kennedy's assassination stands as a significant historical event, even though the effects of the president's death on the course of American history remains uncertain. People widely recognize that the terrorist attacks of September 11th represent an important moment in American history as well; but like the Kennedy assassination, its historical significance remains unclear.

In this regard, this chapter builds on Chapter 7's arguments about the significance of historical events and national tragedies, and how these representations are ways in which Americans engage historical moments of national trauma, seeking historical meaning and understanding in the process. This chapter thus revisits many of the ideas and arguments that focused on historical representations of President Kennedy's assassination as it interrogates historical narratives of 9/11. In fact, this chapter draws upon the principal academic and filmmaker from Chapter 7, namely Peter Dale Scott and Oliver Stone, and their interpretations of the events of September 11th. Perhaps we should not be surprised that Scott and Stone would examine the issues surrounding 9/11 given the ways Americans have yet to achieve historical understanding of this national tragedy, much as they have not with President Kennedy's assassination. And despite the work of the 9/11 National Commission and the lengthy report it published, there are still unanswered questions regarding the secrecy that shrouds intelligence information provided by government agencies such as the CIA and FBI. Questions also remain about these agencies' previous knowledge of potential terrorist threats against the United States and what counterterrorist efforts were made by the government to defend Americans. Because the 9/11 National Commission respected the need for government secrecy regarding intelligence information, and thus refused to provide classified information to the public in its report (thereby protecting the clandestine activities of intelligence agencies),[2] the *9/11 Commission Report* practically invited conspiracy theories and alternative historical narratives that provided answers to questions the report left unresolved.

Like the Warren Commission that investigated the assassination of President Kennedy and its subsequent report, the 9/11 National Commission and its published report received criticism as it refused to attribute responsibility or blame to any government agency or presidential administration (specifically the Clinton and the Bush administrations) for not defending Americans from the terrorist attacks.[3] In the process, critics such as Peter Dale Scott accuse the 9/11 National Commission of covering-up government activities that might lead to the truth of "what actually happened" on September 11th.[4] Scott believes there may be additional information about the government's knowledge of terrorist activities in the months preceding the attacks that might illuminate why the government was ill equipped to defend the United States from al Qaeda. For Scott, investigating and revealing the activities of the intelligence agencies and the Bush Administration would offer insight into the reasons why the United States supported terrorist organizations such as al Qaeda, particularly during the Soviet–Afghan War in the 1980s.[5] Such an investigation might also reveal the degree to which the Bush administration recognized the significance of an attack against the United States like that which occurred on September 11th, "Another Pearl Harbor" as some administration officials stated, and how it was instrumental to their plans to encourage the American people to support the administration's plan to wage a war against Iraq.[6] Nevertheless, in the end the 9/11 National Commission achieved bipartisan unanimity with its report as well as respect and regard for avoiding contemporary vituperative partisan politics.[7] But it also presented an unsatisfactory report that did not conclusively resolve pressing questions about "what actually happened" on 9/11, and the more profound question for many Americans: "Why do [Islamist extremists] hate us so?"[8] It is particularly this last question that addresses the issue of historical meaning and understanding. And though the 9/11 National Commission attempted to answer these questions by providing the historical context of al Qaeda and the rise of contemporary radical Islamism, it still falls short of addressing fundamental epistemological issues about historical knowing that center on the motivation of the terrorists who hijacked American commercial aircraft on September 11th, 2001.

Both the 9/11 National Commission and Peter Dale Scott recognize that understanding the historical meaning of 9/11 lies in placing this momentous and tragic event in historical context, signifying it as an "historical event." In other words the answers to the pressing questions that perplex Americans lies within "history," and that 9/11 cannot be understood unless it is connected to broader historical events and ideas that explain the emergence of al Qaeda and why the United States' government was ill prepared to defend the American people from domestic terrorist attacks.[9] However, where 9/11 must be understood in the context of postcolonial movements in the Muslim world and the history of American foreign policy in the view of the 9/11 National Commission, Peter Dale

Scott contends that the history of September 11th lies within the broader history of clandestine American intelligence agencies, in addition to the historical issues the National Commission did address. Interestingly, for both the 9/11 National Commission and Peter Dale Scott, the historical meaning and significance of 9/11 lay in the way in which this event has produced challenges to American democracy. But where the 9/11 National Commission believes this to be an external and foreign cultural threat to American values and institutions, Scott contends the "deep state" and its abuse of constitutional power continues to be the major threat to the future of American democracy.[10]

In order for Americans to understand the historical meaning of 9/11, Peter Dale Scott maintains that they need to know the history of the American "deep state." For him, it provides the key to the epistemological crisis of historical knowing that shrouds this national tragedy. He contends that this "deep state" history enables us to resolve the quandary regarding what happened on September 11th, and why it happened. But Scott fails to see the powerful role historical narrative plays in addressing this epistemological dilemma. Here, the *9/11 Commission Report* provides a significant contribution to the emerging literature on 9/11. As noted in Chapter 7, narratives are more than a way to organize data; they constitute stories that provide insight and meaning to help people order and understand their universe. The 9/11 National Commission almost preternaturally recognizes the critical function of narrative as it recounts multiple stories about the events, people, and major issues surrounding the September 11th terrorist attacks in its report. It even self-consciously states that it "presents a narrative of this report," knowing that it needed to represent the events and history of 9/11 fundamentally different from a typical government policy report,[11] otherwise it could be regarded as detached and disinterested to the human tragedy of September 11th. Ernest May, the American historian serving as chief advisor to the 9/11 National Commission, notes that initially the *9/11 Commission Report* was set to begin its narrative with the history of Islam and the contemporary Islamic world in order to understand the emergence of al Qaeda and their jihad against Americans and the United States. As May states:

> The [original] outline [of the report] had called for opening with a chapter on al Qaeda, perhaps beginning with the birth of Islam. Late in the process of drafting the report, [Commission member and former Congressman Tim] Roemer recommended that the first chapter describe what happened on 9/11. [Fellow Commission member Fred] Fielding seconded Roemer's proposal, and all the other commissioners quickly agreed. It was an inspired recommendation that added to the report's narrative power.[12]

The original narrative strategy would have fundamentally addressed the question of "why do they hate us so," providing a level of historical understanding of 9/11 from the terrorists' point-of-view. However, the final draft of the report opens with the narratives of the airplane hijackings seemingly constructed from the passengers' phone calls and reports from air traffic controllers.[13] Additionally, the report narrativizes the chaos and confusion confronting federal agencies as they tried to determine what was transpiring on September 11th, and then the actions they took once they realized that the planes were being hijacked and deployed as deadly missiles aimed at significant American landmarks.[14] While Ernest May recognizes that this last-minute editorial change was a brilliant move that established the narrative tone of the *9/11 Commission Report*,[15] he overlooks how this was also a narrative strategy that undermined the 9/11 National Commission's effort to provide readers with the historical understanding that would have enabled them to empathize with the Muslim world and their complicated relationship with the United States and the West. Then again, perhaps the 9/11 National Commission did understand these narrative strategies and reorganized the report for readers to sympathize with the victims of the terrorist attacks. By ending the report's historical narrative with the horrific experience of the victims trapped in the Twin Towers and Pentagon, as well as those first responders who sought to rescue them, the 9/11 National Commission only reinforced the powerful narrative discourse about American tragedy and heroism.

But the events of September 11th stand outside of history in this final rendition of the report, devoid of political accountability and institutional culpability that might provide insight into pertinent historical questions of "what actually happened" and "how could it have happened." The *9/11 Commission Report* is a compelling story nonetheless, and provides a different kind of narrative discourse about human endurance in the face of horror than a film like *United 93*, and how our relationships with family and friends enable us to confront historical disaster. In this regard, the report is creative non-fiction rather than history, arguably rising to the status of literature. Perhaps filmmakers Paul Greengrass and Oliver Stone recognized this as Greengrass's *United 93* and Stone's *World Trade Center* advance the *9/11 Commission Report* in the narrative discourse of their films. However, these movies either minimize or criticize the politics and historical context of September 11th. As we will see, *United 93* depoliticizes 9/11 to emphasize the tragic and heroic human narratives that defined that day, particularly in the ways the passengers of United 93 rebelled against the hijackers and thwarted their suicide mission. Later in this chapter we will also see how Oliver Stone criticizes the historical and political dimensions of September 11th as he narrates powerful stories about human triumphs overcoming what his film depicts as a near-apocalyptic disaster. Perhaps the film's running criticism with the "historical" nature of 9/11 reflects Stone's disapproval of those leaders who controversially politicized this American calamity to advance their own political agendas, namely the 2003 Iraq War. For Stone, one of the defining moments of September 11th was the way Americans and the world were drawn together into a global community, integrated by modern media, and sharing a collective narrative of suffering and endurance as ordinary men and women were called upon to rescue the victims of the World Trade Center Complex. While televisions chatter with news anchors and pundits discussing the political and historical significance of the terrorist attacks throughout Stone's film, these issues are not the ones that galvanize Americans to help one another through the trauma of 9/11, according to *World Trade Center*. Rather, the significance of that momentous day in September 2001 lies in the way we reached out to one another to embrace humanity as we confronted a profound tragedy.

## The *9/11 Commission Report*: Epistemological Crisis and Dramatic Historical Narrative

Signifying 9/11 as an historical event that provoked an epistemological crisis reminds us of similar moments in human history when people searched for meaning and understanding to explain contemporary cataclysmic events. The "fall" of Rome, for example, prompted people in the late Roman Empire to question how an advanced civilization and once powerful military could succumb to lesser "barbarians." As St. Augustine wrote, some Romans blamed Christians and their faith for undermining Roman ideals, Roman society and the Roman state. Of course St. Augustine dismisses these arguments, but he does so by providing a way out of this contemporary epistemological crisis. Firstly, he presents evil as an epistemological framework to "explain" how and why this catastrophe had befallen the mighty Roman Empire. But he also connects this philosophy of evil to a Christian theory of history in which he describes how the cosmic battle between God and Satan that has manifested in the human world and has produced so much human suffering will one day end, and also how there will be an end to this history of suffering with the advent of the City of God, emancipating Christians from the powers of evil, and producing a world of peace and love. In *The City of God*, St. Augustine thus produces a historical narrative of freedom grounded in Christian theology and teleology that will defeat evil, resolving the epistemological quandary plaguing Roman society in Late Antiquity and recreating a new historical narrative of human freedom.[16]

The connection to the Fall of Rome is not as distant as one might think. In fact, the historian Morris Berman draws a direct connection between the demise of the Roman Empire to the "Twilight of American Empire," with 9/11 as the turning point in American history. Like Augustine, Berman sees the demise of the American Empire as an epistemological crisis as well, with Americans yearning for an understanding of this event as their world crumbles around them. And similar to Augustine, Berman believes contemporary secular knowledge cannot provide a rational explanation for this apocalyptic collapse of civilization. Berman sees how domestic vulnerabilities to external threats coincided with internal social, political, and cultural decay, leading to the end of the Roman Empire in Late Antiquity and now the American Empire in our time. And where the collapse of the Roman Empire led to the Dark Ages controlled by the Roman Catholic Church in

European history, so too does Berman see the United States entering a "dark age" dominated by evangelical Christianity.[17] In both cases, Christianity emerged as an epistemology as much as a theology to provide meaning and understanding for people to make sense of a rapidly transforming world.

Perhaps in this vein, the philosopher Alasdair MacIntyre has noted that when we as humans face an epistemological crisis, and when competing interpretations magnify rather than address our palpable anxieties, dramatic narratives resolve our disequilibrium by reconstituting a traditional narrative to meet the needs of our current epistemological dilemma.[18] In other words, we reorient an old story to make sense of new situations, drawing upon received cultural scripts or schemas to understand our changing circumstance. This is also how we redefine cataclysmic challenges as the foundation of a new narrative that serves as the beginning of a new history that can, in turn, reconstitute a prevailing collective paralysis into a narrative of meaning based upon cultural and intellectual progress. The *9/11 Commission Report* embodies this profound point about the epistemological function of dramatic narratives. The ambition and brilliance of the report revolves around its attempt to provide this kind of reconstituted narrative to address the kinds of epistemological questions surrounding the 9/11 terrorist attacks. Moreover, the *9/11 Commission Report* is a reconstituted narrative structured as a "history," woven as a tapestry of stories grounded in historical context and analysis. The National Commission on Terrorist Attacks self-consciously wrote its report as a historical narrative to address the major issues concerning Americans,[19] emplotted as a series of constituent stories that collectively frame a narrative discourse. The report attempts to provide greater meaning and understanding about the events that led up to the terrorist attacks and the conditions that created the possibility for them to happen.

But if the report offers an explanation about the events on that fateful day in September 2001, and attempts to provide a deeper understanding of those events, it nonetheless fails to provide an historical interpretation about the greater significance of what the National Commission recognized as "an event of surpassing disproportion."[20] The *9/11 Commission Report* is not a traditional historical chronicle where the events and historical actors "speak" for themselves.[21] As narrator and interlocutor, the National Commission influences the way we read the events that unfold in the narrative, and frame the point-of-view of historical actors, employing narrative strategies that collectively inform how we understand the historical context of 9/11. Still, the *9/11 Commission Report* stops short of providing an historical interpretation of September 11th. The report repeatedly compares the 9/11 terrorist attacks to the Japanese surprise attack upon Pearl Harbor on December 7, 1941, and describes the broader historical significance of those attacks that brought the United States into World War II. Yet, the National Commission hesitates to draw similar historical conclusions about September 11th and its significance in American history. Perhaps the National Commission never believed this to be the purpose of its report. But failing to provide this kind of narrative closure to such a traumatic historical event leaves its report open to the kind of criticism wielded against the *Warren Report* on the Kennedy assassination (which failed to provide narrative and historical closure as well). This failure only empowers counter-narratives of September 11th, however specious, that do offer the kind of historical interpretation that Americans yearn for to make sense of this national catastrophe.

   The *9/11 Commission Report* was a unique government publication precisely because it is a "history," and is thus unlike "[p]revious commission reports, largely the work of lawyers, politicians, and bureaucrats, [that] had tended to set forth findings of fact tailored for either accusations of blame or recommended remedies."[22] Senior advisor Ernest May, along with the Commission executive director Philip Zelikow, both of whom are professional historians, "believed the 9/11 Commission's report could be quite different." Rather than producing a document that "resembled courtroom presentations, focusing on the indictment or defense of U.S. officials" as some government reports following the Japanese attack on Pearl Harbor had done, May and Zelikow "agreed that there was at least a chance that the 9/11 Commission could write a history dealing with both al Qaeda and the U.S. government, probing the planning of the attack and why the United States had been so unprepared."[23] Members of the National Commission agreed with this approach, and collectively they produced an informative historical narrative that illuminates the broader historical context about 9/11, providing insight about the conditions that created the opportunity for the September 11th terrorist attacks to evolve. In this regard, three historical developments significantly shaped the political and bureaucratic landscape that enabled foreign hijackers to execute their deadly plan of domestic terrorism, according to the *9/11 Commission Report*. First, the report documents how vitriolic and divisive domestic politics circumscribed the counterterrorism efforts of Presidents Bill Clinton and George W. Bush. Second, it describes the colonial history of the Islamic world and the postcolonial legacy of the West, particularly the presence of the United States in the Middle East. Specifically, the report discusses how the history of foreign and economic policies that produced social, economic and political instability in the region in the recent past encouraged the growth of religious extremism and jihadist movements in the Islamic world. Finally, the report describes how the history and epistemology of the American political and bureaucratic establishment was defined by the Cold War, and geared towards defending the United States from external threats from traditional states like the former Soviet Union.[24]

   More than illuminating this historical context, the *9/11 Commission Report* was framed as a "history" in order to have an immediate political purpose. According to Ernest May, by "couching the report as a history" the 9/11 Commission's leaders, Thomas Kean and Lee Hamilton, thought the report "might help delay a partisan split [among the Commission's members]: If the commissioners debated details about what had happened at specific places and times, they might postpone quarrels about whom to blame and what morals to draw."[25] Despite these political imperatives, though, the report was fundamentally written as an historical narrative for the families of the 9/11 victims and the American public more generally.[26]

Thus, we need to examine the *9/11 Commission Report* together as a "history" and as a "narrative," interrogating the story it is trying to tell. As already noted, the narrative begins with the hijackings of American domestic aircraft, which were then turned into weapons of mass destruction directed towards the Twin Towers, the Pentagon, and another major landmark in Washington, DC, believed by the National Commission to be either the White House or Capitol. The 9/11 Commission (along with other leading government officials) speculated that either one of these latter landmarks was United 93's target before the passengers of this aircraft thwarted the hijackers' mission. After narrating the hijackings, however, the report abruptly shifts its narrative focus to the recent history of the Islamic Middle East, particularly the colonial legacy of the West in the region and the postcolonial resistance to its presence. Specifically, it chronicles the history of jihadist violence and the emergence of Osama bin Laden as the leader of the al Qaeda terrorist movement whose purpose is to repel American influence in Islamic nations and undermine what they perceive to be American international hegemony. The *9/11 Commission Report* then describes the history of US counterterrorism and the ways recent presidential administrations addressed the problem of Islamist terrorism against the United States, before returning to the events of September 11th at the end of the report. The report concludes with the horrific experience of victims in the World Trade Center complex and the Pentagon following the explosive missile attacks, including the harrowing experience of the first responders who led the efforts to rescue the victims from these buildings, primarily the New York Port Authority and Washington, DC police officers and firefighters.

Though the broad outlines of the *9/11 Commission Report* are familiar, the second chapter about the history of the Islamic world addresses one of the major goals of the 9/11 National Commission to explain why the events of September 11th happened. Entitled "The Foundation of the New Terrorism," this chapter begins with the 1998 fatwa issued by al Qaeda leaders Osama bin Laden and Ayman al Zawahiri against Americans and the United States. The report notes that bin Laden and Zawahiri claimed

> that America had declared war against God and his messengers [and] they called for the murder of any American, anywhere on earth, as the "individual duty for every Muslim who can do it in any country in which it is possible to do it."[27]

Opening this chapter with al Qaeda's 1998 fatwa, however specious its source, is critical to the report's historical narrative because it reminds readers of Osama bin Laden's widely publicized threat, how little Americans regarded its warning (except for certain key figures in the American intelligence community), and also how this fatwa attracted recruits for the terrorist organization, culled from a divided, anxious, and impoverished Muslim world standing at a historical crossroads, confronting its colonial past and facing the challenges of modernity at the end of the millennium. According to the National Commission, bin Laden's 1998 fatwa and the emergence of al Qaeda as a serious terrorist organization must be understood within the broader history of the Islamic world stemming back to the golden age of Islam in the eighth century, contemporary geopolitics, and modernity, including the disruptive forces of globalization.[28]

Together, the report's second chapter and the following ones describe the historical context of al Qaeda's plans to attack the United States and the disastrous failure by the American intelligence community to prevent them, providing readers with substantial significant information to explain how the these attacks could happen. However, the 9/11 National Commission's editorial decision to begin and end its report with the tragic events of September 11th clearly reflects that its report has a greater purpose. Arguably, the narrative structure is intentionally constructed to retraumatize readers, forcing them to revisit these events in order for them to emotionally connect with the victims who endured this catastrophe, interestingly in ways very similar to the opening sequence in Oliver Stone's *JFK* discussed in the previous chapter. As earlier noted, the report's first chapter retells the hijackings of commercial aircraft, while the final chapter, entitled "Heroism and Horror," reminds us of the human tragedy of 9/11 from a different perspective, namely that of the first responders who were called upon to rescue survivors following the attacks upon the Twin Towers and Pentagon, often with lethal results.

Had the report begun with the second chapter as originally intended (the one that describes the history of the Islamic world and al Qaeda) our empathies otherwise might lie with the terrorists. To signify the victims' experience, the report disrupts the chronological order of the events of September 11th by abruptly ending with the attacks themselves in the first chapter, and returning to their aftermath in the final chapter. This narrative structure is transparently designed to revisit the national trauma of 9/11 and provoke sympathy for the victims of the terrorist attacks. Concluding with the horrific experience of the first responders may have achieved the Commission's objective to remind readers of the powerful human tragedy of 9/11, but the report terminates without narrative closure, ending without historical resolution. As a result, the *9/11 Commission Report* fails to provide a satisfying narrative that would enable Americans to achieve historical catharsis and work through their national trauma, a necessary psychological step that would enable them to integrate their past with their present and shape a new national identity. Moreover, the report does not resolve the epistemological crisis this historical event engendered, thereby preventing Americans from reconstituting a new national narrative that would place September 11th within the larger framework of American history. In other words, it fails to resolve the psychological dilemma that a dramatic narrative is designed to do.

How can we explain this failure given that the 9/11 National Commission recognized the significance of presenting its report as an emotional historical narrative? The answer probably lies with the commission's refusal to engage in the politically charged issue of assigning culpability for the terrorist attacks. Perhaps had the 9/11 National Commission held either (or both) presidential administrations responsible, or even particular agencies within the American intelligence community, its report might have critically provided the psychological closure Americans need in order to move on. Or perhaps the 9/11 National Commission hoped its policy recommendations in the final chapters of its report would serve this psychological function. Whatever the reason, since neither of the recommendations were implemented and the United States entered two wars connected to September 11th that presently continue, understanding 9/11 as a significant historical event remains difficult. The question is whether films about September 11th help Americans move closer to historical resolution to these tragic events or fall short in reaching this objective like the *9/11 Commission Report*.

## *United 93* and *World Trade Center*: Reliving 9/11 through Film

Paul Greengrass's *United 93* is a powerful and visceral film that reconstructs the events surrounding the hijacking and crash of the fourth commercial aircraft many believe destined to attack a major landmark in Washington, DC, possibly the White House or Capitol. Much like the first chapter of the *9/11 Commission Report*, Greengrass's film revisits the particular details of the hijackings on that day in September 2001, from the terrorists' ability to elude airport security at Logan Airport and board United 93, to the Federal Aviation Administration (FAA) and military response to the collective hijackings of the four airplanes, and then the last-minute phone calls passengers of United 93 made before the plane crash. The film also follows the report's conclusion that some passengers, after hearing from loved ones that the Twin Towers had been attacked, likely stormed the cockpit having concluded that United 93 was likely to meet a similar fate. As with the *9/11 Commission Report, United 93* speculates that this melee attack disrupted the hijackers' objective and led to the plane crash outside Shanksville, Pennsylvania.[29]

However, Paul Greengrass's movie does more than recount the historical facts of United 93's hijacking. It describes the way ordinary people performed extraordinary deeds, whether the malevolent or the heroic, as well as signify the importance of human relationships during the catastrophic events of 9/11. Through film casting, cinematography, and character development, *United 93* emotionally engages viewers in profound ways by provoking us to relive the experience of the hijackers and passengers as they endured the horror and heroism of September 11, 2001. Notably, Greengrass did not cast famed movie actors for *United 93* (unlike Oliver Stone for his film *World Trade Center*). This casting decision advances the film's narrative discourse about the human tragedy of 9/11 in critical ways. As viewers are not distracted by film celebrities, they are unlikely to interpret character identity and development in terms of established acting performances from previous movies. In other words, we concentrate more upon the acting performances in *United 93* and how they are connected to the film's plot, rather than the actors themselves and their previous roles. This is a significant casting decision for the movie, because using unknown performers accentuates how *United 93* is about the incredible feats of ordinary people. Famous celebrities by definition are extraordinary people, and we expect them to perform unbelievable actions in the fantasy world of Hollywood blockbusters. In contrast, Greengrass's choice to cast non-notable actors reminds viewers that average people like most Americans were victims of the hijackings and terrorist attacks. As we watch the movie, we are reminded that any one of us could have been among those who boarded the four planes that were hijacked. Greengrass's casting decision not only humanizes the movie, but also reinforces its realism as well, emotionally connecting us to the tragic events of 9/11.

The film's cinematography reinforces *United 93*'s realism as well. As with Greengrass's other films (such as his *Bourne* movies), many scenes are shot from camera angles or positions that simulate news footage captured by camera operators in the field. For example, as the hijackers move through Boston's Logan Airport, viewers observe their movements from the vantage of handheld cameras, presenting fluttered camera shots as the camera operators walk or jog to keep up with their subjects. Greengrass uses this camera position again as the 9/11 hijackings unfold and FAA and military officials scramble to figure out what is happening.[30] Here these fluttered camera shots accentuate the mania and immediate confusion gripping these officials as they process the events of September 11th. At other times, Greengrass uses camera positions we associate with news interviews when characters speak to one another, where the camera moves quickly back-and-forth between characters so that viewers focus their attention on the person speaking. Filming *United 93* as if the camera is recording news events or interviews, of course, underscores its realism. However, the cinematography achieves a more profound film-viewing experience by making these events primal and visceral. In this way, Greengrass has made a film that enables viewers to live and feel United 93's hijacking. Where films can encourage distance and detachment to observe and interpret a film's narrative discourse, *United 93* demands that we have an intimate association with the passengers, and controversially, the hijackers. According to the film, detachment would only objectify what United 93's passengers and hijackers endured, thereby relegating their experience to an historical fact in the American past, and consequently turning them into a dehumanized statistical casualty.

Thus, the casting and cinematography work together to facilitate an intimate relationship between viewers and the film's characters, enabling the audience to better understand the movie's narrative discourse. Here, however, the film is quite controversial and challenges the narrative approach taken by the *9/11 Commission Report*. Where the National Commission's report centralized the victims' experience throughout their narrative, *United 93* offers a more balanced perspective that encourages empathy with the lead hijacker, Ziad Jarrah, as much as sympathy for the passengers. Though the film does not minimize the human tragedy of 9/11, it chooses to develop the film's characters in fundamental ways that have viewers understand the hijackers' perspective as much as the passengers. Beginning the film from the hijackers' point-of-view, and developing the character of Ziad Jarrah while maintaining passenger anonymity, Greengrass establishes a narrative tone that undermines our attempt to see the hijackers as inherently monstrous, or even the passengers likewise heroic. In this vein, the film's character development provokes us to consider the relationship between historical agency and the events of September 11th. Nothing about the hijackings and the response of the passengers was inevitable nor beyond their control. Both hijackers and passengers made active decisions that proved historic on that day in September 2001.

Greengrass's decision to develop the character of Ziad Jarrah in *United 93* is arguably the film's most controversial narrative device as he emerges as the movie's primary protagonist.[31] He is the character confronted with the central problems that animate the movie's narrative tension. From the film's beginning, he is unsure whether to follow through with the hijackings and terrorist attacks. As mentioned earlier, he places a pre-boarding phone call like his fellow passengers, saying "I love you" to whomever or whatever is on the other end of the line, an emotional gesture that provokes empathy from the audience as we know that he knows his fate once he boards the plane. After United 93 leaves Boston, Jarrah is palpably nervous about hijacking the plan and the planned suicide mission. Ultimately, he chooses to adhere to the plan, leading his fellow hijackers to take over the plane, and piloting it towards its planned destination.[32] Although the film takes dramatic license with Jarrah's character, in many respects it parallels conclusions drawn by the 9/11 National Commission. According to the *9/11 Commission Report* al Qaeda's leaders maintained concerns that Jarrah would not follow through with the terrorist attacks. Unlike his fellow hijackers, he did not break off emotional ties with family and friends once they were chosen for al Qaeda's planned attacks. In fact, Jarrah continued to see his girlfriend until the eve of 9/11 while others disconnected completely from relatives.[33] Thus, *United 93*'s portrayal of Jarrah as a reluctant terrorist who places a pre-flight phone call is within the realm of historical possibility, given the evidence the 9/11 Commission gathered about his past. However, the film uses this evidence to narrate a different story than the *9/11 Commission Report*. In the report, Jarrah's complicity in the terrorist attacks was hardly in doubt. Questions al Qaeda's leaders had about Jarrah's ability to perform his chosen task mostly centered upon their inability to keep track of his where-abouts. Once he arrived in New Jersey and then relocated to Boston, it was clear he was going to participate in the hijackings. The film skillfully uses the evidence gathered by the 9/11 Commission to create a psychological conflict within Jarrah as a way to humanize him and encourage empathy. Despite the efforts of the *9/11 Commission Report* to offer historical context and a measure of historical under-standing about al Qaeda's motivations to attack the United States, the hijackers always remain monsters and villains. This is necessary to maintain readers' sympathies for their victims and deflect our criticisms of the United States government and intelligence agencies for failing to prevent these attacks from happening. In contrast, *United 93* provides a more balanced narrative in order to tell a different kind of story about the historical significance of 9/11.

Jarrah's character development stands in marked contrast to the passengers of United 93. Not only do we know his name and have an understanding of his identity, but also he is the one character in the film who demonstrates the kind of possessive individualism that typically drives the plot of a narrative. Ultimately, he must decide whether to follow through with hijacking United 93 and attack the planned (though unknown) landmark in Washington, DC. The film juxtaposes his individual agency with the collective action of the passengers. Throughout the film, they remain anonymous to the audience and each other until the very end. Just as Jarrah's character development challenges audiences, so too does the anonymity of the passengers. We are not meant to connect with any particular one of them, but all of them. It was not the actions of an individual who determined what the passengers would do to disrupt the hijackers' plans (thereby providing the film with the heroic character we associated with disaster or action adventure movies); rather it was the collective decision of a group of passengers to literally steer the course of history. Just as Jarrah overcomes his fears before making a life-altering decision, so too do the frightened passengers once they determine to storm the cockpit.[34] Here, Greengrass provokes viewers to think about the nature of the American character. Often we associate the American character with the attributes of possessive individualism: in the United States individuals have the opportunity to be whatever they want to be, and control the course of their lives. In *United 93*, however, the individual who possesses this trait, ironically, is the hijacker Ziad Jarrah. The passengers reflect a different dimension of the American character we sometimes overlook: that out of many, we are one. And in this regard, the film's narrative discourse speaks to the larger meaning of September 11th. *United 93* reminds viewers that different constituencies of Americans, many of whom did not know one another, came together as a nation on 9/11 whether huddled over television sets watching the aftermath of the attacks, or banding together in places like New York City and Washington, DC to comfort survivors and rebuild their communities. Just as the passengers in the film *United 93*, anonymous Americans were reminded they were one nation on September 11th. And where the film culminates with the passengers taking action to change history, we are left to ask whether Americans as a people can do the same in a world changed by the events of 9/11.

Where *United 93* is a narrative about the fate of this particular hijacked airplane, Oliver Stone's *World Trade Center* tells the story of two Port Authority police officers trapped in the rubble of Tower 2 of the World Trade Center Complex, and how their disappearance affected their families in the immediate aftermath of the terrorist attacks. Like Greengrass's film, Stone's movie uses the experience of these officers and their family to focus upon the extraordinary actions of ordinary people. For Stone, the historical significance of 9/11 is about the American nation coming together in a moment of catastrophic devastation as well. These similarities aside, the two films differ in meaningful ways. Greengrass's *United 93* focuses upon the specific hijacking of this aircraft, although he uses his narrative to offer general conclusions about the historical significance of 9/11. Consequently, the film takes place either within the airport, on the airplane itself, or in the FAA and military control centers. Stone's *World Trade Center*, in contrast, moves beyond the story of Port Authority officers John McLoughlin (Nicolas Cage) and Will Jimeno (Michael Peña) and their families in order to illustrate how the terrorist attacks affected Americans more generally. The movie shows Wisconsin firefighters, workers from a Connecticut business firm, among other Americans watching the events on television, stunned by the attacks on the Twin Towers and Pentagon. As will be discussed in more detail shortly, repeated images of Americans gripped to their television sets become a central motif in Stone's film to remind viewers how most of us experienced the events of September 11th in much the same way. Paul Greengrass's *United 93* arguably is a technically superior movie, but Stone's *World Trade Center* more successfully examines 9/11 as a significant historical event that deeply affected the American people as a nation.

Like *United 93, World Trade Center* opens with Americans like officers McLoughlin and Jimeno beginning their day, preparing to go to work and following their normal routines, activities that remind us that September 11, 2001 started just as any other day. Where as Greengrass's film presents a story of 9/11 from the vantage of the hijackings, Stone has viewers observe the terrorist attacks from the streets of Port Authority and New York City. We share the point-of-view of New Yorkers as they watch the hijacked planes strike the Twin Towers and try to make sense of the attacks. As mayhem grips Lower Manhattan, Port Authority officers are sent to the World Trade Center Complex as first responders to rescue survivors. As a bus takes them to the Twin Towers, they argue whether a small aircraft veered off course and crashed into Tower 1, echoing a sentiment shared by many Americans in these early moments of the attacks as they watched the burning plane embedded in the World Trade Center tower on their televisions. Only when the second plane hits Tower 2 do the officers begin to realize something more sinister has happened, and that their rescue mission has taken on greater significance. With both towers burning and recognizing the imperative of their mission to rescue survivors before the buildings collapse, McLaughlin asks for volunteers to go with him into Tower 2.[35] As the fear in the Port Authority officers' faces reveal, they know that choosing to follow McLoughlin will likely have lethal consequences.

As the volunteers rush into the World Trade Center Complex, their fear intensifies as they watch people leap from the highest floors of the burning Twin Towers as the buildings begin to collapse and fires rage. Mayhem has turned into sheer terror, further complicated by logistical failures that prevent McLoughlin and his men from communicating with other first responders and knowing what exactly is going on throughout the World Trade Center Complex. With useless two-way radios they do not know how best to proceed with their rescue effort, ultimately deciding to enter the building believing they are needed to assist victims of the crumbling tower. As these Port Authority police officers advance into Tower 2 to rescue survivors, horror replaces heroism as other first responders try to communicate to McLoughlin and his fellow officers to leave the tower before it collapses, but to no avail. Moving deeper into Tower 2, an explosion entraps McLoughlin and his men, leaving only him and Jimeno as the sole survivors buried in the rubble.[36]

At this point, Stone's *World Trade Center* moves beyond McLoughlin and Jimeno's particular experience to connect the film to major themes in the *9/11 Commission Report*, especially the logistical challenges facing New York City's first responders in the immediate period following the planes' crashing into the Twin Towers. In fact, the report describes conditions that border upon anarchy as firefighters, police officers, and paramedics tried to coordinate the rescue effort. Poor communication was complicated by a diffused leadership structure that was clearly confused and unprepared for the terrorist attacks. Although one can understand that New York City's first responders were just as surprised as the rest of the nation by the September 11th terrorist attacks, the 9/11 National Commission made two significant points that should have factored into their preparedness. Firstly, the 1993 World Trade Center attacks demonstrated that the Twin Towers were a target for terrorist attacks, and should have alerted the New York City municipal authorities to prepare for a possible later attack. As with the FBI, the success of minimizing the damage of the 1993 attacks as well as the eventual prosecution of the terrorists only led New York City officials to falsely believe that the city was adequately prepared for future terrorist attacks. Second, New York City's response palled in comparison to the effectiveness with which Washington, DC's first responders dealt with the terrorist attacks upon the Pentagon. In contrast to New York City's municipal authorities, DC authorities had a command structure in place in the event of a terrorist attack. When the terrorists struck the Pentagon, they could execute this plan and maintain effective communication as first responders rescued victims. Consequently, Washington, DC had fewer first responder casualties compared to New York City. As the *9/11 Commission Report* notes, if New York City authorities had had a similar plan in place, many of the heroic first responders would not have needlessly died during the chaos of the rescue effort. Although Olive Stone's *World Trade Center* celebrates the heroism and sacrifice of New York City's first responders, it also reminds us of the horror they faced and the unnecessary deaths as a result of a confused and ineffective command structure.[37]

Yet Stone's film curiously refrains from explicitly criticizing New York City's municipal authorities and the command structure in charge of the first responders. Furthermore, given Stone's reputation for presenting alternative histories based upon conspiracy theories (as in his *JFK*), one is surprised that he avoids counter-narratives of the terrorist attacks in *World Trade Center*. In fact, his movie sidesteps the politics of September 11th altogether. The film's major criticisms are reserved for television pundits reporting and analyzing the terrorist attacks immediately following the second plane crash into Tower 2. Once they recognize that the United States has been attacked, these reporters and pundits rush to conclude who was responsible, why the terrorists attacked, and how they were able to breach American security to execute their plans. Throughout the film, these views are transmitted through television sets as with most information about the 9/11 attacks. However, where Americans watch their televisions with rapt attention to learn about the events themselves and the fate of the rescuers and survivors in the film, they want nothing to do with the pundits' political perspective at this moment of national crisis. Whenever pundits appear to voice their inane opinions, various characters in the film turn away from their televisions, or just shut off their sets in disgust. In *World Trade Center* (as well as in Stone's later film *W.*, as we will see shortly), characters who politicize September 11th appear craven and callous, portrayed as people using this traumatic event to advance their own interests.

In *World Trade Center*, the larger historical meaning of September 11th has little to do with politics. In fact, the film's most poignant moments highlight the ways Americans strengthen their bonds as a national community on 9/11. As people hear about the events, they find ways to come to one another's aid, whether to succor each other as they try to figure out the fate of their loved ones who work in the World Trade Center Complex and Lower Manhattan, or people from disparate parts of the country arriving in New York City to help out the rescue effort any way they can. Here again the motif of the ever present television set signifies how this oft-ridiculed mass technology was a vital vehicle of mass communication that stitched together an American community (and the world, as we see people from places as distant as Africa watching the events of 9/11 on their televisions) bonded by a national tragedy. In practically every scene, either people are watching their televisions, or television sets remain in the background feeding them information as they learn about the fate of their family members. Without our televisions to connect us to the devastation in New York City and Washington, DC, the events of September 11th would have remained local. Instead, our televisions became the tendons that connected the sinews of an American nation, enabling us to receive one another as members of an extended family needing emotional support during this moment of human tragedy. Perhaps this sentiment is best reflected in one of the film's final scenes when Officer McLoughlin's wife Donna (Maria Bello) waits in a hospital after John has been rescued, watching television with other families still waiting to hear about the fate of their loved ones. As Donna stands staring at the television, an African American woman describes how her son who works in the World Trade Center remains missing. She poignantly describes that their last conversation ended in an argument, and that she fears she will never see him again. Listening with compassion, Donna embraces her, and together they cry as they process the devastation of 9/11.

Donna never learns this woman's name (nor do we), but this hardly matters as the events of September 11th was a collective traumatic experience that brought them, and the entire nation, together as one.

When Donna and John McLoughlin are tearfully united in the hospital, we are reminded that precious human relationships enabled people to survive this devastating ordeal. Throughout the movie, Officers McLoughlin or Jimeno and their wives flashback to moments in the past which were probably unimportant at the time, but are fraught with profound significance as John and Will lie trapped in the rubble, uncertain whether they will survive, or as their wives desperately wait for word whether their husbands are still alive. During these flashbacks, the film focuses upon the preciousness of their memories and how simple gestures, such as playful banter between a couple, a wife's laughter, or husband's smile, comfort them at these moments of despair. As John says to Donna once he is brought to the hospital, "you kept me alive."[38] Yet, *World Trade Center* wants viewers to ponder the magnitude of 9/11 beyond its immediate impact upon Officers McLoughlin, Jimeno, and their families. While John is led down the hall for surgery with Donna gripping the gurney, the camera remains behind, slowly panning a hospital wall filled with photos of people still missing, and hand-written notes requesting people to call relatives if they have found a missing family member.[39]

The poignancy of this camera shot is reinforced in the following scene as we see New York City the day after 9/11. In contrast to the opening scenes that show a populated, busy New York City with people riding the subway and ferry as they travel to work, these haunting final scenes show a subway train and ferry still operating without passengers, and finally Lower Manhattan still smoldering with strewn ashes and office paper, empty of people.[40] Here the film provokes us to think about the historical significance of 9/11 in a couple of ways. First, the absence of people traveling the subways and ferries and a vacant Lower Manhattan remind us of that profound human loss as a result of the terrorist attacks. Second, we are also meant to remember that the subways and ferries continued to run on September 12th. After all, time did not stop after the terrorist attacks, and we continue to rebuild and live in the aftermath of this national tragedy. Still, these final scenes in the film prompt us to consider whether we have moved on to such a degree that we have forgotten the historical significance of September 11th, particularly the way Americans bonded together as a nation. When one remembers that *World Trade Center* was released in 2006, during a time when Americans were divided over the 2003 Iraq War, this film questions whether Americans have forgotten how 9/11 was an important event that brought them together as a national community.

Indeed, *World Trade Center*'s reflection upon the historical significance of September 11th becomes even more powerful when juxtaposed to Oliver Stone's 2008 film *W*. Although a rare film about a sitting American president, Stone's often hilarious depiction of President George W. Bush nonetheless criticizes his administration for dividing the American public following unprecedented national unity. The film begins with the young, reckless George W. Bush (Josh Brolin) fumbling though college and young adulthood practically intoxicated, and ever resentful of his accomplished father, the future President George H.W. Bush (James Cromwell). At first, it appears that Stone's *W.* narrates every cliché about George W.: his family's privilege, alcoholism, frat-boy behavior, early business and political failures, and nepotism. Over the course of the film, viewers witness how George W.'s life-changing commitment to abstain from drinking and conversion to evangelical Christianity transforms the inveterate youth into an influential businessman (co-owner of the Texas Rangers baseball team) and politician. Yet Stone's *W.* is also about the influence of people with whom George W. surrounds himself, and the significant role they play in his rise to power.[41]

On one level, Stone's film reflects views held by many of the president's critics: that George W. is dim-witted and at the mercy of much more intelligent and politically skillful advisors, whether they be the Svengali-like Karl Rove (Toby Jones) or Machiavellian Vice-President Dick Cheney (Richard Dreyfuss). Throughout the scenes of his life as governor of Texas or president, men like Rove and Cheney believe they are manipulating W. into supporting their decisions, thinking they have the upper hand. Yet, Stone presents President George W. Bush as much more clever and aware of the decisions his advisors make, almost as if he wants them to think he is dim-witted and oblivious to how they are trying to manipulate him. In one key scene where President Bush and Vice-President Cheney have lunch and discuss administrative politics and policy, the president cautions Vice (as he refers to Cheney) to be careful not to overextend his power, reminding him who is ultimately in charge. Although the Vice-President leaves the lunch with his famous smirk, suggesting he thinks he still is "the real president," the film wants viewers to see that President Bush is actually in control of his administration.[42] Rather than a victim in the power-play among his ministerial minions, he is fully aware of his administration's policies. As a historical agent, then, President Bush is just as culpable for his administration's political decisions as high-level cabinet members such as Secretary of Defense Donald Rumsfeld (Scott Glenn), and lower-level administrators such as Paul Wolfawitz (Dennis Boutsikaris) and Condoleezza Rice (Thandie Newton), and especially Vice-President Cheney. In other words, President Bush's most significant policy decision, the 2003 Iraq War, was not an administrative conspiracy, but one for which the president is actively responsible. According to Stone's film, President Bush is as much to blame for the deceit with which his administration presented evidence to the American public and the international community to justify the 2003 Iraq War as his cabinet members.

Oliver Stone's *W.* derides President Bush and members of his administration (except notably Colin Powell) for linking their plan to invade Iraq with September 11th, dividing the nation in the process. The events of 9/11 brought the nation together following years of venomous and divisive politics that began with

President Clinton's administration and continued through President Bush's disputed 2000 presidential election. The 2003 Iraq War yet again splintered the country as some Americans found its connection to 9/11 dubious, and others uniformly supported the president. The division became so intense that the patriotism of Americans who did not support the war was called into question. In light of the 2003 Iraq War, both of Oliver Stone's films wonder if Americans have forgotten the historical meaning of 9/11 now that we have focused our attention upon the legitimacy of this and the Afghanistan War (a military engagement specifically connected to September 11th), military conflicts that remain unresolved with victory that appears elusive. Yet, as Stone's films attempt to remind us of September 11th's historical significance, they never address the critical historical questions about how and why the terrorist attacks occurred. In fact, neither *World Trade Center* nor *United 93* broach the sensitive political and historical issues that would answer these questions. While these films powerfully evoke the ways the terrorist attacks of 9/11 were a national tragedy, they do not help us have an historical understanding of these events. They force us to relive the trauma of this fateful day in September 2001, but they never provide historical resolution for why the terrorists would attack the United States and what these events mean in the broader spectrum of American history. Perhaps if Oliver Stone's more paranoid and conspiratorial mind considered these issues, his films might move us a step forward to finding historical meaning in 9/11. Like the *9/11 Commission Report, United 93* and *World Trade Center* fail to resolve critical historical issues about the terrorist attacks that continue to haunt Americans. Maybe that is why alternative histories based upon conspiracy theories such as those written by Peter Dale Scott and others have begun to find a legitimate audience among the American public.

## Conspiracy Theories or Alternative Histories: Counter-Narratives of 9/11

Whether or not one believes 9/11 conspiracy theories, they are effective counter-narratives to the government's official report. Like the *9/11 Commission Report* they provide a historical context for the terrorist attacks, though one tied to the sordid history of the American intelligence community and its longstanding relationship with al Qaeda. Where the 9/11 National Commission draws historical connections between September 11th and the Japanese attacks on Pearl Harbor, these counter-narratives see closer links between 9/11 and the JFK assassination. For scholars such as Peter Dale Scott, David Ray Griffin, Paul Zarembeka, and others, the 9/11 National Commission is the modern manifestation of the Warren Commission, and its report is intended to deceive the American public and protect responsible government and intelligence officials just as the *Warren Report*. Linking September 11th with President Kennedy is incredibly significant for these scholars because this comparison provides fundamental legitimacy to their alternative histories. Precisely because more Americans believe the counter-narratives of the

JFK assassination,[43] Scott, Griffin, and Zarembeka hope their alternative histories will replace the *9/11 Commission Report* as the dominant historical narrative of September 11th. However, the more significant comparison is how the mood of the American public has shifted in recent years to entertain alternative histories to the *9/11 Commission Report* as it did in the late 1960s and early 1970s when Americans began to question the legitimacy of the *Warren Report*. Just as they began to challenge their government in light of Vietnam, Watergate, and the Church hearings that revealed the extent of the CIA's activities, they are now questioning their political institutions in light of the 2003 Iraq War and Hurricane Katrina. While alternative histories claim to tell the "truth" about 9/11, they better succeed as historical narratives that offer historical resolutions to persistent epistemological questions that neither the *9/11 Commission Report* or 9/11 movies have.

Much as his *Deep Politics and the Death of JFK*, Peter Dale Scott's *The Road to 9/11* tells the story about the covert activities of the American intelligence community and its complicity with nefarious people and organizations in order to advance its interests. Just as Scott develops his theory of "deep politics" to explain the ways government agencies like the CIA operated during the Cold War, he similarly establishes the idea of the "deep state" to understand the activities of political officials as well as the CIA in recent history. In both cases, the term "deep" defines the unaccountable shadow politics and actions of government institutions and agencies conducted away from the public domain. Peter Dale Scott establishes the premise that covert institutions would assassinate President Kennedy because he stood in their way as they attempted to conduct military actions against Castro's Cuba and wage a war in Vietnam. Likewise these same government agencies worked with Islamist terrorists to fight the Cold War and then allowed them to attack the United States in order to implement their plan to wage a war against Iraq.[44] *Deep Politics and the Death of JFK* proposed that our government officials practiced "deep politics," deceiving the American public in order to wage their war against Cuba, Vietnam, and even undermined democratically elected officials such as Chile's Salvador Allende by supporting military coups.[45] Should we therefore be surprised that our government would work with Islamist terrorists and even leave the American people vulnerable to their attacks in order to advance their interests as well?

For Peter Dale Scott, the *9/11 Commission Report* has left more questions unanswered and has protected government officials and the CIA just as the *Warren Report* did in the 1960s. Although both reports state that these officials and intelligence agents purposely withheld information to protect national security, Scott maintains that this is a ruse in order to hide the real truth from the American people. He contends that the CIA and President Bush's administration were aware of al Qaeda's intentions to attack the United States, but allowed the terrorist attacks to happen because they needed such an attack to happen (as they said, "another Pearl Harbor") in order to convince the American people that Saddam Hussein was partly responsible for the September 11th attacks, and thus needed to be overthrown.[46] According to Scott, both 9/11 and 2003 Iraq War would allow the Bush Administration to implement their plans via Continuity of Government and the Federal Emergency Management Agent (FEMA), plans developed years before with the Project for a New American Century. For Peter Dale Scott, 9/11 is a major historical event because it reflects the ways the United States has veered from its democratic principles and is part of long history connected to covert politics since the days of President Kennedy's administration.[47] Whatever one believes of Scott's alternative history, his book offers the kind of historical understanding of September 11th that resolves persistent epistemological questions concerning why and how the terrorist attacks occurred that the *9/11 Commission Report* has not.

Similarly, David Ray Griffin, Paul Zarembeka, and Jay Kolar question the veracity and intentions of the 9/11 National Commission, although they focus more upon particular details of the 9/11 attacks than Peter Dale Scott. Like Scott, the premise of their studies is that the government has historically deceived the American people to advance specific interests, and 9/11 is no different in this regard than the JFK assassination. However, they point to specific issues within the *Warren Report* such as the Lone Gunman and Magic Bullet theories as evidence that the government was willing to advance lies in order to hide the truth as to what happened on November 22, 1963, who was involved, and why they assassinated the president. Likewise, Griffin and Zarembeka contend that there are too many questions left unresolved in the *9/11 Commission Report*, and the more one investigates these questions, the more the details reveal that we still do not know what actually happened on September 11th, who was involved, and why it happened. Griffin and Zarembeka call into question the collapse of the Twin Towers of the World Trade Center, for example, which some physicists have maintained was impossible unless explosives were planted and detonated at the foundations of Towers 1 and 2.[48] And just as conspiracy theorists have advanced a "multiple Oswald" argument to explain how Lee Harvey Oswald could be in so many places simultaneously as he prepared his plans to assassinate President Kennedy and then escape to Cuba, so too does Jay Kohler argue that the CIA planted multiple Ziad Jarrahs to account for how Jarrah could be in several places simultaneously before he participated in the September 11th attacks.[49] Scholars such as David Ray Griffin, Paul Zarembeka, and Jay Kohler never maintain that they have the complete answers as much as they argue that the official government report fails to answer persistent questions. They believe that because the government kept tight control of the investigation, the 9/11 National Commission would lose its credibility if the truth was revealed. They, thus, offer their academic studies as alternative histories to understand what happened and why it happened. Just as Peter Dale Scott, these academics connect 9/11 to a longstanding history of government deception to encourage military actions, a history that began with the attack against the American ship *Lusitania* and the eventual American entry into World War I in 1917 and continued through the 2003 Iraq War.[50]

Collectively these alternative histories are powerful counter-historical narratives to the *9/11 Commission Report* because they signify September 11th as a major historical event, one that is connected to others such as President Kennedy's assassination, the Vietnam War, and the history of American foreign policy. For all these scholars, the events of September 11th must be understood in the context of the 2003 Iraq War. Whatever one makes of this explanation, it resolves our epistemological crisis by reconstituting a national narrative that gives historical meaning to the events of September 11th in the broader spectrum of American history. Similarly, superhero movies such as *Batman Begins* and *Iron Man* are alternative histories of 9/11 that examine the historical issues surrounding the terrorist attacks, though in a much more philosophical context. Unlike the more transparent September 11th movies *United 93* and *World Trade Center*, these superhero movies do not avoid the broader political questions associated with 9/11, and as such better provide an understanding of this historical event, and the ways it transformed American life in the aftermath of the terrorist attacks. Like the academic alternative histories, *Batman Begins* and *Iron Man* provoke us to consider the history of terrorism and counterterrorism in relation to American foreign policy in the post-9/11 world. However, before we explore these two particular films, we will first examine the ways Hollywood has approached the issue of terrorism in movies such as the James Bond films *Casino Royale* and *Quantum of Solace*. While superhero movies such as *Batman Begins* and *Iron Man* are based upon comic-book characters inhabiting worlds of fantasy, the two James Bond movies are fictional narratives that nonetheless draw their plot lines from our contemporary dangerous world. This does not diminish the narrative power of these superhero movies, however, as they are powerful allegories of the post-9/11 American landscape.

## James Bond, Batman, and Iron Man: Confronting Terrorism in the Aftermath of September 11th

*Casino Royale* (2006) and especially *Quantum of Solace* (2008) portray a world where terrorist organizations and an international syndicate prey upon innocent civilians, requiring intelligence agents from MI6 such as James Bond (Daniel Craig), or those working for the CIA, to protect British and American citizens from terrorists and the financial networks that support their operations.[51] As one watches these films, one cannot escape the questions they raise about the legality and ethics of counterterrorist tactics taken by the Anglo-American intelligence communities, and the extraordinary human and political cost required to fight international terrorism. Though seemingly innocuous high-octane action films marketed to a young male audience, *Casino Royale* and *Quantum of Solace* actually stimulate audiences to consider how much the civilized world will strengthen government power in order to eliminate global terrorism, especially in terms of supporting increased government surveillance of its citizens.

Significantly, the villains in these two James Bond films are financial operatives such as Le Chiffre (Mads Mikkelsen), Mr. White (Jesper Christensen), and Dominic Greene (Mathieu Amalric) and the international syndicate with whom they are powerfully connected. Since September 11th and the Patriot Act (2001), Americans have debated the issue of government surveillance (especially wire-tapping citizens and accessing their personal information), and the degree to which they are willing to sacrifice civil liberties to fight terrorism and the elaborate international economic infrastructure that finances it. *Casino Royale* and *Quantum of Solace* rationalize such government surveillance as necessary to undermine the powerful capabilities of well-connected and powerful financiers like Le Chiffre, Mr. White, and Dominic Greene who enrich terrorists and themselves by pro-viding terrorists with the economic means to inflict mass violence. As M (Judi Dench) points out to James Bond, without rogues like Le Chiffre who make money for terrorists by shrewdly investing their financial holdings, terrorists would not have the means to finance their violent operations.

Indeed, it is M who draws *Casino Royale*'s direct link to 9/11 when she describes the ways people profited from selling commercial airline stocks just prior to the explosion of the hijacked airplanes on September 11, 2001, a fact noted by scholars who have written 9/11 counter-narratives.[52] In the film, the villain Le Chiffre anticipates earning profits for himself and his clients by selling short on stocks invested in a commercial airline company whose celebrated new plane he plans to explode. Although these sequences involving the potential destruction of a commercial airplane are fictional, they inevitably draw upon our collective memory of the airplanes that were hijacked on September 11, 2001, exploding as they crashed into the Twin Towers and the Pentagon. Indeed, the anxiety and terror intensify during this dramatic sequence for those viewers who recall the 9/11 terrorist attacks, watching James Bond manically diffuse the terrorist plot to explode the airplane at Miami International Airport. Inevitably Bond succeeds in saving the airplane from destruction, a heroic action that increases his stature within the MI6 organization. And though some within the British intelligence com-munity question Bond's tactics and see him as a renegade and mercurial, his ability to prevent widespread disaster at a major American airport prompts his superiors to promote him from a low-level intelligence operative to an agent with the elite 00 status—becoming the famed British spy, 007.[53]

After Bond thwarts Le Chiffre's plan, Le Chiffre must enter a high-stakes, multimillion dollar poker game in Montenegro to win back his clients' money, otherwise they will kill him. Again, James Bond foils Le Chiffre's plan as he shrewdly outplays him during the poker game, forcing Le Chiffre to turn himself over to the CIA,[54] which is willing to provide him immunity and protection in exchange for information about his terrorist clients. Of course Le Chiffre is killed by the mysterious Mr. White before he can provide this information to the CIA. With Le Chiffre dead, Bond must now look for Mr. White to stop him and his global network,[55] a hunt that continues into the film's sequel, *Quantum of Solace*.

This sequel presents other plot lines about personal vengeance, human dependency upon natural resources, political corruption, and failed South American states besides the narrative that focuses upon Bond's pursuit of Mr. White.[56] By the end of *Quantum of Solace*, however, these two James Bond films have already made their critical point about the politics of counterterrorism in our contemporary world. Even though these Bond movies may vilify cosmopolitan stockbrokers and accountants who have foreign names and accents, and who are also connected to an international network that profits from terrorism (somewhat like al Qaeda without the religious affiliation), these two films ultimately reinforce the political argument that governments in the post 9/11 world require extensive surveillance powers in order to effectively eliminate the financial apparatus that empower terrorist organizations and their violent operations.

Though *Casino Royale* and *Quantum of Solace* confront actual social and political issues defining the post-9/11 landscape, Christopher Nolan's *Batman Begins* engages deeper philosophical and historical issues about modern terrorism and the criminal justice system.[57] Created by Bob Kane in 1939, the Batman character has had many permutations in comic-books, graphic novels, television shows, and films. While the first Batman movie directed by Tim Burton was released in 1989 and recalls Frank Miller's popular graphic novel *The Dark Knight Returns*, subsequent Batman films drifted from this literary source.[58] Miller's graphic novel (including its sequels) challenges readers to consider the ethics surrounding the nature of criminal justice, vigilantism, and the psychology of masked identities. Tim Burton's *Batman* and *Batman Returns* (1992) engage these ideas with some success, but the later Batman films moved away from the intelligence of Burton's movies, becoming parodies that increasingly turned off viewers. Christopher Nolan's *Batman Begins* returns to the philosophical issues provoked by Miller and the other Batman novels he inspired,[59] although exploring these ideas in the contemporary context of modern terrorism, urban decay, and the decline of Western civilization.

Nolan's *Batman Begins* is nominally the story about the transformation of Bruce Wayne (Christian Bale) from wealthy orphan into the Batman, Gotham City's notorious masked crime fighter. Like Tim Burton's Batman movies, Nolan's film initially focuses upon the death of Bruce's parents when he was only a boy, stressing how the critical role of their murder informed his psychological development and was the catalyst for his lifelong crusade against crime.[60] Unlike the Tim Burton Batman films, however, Nolan's *Batman Begins* devotes significant time to Bruce's privileged orphaned adolescence in order to reveal his festering hunger for vengeance, even if it requires killing his parents' convicted murderer, the desperate mugger Joe Chill (Richard Brake). This extended sequence about Bruce's youth enables viewers to see the degree to which bats factor into Bruce's traumatic experiences, and the ways they will continue to haunt young Bruce. As master Bruce matures, he believes that only killing Chill will release him from the trauma of his youth. Home from Princeton for Chill's parole hearing, Bruce plans to assassinate him because he suspects Chill will be released for his cooperation with Gotham's district attorney and their investigation to convict the leader of the local organized crime syndicate, Carmine Falcone (Tom Wilkinson). Before he leaves for the parole hearing, Bruce tells the family butler (and nominal father figure) Alfred (Michael Caine) that he will not be returning to Princeton, recognizing that his planned act of vigilantism may have criminal consequences. However, Bruce's effort to kill Chill is thwarted when an assassin kills him after he is released, producing a psychological crisis for Bruce now that his lifelong ambition has just been taken away from him. Emotionally distraught, Bruce initially plans to kill Falcone to redress his stolen opportunity to kill Chill, only to discover that Falcone's power reaches deep into Gotham's judicial system, including judges and police officers who protect him from criminal investigations and prosecutions.[61]

Disillusioned by the corrupt world around him, Bruce disappears into anonymity, living as an aimless pauper and thief throughout the world, eventually arrested in China for stealing cargo (products actually manufactured by Wayne Enterprises). As Bruce later confesses to Henri Ducard (Liam Neeson), a prominent member of the mysterious vigilante international organization the League of Shadows, who visits Bruce in prison, he has drifted through the world's seedier places in order to understand the criminal mind and motives that drive criminal behavior. Ducard tells Bruce that he similarly deplores a world that allows and protects rampant criminality, and has actually come to recruit him into his organization. Ducard uses his connections to have Bruce released from jail, encouraging him to seek out Ra's al Ghul (Ken Watanabe), the leader of the League of Shadows, who also shares Bruce's commitment to fight the crime and moral corruption that has led to the decay of human civilization. Together, Ra's al Ghul and Ducard become Bruce's spiritual guides, helping him find his psychological and ethical purpose, and teaching him martial arts and the stealth use of weapons, skills that will enable Bruce to become a powerful warrior to avenge justice.[62]

Although initially attracted to the ideologies of the League of Shadows, Bruce ultimately disagrees with Ra's al Ghul's and Ducard's objectives when they demand that he execute a criminal to complete his training and join their organization. They inform Bruce that this man is a murderer who deserves to be executed for his crime. Though Bruce agrees with their principles, he states, "This is not justice, this man should be tried."[63] Ra's al Ghul and Ducard passionately argue that such legal institutions are systematically corrupt, reminding Bruce that the criminal justice system protected murderers like those who killed his parents. By rejecting their demand, Bruce refuses to convert to the League of Shadows as he recognizes the fanaticism of their ideology, a fatal decision that forces him to fight for his escape. The ensuing battle leaves Ra's al Ghul dead, the organization's headquarters destroyed, and Ducard severely wounded and unconscious, surviving the ordeal only because Bruce saved him from a near perilous fall. Following his confrontation with the League of Shadows, Bruce returns to his public life in Gotham City and assumes an executive position in his family's corporation, Wayne Enterprises. Though he purports to work for the company, his life's true purpose is to fight the crime and corruption that plagues Gotham. In order to advance his new ambition, he assigns himself to Wayne Enterprises' Applied Sciences division, working with Lucius Fox (Morgan Freeman), the clever and talented supervisor who has been demoted to this ignored division for crossing the corporation's chief executive officer Earle (Rutger Hauer). Together, Bruce and Lucius explore research products rejected by Wayne Enterprises' executives (though we discover they are quite sophisticated and powerful), weapons that ultimately enable Bruce to lead his secret, but true life as the Batman.[64]

While *Batman Begins* provokes the audience to contemplate the ethics of paralegal justice at this point in the movie, the film nevertheless affirms the Batman's commitment to using the legal system to prosecute criminals. Once the Batman begins his career as a masked vigilante, he develops trusting relationships with Officer Jim Gordon (Gary Oldman) who has valiantly rejected the powerful corrupting influences infecting Gotham's police department, and Rachel Dawes (Katie Holmes), the idealistic Assistant District Attorney and Bruce Wayne's longtime friend who heroically fights the city's powerful criminal underworld. As Officer Gordon and Rachel work with the Batman, they remain ambivalent about his vigilantism, sometimes questioning his commitment to Gotham's criminal justice system. Their ambivalence, however, reflects Bruce Wayne's tortured soul that continues to struggle between his father's optimistic faith in public service and institutional reform and Henri Ducard's nihilism that has condemned civic institutions for perpetuating criminality and moral decay. Indeed, the Batman's vigilantism reflects Bruce Wayne's ongoing psychological battle between his public and secret lives.

Though the aggrieved young Bruce Wayne had recklessly pursued vigilante justice to avenge his parents' murder, as the Batman he reorients his vigilantism to restore public faith in Gotham City's judicial system and the rule of law. The myriad psychological and philosophical contradictions regarding the Batman's paralegal methods reflect Bruce's internal conflicts about his identity and allegiances to his biological father, Thomas Wayne (Linus Roache) and the father-figure Henri Ducard, two men who have instilled Bruce with fundamentally different worldviews about justice and the fate of American civilization. While Thomas Wayne had faith that civic institutions could be reformed to address social injustice and affirm the positive potential of human civilization, Ducard believes that these institutions remain inherently corrupt and perpetuate injustice. For Ducard, vigilantism is the only way to save civilization from endemic crime and systematic corruption. Even though Bruce had articulated his differences with the League of Shadows when he rejected Ra's al Ghul's and Ducard's demand to execute a criminal, the organization's fundamental worldview about the necessity of paralegal justice in a corrupt world and his training as a lethal warrior continue to shape his life as a masked crime fighter stalking the streets of Gotham. As much as Bruce rejects the League of Shadows' nihilistic view about the history of human civilization, he nonetheless remains tethered to their philosophy of vigilantism as long as he fights Gotham's criminals in the shadows of the night as the Batman.[65]

Although his life as the Batman absorbs Bruce's life, he must also maintain a public image as the scion of Thomas Wayne and nominal head of Wayne Enterprises. Instead of projecting himself as Gotham City's public benefactor and upstanding citizen like his father, however, Bruce chooses to live a public life of decadence and debauchery, shaming the Wayne legacy in the eyes of Gotham City's financial and political elite. Of course unbeknown to them, he is privately living up to his father's impressive reputation as the Batman, but only he, Alfred, and Lucius are aware of Bruce's secret life. Bruce's internal conflict intensifies when Henri Ducard resurfaces with his League of Shadow soldiers at a gala birthday party held for Bruce with plans to destroy Gotham City. When Bruce realizes that Ducard's plans include killing his guests, Bruce feigns public drunkenness in order to horrify his guests, who believe his ruse, and then leave Wayne Manor embarrassed and shocked by his behavior. Indeed, during this sequence one of Bruce's guests confronts him to tell him how he has blemished Thomas Wayne's legacy with his atrocious behavior. Bruce appears emotionally wounded by this confrontation, but he also knows that his public display at his birthday party, like his notorious decadent life, is necessary to deflect his life as the Batman.[66]

Alone with Ducard and the League of Shadows, Bruce learns that they have long plotted Gotham's destruction. Despite the League's manifesto to rid the world of decadence and corruption, it actually has been encouraging Gotham's demise by undermining its institutions. As Ducard describes the League of Shadows' purpose and its plans to destroy Gotham, viewers begin to see the film's connections to 9/11 as the League's philosophy and methods eerily reflect those of terrorist organizations like al Qaeda. Ducard tells Bruce that the League was responsible for the fall of Rome after years of moral and institutional decline as well as Constantinople when it too reached the end of its prominence. As Rome and Constantinople had to be destroyed to purge moral decay and corruption, so too must Gotham face a similar historical fate, according to Ducard. In fact, the League of Shadows had conspired to undermine Gotham for years, but had faced a formidable adversary in Thomas Wayne whose public contributions such as the mass transit train system and Wayne Tower sustained the city's civic life. Thomas Wayne's death resurrected the League's conspiracy, and accelerated Gotham's civic suicide. Ducard and the League now have arrived to complete their plan, and watch the citizens of Gotham destroy their once magnificent city. The League actually plans to use a weapon developed by Wayne Enterprises that will evaporate the city's water supply while releasing a hallucinogenic toxin that simultaneously promotes terror and violent behavior. Once detonated, this weapon will produce a paranoid atmosphere where Gotham's residents will eventually kill each other in fear of the monstrous visions the hallucinogen has created. Ducard's plan is to detonate this powerful weapon by planting it aboard the city's mass transit train and drive it straight through Wayne Tower, which sits above the control center that operates Gotham's water supply.[67]

Upon describing the League of Shadows' plan, Ducard and his soldiers proceed to attack Bruce while setting fire to Wayne Manor. Bruce is overwhelmed by the League's soldiers, and is left apparently unconscious to burn along with the Wayne estate. However, Bruce awakens in time to escape, making his way to his Batcave and transforming into the Batman. As he heads toward Gotham to thwart Ducard's plans, he looks for Rachel Dawes to give her the antidote to the toxic hallucinogen which has been released throughout the city in order for mass quantities to be made for Gotham's afflicted residents. The Batman also connects with Officer Gordon to coordinate their effort to stop Ducard, who has now hijacked the mass transit train and is hurtling it towards Wayne Tower. While the Batman will board the train to challenge Ducard, Gordon will drive the Batmobile to stop the train from reaching Wayne Tower. Although the fight between the Batman and Ducard nominally completes Bruce's training as a crime fighter and emerge from the shadows of his father-figure Ducard, Nolan also uses this sequence to complete the juxtaposition between Ducard and Thomas Wayne. Just as Thomas Wayne had built the mass transit train system and Wayne Tower to promote Gotham's civic institutions and life, Ducard uses them as weapons of mass destruction to annihilate the city. During this sequence, Ducard always calls the Batman by his birth name, and during the intense fighting, says, "You have nothing to fear Bruce," repeating the same line Thomas Wayne once said to young Bruce when bats were flying in his room following his frightening ordeal trapped in a well in the grounds of Wayne Manor. When Ducard says that Bruce cannot kill him, the Batman agrees, pinning him to the train as it accelerates towards Wayne Tower. But the train never reaches the tower, as Officer Gordon rams the Batmobile into the rails supporting the train's tracks, and the train explodes before crashing into the tower.[68]

In this climactic scene, Christopher Nolan draws the starkest connections between *Batman Begins* and the terrorist attacks of September 11th. Watching the hijacked mass transit train planted with an explosive device hurling towards Wayne Tower, viewers are reminded of the hijacked commercial airplanes crashing into the Twin Towers. In both cases, passenger vehicles were transformed into weapons of mass destruction directed towards major civic landmarks. Critically, however, Gotham City's train never reaches Wayne Tower, and the city is saved from catastrophic devastation. In this regard, viewers experience an alternative history of 9/11 where citizens are saved from a terrorist attack and feel virtual resolution and relief along with the people of Gotham City. The following scene also recalls the events of September 11th as Bruce moves through the smoldering rubble of Wayne Manor surrounded by men in hard hats cleaning up debris the day after the League of Shadows' terrorist attacks. He tells Alfred that they will rebuild the estate, but this time with a stronger foundation.[69]

For the film's narrative discourse, this sequence resolves Bruce's psychological conflict between his biological father's legacy and the relationship he developed with his father-figure Ducard. While two symbols of Thomas Wayne's legacy have been destroyed, the mass transit train system and Wayne Manor, Bruce has decided to become like his father, a creative force who works on behalf of the pubic good. Having reached his personal catharsis, Bruce has integrated his past with his present life, achieving an understanding that his personal history is part of his identity and enables him to live a fulfilling life in the present. However, as the following sequence between (now) Lieutenant Gordon and the Batman reveals, Gotham has yet to reach the same point as Bruce, and the city continues to need the Batman as a necessary instrument of justice in a world still plagued by criminals and their terrorist methods.[70]

Watching the men in hard hats move through the smoldering rubble of Wayne Manor provokes viewers to draw further parallels to the fallen Twin Towers and how it devastated Lower Manhattan in the days following the 9/11 terrorist attacks. As in *Batman Begins*, men in hard hats moved through the destruction in the aftermath of the attacks, removing rubble around the World Trade Center as the city and nation tried to process the horrific trauma, looking to its civic and national leaders to help them understand what happened. Significantly, when President Bush visited the smoldering remains of the Twin Towers and resolved to pursue the perpetrators of the attacks and bring them to justice, the psychological disorientation that gripped the nation abated. As the *9/11 Commission Report* notes, the Japanese attack on Pearl Harbor remains the only other historical event in recent American history that similarly traumatized Americans.[71] Furthermore, much as the war against Japan following the attacks helped Americans to achieve catharsis after Pearl Harbor, the United States went to war against al Qaeda (and its supporters the Taliban) in Afghanistan to achieve a similar result. However, Americans have yet to reach total victory in the Afghanistan War, inhibiting them from working through their trauma and find historical understanding in the 9/11 terrorist attacks like they did in World War II.

Following Hiroshima and Japanese surrender, Americans integrated a traumatic event to redefine a new post-war identity that shaped American life and foreign policy through September 11, 2001. Until the United States satisfactorily reaches a similar kind of victory, historical understanding remains elusive. In some ways, superhero movies like *Batman Begins* and *Iron Man* provide a space to revisit the psychological issues surrounding 9/11 and feel a measure of catharsis in a metaphorical context as they provide narrative closure to traumatic issues affecting the film's characters. Yet, these movies also remind us how far removed we are from achieving an actual psychological resolution to 9/11 as long as the Afghanistan War rages. And though *Iron Man* specifically addresses the Afghanistan conflict and narrates a superhero story that confronts global terrorism and promotes the United States as a positive force in the international arena, it also provokes viewers to consider the questionable role it played in creating the conditions for the emergence of terrorism in the Islamic world.

Released the same year as Nolan's *The Dark Knight*, Jon Favreau's *Iron Man* also presents a superhero narrative that engages themes connected to the events of 9/11.

Where Nolan's Batman films are allegories of post-9/11 America, however, Favreau's *Iron Man* directly confronts ideas about modern terrorism in recent history, and how they have shaped our contemporary world. For example, Favreau's film addresses some of the critical issues that the *9/11 Commission Report* examined. Specifically, *Iron Man* addresses the role the United States played in creating the conditions that led to the emergence of militant Islamism in recent history, particularly how it supported terrorist insurgents in Afghanistan in order to advance American interests during the Cold War. Just as the report describes the relationship between the CIA and the Afghani Mujahadeen in the Soviet–Afghan conflict,[72] Favreu's *Iron Man* similarly presents a narrative where American interests rival American ideals, and how the priority of the former justifies collusion with international terrorism. Along with the film's protagonist Tony Stark (Robert Downey Jr.), viewers discover that his business partner, Obadiah Stane (Jeff Bridges), has been selling weapons manufactured by Stark Industries to the Ten Rings terrorist group based in Afghanistan.

More than a simplistic comic-book narrative about the transformation of playboy and weapons designer Tony Stark into a superhero, *Iron Man* presents a complex story about American involvement in the Afghanistan War. Favreu's film is thus a provocative story about contemporary American foreign policy in the aftermath of September 11th, and the longstanding debate regarding advancing American interests or American ideals in global geopolitics. Where interests and ideals can work simultaneously, at times they conflict in the international arena, particularly in the case of American business and foreign policy interests. *Iron Man* chiefly focuses upon the role of American capitalism, and the ways its imperatives corrupt those who seek profit above the ideal that the United States is a force for moral good in the world.

In perhaps the film's most arresting opening scenes, viewers observe the jovial camaraderie shared between Stark and American soldiers until a terrorist ambush ruptures their conviviality, leaving all the soldiers dead, and Stark critically wounded. Favreau directs these scenes of accelerating staccato violence with camera shots that simulate news-camera footage, making the violence shockingly intimate and familiar while reminding viewers of the real military challenges American soldiers face everyday from insurgents in Iraq and Afghanistan.[73] By representing the realities of current military conflicts, *Iron Man* demands viewers to consider the actual dangers American soldiers encounter in military combat. However, as it portrays the story of Tony Stark's moral evolution from arrogant, callous, and self-interested war designer into an idealistic superhero, it links his narrative to a historical one that accepts America's culpability for the conditions that have enabled global terrorists to thrive. Specifically, it recalls the themes within the *9/11 Commission Report* that describe the ways Islamist extremists considered the United States decadent and arrogant, a corrupt civilization responsible for the manifold problems in the Muslim world.[74]

More significant, the film narrates the hypocrisies that arguably define contemporary American foreign policy: one that is willing to work with terrorists, dictators, and other people with nefarious goals in order to advance its agenda. The film *Iron Man* suggests that once America, like Tony Stark, confronts its responsibility for the violent world it has created, it can then act to defeat terrorism, and once again be a force for greater good.

After the terrorists ambush the military convoy, Tony Stark is taken hostage, and another hostage, the Afghani Wellington Yinsen (Shaun Toub), surgically attaches an electromagnetic device powered by a car battery to Tony's heart. As Yinsen later tells Tony, this device and the connected car battery keep Tony alive, preventing shrapnel from a Stark-made missile from entering Tony's heart, thereby killing him. While Yinsen performs this operation, Tony recalls the last 36 hours of his life. In these flashback scenes, viewers see the self-centered life Tony has lived, arrogantly snubbing his awards ceremony that honors his contributions to the American defense industry, drinking liquor excessively, and carousing with beautiful women. Moreover, he repudiates and dismisses those around him who apparently worry about the way Tony recklessly lives his life, particularly his personal secretary Pepper Potts (Gwyneth Paltrow) and his colleague Lieutenant Colonel James Rhodes (Terrence Howard), also known as Rhodey. During one of these flashback scenes, Pepper finds Tony in his laboratory, telling him that he is running excessively late for a scheduled plane flight to Afghanistan. Tony dismisses Pepper's concern, noting that his plane awaits him. However, we discover that Rhodey has been waiting for him for nearly three hours by the time Tony arrives at his plane, visibly angry since they both have an important meeting with military officials to demonstrate Stark Industries' new and most powerful weapon, the Jericho Missile.[75] During the plane flight, Rhodey reprimands Tony for his callousness, and how he is oblivious to the ways his cavalier lifestyle affects others.[76]

In these flashback scenes we observe the young, brilliant, and rich Tony Stark, who has expanded upon his father's initial vision for Stark Industries since he took over the company after his father's death, boasting how his company manufactures the most sophisticated and powerful weapons in the world. Though Tony's father had founded the company with his colleague, and Tony's mentor, Obadiah Stane, his father's mission was to develop weapons as deterrents during the Cold War. Having worked on the Manhattan Project that developed the atomic bomb, Tony's father apparently was humbled by the ethical responsibility that he believed went along with producing weapons of mass destruction, especially as he became closely tied to the military industrial complex. Tony admires his father's ethics, and attempts to convey this point to a churlish reporter, Christine Everhart (Leslie Bibb), and tries to persuade her (and viewers) that he has adopted a similar moral position. As Tony attempts to leave his opulent awards ceremony, the reporter confronts him about the human casualties caused by weapons produced by Stark Industries. More concerned with sleeping with the reporter, Tony is unsympathetic to the death of those dead innocent civilians she has tried to bring to his attention.[77]

Whatever ethics Tony's father may have had about the responsible use of the advanced military technology his company manufactured, Tony's capitalistic imperative and self-centered interest largely dismisses the reporter's accusations, pointing out that those with the most powerful weapons ultimately control and rule over others, deterring any threat.[78] Of course this was the United States' rationale for its defense policies during the Cold War, particularly during the Reagan Administration when the United States accelerated its weapon's production (and forcing the Soviet Union to do likewise) in the 1980s, justifying increasing its defense arsenal in America and Western Europe as working for "peace through strength." Reagan's policy arguably forced the Soviet Union to try to maintain pace with the United States. The actions of the Reagan administration initially heightened the Cold War, but its policies, along with the costly and unpopular war in Afghanistan, contributed to the economic collapse of the Soviet Union, ultimately leading to its demise, ending the Cold War, and leaving the United States as the sole military superpower. During the Cold War, the Reagan Administration shipped some of these weapons to insurgent groups working in its interests to undermine the Soviet Union, such as Islamist radicals during Afghanistan's civil war during the 1980s, strengthening positions of extremist groups like the Taliban.[79] In *Iron Man*, Tony sees, and Yinsen reminds him, that the terrorists holding him hostage have become incredibly powerful because they have amassed weapons from Stark Industries, enabling them to attack and kill Americans like those who were ambushed in the military convoy assigned to transport him.[80] Here, Favreau's film draws a parallel to the *9/11 Commission Report* and one of its more startling conclusions about the history of American foreign policy: its culpability in supporting terrorism to advance its interests. And as the report describes, the United States would later discover that years of sending powerful military weapons to insurgents in places like Afghanistan to fight the Cold War ultimately empowered terrorists and lethal organizations like Osama bin Laden and al Qaeda whose collective intention is to attack and kill Americans, waging a global war against the United States.[81]

Although geographically located in Afghanistan, the Ten Rings' oblique political and religious affiliations actually enable it to represent the idea of terrorism more powerfully than if it was identified with any specific organization in the modern Middle East such as al Qaeda. Moreover, alluding to the organization's religious faith but clearly noting its political intentions for global domination, the film presents the Islamic Middle East in a much more complex, provocative way, especially as it establishes the friendship between Tony and Yinsen, and in later scenes that depict the terrorists attacking Afghani communities. The terrorist leaders keeping Tony hostage want him to build the powerful Jericho Missile he just demonstrated for the American military, to be assembled from various parts of other Stark weapons they have stockpiled. Of course, Tony's initial response to the terrorist leaders is to adamantly decline their order. However, Yensin convinces him to acquiesce to their demands to save Tony's life. Together they first build a more powerful electromagnetic device for Tony, and then a powerful metal suit that will enable Tony and Yensin to escape their captors. During these scenes, Tony undergoes a personal and moral transformation as he realizes that the weapons he designed has supported the horrific actions of these terrorists. Initially he wants to die, a consequence for his "sins." Yinsen, however, persuades him that the brilliance, wealth, and power that made him the premier weapons' designer in the world can actually be used for good by stopping the proliferation of Stark weapons and from getting into the grasp of terrorists.[82]

Tony is not beyond redemption in Yinsen's eyes. As he forces Tony to confront his egoism, he also reminds Tony about the significance of friends and family, and how they enable us to get through life's challenges and the world's horrors. Throughout these hostage scenes, Yinsen and Tony develop a powerful emotional bond. Though Yinsen's religious faith is ambiguous, his ethnic background suggests he is probably Afghani Muslim, and it is significant that the person who saves Tony's life and shows him the path towards personal redemption is someone from the Middle East. Indeed, as they attempt their escape from their captors, Yinsen fights them off in order to give Tony more time to assemble the iron suit, sacrificing himself so that Tony can fight the terrorists who have killed Yinsen's family and ravaged his community. Rather than present the Middle East as monochromatically evil, *Iron Man* portrays it as both the victim and incubator of terrorism.

Yet, as Tony and viewers discover, the real villain is not the Ten Rings terrorist organization after all, but Tony's mentor Obadiah Stane. Along with Tony, we learn that Obadiah has been selling an incredible arsenal of sophisticated weapons to the terrorists, treating them as if they are just among the many buyers of Stark Industries' products that also includes the United States military. In this regard, Obadiah embodies a capitalist ethos that reifies the profit imperative above all ethical considerations, including a corporation's responsibility for the consequences of its potentially lethal actions. Indeed, we discover that Obadiah actually encouraged the terrorists to kidnap Tony, whom he wanted assassinated, and who now wants the remains of Tony's iron suit which the terrorists collected after Tony's escape in order to create an even more powerful military weapon. Earlier, Tony's reckless lifestyle was an embarrassment for the company, but not an impediment to Obadiah's plans for global control of the weapons industry. However, Tony and Obadiah emerge as mortal enemies once Tony returns from his ordeal in Afghanistan, and decides to shut down the profitable weapons development division in Stark Industries. Obadiah maneuvers to have the corporation's board marginalize Tony's ownership power, allowing Obadiah to pursue Stark Industries' primary objective—to control the global market in military weapons.

Not surprisingly, the film's climax depicts the redeemed, idealistic Tony and his superhero identity, Iron Man,[83] confronting the morally bankrupt Obadiah, the depraved global capitalist who profits from terrorism (in his über-iron suit made from Tony's earlier plans). By this point in the film, Tony has developed a more sophisticated metallic suit that he immediately uses to undermine the terrorist organization that held him hostage and now threatens an Afghani village, saving innocent civilians while deploying even more sophisticated weapons against the nefarious terrorists. Significantly, the film does not dismiss powerful military technology in these scenes; in fact, it illustrates how this technology can be used to advance moral good, rather than simply protecting one's (or a country's) "interests." In this regard, *Iron Man* provokes viewers to confront a panoply of profound issues facing Americans in the post-9/11 world, including its defense policies, the military industrial complex, global terrorism, and the ethics of capitalism.

Thus, Favreau's film forces viewers to reflect upon the recent history of American foreign policy, and the economic philosophy that defines the American way of life. *Iron Man* challenges viewers to consider whether we are going to follow the path of the redeemed Tony Stark who wants to use weapons (as Iron Man) as a force of good in the world; or whether we take (continue?) the path of Obadiah Stane who uses his company's powerful military capacity to advance corporate interests, regardless of the ethical consequences, dealing with terrorists or other morally questionable organizations or leaders if necessary. Arguably, the honesty with which Americans need to confront these issues comes at the film's ending, when the government encourages Tony to lie about his superhero identity at a press conference. Tony debates with Pepper whether or not he should be a secret superhero leading a dual life (a common decision superheroes have made in comic-book series such as *Batman* and *Superman*). Like the government, Rhodey wants Tony to "stick to the script" and deny his superhero identity. However, Tony ultimately decides to be honest about who he is, and confront the truth that he is the "Iron Man," the name given to the celebrated superhero by the press.[84]

That the film ends with Tony's confession and the press shouting questions without receiving answers leaves the film very open-ended (and nicely setting it up for a sequel), prompting viewers to wonder why Tony would dismiss the government's and his friend Rhodey's plea, and divulge his "true" identity. Perhaps the film wants Americans to consider their "true" identity as well. Maybe *Iron Man* asks them to be honest about their nation's past, accept the United States' identity as a "superpower," and to use its powerful global position as economic and military leader to advance American ideals, making the world a safer and better place in the process.

Telling stories remains one of the primary means by which human beings attempt to make sense of their world. As Hayden White notes,

> narrative might well be considered a solution to a problem of general human concern, namely, the problem of how to translate knowing into telling, the problem of fashioning human experience into a form assimilable to structures of meaning that are generally human.[85]

We should then not be surprised that Americans have turned to narratives to help them understand the traumatic events of September 11th. Moreover, transforming a narrative of 9/11 into a history enables us to work through an epistemological crisis that will help us comprehend "why this happened" as much as knowing "how this happened." The terrorist attacks shattered a fundamental worldview Americans believed about themselves: namely that they represented the pinnacle of a human civilization defined by freedom, democracy, and economic opportunity. After triumphing over the Soviet Union and celebrating the demise of global communism (with China as the major exception, and the degree to which it remains an orthodox communist regime is questionable), some Americans imagined that the world had even achieved "the end of history."[86] Without a viable opposing ideological system, the United States was celebrated as a model liberal capitalist democracy for other nations to emulate, particularly developing countries wanting to lift their people out of poverty and promote political freedom. To be sure, there were critics of the American system, but they largely demanded a fairer and more equitable distribution of economic and political resources rather than reject the ideological foundations of liberalism and modernity associated with the American way of life. Yet, these views of American values and culture were rooted in a Cold War epistemology. Of course the United States was aware of emerging radical Islamism following the end of the Cold War, and aims of jihadist terrorists to challenge what they viewed as American hegemony and decadence. But extreme Islamism and its goals of global terrorism were viewed as a fringe movement and containable, particular after the FBI successfully prosecuted al Qaeda terrorists after the 1993 World Trade Center bombing. The events of 9/11 thus shook Americans to their core, forcing them to reconstitute their Cold War epistemology in light of new global conditions and a different kind of ideological conflict.

To its credit, the 9/11 National Commission recognized this epistemological crisis, and presented its report as a narrative in part to provide the kind of meaning that would enable Americans to understand the political and historical context of the September 11th attacks. However, its efforts tragically fall short of these goals for two main reasons: first, the decision to privilege the horrific experience of the victims of the hijackings, the Twin Towers, and the Pentagon above the history of the Muslim world and rise of radical Islamism, and second, the refusal to assign culpability to either the Clinton or Bush administrations as well as the American intelligence community. As such, the *9/11 Commission Report* lacks the necessary narrative closure that would resolve persisting issues that would allow Americans to see this as a significant historical event and help them understand what 9/11 means in the broader narrative of American history.

Films directly about the 9/11 terrorist attacks like Paul Greengrass's *United 93* and Oliver Stone's *World Trade Center* similarly refuse to address these important historical issues. While these movies demonstrate how September 11th reflected the indomitable human spirit in the face of terror and tragedy, the ultimate significance of 9/11 lies in the ways Americans united as a national community in these moments of catastrophe and devastation. *United 93* and *World Trade Center* are emotionally gripping films and address a critical dimension of this momentous day in recent American history. These movies, however, refrain from probing the importance of the terrorist attacks any further. The broader political and historical meaning of 9/11 is noticeably absent, thereby preventing viewers from seeing these films beyond anything more than direct representations of that tragic day. Because the *9/11 Commission Report* and these 9/11 movies do not resolve the epistemological questions about why these events happened and why the Muslim world remains hostile to American civilization, counter-narratives that do assign responsibility to political leaders and intelligence agencies have found a legitimate audience (including reputable university book publishers) that is willing to entertain alternative histories. The competition between the official history (the *9/11 Commission Report*) and alternative histories (conspiracy theories that vilify corrupt American institutions) illustrates that Americans are caught between conflicting histories, and recalls the ideological and cultural battles surrounding the *Warren Report* and the counter-narratives it spawned following President Kennedy's assassination. Just as Americans questioned the *Warren Report* in light of government deceit regarding Vietnam and Watergate, we may be in a similar historical circumstance whereby Americans doubt the official 9/11 government report because of intentional government misinformation about the 2003 Iraq War.

Will the 9/11 counter-narratives become the legitimate history of September 11th? Perhaps this answer will be resolved once the Afghanistan and Iraq wars are over and we find closure to the traumatic events of 9/11. For now, however, the best way for us to find historical meaning and understanding to the terrorist attacks may lie with superhero allegorical films that can engage epistemological and historical issues in an alternative fantasy universe to interrogate pressing questions about our post-9/11 society. Already, movies such as *Batman Begins* and *Iron Man* have shown that superhero films can successfully probe profound issues about the relationship between terrorism and justice as well as the legacy of American foreign policy and global capitalism in recent history. *Batman Begins* and *Iron Man* demonstrate that narratives remain the critical way to find historical meaning in the devastating events of 9/11. Perhaps other films will follow their lead and navigate us through our epistemological crisis so that we may construct a new American narrative that helps us understand where September 11th stands in relation to the broader currents of American history.

# NOTES

## Introduction

1  Martin Scorsese, dir., *Gangs of New York* (Miramax, 2002).
2  Scorsese, *Gangs of New York*.
3  Scorsese, *Gangs of New York*.
4  Charles Beard, "Written History as an Act of Faith," *American Historical Review*, vol. 39, no. 2 (1934): 219–231, 219.
5  Victor Fleming, dir., *Gone with the Wind* (MGM, 1939).
6  Arguably, Scarlett's return to Tara is an effort to engage with her past, but I would maintain that this is about returning to the place that defined hers and her family's values, and is a resource of identity and spirit. After all, it was at Tara where she endured suffering following the South's defeat, and where she determined that she "will never go hungry again." Going to Tara reflects Scarlett's acknowledgement of the source of her identity, allowing her to escape her past in Atlanta, and giving her the strength to pursue Rhett. See Fleming, dir., *Gone with the Wind.*
7  Mark Twain, *The Adventures of Huckleberry Finn: The Authoritative Text*, ed. Victor Fischer and Lin Salamo (Berkeley, CA: University of California Press, 1997), 363.
8  Peter Novick, *That Noble Dream: The "Objectivity Question" and the American Historical Profession* (New York: Cambridge University Press, 1988, 1991), 43–46.
9  Novick, *That Noble Dream*, 47–60.
10  Novick, *That Noble Dream*, 47–60.
11  J.H. Hexter, *Doing History* (Bloomington, IN: Indiana University Press, 1971), 77–106.
12  Robert Rosenstone, *Visions of the Past: The Challenge of Film to Our Idea of History* (Cambridge, MA: Harvard University Press, 1996), 19–44.
13  Rosenstone, *Visions of the Past*, 19–44.
14  National Commission on Terrorist Attacks Upon the United States, *The 9/11 Commission Report: Final Report of the National Commission on Terrorist Attacks Upon the United States* (New York: Norton, 2004), xv; Ernest R. May, ed., *The 9/11 Commission Report with Related Documents* (Boston, MA: Bedford/St. Martin's Press, 2007), 2, 15–17.

## 1 Exorcising the Demons Within

1 Mark Kermode, *The Exorcist*, 2nd edn (London: British Film Institute, 1997, 1998), 8–10.

2 William Peter Blatty wanted to affirm a more positive spiritual message in the film's ending than the one that is more ambivalent in the original 1973 release of the film, but his perspective was dismissed by Friedkin. Viewers can now see Blatty's original vision of the film's ending in the re-released version of the film in 2000. For the dispute about the film's ending, see Kermode, *The Exorcist*, 2nd edn.

3 Kermode, *The Exorcist*, 2nd edn, 10.

4 Some have interpreted Father Karras's invocation of the demon to possess him and then jump through the bedroom window as a Christian act of sacrifice, resurrecting Karras's faith, suggesting the ability of Christianity and its believers to triumph over evil. That Father Karras is given the last rites by Father Dyer further supports the idea that he has been absolved of his sins, affirming his Christian faith. As I will argue later in this chapter, the original theatrical release is more equivocal about the power of Christianity to exorcise the demon that possesses Regan. Arguably, that Father Karras implores the demon to possess him, not to mention having triumphed over Father Merrin, reveals the inadequacy of Christianity to exorcise the demon. Mark Kermode describes the two versions of *The Exorcist*, the 1973 theatrical release and the later re-release (Kermode was able to view the re-released version prior to its 2000 release as he wrote the second edn of his book, *The Exorcist*). See Kermode, *The Exorcist*, 2nd edn, 89–99.

5 William Friedkin, dir., *The Exorcist* (Warner Bros., 1973, 2000).

6 Clifford Geertz, "Religion as a Cultural System," in Clifford Geertz, *The Interpretation of Cultures: Selected Essays* (New York: Basic Books, 1973), 87–125.

7 Thomas Luckman, *The Invisible Religion: The Problem of Religion in Modern Society* (New York: Macmillan, 1967), 52–54, 61.

8 Jon Butler, *Awash in a Sea of Faith: Christianizing the American People* (Cambridge, MA: Harvard University Press, 1988), 3.

9 Randy Kennedy, "2 Jewish Leaders Upset After Viewing 'Passion'," *New York Times*, January 23, 2004; Sharon Waxman, "Gibson to Delete a Scene in 'Passion'," *New York Times*, February 2, 2004.

10 Matthew Frye Jacobson, *Whiteness of a Different Color: European Immigrants and the Alchemy of Race* (Cambridge, MA: Harvard University Press). I place "ethnicity" in quotation marks because Jacobson cautions us about this term. Although "ethnicity" currently has social, political, and cultural currency, Jacobson rightly challenges this cultural category as it minimizes the contested history of whiteness that is central to the history of race in American history.

11 At the end of 2004, the film had grossed over $370 million. See Frank Rich, "2004: The Year of 'The Passion'," *New York Times*, December 19, 2004.

12 Frank Rich, "Mel Gibson Forgives Us for His Sins," *New York Times*, March 7, 2004.

13 Paul Boyer and Stephen Nissenbaum, *Salem Possessed: The Social Origins of Witchcraft* (Cambridge, MA: Harvard University Press, 1974); John Demos, *Entertaining Satan: Witchcraft and the Culture of Early New England* (New York: Oxford University Press, 1982); Carol F. Karlsen, *The Devil in the Shape of a Woman: Witchcraft in Colonial New England* (New York: Norton, 1987, 1998); Butler, *Awash in a Sea of Faith*, 67–97; Mary Beth Norton, *In the Devil's Snare: The Salem Witchcraft Crisis of 1692* (New York: Norton, 2002).

14 Christopher Bigsby, "Introduction," in Arthur Miller, *The Crucible: A Play in Four Acts* (New York: Viking, 1952, 1995), vii–xxv, ix.

15 Quoted from Christopher Bigsby's introduction to Arthur Miller's *The Crucible*. See Bigsby, "Introduction," ix.

16 Karlsen, *The Devil in the Shape of a Woman*, 222–251.

17 Norton, *In the Devil's Snare*, 11–12.
18 Boyer and Nissenbaum, *Salem Possessed*, 22–36.
19 Boyer and Nissenbaum, *Salem Possessed*, 22.
20 Of course the literature on New England town studies is quite large. Two classics in the field remain Philip Greven, *Four Generations: Population, Land, and Family in Colonial Andover, Massachusetts* (Ithaca, NY: Cornell University Press, 1970) and Kenneth Lockridge, *A New England Town: The First Hundred Years, Dedham, Massachusetts, 1636–1736* (New York: Norton, 1970). Paul Boyer and Stephen Nissenbaum's *Salem Possessed* remains among the classics of these community studies that emphasize decline from the Puritan ideal, but see also Richard Bushman, *From Puritan to Yankee: Character and the Social Order in Connecticut* (Cambridge, MA: Harvard University Press, 1968) and Darrett Rutman, *John Winthrop's Boston: Portrait of a Puritan Town, 1630–1649* (Chapel Hill, NC: University of North Carolina Press, 1969). For examples of community studies that stress social and cultural continuities instead of declension, see James Henretta, "Farms and Families: Mentalité in Pre-Industrial America," *William and Mary Quarterly*, 3rd series, vol. 35, no. 1 (1978): 3–32; Michael Zuckerman, *Peaceable Kingdoms: New England Towns in the Eighteenth Century* (New York: Vintage, 1970). For a variation on Atlantic commerce and the declension model, see Christine Leigh Heyrman, *Commerce and Culture: The Maritime Communities of Colonial Massachusetts, 1690–1750* (New York: Norton, 1984).
21 Boyer and Nissenbaum, *Salem Possessed*, 27–28.
22 Boyer and Nissenbaum, *Salem Possessed*, 22–36.
23 Boyer and Nissenbaum, *Salem Possessed*, 179–216.
24 Norton, *In the Devil's Snare*, 3–12.
25 Butler, *Awash in a Sea of Faith*, 67–97.
26 Richard Godbeer, *The Devil's Dominion: Magic and Religion in Early New England* (New York: Cambridge University Press, 1994), 1–23.
27 Richard Godbeer, *Escaping Salem: The Other Witch Hunt of 1692* (New York: Oxford University Press, 2005).
28 Norton, *In the Devil's Snare*, 295–304.
29 Norton, *In the Devil's Snare*, 13.
30 Hayden White, "The Question of Narrative in Contemporary Historical Theory," *History and Theory*, vol. 23, no. 3 (1984): 1–33.
31 Hayden White, "Interpretation in History," *New Literary History*, vol. 4, no. 2 (1973): 281–314; Hayden White, *Metahistory: The Historical Imagination in Nineteenth-Century Europe* (Baltimore, MD: Johns Hopkins University Press, 1973).
32 For a discussion about historical narrative and historical catharsis, see White, "The Question of Narrative in Contemporary Historical Theory."
33 Norton, *In the Devil's Snare*, 3–13, 305–308.
34 Karlsen, *The Devil in the Shape of a Woman*, 1–45.
35 Karlsen, *The Devil in the Shape of a Woman*, 14–19.
36 Karlsen, *The Devil in the Shape of a Woman*, 1–45, 77–116.
37 Karlsen, *The Devil in the Shape of a Woman*, 117–152.
38 Jane Kamensky, *Governing the Tongue: The Politics of Speech in Early New England* (New York: Oxford University Press, 1997); Jane Kamensky, "Words, Witches, and Women Trouble: Witchcraft, Disorderly Speech, and Gender Boundaries in Puritan New England," *Essex Institute Historical Collections*, vol. 128, no. 3 (1992): 286–307.
39 Arthur Miller, *The Crucible* (New York: Penguin, 1976, 1995), 9–11.
40 Nicholas Hytner, dir., *The Crucible* (Twentieth Century Fox, 1996, 2005).
41 The historical literature on the history of European witchcraft is of course quite extensive. Among the classics on the topic is Keith Thomas, *Religion and the Decline of Magic* (New York: Scribner, 1971). In addition to Keith Thomas's book, I have drawn upon the history of European witchcraft from the essays in Darren Oldridge's

*The Witchcraft Reader.* See Darren Oldridge, ed., *The Witchcraft Reader* (New York: Routledge, 2002).

42   As in the historiography of women and witchcraft in colonial America, the scholarly literature on gender and European witchcraft has grown in recent years. For gender and European witchcraft, see Christina Larner, "Was Witch-Hunting Women-Hunting?", in *The Witchcraft Reader*, ed. Oldridge, 273–275. See also Marianne Hester, "Patriarchal Reconstruction and Witch-Hunting," in *The Witchcraft Reader*, ed. Oldridge, 276–288; Jim Sharpe, "Women, Witchcraft, and the Legal Process," in *The Witchcraft Reader*, ed. Oldridge, 289–302; Clive Holmes, "Women: Witches and Witnesses," in *The Witchcraft Reader*, ed. Oldridge, 303–322; Louise Jackson, "Witches, Wives and Mothers: Witchcraft Persecutions and Women's Confessions in Seventeenth-Century England," in *The Witchcraft Reader*, ed. Oldridge, 353–366.

43   For witchcraft and the Reformation, see Stuart Clark, "Protestant Witchcraft and Catholic Witchcraft," in *The Witchcraft Reader*, ed. Oldridge, 165–178. See also Gary K. Waite, "Between the Devil and the Inquisitor: Anabaptists, Diabolical Conspiracies and Magical Beliefs," in *The Witchcraft Reader*, ed. Oldridge, 189–199.

44   Philip A. Kuhn, *Soulstealers: The Chinese Sorcery Scare of 1768* (Cambridge, MA: Harvard University Press, 1990), 225.

45   Kuhn, *Soulstealers*, 223–232.

46   Max Weber, *Economy and Society*, 2 vols, trans. and ed. Guenther Roth and Claus Wittich (Berkeley, CA: University of California Press, 1978), 217–226, 956–1005, 1393–1405.

47   Kuhn, *Soulstealers*, 232.

48   Geertz, "Religion as a Cultural System," 105–108.

49   Laurence Thompson, *Chinese Religion: An Introduction* (Belmont, CA: Wadsworth, 1989), 25–30.

50   Thompson, *Chinese Religion*, 25–30.

51   Thompson, *Chinese Religion*, 25–30.

52   Barend J. Ter Haar, *Telling Stories: Witchcraft and Scapegoating in Chinese History* (Boston, MA: Brill, 2006), 30–36.

53   Elaine Pagels, *The Origin of Satan* (New York: Vintage, 1996), 35–62.

54   Pagels, *The Origin of Satan*, 35–62.

55   Pagels, *The Origin of Satan*, 35–62.

56   Pagels, *The Origin of Satan*, xvi.

57   Pagels, *The Origin of Satan*, xvi–xxiii.

58   Pagels, *The Origin of Satan*, 3–34.

59   Pagels, *The Origin of Satan*, 3–34.

60   Pagels, *The Origin of Satan*, 3–34.

61   Pagels, *The Origin of Satan*, 3–34.

62   Pagels, *The Origin of Satan*, 3–34.

63   Pagels, *The Origin of Satan*, 3–34.

64   Pagels, *The Origin of Satan*, 3–34; Caroline Walker Bynum, *Holy Feast and Holy Fast: The Religious Significance of Food to Medieval Women* (Berkeley, CA: University of California Press, 1987), 251–259.

65   Pagels, *The Origin of Satan*, 111.

66   Bynum, *Holy Feast and Holy Fast*, 251–259.

67   Bynum, *Holy Feast and Holy Fast*, 251–259.

68   Frank Rich, "Mel Gibson Forgives Us for His Sins," *New York Times*, March 7, 2004.

69   Sharon Waxman, "Gibson to Delete a Scene in 'Passion'," *New York Times*, February 4, 2004.

70   Jacobson, *Whiteness of a Different Color*, 171–199.

71   Pagels, *The Origin of Satan*, 89–111.

72   Jacobson, *Whiteness of a Different Color*, 171–199.

73  Jacobson, *Whiteness of a Different Color*, 13–39.

74  Jacobson, *Whiteness of a Different Color*, 246–273.

75  The early Christian movement was quite diverse. Multiple gospels circulated throughout the ancient Mediterranean world, and perhaps deep into Asia. Churches were mostly locally organized during Christianity's early history. The Christian Church in Rome attempted to impose theological and ecclesiastical authority by asserting theological orthodoxy and establishing an Episcopal Church structure that was integrated and hierarchical, claiming to be the legitimate heir to the Apostle Peter and the first Christian Church. Gnostic Christians, who might be members and perhaps even religious leaders within the Roman Church, fundamentally dismissed the orthodox belief that the Roman ecclesiastical structure and apostolic succession were the ultimate theological authorities for Christians. Some of these Gnostics, such as the adherents to the Gospel of Thomas, saw churches as initially necessary to help guide Christians along a spiritual path, but eventually believers were to look within themselves to discover the essence of their Christian spirituality, and use this spiritual knowledge to develop a closer relationship with God. More than heterodoxy, the Roman Church viewed Gnostics as heretics because they rejected Papal and Episcopal authority to define Christian faith and practices for the Christian world. See Pagels, *The Origin of Satan*, 149–178.

76  Stuart Wright, "Satanic Cults, Ritual Abuse, and Moral Panic: Deconstructing a Modern Witch-Hunt," in *Witchcraft and Magic: Contemporary North America*, ed. Helen A. Berger (Philadelphia, PA: University of Pennsylvania Press, 2005), 120–136.

77  Wright, "Satanic Cults, Ritual Abuse, and Moral Panic."

78  Gregory A. Waller, "Introduction," in *American Horrors: Essays on the Modern American Horror Film*, ed. Gregory A. Waller (Urbana, IL: University of Illinois Press, 1987), 1–13; Vivian Sobchack, "Bringing It All Back Home: Economy and Generic Exchange," in *American Horrors*, ed. Waller, 175–194.

79  Waller, "Introduction," in *American Horrors*, ed. Waller, 1–13.

80  Marsha Kinder and Beverle Houston, "Seeing Is Believing: *The Exorcist* and *Don't Look Now*," in *American Horrors*, ed. Waller, 44–61.

81  Arguably, perceiving *The Exorcist* as a film about satanic possession is reinforced by Father Merrin's and Father Karras's exorcism, and the Christian rituals and symbols they deploy throughout the film. Moreover, scholarship on *The Exorcist* has been mostly produced in the disciplines of film and literary studies and present cursory and discursive discussions about Christian theology and American religious history. Perhaps because these studies are not about the film's religious themes and center on other themes such as the horror film genre, gender, among others, scholars rarely examine the movie's substantive religious dimensions. See particularly Kinder and Houston, "Seeing Is Believing"; Carol Clover, *Men, Women, and Chainsaws: Gender in the Modern Horror Film* (Princeton, NJ: Princeton University Press, 1992), 65–113.

82  See Jürgen Habermas, *The Philosophical Discourse of Modernity: Twelve Lectures*, trans. Frederick Lawrence (Cambridge, MA: The MIT Press, 1987). See also Jürgen Habermas, "Modernity: An Unfinished Project," and the accompanying critical essays in *Habermas and the Unfinished Project of Modernity: Critical Essays on the Philosophical Discourse of Modernity*, ed. Maurizio Passerin d'Entrèves and Seyla Benhabib (Cambridge, MA: The MIT Press, 1997).

83  Walter Benjamin, "Paris, Capital of the Nineteenth Century," in Walter Benjamin, *The Arcades Project*, trans. Howard Eiland and Kevin McLaughlin (Cambridge, MA: Belknap Press of Harvard University Press, 2002), 14–26.

84  Clover, *Men, Women, and Chainsaws*, 65–113.

85  Kermode, *The Exorcist*, 2nd edn, 24.

86  Kermode, *The Exorcist*, 2nd edn, 53.

87  In narrative theory, point-of-view is a narrative device to align the reader or viewer with ways a particular character sees the world, sometimes simply in terms of

perception, sometimes epistemologically. See H. Porter Abbott, *The Cambridge Introduction to Narrative*, 2nd edn (New York: Cambridge University Press, 2008), 67–82.

88   Kermode, *The Exorcist*, 2nd edn, 58.

89   For a more detailed discussion about camera angles and character perspective in *The Exorcist*, see Kermode, *The Exorcist*, 2nd edn, 62.

90   Morris Berman, *The Reenchantment of the World* (Ithaca, NY: Cornell University Press, 1981).

91   Claude Lévi-Strauss, *Structural Anthropology* (New York: Basic Books, 1963), 167–185.

92   Lévi-Strauss, *Structural Anthropology*, 167–185.

93   My understanding of modernity has been influenced not only by theorists such as Jürgen Habermas, but also by critics of modernity such as Dipesh Chakrabarty and Ian Baucom. For Habermas's positions about modernity and the Enlightenment Project, see Jürgen Habermas, *The Philosophical Discourse of Modernity: Twelve Lectures*, trans. Frederick Lawrence (Cambridge, MA: The MIT Press, 1987); Habermas, "Modernity: An Unfinished Project," in *Habermas and the Unfinished Project of Modernity: Critical Essays on the Philosophical Discourse of Modernity*, ed. Maurizio Passerin d'Entrèves and Seyla Benhabib (Cambridge, MA: The MIT Press, 1997), 38–58. For a critique of Habermas's Enlightenment Project, see Fred Dallmayr, "The Discourse of Modernity: Hegel, Nietzsche, Heidegger, and Habermas," in *Habermas and the Unfinished Project of Modernity*, ed. Passerin d'Entrèves and Benhabib, 59–96. For a critique of modernity, scientific empiricism, and Enlightenment visions of progress and emancipation, see Dipesh Chakrabarty, *Habitations of Modernity: Essays in the Wake of Subaltern Studies* (Chicago, IL: University of Chicago Press, 2002). For ideas about historical subjectivity, historical agency, and Enlightenment philosophies, see Ian Baucom, *Specters of the Atlantic: Finance Capital, Slavery, and the Philosophy of History* (Durham, NC: Duke University Press, 2005), 35–79. David Harvey's *The Condition of Postmodernity* remains a good survey of the major themes of modernity, particularly as it relates to technology, progress, and philosophies of human emancipation. See David Harvey, *The Condition of Postmodernity: An Enquiry into the Origins of Cultural Change* (Cambridge, MA: Blackwell, 1990).

94   Habermas, "Modernity: An Unfinished Project," 38–58.

95   Friedken, dir., *The Exorcist*.

96   In narrative theory, narrative discourse is the broader thread that connects the stories and event sequences within the narrative. Throughout this chapter I utilize the term "constituent story or constituent event" to denote a particular story or event-sequence in the film. Where stories are embedded within a narrative to complement or advance narrative discourse, we need to think about narrative discourse as the metanarrative, the totality of the entire narrative. Sometimes story and narrative are distinguished by the terms fabula for story and sujet (also sjuzet) for narrative. See Abbott, *The Cambridge Introduction to Narrative*, 13–27.

97   Wright, "Satanic Cults, Ritual Abuse, and Moral Panic."

98   Friedkin, dir., *The Exorcist*.

99   Michel Foucault, *Madness and Civilization: The History of Insanity in the Age of Reason*, trans. Richard Howard (New York: Vintage, 1965, 1988); Michel Foucault, *Discipline and Punish: The Birth of the Prison*, trans. Alan Sheridan (New York, Vintage, 1979); Michel Foucault, *The History of Sexuality*, vol. 1, trans. Robert Hurley (New York: Vintage, 1980), 115–150.

100  Friedkin, dir., *The Exorcist*. See also Kermode, *The Exorcist*, 2nd edn, 58–62.

101  Clover, *Men, Women, and Chainsaws*. In this interpretation, Carol Clover draws upon Thomas Laqueur's interpretation of one-sex and two-sex modalities as scientific and sexual modes of discourse deployed to understanding sex, gender, and our bodies. The one-sex model postulates that the male sex is the biological paradigm to understanding sexual organs and sexuality, where the female body is an inversion of

the male (thus the uterus is a variation of the penis and the ovaries a variation of the testes). The two-sex model postulates that men and women are two distinct sexes with discrete sexual organs. Laqueur argues that Freudian psychoanalysis returned to the one-sex model with its constructions of hysteria and penis envy. Clover argues that possession films reverse the one-sex model where the female body becomes the sexual paradigm, and male figures such as Father Karras are inversions of the female sex, becoming opened vessels as their bodies adopt characteristics of the vulva, vagina, and uterus. See Clover, *Men, Women and Chainsaws*, 65–113. See also Thomas W. Laqueur, *Making Sex: Body and Gender from the Greeks to Freud* (Cambridge, MA: Harvard University Press, 1990).

102 Foucault, *The History of Sexuality*, vol. 1, 155–159.
103 Ronald Reagan, "Farewell Address to the Nation," January 11, 1989. See www. ronaldreagan.com/sp_21.html

## 2 Redeeming the South, Redeeming the Nation

1 From Barry Schwartz, "Collective Memory and History: How Abraham Lincoln Became a Symbol of Racial Equality," *Sociological Quarterly*, vol. 38, no. 3: 469–496.
2 From Schwartz, "Collective Memory and History."
3 Eric Foner, *Reconstruction: America's Unfinished Revolution, 1863–1877* (New York: HarperCollins, 1988), Chapters 5 and 6.
4 The historiography on Jeffersonian ideology and political economy is, of course, quite lengthy. However, three texts that inform this chapter on Jeffersonian economic and political thought are Richard Hofstadter's *The American Political Tradition*, which actually connects Jefferson and Lincoln to the political tradition of classical liberalism in American political ideology, and more recent studies such as Drew McCoy's *The Elusive Republic* and Joyce Appleby's *Capitalism and the New Social Order*. See Richard Hofstadter, *The American Political Tradition and the Men Who Made It* (New York: Vintage, 1948); Drew McCoy, *The Elusive Republic: Political Economy in Jeffersonian America* (New York: Norton, 1980); Joyce Appleby, *Capitalism and the New Social Order* (New York: New York University Press, 1984).
5 For the role John Burgess and William Dunning played in shaping Reconstruction historiography, see Foner, *Reconstruction*, xix–xxi; Peter Novick, *That Noble Dream: The Objectivity Question and the American Historical Profession* (New York: Oxford University Press, 1988), Chapter 2.
6 W.E.B. DuBois, *Black Reconstruction: An Essay Toward a History of the Part which Black Folk Played in the Attempt to Reconstruct Democracy in America, 1860–1880* (New York: Harcourt, Brace, 1935). A landmark study of Reconstruction, DuBois's study was initially dismissed by the historical profession because of its neo-Marxist analysis. See Novick, *That Noble Dream*, 232. August Meir and Elliot Rudwick, *Black History and the Historical Profession* (Urbana, IL: University of Illinois Press, 1986); Foner, *Reconstruction*, xxi. For how DuBois's work has led revisionist scholarship on Reconstruction, see Foner, *Reconstruction*, xxiv–xxv.
7 David Shepard, *The Making of "The Birth of a Nation"* (Film Preservation Associates, 1992).
8 Michael Rogan, "'The Sword Became a Flashing Vision': D.W. Griffith's *The Birth of a Nation*," in *The Birth of a Nation, D.W. Griffith Director*, ed. Robert Lang (New Brunswick, NJ: Rutgers University Press, 1994), 250–293, 250.
9 Shepard, *The Making of "The Birth of a Nation."*
10 David W. Blight, *Race and Reunion: The Civil War in American Memory* (Cambridge, MA: Belknap Press of Harvard University Press, 2001), 224, 227–231.
11 D.W. Griffith, dir., *The Birth of a Nation, or The Clansman* (David W. Griffith Corp., 1915). See also *The Birth of a Nation, D.W. Griffith Director*, ed. Lang, 44.

12 Griffith, dir., *The Birth of a Nation*.

13 Abraham Lincoln, "Speech Given at the Illinois Republican State Convention," June 16, 1858. See http://showcase.netins.net/web/creative/lincoln/speeches/house.html.

14 The following is a more complete summary of the film, providing the reader with a better understanding of the strong personal connections between the regions. As the war ensues, Ellen has become a spy for the South, and her brother Tom sees her pass a message to her lover Frank Carey, Ethel's brother and Confederate soldier. Tom seizes the note, but allows Frank to leave. The note is later discovered in Tom's hands, and Union Army officers declare him a traitor and sentence him to death, despite his heroic efforts at the Battle of Shiloh. The execution is commuted when Frank admits that the letter was intended for Tom. Before he is executed, Frank escapes, but then he is recaptured. Meanwhile, Tom has been captured by Southern troops when visiting his sister. Ethel and Ellen promote the exchange of their imprisoned brothers, and the film ends with the lovers Frank and Ellen heading South, and Tom and Ethel going North. The confusing narrative parallels the internecine and discombobulated nature of the Civil War. Family and love are the only rational and loyal relationships established in the conflict. Politics and war are not only disconnected, but also artificial compared to blood relationships. Whether the modern viewer believes this interpretation, it must be taken into account that contemporaries saw the Civil War as a human tragedy (and in some cases, the apocalypse), and reaching for human understanding was central to rationalizing what transpired. As much as we see political instruction from the conflict, contemporaries sought to distance themselves from such claims because of the immediate emotional dimension of their experience with the war. Joseph W. Smiley, dir., *The Battle of Shiloh* (Lubin Mfg Co. Distribution Co. General Film Co., 1913). Plot summary from *American Film Institute Catalog*.

15 Colin Campbell, dir., *The Crisis* (Selig Polyscope, 1919). Plot summary from *American Film Institute Catalog*.

16 See, in general, DuBois, *Black Reconstruction*.

17 Rogan, "'The Sword Became a Flashing Vision'," 254.

18 Foner, *Reconstruction*, 6.

19 Other than President Lincoln, Austin Stoneman is the closest representation to a historical figure in the film, in this case Thaddeus Stevens, a staunch abolitionist Republican from Pennsylvania. Thaddeus Stevens embodied much of the "radical" sentiments of the Republican party, including emancipation, black suffrage, and racial equality. Stoneman's likeness to Stevens is quite clear, including the pursed lips and club foot. One can only speculate that giving Stevens a pseudonym in the film enabled Griffith to develop the fictionalized narrative of the Northern family. Arguably, the similarity to Stevens allows Griffith to further connect history and fiction, confusing the two even further. On the other hand, given that Griffith believed his representation of Reconstruction was "history," he probably thought he was giving an accurate portrayal of Stevens' plans for Southern Reconstruction.

20 Griffith, dir., *The Birth of a Nation*.

21 Griffith, dir., *The Birth of a Nation*.

22 Griffith, dir., *The Birth of a Nation*.

23 Griffith, dir., *The Birth of a Nation*.

24 Griffith, dir., *The Birth of a Nation*.

25 Schwartz, "Collective Memory and History," 1, 5–7.

26 Blight, *Race and Reunion*, 2, 64–93.

27 Robert Lang, "*The Birth of a Nation*: History, Ideology, Narrative Form," in *The Birth of a Nation, D.W. Griffith Director*, ed. Lang, 3–24.

28 Griffith, dir., *The Birth of a Nation*, shots 621–625; *The Birth of a Nation, D.W. Griffith Director*, ed. Lang, 94; Woodrow Wilson, *The History of the American People*, vol. 5, *Reunion and Nationalization* (New York: Harper and Brothers, 1901), 19–20, 49–50, 60.

29  Rogan, "'The Sword Became a Flashing Vision'," 251.

30  John Burgess, *Reconstruction and the Constitution: 1866–1876* (New York: Scribner's Sons, 1902), 10–11. States are placed in quotation marks as they are in Burgess's text.

31  Burgess, *Reconstruction and the Constitution.*

32  Burgess, *Reconstruction and the Constitution,* 11, 13.

33  Burgess, *Reconstruction and the Constitution,* 11, 13.

34  Claude Bowers, *The Tragic Era: The Revolution after Lincoln* (Cambridge, MA: Harvard University Press, 1929), 4.

35  Bowers, *The Tragic Era,* v.

36  Bowers, *The Tragic Era,* v.

37  William Archibald Dunning, *Essays on the Civil War and Reconstruction* (New York: Macmillan, 1904), 65–66.

38  Dunning, *Essays on the Civil War and Reconstruction,* 65–66.

39  Dunning, *Essays on the Civil War and Reconstruction,* 65–66.

40  Dunning, *Essays on the Civil War and Reconstruction,* 70–77.

41  Dunning, *Essays on the Civil War and Reconstruction,* 77.

42  Dunning, *Essays on the Civil War and Reconstruction,* 73, 75.

43  Novick, *That Noble Dream,* 75.

44  Novick, *That Noble Dream,* 75.

45  Novick, *That Noble Dream,* 77.

46  Novick, *That Noble Dream,* 77.

47  Kenneth M. Stampp, *The Era of Reconstruction, 1865–1867* (New York: Alfred A. Knopf, 1966).

48  Tamara Venit, "A Squatter's Republic: Land Rights, Reform, and Anti-Monopoly in California and the Nation, 1890–1920" (PhD Dissertation, Stanford University, 2008).

49  Nell Irvin Painter, *Standing at Armageddon: The United States, 1877–1919* (New York: Norton, 1987).

50  Victor Fleming, dir., *Gone with the Wind* (Metro-Goldwyn-Meyer, 1939).

51  Fleming, dir., *Gone with the Wind.*

52  Fleming, dir., *Gone with the Wind.*

53  Fleming, dir., *Gone with the Wind.*

54  The historical literature on modernity and the American South is quite extensive. A few noteworthy studies that provide different interpretations about whether the South challenged or encouraged modernity include Eugene D. Genovese, *The Political Economy of the Slavery: Studies in the Economy and Society of the Slave South* (New York: Vintage, 1967); Elizabeth Fox-Genovese and Eugene D. Genovese, *The Fruits of Merchant Capital: Slavery and Bourgeois Property in the Rise and Expansion of Capitalism* (New York: Oxford University Press, 1983); Steven Hahn, *The Roots of Southern Populism: Yeoman Farmers and the Transformation of the Georgia Upcountry, 1850–1890* (New York: Oxford University Press, 1983); Peter Coclanis, *The Shadow of a Dream: Economic Life and Death in the South Carolina Low Country, 1670–1920* (New York: Oxford University Press, 1989); Joyce E. Chaplin, *An Anxious Pursuit: Agricultural Innovation and Modernity in the Lower South, 1730–1815* (Chapel Hill, NC: University of North Carolina Press, 1993); Manisha Sinha, *The Counter-Revolution of Slavery: Politics and Ideology in Antebellum South Carolina* (Chapel Hill, NC: University of North Carolina Press, 2000).

55  Howard Beale, *The Critical Year: A Study of Andrew Johnson and Reconstruction* (New York: Frederick Ungar, 1930, 1958), 1–9. I am indebted to Rob Brown for bringing Beale's book to my attention in his historiography paper on Reconstruction for my theory and methods course at Colorado College.

56  Historical interpretations about Jeffersonian ideology have of coursed changed since the publication of Beale's book and the release of *Gone with the Wind.* Yet there is

still much debate whether Jefferson would be considered pre-modern in his critique of liberal capitalism and industrialization, or despite his criticisms of urban centers and industrialization, he favored liberal capitalism in the realm of agro-business. See Drew McCoy, *The Elusive Republic: Political Economy in Jeffersonian America* (New York: Norton, 1980); Appleby, *Capitalism and the New Social Order.*

57 Foner, *Reconstruction*, xxii–xxiv. See also James McPherson, *Battle Cry of Freedom: The Civil War Era* (New York: Oxford University Press, 1988).

58 This debate has arisen in the context of recent research on the role slaves played in the emancipation process. For an overview of these arguments, see Ira Berlin et al., *Slaves No More: Three Essays on Emancipation and the Civil War* (New York: Cambridge University Press, 1989). For a response to these perspectives, see James McPherson, "Who Freed the Slaves?", *Proceedings of the American Philosophical Society*, vol. 139, no. 1 (1995): 1–10.

59 As described in Chapter 1, in narrative theory, intertextuality is the idea that all texts are "made" out of other texts, and are thus in dialogue with these other texts, whether in direct engagement or the ways they draw upon or allude to motifs and themes in the engaged texts. For intertextuality and narrative theory, see H. Porter Abbott, *The Cambridge Introduction to Narrative Theory*, 2nd edn (New York: Cambridge University Press, 2008), 100–111.

60 Andrew McLaglen, dir., *The Blue and the Gray* (Columbia Pictures Television, 1982, 2001).

61 David L. Wolper, prod., *John Jakes' North and South, Book I: North and South* (Warner Bros., 1985, 2004); David L. Wolper, prod., *John Jakes' North and South, Book II: Love and War* (Warner Bros., 1986, 2004); David L. Wolper, prod., *John Jakes' North and South, Book III: Heaven and Hell* (Warner Bros., 1991, 2004).

62 McLaglen, dir., *The Blue and the Gray.*

63 McLaglen, dir., *The Blue and the Gray.*

64 McLaglen, dir., *The Blue and the Gray.*

65 McLaglen, dir., *The Blue and the Gray.*

66 McLaglen, dir., *The Blue and the Gray.*

67 The issue of slaves' emancipating themselves during the Civil War is a longstanding question. For one of the more recent scholarly accounts about this issue, see Berlin et. al., *Slaves No More.*

68 Blight, *Race and Reunion*, 1–5.

69 Although briefly mentioned earlier, Southern Redemption was the political effort by white Southerners which overturned reconstructed governments that protected black freedmen and women, revoked black civil rights, and institutionalized white supremacy. See Foner, *Reconstruction*, 564–601.

70 Wolper, prod., *North and South, Book I: North and South.*

71 Wolper, prod., *North and South, Book I: North and South.*

72 Wolper, prod., *North and South, Book I: North and South.*

73 Wolper, prod., *North and South, Book II: Love and War.*

74 Wolper, prod., *North and South, Book III: Heaven and Hell.*

75 Foner, *Reconstruction*, 106–108.

76 Wolper, prod., *North and South, Book III: Heaven and Hell.*

77 Wolper, prod., *North and South, Book III: Heaven and Hell.*

78 Foner, *Reconstruction*, 564–601.

79 Foner, *Reconstruction*, 564–601.

80 Lamont Johnson, dir., *Gore Vidal's Lincoln* (Finnegan/Pinchunk, 1988; Echo Bridge Entertainment, 2004).

81 Johnson, dir., *Gore Vidal's Lincoln.*

82 McPherson, "Who Freed the Slaves?"

83 Foner, *Reconstruction*, xix–xxvii.

84 Ronald Maxwell, dir., *Gettysburg* (Warner Bros., 1993, 2000).

85 Edward Zwick, dir., *Glory* (TriStar Pictures, 1989, 1997).

86 Anthony Minghella, dir., *Cold Mountain* (Miramax, 2003).

87 J. Mills Thornton, *Politics and Power in a Slave Society: Alabama, 1800–1860* (Baton Rouge, LA: Louisiana State University Press, 1978); Lacy K. Ford, *The Origins of Southern Radicalism: The South Carolina Upcountry, 1800–1860* (New York: Oxford University Press, 1988). Thornton and Ford, among others, developed an historical interpretation about white yeoman independence, slavery, and republican politics initially advanced by Edmund S. Morgan in his seminal book, *American Slavery, American Freedom: The Ordeal of Colonial Virginia* (New York: Norton, 1975). For a study that challenges this Jeffersonian republican thesis, see Manisha Sinha, *The Counterrevolution of Slavery: Politics and Ideology in Antebellum South Carolina* (Chapel Hill, NC: University of North Carolina Press, 2000).

88 Ford, *The Origins of Southern Radicalism*, 1–4.

89 Foner, *Reconstruction*, xxiv–xxvii.

90 Berlin et al., *Slaves No More*; McPherson, "Who Freed the Slaves?", 1–10.

91 Michael Kammen, *People of Paradox: An Inquiry Concerning the Origins of American Civilization* (New York: Cornell University Press, 1972, 1975).

92 Gary Wills, *Lincoln at Gettysburg: The Words that Remade America* (New York: Simon & Schuster, 1992).

93 Ken Burns, dir., *The Civil War* (Florentine Films, 1990, 2004).

## 3 Envisioning and Re-visioning America

1 The significance of Hawkeye's name will be discussed in more detail later in the chapter. His Mohawk father and brother Uncas know him as Hawkeye, but whenever he is among Anglo-American colonists and the English, he is referred to as Nathaniel. As most of the film takes place with Hawkeye among these people, we rarely hear him called Hawkeye. The main indicator that Hawkeye is his primary name is in the credits, which identifies the character with the actor Daniel Day-Lewis and does not refer to his anglicized name Nathaniel whatsoever. See Michael Mann, dir., *The Last of the Mohicans* (Twentieth Century Fox, 1992).

2 Mann, dir., *The Last of the Mohicans*.

3 Patricia Nelson Limerick, *The Legacy of Conquest: The Unbroken Past of the American West* (New York: Norton, 1987), 19–21.

4 Limerick, *The Legacy of Conquest*, 20–21.

5 Limerick, *The Legacy of Conquest*, 21–25.

6 Limerick, *The Legacy of Conquest*, 25–32.

7 Limerick, *The Legacy of Conquest*, 26.

8 Richard White, *The Middle Ground: Indians, Empires, and Republics in the Great Lakes Region* (New York: Cambridge University Press, 1991), ix–xv, 50–93.

9 William Cronon, *Changes in the Land: Indians, Colonists, and the Ecology of New England* (New York: Hill & Wang, 1983), 54–81.

10 Jill Lepore, *The Name of War: King Philip's War and the Origins of American Identity* (New York: Alfred A. Knopf, 1998), 29–47.

11 Lepore, *The Name of War*, ix–xxiii. Lepore contends that King Philip's War produced the most casualties when we count the per capita population. Of course, the American Civil War generated the most casualties when we account for the total population.

12 Lepore, *The Name of War*, 125–170.

13 John Demos, *The Unredeemed Captive: A Family Story from Early America* (New York: Vintage, 1995), 12–39.

14 Demos, *The Unredeemed Captive*, 214–236.

15 Mann, dir., *The Last of the Mohicans*.

16  Jack Greene, *Pursuits of Happiness: The Social Development of Early Modern British Colonies and the Formation of American Culture* (Chapel Hill, NC: University of North Carolina Press, 1988).

17  Mann, dir., *The Last of the Mohicans*.

18  Mann, dir., *The Last of the Mohicans*.

19  Mann, dir., *The Last of the Mohicans*.

20  T.H. Breen, *The Marketplace of Revolution: How Consumer Politics Shaped American Independence* (New York: Oxford University Press, 2004), 33–147.

21  Mann, dir., *The Last of the Mohicans*.

22  Mann, dir., *The Last of the Mohicans*.

23  Mann, dir., *The Last of the Mohicans*.

24  Mann, dir., *The Last of the Mohicans*.

25  James Merrell, *The Indian's New World: Catawbas and their Neighbors from European Contact through the Era of Removal* (New York: Norton, 1989); Colin Calloway, *New Worlds for All: Indians, Europeans and the Remaking of America* (Baltimore, MD: Johns Hopkins University Press, 1997).

26  See especially Merrell, *The Indian's New World*, 92–133.

27  Mann, dir., *The Last of the Mohicans*.

28  Mann, dir., *The Last of the Mohicans*.

29  Mann, dir., *The Last of the Mohicans*.

30  See generally Daniel Richter, *The Ordeal of the Longhouse: The Peoples of the Iroquois League in the Era of European Colonization* (Chapel Hill, NC: University of North Carolina Press, 1992).

31  Richter, *The Ordeal of the Longhouse*, 271.

32  Drew McCoy, *The Elusive Republic: Political Economy in Jeffersonian America* (Chapel Hill, NC: University of North Carolina Press, 1980), 13–47, 185–208.

33  Thomas Jefferson, *Notes on the State of Virginia with Related Documents*, ed. David Waldstreicher (Boston, MA: Bedford/St. Martin's, 2002), 197.

34  Jefferson, *Notes on the State of Virginia with Related Documents*, 197.

35  Thomas Jefferson to William Henry Harrison, 2/171803, in *Major Problems in the Early Republic*, 2nd edn, ed. Sean Wilentz and Jonathan H. Earle (New York: Houghton Mifflin, 2008), 109.

36  Thomas Jefferson to William Henry Harrison, 2/171803, in *Major Problems in the Early Republic*, ed. Wilentz and Earle, 109.

37  Mann, dir., *The Last of the Mohicans*.

38  Mann, dir., *The Last of the Mohicans*.

39  Adam Rothman, *Slave Country: American Expansion and the Origins of the Deep South* (Cambridge, MA: Harvard University Press, 2005), 128–139.

40  Andrew Jackson, "Second Annual Speech" (1830), in *Major Problems in the Early Republic*, ed. Wilentz and Earle, 247–248.

41  Jackson, "Second Annual Speech," 247–248.

42  John Ford, dir., *The Searchers* (Warner Bros., 1956).

43  Ford, dir., *The Searchers*.

44  Ford, dir., *The Searchers*.

45  Ford, dir., *The Searchers*.

46  Ford, dir., *The Searchers*.

47  Ford, dir., *The Searchers*.

48  Ford, dir., *The Searchers*.

49  Ford, dir., *The Searchers*.

50  Ford, dir., *The Searchers*.

51  Ford, dir., *The Searchers*.

52  Ford, dir., *The Searchers*.

53  Ford, dir., *The Searchers*.

54  Ford, dir., *The Searchers*.

55  Ford, dir., *The Searchers*.
56  Henry Hathaway et al., dirs., *How The West Was Won* (Warner Bros., 1962).
57  Thomas Jefferson, *Notes on the State of Virginia with Related Documents*, 121–125.
58  Hathaway et al., dirs., *How The West Was Won*.
59  John Ford, dir., *Stagecoach* (United Artists, 1939).
60  Hathaway et al., dirs., *How The West Was Won*.
61  Hathaway et al., dirs., *How The West Was Won*.
62  Hathaway et al., dirs., *How The West Was Won*.
63  Thomas Jefferson to William Henry Harrison, 2/17/1803, in *Major Problems in the Early Republic*, ed. Wilentz and Earle, 109.

## 4 Historicizing Triumphs and Tragedies in the American West

1  Patricia Nelson Limerick, *The Legacy of Conquest: The Unbroken Past of the American West* (New York: Norton, 1987), 324–325.
2  *Brown v. Board of Education*, May 17, 1954, *Brown v. Board of Education: A Brief History with Documents* (Boston, MA: Bedford/St. Martin's, 1998), 168–174; *Ruling in Relief*, May 31, 1955, *Brown v. Board of Education: A Brief History with Documents*, 194–198.
3  John Ford, dir., *The Searchers* (Warner Bros. 1956).
4  Ford, dir., *The Searchers*.
5  Ford, dir., *The Searchers*.
6  Ford, dir., *The Searchers*.
7  Ford, dir., *The Searchers*.
8  D.W. Griffith, dir., *The Birth of a Nation* (Alpha Video, 1915, 2005); Ford, dir., *The Searchers*.
9  Eric Foner, *Reconstruction: America's Unfinished Revolution, 1863–1877* (New York: Harper & Row, 1988), 564–601; Glenda Gilmore, *Gender and Jim Crow: Women and the Politics of White Supremacy in North Carolina, 1896–1920* (Chapel Hill, NC: University of North Carolina Press), 31–60.
10  Ford, dir., *The Searchers*.
11  Ford, dir., *The Searchers*.
12  Ford, dir., *The Searchers*.
13  Ford, dir., *The Searchers*.
14  Thomas Jefferson, *Notes on the State of Virginia with Related Documents*, ed. David Waldstreicher (Boston, MA: Bedford/St. Martins, 2002), 197.
15  Henry Hathaway et al., dirs., *How The West Was Won* (Warner Bros., 1962).
16  Hathaway et al., dirs., *How The West Was Won*.
17  Hathaway et al., dirs., *How The West Was Won*.
18  Hathaway et al., dirs., *How The West Was Won*.
19  Hathaway et al., dirs., *How The West Was Won*.
20  Hathaway et al., dirs., *How The West Was Won*.
21  Hathaway et al., dirs., *How The West Was Won*.
22  Hathaway et al., dirs., *How The West Was Won*.
23  Hathaway et al., dirs., *How The West Was Won*.
24  Hathaway et al., dirs., *How The West Was Won*.
25  Hathaway et al., dirs., *How The West Was Won*.
26  Hathaway et al., dirs., *How The West Was Won*.
27  Hathaway et al., dirs., *How The West Was Won*.
28  Hathaway et al., dirs., *How The West Was Won*.
29  Arthur Penn, dir., *Little Big Man* (CBS Productions, 1970).
30  Penn, dir., *Little Big Man*.
31  Penn, dir., *Little Big Man*.
32  Penn, dir., *Little Big Man*.

33  Penn, dir., *Little Big Man*.
34  Penn, dir., *Little Big Man*.
35  Limerick, *The Legacy of Conquest*, 181–221.
36  Philip Deloria, *Playing Indian* (New Haven, CT: Yale University Press), 1–9, 154–180.
37  Penn, dir., *Little Big Man*.
38  Ford, dir., *The Searchers*; Penn, dir., *Little Big Man*.
39  Clint Eastwood, dir., *Unforgiven* (Warner Bros., 1992).
40  Eastwood, dir., *Unforgiven*.
41  Eastwood, dir., *Unforgiven*.
42  Eastwood, dir., *Unforgiven*.
43  Eastwood, dir., *Unforgiven*.
44  Eastwood, dir., *Unforgiven*.

## 5 Immigration, the American Dream, and the Problem of the Irish American Experience

1  Ron Howard, dir., *Far and Away* (Universal Studios, 1992).
2  Thomas Sowell, *Ethnic America: A History* (New York: Basic Books, 1981), 17–42.
3  Matthew Frye Jacobson, *Whiteness of a Different Color: European Immigrants and the Alchemy of Race* (Cambridge, MA: Harvard University Press), 39–134, 246–273.
4  As will be further discussed in Chapter 6, Mexican Americans are purposely not hyphenated as various European Americans sometimes are; scholars of Mexican American history are sharply divided about the issue of hyphenation and the political and cultural implications connected with it. See particularly George Sanchez, *Becoming Mexican American: Ethnicity, Culture and Identity in Chicano Los Angeles, 1900–1945* (New York: Oxford University Press, 1993), 9–14.
5  Alexis de Tocqueville, *Democracy in America*, ed. J.P. Mayer, trans. George Lawrence (New York: Harper Perennial, 1968), 9.
6  Hector St. Jean de Crèvecoeur, "Letter III: What is an American," www.civics-online.org/library/formatted/texts/crevecoeur.html
7  Dorothy Ross, *The Origins of American Social Science* (New York: Cambridge University Press, 1991).
8  Oscar Handlin, *The Uprooted: The Epic Story of the Great Migrations that Made the American People* (Boston, MA: Little, Brown, 1952), 3.
9  Oscar Handlin, *Boston's Immigrants*, revised and enlarged edn (New York: Atheneum, 1941, 1976).
10  Possessive individualism is the idea associated with Lockean liberalism whereby individuals are political subjects endowed with particular natural and constitutional rights, particularly life, liberty, and property. As individual agents possessed with these rights and protected by the state, they are free to determine the course of their own particular history.
11  Handlin, *Boston's Immigrants*, 207–229.
12  Oscar Handlin, *Race and Nationality in American Life* (Boston, MA: Little, Brown, 1948, 1957), 3–50.
13  Handlin, *Race and Nationality in American Life*, 51–67, 93–138, 188–254. See also Barbara Jean Fields, "Slavery, Race, and Ideology in the United States of America," *New Left Review*, no. 181 (May–June): 97–118; David Roediger, *The Wages of Whiteness: Race and the Making of the American Working Class* (New York: Verso, 1993), 3–25; Matthew Frye Jacobson, *Whiteness of a Different Color: European Immigrants and the Alchemy of Race* (Cambridge, MA: Harvard University Press, 2001), 3–12. To be fair, none of these historians maintains they have written path-breaking scholarship, although this is how their work has been treated by their colleagues in the historical

profession. Barbara Jean Fields notes that she has been influenced by historians such as Edmund Morgan and his seminal book, *American Slavery, American Freedom: The Ordeal of Colonial Virginia* (New York: Norton, 1975). David Roediger acknowledges his intellectual debt to W.E.B. DuBois, who initially described race as a "psychological wage" for working-class white Americans and whose Marxist methodology and analysis Handlin apparently disagrees. See Fields, "Slavery, Race, and Ideology in the United States of America," 101–103; Roediger, *The Wages of Whiteness: Race and the Making of the American Working Class*, 12–15.

14  Handlin, *The Uprooted*.
15  Peter Novick, *That Noble Dream: The "Objectivity Question" and the American Historical Profession* (New York: Cambridge University Press, 1988, 1991). For the influence of World War II and the Cold War on the historical profession, see Novick, *That Noble Dream*, 281–360.
16  Quoted in Novick, *That Noble Dream*, 391–392.
17  Novick, *That Noble Dream*, 281–360.
18  Thomas Sowell, *Ethnic America: A History* (New York: Basic Books, 1981), 273–296.
19  Sowell, *Ethnic America*, 17–42.
20  Sowell, *Ethnic America*, 42.
21  Nicholas Canny, "In Search of a Better Home? European Oversees Migration, 1500–1800," in *Europeans on the Move: Studies on European Migration, 1500–1800*, ed. Nicholas Canny (New York: Oxford University Press, 1994), 263–283; Bernard Bailyn, *The Peopling of British North America: An Introduction* (New York: Vintage, 1986, 1988); Bernard Bailyn, *Voyagers of the West: A Passage in the Peopling of the America on the Eve of the Revolution* (New York: Vintage, 1986), 3–5.
22  Bailyn, *The Peopling of British North America*, 89–131.
23  Ron Howard, dir., *Far and Away* (Universal, 1993).
24  Howard, dir., *Far and Away*.
25  Howard, dir., *Far and Away*.
26  Handlin, *Boston's Immigrants*, 151–176; Liz Cohen, *Making a New Deal: Industrial Workers in Chicago, 1919–1939* (New York: Cambridge University Press, 1990), 54–97; Jacobson, *Whiteness of a Different Color*, 39–90.
27  Handlin, *Boston's Immigrants*, 178–206; Cohen, *Making a New Deal*, 12–42; Jacobson, *Whiteness of a Different Color*, 39–90.
28  Howard, dir., *Far and Away*.
29  Howard, dir., *Far and Away*.
30  Howard, dir., *Far and Away*.
31  As the film notes, in September 1893, the federal government offered American settlers free homestead in Oklahoma Territory by launching a race to claim staked land. Once the homesteader found the staked land he wanted, he was to replace the staked marker with the one given to him by the federal officer. This land of course had already been granted to Native Americans following President Andrew Jackson's removal policies in the 1840s, but the federal government once again broke its treaties with Native Americans living in Indian Territory in order to encourage American settlement. Howard, dir., *Far and Away*.
32  Howard, dir., *Far and Away*.
33  Howard, dir., *Far and Away*.
34  Howard, dir., *Far and Away*.
35  Howard, dir., *Far and Away*.
36  Sowell, *Ethnic America*, 273–296.
37  Handlin, *The Uprooted*, 304–307.
38  Handlin, *The Uprooted*, 304–307; Sowell, *Ethnic America*, 273–296.
39  Handlin, *Boston's Immigrants*, 178–206.
40  Handlin, *Boston's Immigrants*, 207–212.

41 The terms nativist and nativism refer to native-born Americans and their movement to resist the influx of immigrants in the mid-nineteenth century, particularly the Irish. As Matthew Frye Jacobson illustrates, nativists believed in the superiority of Anglo-Saxonism, a loosely defined ideology based on the perceived premise that the United States was founded upon Anglo-American cultural and political traditions, which in their mind were threatened by the growing presence of ethnic immigrants unaffiliated with these traditions. As the first major wave of immigrants, the Irish were viewed as the most salient threat because they were Catholics and perceived to ultimately owe their allegiance to the Pope instead of any secular government. See John Higham, *Strangers in the Land: Patterns of American Nativism, 1860–1925* (New Brunswick, NJ: Rutgers University Press, 1955, 1994), 3–11; Jacobson, *Whiteness of a Different Color*, 39–90; Roediger, *The Wages of Whiteness*, 133–163.
42 Martin Scorsese, dir., *Gangs of New York* (Miramax, 2002).
43 Scorsese, dir., *Gangs of New York.*
44 Scorsese, dir., *Gangs of New York.*
45 Scorsese, dir., *Gangs of New York.*
46 Scorsese, dir., *Gangs of New York.*
47 See Higham, *Strangers in the Land*, 3–11; Jacobson, *Whiteness of a Different Color*, 39–90.
48 Originally, Amsterdam planned to work for Bill in order to get close to him and fulfill his pledge to kill him. But now that he has benefited from Bill's patronage and moves within his inner circle, he has become psychologically conflicted and questions his own loyalties. See Scorsese, dir., *Gangs of New York.*
49 Scorsese, dir., *Gangs of New York.*
50 Scorsese, dir., *Gangs of New York.*
51 Scorsese, dir., *Gangs of New York.*
52 Scorsese, dir., *Gangs of New York.*
53 Eric Foner, *Reconstruction: America's Unfinished Revolution, 1863–1877* (New York: Harper & Row, 1988), 31–33.
54 Jacobson, *Whiteness of a Different Color*, 39–90.
55 Scorsese, dir., *Gangs of New York.*
56 Roediger, *Wages of Whiteness*, 133–163; Jacobson, *Whiteness of a Different Color*, 39–90.
57 Roediger, *Wages of Whiteness*, 133–163.
58 Scorsese, dir., *Gangs of New York.*
59 Griffith, dir., *The Birth of a Nation*; Scorsese, dir., *Gangs of New York.*
60 Scorsese, dir., *Gangs of New York.*

## 6 The European American and Mexican American Immigration Experience

1 Francis Ford Coppola, dir., *The Godfather* (Paramount, 1972).
2 Coppola, dir., *The Godfather.*
3 Francis Ford Coppola, dir., *The Godfather, Part II* (Paramount, 1974).
4 Drew McCoy, *The Elusive Republic: Political Economy in Jeffersonian America* (Chapel Hill, NC: University of North Carolina Press, 1981), 185–208.
5 Matthew Frye Jacobson, *Whiteness of a Different Color: European Immigrants and the Alchemy of Race* (Cambridge, MA: Harvard University Press), 91–135.
6 Joyce Appleby, Lynn Hunt, and Margaret Jacob, *Telling the Truth about History* (New York: Norton, 1994), 291–302.
7 Joan Wallach Scott, *Gender and the Politics of History* (New York: Columbia University Press, 1988), 28–50.
8 George Sanchez, *Becoming Mexican American: Ethnicity, Culture and Identity in Chicano Los Angeles, 1900–1945* (New York: Oxford University Press, 1993), 10–14,

253–269, 271–274. Sanchez draws similar conclusions as Liz Cohen in her study of mid-twentieth century Chicago. See Liz Cohen, *Making a New Deal: Industrial Workers in Chicago, 1919–1939* (New York: Cambridge University Press, 1990), 100–158. Mathew Frye Jacobson complicates this historical trajectory in his study of European immigrants. See generally Jacobson, *Whiteness of a Different Color.*

9   Douglas Monroy, *Rebirth: Mexican Los Angeles from the Great Migration to the Great Depression* (Berkeley, CA: University of California Press, 1999), 257–269.

10  Jacobson, *Whiteness of a Different Color*, 1–12.

11  Jacobson, *Whiteness of a Different Color*, 246–273.

12  Coppola, dir., *The Godfather.*

13  Coppola, dir., *The Godfather.*

14  Coppola, dir., *The Godfather.*

15  Coppola, dir., *The Godfather, Part II.*

16  Coppola, dir., *The Godfather, Part II.*

17  Coppola, dir., *The Godfather, Part II.*

18  Coppola, dir., *The Godfather, Part II.*

19  Cohen, *Making a New Deal*, 100–158; Monroy, *Rebirth*, 165–207; Sanchez, *Becoming Mexican American*, 171–187.

20  Coppola, dir., *The Godfather, Part II.*

21  Coppola, dir., *The Godfather, Part II.*

22  Coppola, dir., *The Godfather, Part II.*

23  Coppola, dir., *The Godfather, Part II.*

24  The scene in many ways recalls the character attributes of all the Corleone children exhibited in both *Godfather* films: Sonny as dominant, impassioned, and hot-tempered; Tom as cerebral, diplomatic, and managerial; Fredo as passive, even emasculated in this hyper-masculine world; and Connie as equally passive, but quiet and shy as well. See Coppola, dir., *Godfather Part II.*

25  Coppola, dir., *The Godfather, Part II.*

26  Coppola, dir., *The Godfather, Part II.*

27  Coppola, dir., *The Godfather, Part II.*

28  See generally Cohen, *Making a New Deal.*

29  See generally Cohen, *Making a New Deal*; Jacobson, *Whiteness of a Different Color.*

30  Coppola, dir., *The Godfather.*

31  Coppola, dir., *The Godfather.*

32  Coppola, dir., *The Godfather.*

33  Coppola, dir., *The Godfather.*

34  Coppola, dir., *The Godfather.*

35  Coppola, dir., *The Godfather.*

36  Although this chapter has not discussed *The Godfather, Part III*, one could look at this film as Michael embracing his ethnic past as he returns to New York and rebuilds the Corleone family empire. And though his dream remains to legitimize the Corleone family, he no longer intends to redeem the family in the eyes of America. In fact, he turns to even more traditional Italian institutions to absolve his family's past, namely the Catholic Church. Michael initially achieves this goal as he finances the cash-strapped Church, and turns over the family business to his nephew Vincent Mancini (Andy Garcia), Sonny's bastard son. But just as Michael believes he disconnected from his mafia past and thought his sins were absolved, tragedy strikes as his long-standing enemies kill his daughter, Mary (Sophia Coppola). Ultimately, Michael was never able to escape his history, dying a lonely man in Sicily, never able to achieve his American Dream. See Francis Ford Coppola, dir., *The Godfather, Part III* (Paramount, 1990).

37  Joel Zwick, dir., *My Big Fat Greek Wedding* (HBO Video, 2002).

38  Zwick, dir., *My Big Fat Greek Wedding.*

39 Zwick, dir., *My Big Fat Greek Wedding.*
40 Zwick, dir., *My Big Fat Greek Wedding.*
41 Zwick, dir., *My Big Fat Greek Wedding.*
42 David A. Hollinger, *Postethnic America: Beyond Multiculturalism* (New York: Basic Books, 1995), 14.
43 Matthew Frye Jacobson, *Roots Too: White Ethnic Revival in Post-Civil Rights America* (Cambridge, MA: Harvard University Press, 2006), 11–71.
44 Thomas Sowell, *Ethnic America: A History* (New York: Basic Books, 1981), 273–296.
45 Douglas Monroy, *Thrown Among Strangers: The Making of Mexican Culture in Frontier California* (Berkeley, CA: University of California Press, 1990), 163–183; Tomás Almaguer, *Racial Fault Lines: The Historical Origins of White Supremacy in California* (Berkeley, CA: University of California Press, 1994), 75–104.
46 Sanchez, *Becoming Mexican American*, 17–62; Monroy, *Rebirth*, 67–111.
47 Gregory Nava, dir., *My Family/Mi Familia* (New Line, 1995).
48 Sanchez, *Becoming Mexican American*, 3–14.
49 Nava, dir., *My Family/Mi Familia.*
50 Nava, dir., *My Family/Mi Familia.*
51 Nava, dir., *My Family/Mi Familia.*
52 Nava, dir., *My Family/Mi Familia.*
53 Nava, dir., *My Family/Mi Familia.*
54 Sanchez, *Becoming Mexican American*, 87–107.
55 Nava, dir., *My Family/Mi Familia.*
56 Patricia Cardoso, dir., *Real Women Have Curves* (HBO Video, 2002).
57 Cardoso, dir., *Real Women Have Curves.*
58 Cardoso, dir., *Real Women Have Curves.*
59 Sanchez, *Becoming Mexican American*, 87–107; Monroy, *Rebirth*, 165–207.
60 Cardoso, dir., *Real Women Have Curves.*
61 Cardoso, dir., *Real Women Have Curves.*
62 Cardoso, dir., *Real Women Have Curves.*
63 Cardoso, dir., *Real Women Have Curves.*
64 Monroy, *Rebirth*, 261–269.
65 Monroy, *Rebirth*, 257–261.
66 Monroy, *Rebirth*, 261–266.
67 Sanchez, *Becoming Mexican American*, 271–274.

# 7 Beyond Dallas

1 Oliver Stone, dir., *JFK* (Warner Bros., 1991, 2003).
2 Stone, dir., *JFK.*
3 Stone, dir., *JFK.*
4 Throughout this chapter I will place "historical event" in quotation marks to draw attention to the ways we signify these historical moments with greater value than normal historical episodes, and how they are allegories for something we deem to have greater meaning than other moments we do not consider as important. For an elaboration of the "historical event" as allegory, see Hayden White, "The Question of Narrative in Contemporary Historical Theory," *History and Theory*, vol. 23, no. 3 (1984): 1–33.
5 Max Holland, "After Thirty Years: Making Sense of the Assassination," *Reviews in American History*, vol. 22, no. 2 (1994): 191–209, 191.
6 Holland, "After Thirty Years," 191.
7 Peter Novick, *That Noble Dream: The "Objectivity Question" and the American Historical Profession* (New York: Cambridge University Press, 1988), 21–46.

8   Charles Beard, "Written History as an Act of Faith," *American Historical Review*, vol. 39, no. 2 (1934): 219–231.

9   J.H. Hexter, "The Historian and his Society: A Sociological Inquiry—Perhaps," in J.H. Hexter, *Doing History* (Bloomington, IN: Indiana University Press, 1971), 77–106.

10  Holland, "After Thirty Years."

11  Holland, "After Thirty Years."

12  Jürgen Habermas, "Modernity: An Unfinished Project," in *Habermas and the Unfinished Project of Modernity: Critical Essays on the Philosophical Discourse of Modernity*, ed. Maurizio Passerin d'Entrèves and Seyla Benhabib (Cambridge, MA: The MIT Press, 1997), 38–55. See also Jürgen Habermas, *The Philosophical Discourse of Modernity: Twelve Lectures*, trans. Frederick G. Lawrence (Cambridge, MA: The MIT Press, 1990).

13  Holland, "After Thirty Years."

14  White, "The Question of Narrative in Contemporary Historical Theory," 1–33.

15  Edward Branigan, *Narrative Comprehension and Film* (New York: Routledge, 1992), 1–33.

16  H. Porter Abbott, *The Cambridge Introduction to Narrative Theory*, 2nd edn (New York: Cambridge University Press, 2008), 3.

17  White, "The Question of Narrative in Contemporary Historical Theory," 24–30.

18  Historiography has multiple definitions, including the study of history, the philosophy of history, the history of historical thinking and the historical profession, the debates that animate particular fields within the discipline of history, and the practice of writing history. Throughout this chapter, I will use "historiography" to denote these various meanings. In this particular case, I am referring to historiography or the "historiographic" in the last definition to distinguish between the historical narratives that professional historians write and those that novelists and filmmakers produce.

19  White, "The Question of Narrative in Contemporary Historical Theory," 1–33; Michael Oakeshott, *On History and Other Essays* (Indianapolis, IN: Liberty Fund, 1999), 3–48.

20  G.W.F. Hegel, "The Philosophy of History," in *Theories of History*, ed. Patrick Gardiner (Glencoe, NY: The Free Press, 1959), 58–73; Oakeshott, *On History and Other Essays*, 3–48; Walter Benjamin, "Paris, Capital of the Nineteenth Century," in Walter Benjamin, *The Arcades Project*, trans. Howard Eiland and Kevin McLaughlin (Cambridge, MA: Harvard University Press, 2002), 14–26; Hayden White, "Interpretation in History," *New Literary History*, vol. 4, no. 2 (1973): 281–314; White, "The Question of Narrative in Contemporary Historical Theory," 1–33; Dominick LaCapra, *History in Transit: Experience, Identity, and Theory* (Ithaca, NY: Cornell University Press, 2004), 106–143.

21  Oakeshott, *On History*, 3–48.

22  Beard, "Written History as an Act of Faith," 219–231.

23  Hegel, "The Philosophy of History," 58–73.

24  Hegel, "The Philosophy of History," 58–73.

25  Oakeshott, *On History*, 3–48.

26  Benjamin, "Paris, Capital of the Nineteenth Century."

27  Don DeLillo, *Libra* (New York: Penguin, 1988, 2006), 59.

28  White, "Interpretation in History," 281–314; White, "The Question of Narrative in Contemporary Historical Theory," 1–33.

29  White, "Interpretation in History," 281–314.

30  White, "The Question of Narrative in Contemporary Historical Theory," 1–33.

31  White, "The Question of Narrative in Contemporary Historical Theory," 1–33.

32  White, "The Question of Narrative in Contemporary Historical Theory," 1–33.

33  LaCapra, *History in Transit*, 106–143.

34  LaCapra, *History in Transit*, 106–143.
35  Holland, "After Thirty Years," 191–192.
36  Holland, "After Thirty Years," 200–207.
37  Holland, "After Thirty Years," 193–209.
38  Holland, "After Thirty Years," 191–192.
39  Peter Dale Scott, *Deep Politics and the Death of JFK* (Berkeley, CA: University of California Press, 1993, 1996), 24–37.
40  Peter Dale Scott, *Crime and Cover-Up: The CIA, the Mafia, and the Dallas–Watergate Connection* (Berkeley, CA: Westworks, 1977).
41  Scott, *Deep Politics and the Death of JFK*.
42  Scott, *Deep Politics and the Death of JFK*, xi–xxvi, 6–10, 18–21.
43  Scott, *Deep Politics and the Death of JFK*, xi–xxvi, 6–10, 18–21.
44  Holland, "After Thirty Years," 191–192.
45  Holland, "After Thirty Years," 191–192.
46  Scott, *Deep Politics and the Death of JFK*, 22–23.
47  Marita Sturken, "Reenactment, Fantasy, and the Paranoia of History: Oliver Stone's Docudramas," *History and Theory*, vol. 36, no. 4 (1997): 64–79.
48  Holland, "After Thirty Years," 193–207; Scott, *Deep Politics and the Death of JFK*, 24–37; Oliver Stone, *JFK* (Warner Bros., 1991, 2003).
49  Scott, *Deep Politics and the Death of JFK*, xi–xxvi, 3–37; Stone, dir., *JFK*.
50  Holland, "After Thirty Years," 195–197.
51  Holland, "After Thirty Years," 197–200.
52  Holland, "After Thirty Years," 197–200.
53  Holland, "After Thirty Years," 203–209.
54  Holland, "After Thirty Years," 203–209.
55  The scholarly literature on *JFK* is quite extensive, although perhaps not surprising since it is such a controversial film. The following scholarship informs this particular chapter: Hayden White, "The Modernist Event," in *The Persistence of History: Cinema, Television, and the Modern Event*, ed. Vivian Sobchack (New York: Routledge, 1996), 17–38; Janet Staiger, "Cinematic Shots: The Narration of Violence," in *The Persistence of History*, ed. Vivian Sobchack, 39–54; Robert Burgoyne, "Modernism and the Narrative of Nation in JFK," in *The Persistence of History*, ed. Vivian Sobchack, 113–126; Robert Rosenstone, *Visions of the Past: The Challenge of Film to our Idea of History* (Cambridge, MA: Harvard University Press, 1996), 120–131; Robert Brent Toplin, *History by Hollywood: The Use and Abuse of the American Past* (Urbana, IL: University of Illinois Press, 1996), 45–78.
56  Abbott, *The Cambridge Introduction to Narrative*, 83–111.
57  White, "The Modernist Event"; Staiger, "Cinematic Shots: The Narration of Violence."
58  White, "Interpretation in History"; White, "The Question of Narrative in Contemporary Historical Theory."
59  Sturken, "Reenactment, Fantasy, and the Paranoia of History."
60  Novick, *That Noble Dream*, 21–46.
61  Novick, *That Noble Dream*, 21–46.
62  Novick, *That Noble Dream*, 21–46.
63  Beard, "Written History as an Act of Faith," 219–231.
64  Beard, "Written History as an Act of Faith," 219–231.
65  Stone, dir., *JFK*.
66  Burgoyne, "Modernism and the Narrative of Nation in *JFK*."
67  Sturken, "Reenactment, Fantasy, and the Paranoia of History: Oliver Stone's Docudramas." For a discussion about the cultural significance of the Zapruder film as an iconic text, see David M. Lubin, *Shooting Kennedy: JFK and the Culture of Images* (Berkeley, CA: University of California Press, 2003), 1–37.

68 For a discussion of intertextuality and how it informs narrative theory, see Abbott, *The Cambridge Introduction to Narrative*, 100–111.

69 Toplin, *History by Hollywood*, 46–78.

70 Stone, dir., *JFK*.

71 Stone, dir., *JFK*.

72 Stone, dir., *JFK*.

73 Stone, dir., *JFK*.

74 In his essay "The Modernist Event," Hayden White describes the ways in which twentieth-century traumatic "historical events" such as the Kennedy assassination and the Holocaust signify historical meaning but resist the kind of narrative closure typical of "modernist" narratives. Films such as *JFK* and *Schindler's List* may attempt narrative closure but cannot provide the typical closure or catharsis for viewers because films cannot do what people must do for themselves, that is take historical agency in order to work-through their own trauma. See White, "The Modernist Event."

75 Stone, dir., *JFK*.

76 Abbott, *The Cambridge Introduction to Narrative*, 100–111.

77 Plato, *The Republic*, trans. Desmond Lee (New York: Penguin, 1955, 2003), 240–248.

78 White, "The Question of Narrative in Contemporary Historical Theory," 1–33.

79 White, "The Modernist Event"; Staiger, "Cinematic Shots."

80 David Harvey, *The Condition of Postmodernity: An Enquiry into the Origins of Cultural Change* (Oxford: Blackwell, 1990), 3–9, 39–65.

81 See Emily Rosenberg, *Spreading the American Dream: American Economic and Cultural Expansion, 1890–1945* (New York: Hill & Wang, 1982).

82 DeLillo, *Libra*, 3.

83 DeLillo, *Libra*, 13.

84 DeLillo, *Libra*, 369–370.

85 DeLillo, *Libra*, 330.

86 DeLillo, *Libra*, 11.

87 DeLillo, *Libra*, 435.

88 Max Weber, *Economy and Society: An Outline of Interpretive Sociology*, vol. 2, ed. Gunther Roth and Claus Wittich (Berkeley, CA: University of California Press, 1978), 956–1005.

89 DeLillo, *Libra*, 19–28.

90 DeLillo, *Libra*, 378.

91 DeLillo, *Libra*, 379.

92 DeLillo, *Libra*, 445.

# 8 "We Are Alive in Hell"

1 Whether Ziad Jarrah was the actual leader of the group who hijacked United 93 is uncertain, but the *9/11 Commission Report* draws this conclusion and identifies him as the pilot of the hijacked airplane as the National Commission determined he had flight training. See National Commission on Terrorist Attacks Upon the United States, *The 9/11 Commission Report: Final Report of the National Commission on Terrorist Attacks Upon the United States* (New York: Norton, 2004), 12, 223–253. As will be discussed in further detail later in this chapter, Greengrass's *United 93* arguably presents an empathetic portrait of Jarrah precisely because the *9/11 Commission Report* narrates a similar characterization of him. The *9/11 Commission Report* suggests that Jarrah maintained doubts about the attacks until the summer of 2001, and unlike the other hijackers, he continued to remain in close contact with loved ones, even visiting his family until the months preceding the 9/11 terrorist attacks. Greengrass's *United 93* only dramatizes what the *9/11 Commission Report* concludes. See particularly National

Commission on Terrorist Attacks Upon the United States, *The 9/11 Commission Report*, 223–253.

2 Ernest R. May, "Introduction," *The 9/11 Commission Report with Related Documents* (New York: Bedford/St. Martin's, 2007), 1–26.

3 May, "Introduction," *The 9/11 Commission Report with Related Documents*, 1–26.

4 Peter Dale Scott, *The Road to 9/11: Wealth, Empire, and the Future of America* (Berkeley, CA: University of California Press, 2008), 212–235.

5 Scott, *The Road to 9/11*, 114–137.

6 Scott, *The Road to 9/11*, 194–211.

7 May, "Introduction," *The 9/11 Commission Report with Related Documents*, 1–26.

8 May, "Introduction," *The 9/11 Commission Report with Related Documents*, 19–25.

9 May, "Introduction," *The 9/11 Commission Report with Related Documents*, 1–26; Scott, *The Road to 9/11*, 1–25.

10 National Commission on Terrorist Attacks Upon the United States, *The 9/11 Commission Report*, 47–70; Scott, *The Road to 9/11*, 1–25, 246–266.

11 May, "Introduction," *The 9/11 Commission Report with Related Documents*, 17.

12 May, "Introduction," *The 9/11 Commission Report with Related Documents*, 17.

13 May, "Introduction," *The 9/11 Commission Report with Related Documents*, 15–19.

14 May, "Introduction," *The 9/11 Commission Report with Related Documents*, 15–19.

15 May, "Introduction," *The 9/11 Commission Report with Related Documents*, 15–19.

16 St. Augustine, *The City of God: An Abridged Version from the Translation by Gerald J. Walsh, Demetrius B. Zema, Grace Monahan, and Daniel J. Honan*, ed. Vernon J. Bourke (Garden City, NY: Image Books, 1958), 39–49, 427–450, 540–545.

17 Morris Berman, *Dark Ages America: The Final Phase of Empire* (New York: Norton, 2006), 1–11.

18 Alasdair MacIntyre, "Epistemological Crisis, Dramatic Narrative, and the Philosophy of Science," in *Knowledge and Postmodernism in Historical Perspective*, ed. Joyce Appleby et al. (New York: Routledge, 1996), 357–367.

19 May, "Introduction," *The 9/11 Commission Report with Related Documents*, 15.

20 National Commission on Terrorist Attacks Upon the United States, *The 9/11 Commission Report*, 339.

21 Hayden White, "The Value of Narrativity in the Representation of Reality," *Critical Inquiry*, vol. 7, no. 1 (1980): 5–27.

22 May, "Introduction," *The 9/11 Commission Report with Related Documents*, 15.

23 May, "Introduction," *The 9/11 Commission Report with Related Documents*, 15.

24 National Commission on Terrorist Attacks Upon the United States, *The 9/11 Commission Report*, 339–360; May, "Introduction," *The 9/11 Commission Report with Related Documents*, 1–26.

25 May, "Introduction," *The 9/11 Commission Report with Related Documents*, 15–16.

26 May, "Introduction," *The 9/11 Commission Report with Related Documents*, 6–15.

27 National Commission on Terrorist Attacks Upon the United States, *The 9/11 Commission Report*, 47. The *9/11 Commission Report* points out that a "fatwa is normally an interpretation of Islamic law by a respected Islamic authority" but that "neither Bin Laden, Zawahiri, nor the three others who signed this statement were scholars of Islamic law." Nevertheless, the 1998 fatwa found fertile ground from which to attract followers who supported Bin Laden and Zawahiri's terrorism against Americans. See National Commission on Terrorist Attacks Upon the United States, *The 9/11 Commission Report*, 47.

28 National Commission on Terrorist Attacks Upon the United States, *The 9/11 Commission Report*, 47–70.

29 Paul Greengrass, dir., *United 93* (Universal, 2006); National Commission on Terrorist Attacks Upon the United States, *The 9/11 Commission Report*, 1–46.

30 Greengrass, dir., *United 93*.

31  As H. Porter Abbott notes, the protagonist is the classical hero who undergoes personal transformation connected to narrative tension animating the plot. He is not necessarily the "good guy." See H. Porter Abbott, *The Cambridge Introduction to Narrative*, 2nd edn (New York: Cambridge University Press, 2008), 240.

32  Abbott, *The Cambridge Introduction to Narrative*, 240.

33  National Commission on Terrorist Attacks Upon the United States, *The 9/11 Commission Report*, 163, 223–225, 229–230, 244, 246–249.

34  National Commission on Terrorist Attacks Upon the United States, *The 9/11 Commission Report*, 163, 223–225, 229–230, 244, 246–249.

35  Oliver Stone, dir., *World Trade Center* (Paramount, 2006).

36  Stone, dir., *World Trade Center*.

37  Stone, dir., *World Trade Center*.

38  Stone, dir., *World Trade Center*.

39  Stone, dir., *World Trade Center*.

40  Stone, dir., *World Trade Center*.

41  Oliver Stone, dir., *W.* (Universal, 2008).

42  Stone, dir., *W.*

43  Max Holland, "After Thirty Years: Making Sense of the Assassination," *Reviews in American History*, vol. 22, no. 2 (1994): 191–232.

44  Scott, *The Road to 9/11*, 114–137.

45  Scott, *The Road to 9/11*, 26–49.

46  Scott, *The Road to 9/11*, 19–24, 246–266.

47  Scott, *The Road to 9/11*, 19–24.

48  David Ray Griffin, "Sixteen Reasons to Question the Official Story of 9/11," in *The Hidden History of 9/11*, ed. Paul Zarembka (New York: Seven Stories Press, 2006, 2008), xvii–xix.

49  Jay Kolar, "What We Know about the Alleged Hijackers," in *The Hidden History of 9/11*, ed. Zarembka, 21–26.

50  Paul Zarembka, ed., *The Hidden History of 9/11*, xi–xiii.

51  See Martin Campbell, dir., *Casino Royale* (MGM/Columbia Pictures, 2006); Marc Forster, dir., *Quantum of Solace* (MGM/Columbia Pictures, 2008).

52  See Campbell, dir., *Casino Royale*. For arguments about insider trading and the selling of airplane stocks before the terrorist attacks, see Paul Zarembka, "Initiation of the 9–11 Operation, with Evidence of Insider Trading Beforehand," in *The Hidden History of 9/11*, ed. Zarembka, 47–74.

53  See Campbell, dir., *Casino Royale*; Forster, dir., *Quantum of Solace*.

54  During the poker game sequence, Bond loses the money provided by the British government to Le Chiffre. The CIA agent Felix Leiter (Jeffrey Wright), with the same intentions as Bond to defeat Le Chiffre, has also entered this high-stakes card game. However, agent Leiter realizes he cannot beat Le Chiffre, and extends Bond the credit he needs to stay in the game in exchange for the right to Le Chiffre's intelligence about the terrorist organizations with whom he has worked once Bond beats Le Chiffre in the poker game. See Campbell, dir., *Casino Royale*.

55  See Campbell, dir., *Casino Royale*.

56  This is also a personal issue for Bond since Mr. White is partly responsible for the death of Bond's girlfriend, Vesper Lynd (Eva Green), driving his need to avenge her death while pursuing his professional duty to undermine Mr. White's international organization, despite the orders from MI6 only to capture him. The narrative tension between Bond's personal and professional motives that begin in *Casino Royale* is the primary plot line in the next film, *Quantum of Solace*. See Forster, dir., *Quantum of Solace*.

57  Christopher Nolan's *The Dark Knight* engages with these issues and in arguably more direct ways. However, as film critics drew these connections when the movie was

released in 2008, it is not necessary to elaborate upon them in detail in this chapter. In short, the principal villain, the Joker (Heath Ledger), terrorizes Gotham City for the sheer purpose of provoking terror. Or as Alfred says, he is someone who "enjoys watching the world burn." While other criminals in the film are motivated by money and power, the Joker is motivated only by the pleasure of terrorizing Gotham's citizens. Here the film asks viewers to consider the rationale that inspires terrorists to use violence in order to achieve their ends. Furthermore, it demands us to think about the lengths to which citizens are willing to surrender their civil liberties in order to fight terrorism. In a critical scene, the Batman asks Lucius Fox to use powerful surveillance equipment to tap into the private phone calls of Gotham's citizens in order to find the Joker before he unleashes violent mayhem. Displeased and ambivalent that he has been asked to violate privacy rights, Lucius agrees only because he will destroy the equipment once he finds the Joker. Where *Casino Royale* and *Quantum of Solace* do not question the legitimacy of surveillance power if these means are required to achieve the ends of effectively combating terrorism as earlier mentioned in this chapter, *The Dark Knight* provokes viewers to think more carefully about these issues as it makes the political ethics of surveillance power much more problematic and sinister. See Christopher Nolan, *The Dark Knight* (Warner Bros., 2008).

58  Tim Burton, dir., *Batman* (Warner Bros., 1989); Frank Miller, *Batman: The Dark Knight Returns* (New York: DC Comics, 1986, 2002); see also Frank Miller, *Batman: The Dark Knight Strikes Again* (New York: DC Comics, 2004).

59  Although there are a number of sequels to Miller's revisionist interpretation of the Batman narrative, Grant Morrison and Dave McKean's *Arkham Asylum* would arguably have as much influence as Miller's work upon the Batman films. See Grant Morrison and Dave McKean, *Arkham Asylum: A Serious House on Serious Earth* (New York: DC Comics, 1989, 2004).

60  While Tim Burton's *Batman* and Christopher Nolan's *Batman Begins* both use the murder of Bruce's parents by desperate petty criminals as a plot device, they structure this critical episode in Bruce Wayne's young life differently to inform the narrative discourse of their respective films. In both films Bruce and his parents leave the alley exit of a theater and are assaulted by armed muggers. However, in Burton's movie one of the attackers is a young Jack Napier, the criminal who will later emerge as an influential player in Gotham City's underworld and eventually become Bruce Wayne/the Batman's nemesis and alter ego, the Joker (Jack Nicholson). As the Joker points out, he and the Batman (Michael Keaton) are two sides of the same psychological coin, living a life of masked identities that they have mutually defined for each other. See Tim Burton, dir., *Batman* (Warner Bros., 1989). While Christopher Nolan's *The Dark Knight* draws upon this version of the Batman–Joker relationship, his Joker (Heath Ledger) is much more of an enigma. In Nolan's film, the Joker's birth name is vaguely suggested and his original identity remains mysterious, largely because the Joker constantly retells the story of his previous life and the origins of his frightening facial scars. See Christopher Nolan, *The Dark Knight* (Warner Bros., 2008). In Nolan's *Batman Begins*, Joe Chill is the mugger who kills Bruce's parents, serving two roles to advance the film's narrative discourse. First, he is a psychological force that incubates young Bruce's drive for vengeance. Second, Chill's parole trial, potential testimony against Carmine Falcone, and eventual murder by one of Falcone's assassins introduces viewers to the Gotham criminal underworld controlled by Falcone. See Christopher Nolan, dir., *Batman Begins* (Warner Bros., 2005).

61  Nolan, dir., *Batman Begins*.

62  Nolan, dir., *Batman Begins*.

63  Nolan, dir., *Batman Begins*.

64 As viewers learn from the beginning of *Batman Begins*, Bruce was traumatized when he fell down a dried-up well while playing with his friend Rachel Dawes in the vast grounds of Wayne Manor as a young boy. After sustaining a leg injury during the fall, he is attacked and terrified by a swarm of bats. As his father, a medical doctor, examines his leg in his bedroom, Bruce sights a flying bat, cringing in fear even though his father assures him that he is safe. Later, when Bruce and his parents attend an opera, he relives his trauma when a bat-like character in the opera descends on stage, frightening Bruce, who implores his parents that they leave the opera. When they exit a backstage door into a dark alley, the desperate mugger Joe Chill murders his parents, further traumatizing Bruce, who now feels guilty and responsible for their deaths. At the League of Shadows, Ducard encourages Bruce to confront his deepest fears in order to become a formidable warrior whom criminals will fear. Once he returns home, Bruce explores the underground caves of Wayne Manor, confronting the legion of bats that have haunted his nightmares ever since the day he fell and injured his leg. Nolan directs this scene as a moment of rebirth for Bruce, suggesting that the caves are a symbolic womb that Bruce must re-enter in order to be reborn as a new man, the Batman. He shoots this scene with minimal light as Bruce moves through the darkness and shadows until he reaches the only source of light, where he is again attacked by flying bats. Unafraid, Bruce remains among them as they swirl around him, finally confronting and overcoming the trauma that has haunted him since childhood. Bruce chooses the caves as the home of the Batman, descending there whenever he must leave his public identity and re-emerge as the masked crime fighter. Becoming the Batman, Bruce signals to criminals that they will now fear that which terrified him for so long. Nolan, dir., *Batman Begins*.

65 Nolan, dir., *Batman Begins*.

66 Nolan, dir., *Batman Begins*.

67 Nolan, dir., *Batman Begins*.

68 Nolan, dir., *Batman Begins*.

69 Nolan, dir., *Batman Begins*.

70 Nolan, dir., *Batman Begins*.

71 National Commission on Terrorist Attacks Upon the United States, *The 9/11 Commission Report*, 339.

72 National Commission on Terrorist Attacks Upon the United States, *The 9/11 Commission Report*, 55–57.

73 Jon Favreau, dir., *Iron Man* (Paramount, 2008).

74 National Commission on Terrorist Attacks Upon the United States, *The 9/11 Commission Report*, 47–70.

75 Favreau, dir., *Iron Man*.

76 Favreau, dir., *Iron Man*.

77 Favreau, dir., *Iron Man*.

78 Favreau, dir., *Iron Man*.

79 National Commission on Terrorist Attacks Upon the United States, *The 9/11 Commission Report*, 55–57.

80 Favreau, dir., *Iron Man*.

81 National Commission on Terrorist Attacks Upon the United States, *The 9/11 Commission Report*, 59–70.

82 Favreau, dir., *Iron Man*.

83 Despite the clear connection between his stealth and powerful iron suit and the film's title *Iron Man*, the actual "Iron Man" name will not be given to the superhero until the end of the movie.

84 Favreau, dir., *Iron Man*.

85 White, "The Value of Narrativity in the Representation of Reality," 5.

86 The notion of the "end of history," comes from Francis Fukuyama's controversial essay that celebrates the triumph of liberal capitalist democracies over communism

following the fall of the Berlin Wall in 1989 and the end of the Cold War. History in this context is defined as a Hegelian dialectic between competing ideological systems. With liberalism's triumph, only economic activity will characterize life in the post-Cold War era. While Fukuyama's essay has been well received in some quarters, it has been viewed as hopelessly naive in others. Whatever the case, 9/11 would signify that we are once again back in history now defined by a new conflict between Western modernity and radical fundamentalist Islamism. For Fukuyama's views, see Francis Fukuyama, "The End of History?", *National Interest* (Summer, 1989): 3–18.

# INDEX